MW00655755

Schizophrenia

SCHIZOPHRENIA

An Unfinished History

Orna Ophir

polity

Copyright © Orna Ophir 2022

The right of Orna Ophir to be identified as Author of this Work has been asserted in accordance with the UK Copyright, Designs and Patents Act 1988.

First published in 2022 by Polity Press

Polity Press
65 Bridge Street
Cambridge CB2 1UR, UK

Polity Press
101 Station Landing
Suite 300
Medford, MA 02155, USA

All rights reserved. Except for the quotation of short passages for the purpose of criticism and review, no part of this publication may be reproduced, stored in a retrieval system or transmitted, in any form or by any means, electronic, mechanical, photocopying, recording or otherwise, without the prior permission of the publisher.

ISBN-13: 978-1-5095-3647-4

A catalogue record for this book is available from the British Library.

Typeset in 11.5 on 14 pt Adobe Garamond
by Cheshire Typesetting Ltd, Cuddington, Cheshire
Printed and bound in Great Britain by CPI Group (UK) Ltd, Croydon

The publisher has used its best endeavors to ensure that the URLs for external websites referred to in this book are correct and active at the time of going to press. However, the publisher has no responsibility for the websites and can make no guarantee that a site will remain live or that the content is or will remain appropriate.

Every effort has been made to trace all copyright holders, but if any have been overlooked the publisher will be pleased to include any necessary credits in any subsequent reprint or edition.

For further information on Polity, visit our website:
politybooks.com

Contents

Figures

Preface

The first time I encountered a person diagnosed with schizophrenia in a psychiatric hospital, I was 16 years old. My mother took me to visit Orlean, her friends' daughter, who was only three years older than I was. A bright, beautiful, outgoing young woman, Orlean, so I was told, had a "mental breakdown" following a breakup with her high school sweetheart. This young woman, whom I admired and looked up to, was in a one-size-fits-all pink, tattered hospital gown. Her long black hair somewhat unkempt, her lips chapped and blood-red, her pupils so dilated that her big hazel eyes were almost invisible. She had a very strange expression on her face, as if she was there, with us, but uncannily also absent. The three of us sat outside on the lawn, next to the "adult semi-open ward" of Shalvata Hospital. Shalvata stands for serenity in Hebrew. The hospital looked like a kibbutz. The rural landscape, the wild monk parakeets in the trees, and the plain frugal architecture gave it the appearance of a utopian, peaceful place. As I observed the patients around us, an eerie feeling started to creep in. They seemed different. An older lady was conversing with an unseen other on a bench, a man in his fifties was picking up a cigarette butt, trying to light it, and then there was a deep loud roar, a bellow, that culminated in continuous, repetitive begging: "Get me out of here! Get me out of here!"

Five years after this visit, following a brief detour through the Bezalel Academy of Art in Jerusalem, I decided to become a clinician. As an undergraduate majoring in psychology, I volunteered in the adolescent ward at that very same hospital. For three years, I worked with children aged 12–18. Their stay was always involuntary, and always involved a high risk of suicide. I observed these terrified, haunted, confused kids, living in their own nightmarish universe, seeing things only they could see, and hearing voices no one else could hear. And I saw their broken-hearted, helpless parents. I witnessed many of them receiving help, gently cared for, and being heard. Many left the ward calmer and more organized. Some returned in a state of crisis.

The staff meetings in the director's office, recounting the ups and downs of daily life on the ward, were fascinating. Interviews of patients by senior psychiatrists, followed by extensive discussions and deeply informed by psychoanalytic theory, were simply mesmerizing. In the adjacent room, dangerously agitated patients were restrained to their beds. It wasn't a pleasant sight, and the sounds coming from it made a strong impression on me. Although I worked with the "kiddos" as we called them, every now and then I saw Orlean, who moved between the closed and the semi-open wards, between wearing a hospital gown and her own clothes. She had put on a lot of weight. Her teeth had darkened from the cigarettes she compulsively smoked.

A year later, I returned to the hospital, this time as a graduate student in clinical psychology, to fulfill the requirements of a practicum in the context of the semi-open, adult ward. There, I was assigned patients, offering them psychotherapy and psychodiagnosis. I viewed the – at times, miraculous – immediate effect of tranquilizers on agitated patients who were in severe mental pain, and I saw the deleterious effect of their chronic use. At the same time, I conducted extensive research for my Master of Arts (MA) thesis about schizophrenia and L-tryptophan, a natural amino acid found in many plants and animals that the body turns into the neurotransmitter serotonin. While most drugs for schizophrenia were based on the "dopamine hypothesis," and the need to treat patients' "mad" thoughts and behavior by blocking dopaminergic receptors, this new research offered to study substances that could help with the memory dysfunction many of these patients were suffering from.

Most of the patients I saw at the hospital were diagnosed with schizophrenia. Among them, Ms. M. who did not get out of her bed for three months fearing "the man from the radio" would harm her only son, if she dared to move; Mr. A. who believed he was on a mission with Mossad and insisted that I had the "codes"; and Mr. O. who had been involuntarily committed to the ward after he had tried to kill his mother, whom he believed was an Iraqi spy that had taken her place. It was not easy to establish a therapeutic relationship with these suffering patients, but once it happened, I found their stories to be both intriguing and excruciating. Every week, I saw Orlean, as she came for her treatment at the outpatient clinic. She had begun a relationship with another patient in the clinic (who was also diagnosed with schizophrenia) and told me that she was "doing well."

A couple of years later, when I returned to the same hospital as an intern clinical psychologist, I was assigned one intensive case. Mr. N. was a 56-year-old man, diagnosed with disorganized schizophrenia, who lived with his psychotic mother, a survivor of the Nazi concentration camps, with whom he shared a delusional world in which he was still her little baby. I saw both of them together, as she gradually made the transition to a psychiatric nursing home. Mr. N. almost died due to complications related to his antipsychotic medication, and as a response to the upcoming separation from his mother. I met with him three times a week for an hour and wrote an extensive case study based on this treatment for the State Board exam. As it turned out, this was the first time that a patient diagnosed with schizophrenia was presented in this context. But it was not the last. When I returned to the hospital as a specialist in clinical psychology, I encouraged students, interns, and residents to carefully listen to these patients, as they try and find meaning and purpose in what otherwise sounded so unreasonable and, at times, plainly horrifying. Meanwhile, Orlean got married and the couple moved into a small apartment purchased by her parents. They attended a nearby psychiatric rehabilitation center on a daily basis, and I saw her once in a while when she came for her follow-up sessions at the clinic. Though she had prematurely aged, she seemed content with her relationship.

During the late 1990s, when the older cohort of dynamic psychiatrists was replaced by the younger generation of biologically oriented medical professionals, psychoanalytically informed discussions were gradually phased out, while studies on drugs and somatic psychiatry were more and more prevalent. This is when I witnessed how lethal serious mental illnesses could be: Mr. G., who was new to the ward and only 23 years old, was found hanged inside the greenhouse on the hospital grounds. Mr. Y., who was 35 years old, refused to consume the medications he was offered, and his treatment at the hospital was terminated. He hanged himself in his apartment, leaving a note explaining that he would be reborn and delivered by his real father, the Lord. Mr. S., who was 21 years old, was released from the ward after recovering from an acute catatonic state. He stopped taking his medication since he felt it "killed" his ability to write music and became very laconic in his psychotherapy follow-up sessions. He went missing, and on a frigid winter day, after 12 days of a major search for him, was found dead in a river, far away from where he started his aimless walk. Mr. J., who was 42 years old, set himself on fire in a car, after a young lawyer, an advocate of patients' rights, managed to release him from an involuntary hospitalization. And, finally, Ms. A., a 27-year-old woman, who believed that she was responsible for the mass extinction of whales in the Indian Ocean, was found dead in the Judean desert, after she missed her appointment with an intern psychologist who had diagnosed her as extremely dangerous to herself, based on a battery of projective psychological tests. Orlean, to conclude this sad, long, yet far from complete list, died a few years ago from a complication related to her smoking and the antipsychotic medication she had consumed for years. She was 47 years old.

While continuing to work at the hospital with patients and their families, I went back to graduate school, this time to study the history of my field. More specifically, my interests focused on the shift I experienced firsthand in our thinking, theorizing, and treatment of patients we mostly diagnosed as "schizophrenics." I joined the Cohn Institute for the History and Philosophy of Science and Ideas at Tel Aviv University, where I wrote my first book about the history of psychoanalysis, psychiatry, and psychosis in postwar United States. I also founded the Israeli chapter of ISPS, whose acronym at that time stood for the International Society for the Psychological Treatments of the Schizophrenias and other Psychoses. The name was a mouthful, but aptly defined the work of mental health professionals who were deeply committed to following the psychoanalytic idea of finding meaning in patients' symptoms, not least by establishing a working relationship with them. Our local branch organized conferences in collaboration with the Sigmund Freud Center at the Hebrew University in Jerusalem, with the Israeli Psychoanalytic Society, and with psychiatric hospitals both in Israel and around the world.

As the 2009 international conference of ISPS in Copenhagen started to take shape, a discussion among members called for the removal of the term "schizophrenia" from the association's name, given the stigma it both carried and imposed. Based not least on the failure to validate schizophrenia as a distinct disease entity,[1] efforts to abolish its label and nomenclature mushroomed. Suggestions such as "bury the 'schizophrenia' construct," "abandon the concept of schizophrenia," "abolish schizophrenia," etc., indicated the direction that the association was about to take.

In anticipation of the upcoming publication of the DSM-5, the fifth edition of the *Diagnostic and Statistical Manual of Mental Disorders*, the ISPS leadership tried to press a change that would go beyond its own name and might influence the decision makers of the latest installment of what came to be known as psychiatry's "Bible." Experts argued that schizophrenia was "an idea whose very essence is equivocal," a "category without natural boundaries, a barren hypothesis." They condemned it for being "yesterday's diagnosis,"[2] "a construct with little reliability or predictive validity," precisely because the symptoms used to diagnose it can be understood as extreme versions of normal human experience.[3] Among others, these examples were a source of inspiration for the drive to rename.

It was further suggested that the Japanese term for "integration disorder" that had replaced the word "schizophrenia," offered one example of a name change that was greatly preferred by both patients and caregivers. Yet others claimed that it was not just the name, but the whole nosological enterprise, the attempt to classify so-called psychiatric diseases, that had to be drastically reformed. To do so, it was argued, it would be helpful to introduce a dimensional approach that would jettison the earlier – metaphysical and modern – model, which was based on the increasingly untenable assumption of discrete categories or disease entities. The dimensional model, it was believed, would be compatible with empirical evidence that psychotic symptoms occur on a *continuous spectrum* that ranges from normality, on one end, to severe mental illness (SMI), on the other. Some also called for a hybrid system that would combine the advantages of the categorical system that was associated with known treatment outcomes, on the one hand, and the new dimensional approach that was deemed to have greater explanatory power, on the other.[4]

And then, a further group argued that while the current diagnostic criteria for schizophrenia were admittedly "arbitrary and pseudo-scientific," Bleuler's original concept of "schizophrenia" was still quite valuable, as it could offer "a much broader, dynamic, phenomenological-oriented approach to understanding the schizophrenic patient."[5] Even those who remained intent on renaming the diagnosis searched for a term that would do "adequate justice to the alteration in the person's [i.e., the patient's] relationship with reality."[6]

At the "renaming" conference, the initial idea for my own contributing paper was to present a reasoned challenge to all these various efforts to discard the term schizophrenia. Initially, I thought I might take my lead from the gay rights movement, which by co-opting the originally derogatory term "queer" and transforming it into a positive self-label, had, in fact, succeeded in disarming hordes of homophobes. Others, notably in the fields of feminism, queer theory, and postcolonial theory, spoke of the critical need for "strategic essentialism," a term coined by Gayatri Chakravorty Spivak to describe the political tactic, employed by a minority group that shares an identity in the public sphere, to struggle for its equal rights. In other words, even if schizophrenia as an essence was obsolete, using the term as a means to a different *end* was potentially more useful than putting an *end* to the very concept, then and there.

However, I was not fully convinced that the comparison with other minorities would hold up when it came to "schizophrenia." Although "Mad Pride" activists called for reclaiming terms such as "mad" or "psycho," I never met a suffering patient in real life who proudly adopted the "schizophrenic" label as a badge of honor, much less as a strategic, discursive advantage. Given my reservations, I came up with an alternative proposal, as I had noticed that – together with the call to discard the term schizophrenia – the word "psychoanalysis" had already gone missing from the announced program of the aforementioned congress in Copenhagen. Yet psychoanalysis was the very foundation on which ISPS was established in 1956, when Gaetano Benedetti and Christian Müller cofounded what was then called the International Symposium for the Psychotherapy of Schizophrenia (ISPS), whose first gathering took place at the psychiatric clinic of the University of Lausanne in Switzerland. Dissatisfied with the reductionist orientation of European psychiatry at the time, they sought the aid of psychoanalysis to find a deeper, more comprehensive approach to the medical theorization, clinical diagnosis, and treatment of the so-called schizophrenias. Even if psychoanalysis was not interested in diagnostic categories, and even though the name "schizophrenia" was a term Sigmund Freud, in particular, neither liked nor approved of, psychoanalysis offered an approach that helped understand the symptoms of schizophrenia as meaningful and, indeed, saw in their further exploration a possible path for insight and growth (as the psychoanalyst Ann-Louise Silver, the founder of the American chapter of the ISPS, asserted in this same context). Just as importantly, the premises and method of psychoanalysis allowed for a radically different way of envisioning the putative difference between the states of mental health, on the one hand, and those of serious mental illness, on the other.

The vote was cast, and the international association changed its name, deciding to remove "schizophrenia" from its very title. It was baptized as the International Society for Psychological and Social Approaches to Psychosis, at around the same time as the DSM-5 introduced a "schizophrenia spectrum" that replaced the earlier, more clear-cut, categorical classification of schizophrenia. Simultaneously, the American National Institute of Mental Health (NIMH) established the Research Domain Criteria (RDoC), which suggested an entirely new framework for the classification of mental illnesses, discarding the old psychopathological terms and searching for clues in genes, molecules, cells, and brain circuitry instead.

Given the personal and professional experiences recounted above, and with an eye on the recent trends in our disciplinary fields and institutions, when I was offered the chance to write a book about the history of schizophrenia, I thought of the many excellent, historical depictions of the "rise and fall" genre in this field. But the title of the book ended up being *Schizophrenia: An Unfinished History*, since its aim is not just to present a study of the appearance and possible disappearance of the term "schizophrenia," or of the birth and the possible death of this diagnosis. Rather, its goal is, first and foremost, to inquire into the more perennial ways in which we define and respond to *difference*, mentally and conceptually, but also practically and institutionally.

Acknowledgments

The work that I present here goes back to – and is deeply inspired by – my experience, which extended over two decades, as visitor, student, extern, intern, clinician, and teacher at Shalvata Mental Health Center, near Tel Aviv, in Israel. I owe profound and abiding thanks to the many patients and families, doctor and nurses, therapists and other health care workers I met there, who taught me more about the reality of extreme states of mind than I could possibly imagine and would not have found by consulting books alone. Over the years, the interns, residents, undergraduate, and graduate students in Israel and in the United States – especially recently at the Gallatin School of Individualized Studies at New York University (NYU), where I have been teaching a course on the history of madness since 2017, and at the Humanities Center at Johns Hopkins University, where I taught from 2015 to 2017 – challenged me, helping me clarify my ideas while offering their own insights, based on their experiences, those of their families, and extraordinarily diverse communities. I am deeply grateful to my Dean at NYU's Gallatin School, Susanne Wofford, who welcomed me to this most unique academic institution and kindly offered a space to write when it was much needed.

Much of the work that will be discussed here is drawn from vast quantities of sophisticated scholarship, based on the research of the many psychiatrists, psychoanalysts, historians, anthropologists, philosophers, advocates, and service users, whose work I have encountered and came to admire over the years. It is truly inspiring – and deeply humbling – to see the magnitude and range of these efforts, not only to understand psychological pain on a theoretical level, but also to be of greater practical use to those who suffer, and, in so doing, to cultivate a vocation – an ethics, as I will call it – dedicated to alleviating and, where possible, preventing, psychic suffering. I have greatly learned – and continue to learn – from the extraordinary work of Roy Porter, Tanya Luhrmann, Greg Eghigian, Richard Noll, Ian Hacking, Elyn Saks, Kenneth Kendler, Nick Haslam,

Kay Redfield Jamison, Andrew Scull, German Berrios, Josef Parnas, Susan Lamb, Peter Zachar, Kenneth Schaffner, Rachel Cooper, Jonathan Metzl, Assen Jablensky, Kieran McNally, Anne Harrington, Louis Sass, and Sander Gilman, to name but a few of those whose contributions to the history and philosophy of psychiatry in general – and of schizophrenia in particular – have been both formative and generative. Some of them have generously shared their latest insights with me, going beyond what is already available on the subject in print.

During my years of theoretical studies, practical training, and activist engagement for improved psychological understanding and treatment of those diagnosed with schizophrenia, I have come across brilliant minds, extraordinary clinicians, and committed citizens. I am especially thankful to Dr. Ann-Louise Silver and to the ISPS organization and its chapters, both in Israel and around the world. Our yearly conferences, reading groups, and work groups, bringing together service users, families, and mental health professionals, have always been inspiring and moving.

An in-depth study of the history of the field would not have been possible without the DeWitt Wallace Institute for Psychiatry, History, Policy and the Arts at Weill Cornell Medical College in New York City. Both its working groups, on the *History of Psychoanalysis* and on *Psychoanalysis and the Humanities*, have served as a supportive and facilitating intellectual environment. In my role as the director of the Richardson Seminar at the institute from 2016 to 2019, I was fortunate enough to invite many of the scholars whose work I found intriguing to discuss their research with us. I am immensely grateful to the mentorship and friendship of the director of the institute, George Makari, to its associate director Nathan Kravis, and to its members Rosemary Stevens, Ted Shapiro, Kathy Dalsimer, Bob Michels, Anne Hoffman, Aaron Esman, Nirav Soni, Larry Friedman, and Lenny Groopman. Larry, one of the most passionate and generous scholars of psychoanalysis I have ever met, has been instrumental in making helpful suggestions at a very early stage of this project. Lenny, a brilliant historian and a unique clinician, has always been an extraordinary teacher and a source of constant support and encouragement on this project and on others.

I also want to thank the members of the recently formed group of scholars that make up the *Psychiatry, Psychoanalysis and Society* working group at the DeWitt Wallace Institute for the History of Psychiatry:

Kathryn Tabb, Thomas Dodman, Rachel Aviv, Dagmar Herzog, Alexandra Bacopoulos-Viau, Camille Robcis, Jonas Knatz, Stefanos Geroulanos, Jessica Kovler, Ben Kafka, and Larry McGrath, who provided invaluable comments and asked critical questions at various stages of this project. I especially thank Katie Tabb for her thoughtful contributions to the field overall, and for her specific recommendations for improvement and further reading regarding this specific project.

I am much obliged to Megan Wolf who quite literally runs the institute, and am infinitely in debt to Nicole Topich, the most resourceful librarian of the Oskar Diethelm Library, who never failed to provide me with the necessary sources, no matter how obscure they were.

Last but not least, I would like to pay special thanks to Lucy Bergeret. First as my teaching assistant at the Humanities Center at Johns Hopkins University and, more recently, as my research assistant and a wise editor, Lucy's superb input and wise advice, especially during the last few months of finalizing this book, were indispensable. A philosopher, an intellectual historian, and a scholar of comparative literature, Lucy has made this book a whole lot better than it would have been otherwise.

Thanks to the editorial staff at Polity Press, Ellen MacDonald-Kramer and Stephanie Homer, for shepherding me through this project, and especially to the series editor, Pascal Porcheron, for his undiminished belief in this work, his patience, and his wise counsel. I also want to thank the two anonymous readers of the Polity Press for their thoughtful and rigorous feedback on this manuscript. Their invaluable input helped clarify my argument and improved this book.

The last year of working on this book took place during the COVID-19 pandemic and the barely veiled assault on democracy in the United States, where I was located and found a second home. I am thankful to my family and friends, whose steady stream of expressed interest, care, and concern, and whose blessed sense of humor, contributed to the finalization of this project, keeping me sane along the way.

No one can measure the embracing presence in my life of my mother, Aliza Ophir, my brothers Ori and Arnon Ophir, and my long-time dear friends Sigal Avin, Shiri Broza, Aya Seker Einbinder, Alon Hager, Maya Levi, Michal Kaplan Rokman, Efrat Shamgar, Daphna Spigelman, Gil Talmi, Antal Tzur, and Ruth Weinberg. I feel privileged to have found new neighbors and friends in a welcoming community, and especially the McCollum-Garlins, the Schindler-Schuls, the Kramers, and the Nicosias, all of whom were enormously supportive at the final stages of writing this book.

My most heartfelt gratitude goes to the loves of my life, Britt and Alma, who graciously awaited the completion of this manuscript, and were unbelievably tolerant. By the time its last pages were written and proof-read, they had grown taller, more beautiful, and even more talented. As always, they kept their charming and funny traits intact! I cannot wait to spend much needed time with you again. You are my miracles, and thank you for insisting on getting us Tulip, our pandemic puppy, who quite literally pushed me off my desk chair when it was high time to do so, taking me on daily walks along the bay and in the city.

This book is dedicated to Hent, my toughest reader and my partner in all things worth living for. If it were not for *you*, it would not have been at all.

Introduction: The Ends of a Diagnosis

"It's a word, that's all, a word that covers a large, loose category," the psychiatrist explained, "it's like saying 'tree.' There are all kinds, firs, elms, pines. So there are many kinds and degrees of schizophrenia." (Louise Wilson, *This Stranger, My Son*, 1968)[1]

If You Want a Label

When Tony was discharged from the hospital, his father, Jack Wilson (a surgeon by profession), had enough of the conflicting reports and wanted a "real diagnosis." Dr. Brewster, the psychiatrist, who thought Tony's parents surely realized he was "very sick," concluded: "schizophrenia, if you want to label it. The boy is a paranoid schizophrenic." Shocked by the doctor's response, Tony's mother, Louise, echoed the expert's words: "*schizophrenia, if you want a label*," thinking all the while about her son's dark blue eyes, his beautiful, rare smile, but also about the "ugly contortions of his rage," his terror and fear.

What was this strange phenomenon of Tony's illness? Was it "a thing," of a natural, biological, or ontological, kind? Was it a phenomenon to be understood as a matter of degree, as part of a broader spectrum, a scale or continuum? The psychiatrist's choice to describe it as a "loose category" (just a "word") certainly had not made things easier to decide. Neither had his comparison with the natural kind of a "tree," or his evoking the "many kinds and degrees" of schizophrenia. Did the name "schizophrenia" or "paranoid schizophrenia" offer an adequate characterization in and of itself, a genuine definition, of the ailment Tony appeared to be suffering from? Or did it merely introduce another label (if one "wanted" one), adding on to the numerous, equally apt or vague, preexisting ones? In other words, what is – and what was – "schizophrenia," precisely?

While this book is intended for a broader interested audience, it makes informative excursions here and there into topics that may speak to specialists and therapists alike. It will ask a few simple questions, to shed light on the different ways in which Tony and his family's situation might be understood: can the term schizophrenia be considered as a natural kind in its own right, whose members are constituted by a similar set of biological mechanisms, and can its application to a particular case be determined with certainty? Can paranoid schizophrenia, for instance, be considered as a subspecies of a kind that shares a similar natural causal structure and, hence, as a biological classification rank of schizophrenia (just as an "elm" or a "pine" are types of trees)? Or does schizophrenia have many kinds and (unlike trees), many degrees, as Dr. Brewster seems to suggest? Is it a category (in the same way that "tree" is one), albeit composed of distinct kinds and varying degrees? Was Dr. Brewster diagnosing a natural disease ("schizophrenia") or was he diagnosing Tony as a type of person (a "paranoid schizophrenic"), taking the latter as part of a wider spectrum of mental deviancy that differs only in degree (rather than in kind) from psychological "normalcy," broadly construed? Or should we consider schizophrenia (as did some American psychiatrists in the 1960s) as no more than a "word," that covers a "large, loose, category"?

To answer these questions, we will abstain from trying to draw out some timeless essence of schizophrenia, an implausible enterprise if ever there was one. Rather, we will limit ourselves to examining its genesis as a medical and psychiatric diagnosis, and describe and evaluate its uses in the clinical and therapeutic professions over time. In so doing, we will try to understand not only its history and present characteristics, but also what kind of future this diagnosis and the proposed treatment for it might still hold in store. In other words, we will aim to see what picture emerges once one no longer takes the diagnosis of schizophrenia to be that of a stable identity per se, but also one of perspective. At times, the diagnosis will be, and perhaps needs to be, placed on a continuum or a spectrum with the normal and, at other times, be seen and appreciated as if it were a fixed category of illness, a natural kind, of sorts.

This dual vision of one and the same phenomenon recalls the picture shown in figure 1, which Thomas Kuhn, the philosopher and historian of science, following Ludwig Wittgenstein, borrowed from the psychologist

Figure 1 Joseph Jastrow, The duck–rabbit illusion (1899)
Source: Wikimedia Commons

Joseph Jastrow, to demonstrate "the structure of scientific revolutions." According to Kuhn, even when nothing in the environment has changed, the shift of attention of the scientific community transforms its perception of the phenomenon all at once, and "[w]hat were ducks in the scientist's world before the revolution are rabbits afterwards."[2] The relationship between the two distinct paradigms of diagnosing schizophrenia may be just that, with the important difference that in the case of the latter it is increasingly evident that the two pictures somehow continue to alternate – that is, flip back and forth – throughout history.

Carving Nature at Its Joints

Schizophrenia, also known as the paradigmatic form of madness,[3] the "sacred symbol,"[4] or "heartland"[5] of psychiatry, was first used as a medical classification by the Swiss psychiatrist Paul Eugen Bleuler in 1908.[6] It was coined as a diagnosis exactly a century after the name "psychiatry" (from *psykhe*, meaning soul, and *iatreia*, connoting medical treatment) was first used by the German physician Johann Christian Reil. In his seminal 1808 paper, "On the Term of Medicine and its Ramifications, Particularly with Regard to the Revision of the Topic in Psychiatry," Reil called for the establishment of a specific subdivision of medicine to treat mental illnesses.[7] Ever since, psychiatrists in Europe and around the world have been engaged in an ongoing collective effort to classify – that is, to identify and name, describe, and treat – such psychological ailments.

Nevertheless, attempts to classify specific mental disturbances and the ways in which they affect the behavior of those suffering from them have a much longer history. One of the first attempts to classify different types of *mania* – the Greek term for madness – can be found in Plato's dialogue *Phaedrus* (*c.*370 BC). In the text, Socrates defines *eros* or Love as a form of madness, and thus as a disturbance of our conventions and conducts.[8] Socrates then distinguishes between madness that is caused by human ailments, and madness that is sent by the gods:[9]

> SOCRATES: … we said did we not that love is a kind of madness, didn't we?
> PHAEDRUS: Yes.
> SOCRATES: And that there are two kinds of madness, one caused by human illnesses, the other from a divine release from the norms of conventional behavior.
> PHAEDRUS: Quite so.
> SOCRATES: And we divided the divine kind of madness into four parts, each with its own deity. We attributed prophetic inspiration to Apollo, mystical inspiration to Dionysus, poetic inspiration to the Muses, and the fourth kind to Aphrodite and to Eros.[10]

In *Phaedrus*, Plato derives his definitions of *mania* from contemporary Greek medical writings, which began with the generic concept of madness, before proceeding to differentiating its species. Just as he distinguishes between two methods of reasoning, Plato defines the method of collecting diverse elements under a single generic term as one method, and that of dividing this genus into further species as the other. However, this second method of division should not be applied crudely, like an unskilled butcher indistinctly carving up an animal. Rather, Socrates claims, when we make divisions or classifications, we should *carve nature at its joints*. Even when we think we are looking at a single physical body, on closer scrutiny, we see that it contains pairs of organs. And even though these separate organs may share the same name, they are still distinct, in the same way that a left hand is distinct from a right hand. The same holds true for madness, as Socrates argues. Although we have a single name for it (a generic form), we can carefully divide it into further parts, "carving its nature at the joints."

During the Enlightenment, attempts to order elements in the natural world expanded significantly. These efforts were undertaken in different disciplines, from chemistry to mathematics, and applied to various objects of study, from minerals and animals, to human diseases. The first psychiatric classifications of mental diseases followed the early medical nosology (from the Greek *nosos*, "disease"), which was inspired not by anatomy but by botany. Indeed, they drew on the model of plant taxonomy, or classification.[11] Despite these systematic ambitions, however, it was soon realized that when it comes to mental illnesses, constructing a valid "family, genus, species" along the lines of classification in the natural world was a difficult task. The combination of body and soul (with all its variations, distortions, and pathologies) does not always follow the same patterns as the rest of the natural world. Most importantly, mental phenomena rarely fit into the predictable models of natural laws and probabilities that regulate causes and effects in the material world. While metaphysicians have long employed the idea of *carving nature at its joints* in relation to the phenomenon of madness, when it comes to rapidly changing psychiatric diagnoses like schizophrenia, it is far from obvious that there even *is* a natural essence – with presumably decisive, descriptive, and classificatory categories – to be carved out.

In his criticism of the American psychiatric classification system, the *Diagnostic and Statistical Manual of Mental Disorders* (DSM), the philosopher Ian Hacking shows how psychiatry encountered insurmountable problems in its early modern endeavor to emulate botany. As Hacking notes, these difficulties occur not so much on the level of assessing different "trees" (the various diagnoses found in the DSM), but rather, of encountering the "wood itself" (that is, the classificatory enterprise as such).[12] For him, there is a flawed logic at the heart of an enterprise that tries to think about mental illnesses in terms of natural categories. First of all, unlike other medical fields, in psychiatry – or, for that matter, in psychology, psychotherapy, and psychoanalysis – the object one tries to observe, classify, and heal, is not always easily identifiable or recognizable. It might not even be a *unitary* object at all. Furthermore, while in animals and plants the various aspects which are classified arise *naturally* by evolutionary descent, the abnormal behaviors that psychiatry sets out to classify and heal have no such shared genealogy or pathogenesis. As a consequence, "paranoid schizophrenia" cannot be traced back to "schizophrenia," just as schizophrenia does not derive from a "schizophrenic spectrum." On the other hand, an "American elm" can be traced back to the genus of "ulmus/elm" and to the family of "ulmaceae/elms," in the same way that "sugar pine" can be traced back to the genus of "pinus/pine" and to the family or differentiated species of "pinaceae/pines."

In retrospect, as Hacking shows, the reason for psychiatry's failure in properly identifying – and thus, treating – mental illnesses was as simple as it was compelling. This endeavor was fundamentally flawed in its attempt to use the botanical, naturalist model as a foundation for its method of classification. Rather than referring to a single and permanent object, our concepts of madness, mental deviance, and, *a fortiori*, schizophrenia, refer to an unstable state or episode, whose symptoms can change, both throughout history and in an individual's lifetime. Schizophrenia is not a stable object, Hacking concludes, but "a moving target."[13]

In their alternative reading of the botanical metaphor of mental illnesses, the psychiatrists Daniel Mason and Honor Hsin refer to yet a different way in which their field used this model in its effort to classify mental illnesses. They demonstrate how the American neurologist George Beard (1881), in his *American Nervousness: Its Causes and Consequences*, offered a radical conceptual departure from the botanical metaphors used by eighteenth-century taxonomists, with his "evolutionary tree" of nervousness. According to Beard, all mental illnesses are branches on the same tree. They share the same trunk, the same roots, the same soil, indeed the same ecosystem, in which psychiatric illnesses can thrive.[14] Ecosystems, or more precisely "ecological niches," in which mental illnesses flourish, were the better metaphors offered by Hacking to describe the many elements that make a new type of diagnosis possible, and in the absence of which the diagnosis cannot survive.[15]

The End of a Diagnosis?

While in the late 1960s Tony Wilson could be diagnosed with paranoid schizophrenia, coded 295.3 by the 1968 version of the American

Psychiatric Association's DSM-II,[16] this diagnosis is no longer permitted by the newest version of the manual (the 2013 DSM-5). Is this to say that there are no longer any "paranoid schizophrenics" among us? Have these individuals changed their nature? Or rather, has psychiatry changed its way of classifying and ordering disturbances in human psychological behavior?

Given the fundamental uncertainty that now surrounds the idea of *carving nature at its joints* when it comes to mental illnesses, most psychiatrists tend to reach their clinical diagnoses and proposed therapies by *cutting to the chase*, as Dr. Brewster did with Tony. After all, as *The History of Nosography* aptly noted in 1923, most physicians "cannot live, cannot speak or act without the concept of morbid categories."[17] They have no choice but to chop up the organic whole of mental illness into ill-defined parts, at times like clumsy butchers. Whether in the research lab or clinic, to make a diagnosis, psychiatrists are driven by their own pragmatic and bureaucratic needs, in addition to the urgency of their patients' suffering. Furthermore, patients and their families – like Tony's – are often just as eager as psychiatrists, in wanting a clearly defined, definitive, medical category. A diagnosis gives one something to hold onto, to replace the perplexing and, at times, terrifying experience of mental illness.

In his 2007 book, *Our Present Complaint: American Medicine Then and Now*, historian of medicine Charles Rosenberg argues that "the act of diagnosis links the individual to the social system."[18] Not only does a diagnosis serve a bureaucratic need (keeping records, setting up reimbursements, coordinating between professionals and institutions), it also serves an emotional necessity, offering patients and their families the security of a narrative. It gives a sense of solid ground to stand on, where previously uncertainty and anxiety prevailed. Patients want to know what they are suffering from: "What is wrong with me?," as Anisha asked Amy June Sousa, who conducted her fieldwork in Lucknow, India, "Do you know if my illness has a name?,"[19] she persisted. Or just as another patient diagnosed with schizophrenia who otherwise was not entirely comfortable with the diagnosis of the disease wrote: "The label has helped me, though, to feel less guilt about my inability to 'conquer' my problems, and to learn to make some allowances for my difficulties in handling situations."[20]

In his book, Rosenberg describes diagnoses as passwords that grant access to the institutional software managing contemporary medicine. In this way, a diagnosis connects the individual to the collective, and vice versa. The problem, however, is that diagnoses then become "part of reality as much as our clogged arteries or dysfunctional kidneys."[21] In other words, for all its shaky grounds, not only does the clinical classification become "real," but from there on, it wields a tyrannical power over our minds. This is fatefully illustrated by the astonishing willingness of physicians and psychiatrists to keep using categories of so-called "nosologies," despite the wealth of clinical and therapeutic reasons to doubt their fundamental validity.

Dr. Brewster and other clinicians who still use the DSM understand this *end* of a diagnosis. Significantly, the DSM itself – also known as the Bible, the Rosetta Stone,[22] and even the Chinese Menu[23] of psychiatry – changes every few years, introducing new categories and putting an *end* to earlier diagnoses. Indeed, diagnoses are removed from the DSM when they fail to stand the test of time, that is, when the accumulated critical experience of doctors, patients, and families calls for a fresh look and a revision of previously established criteria. Collective disappointment thus produces a renewed effort to identify and classify madness or mental deviance – including schizophrenia – which then allows for completely new ways of diagnosing them. Together with disorganized schizophrenia, catatonic schizophrenia, undifferentiated schizophrenia, and residual schizophrenia, the diagnosis of paranoid schizophrenia became obsolete in the DSM-5. Formally speaking, there are no longer any "paranoid schizophrenics" among us. Since 2013, the *kind* or *type* of people (genus and species) that Dr. Brewster had labeled Tony with is nowhere to be found.

According to Hacking, the human sciences (including psychology, psychiatry, the social sciences, and clinical medicine) are driven by nine engines of discovery, and involved in a process of "making up people."[24] By *counting* people (say, 1 per 100 people in America suffers from schizophrenia); by *quantifying* them (age of onset before 45, duration of psychotic symptoms longer than a month), by *creating norms*; by *correlating* data about them (schizophrenics are 10% more likely to die of suicide); by *medicalizing*, *biologizing*, and *geneticizing* these subjects while trying to *normalize* deviance, by *bureaucratizing* these individuals, they invent new kinds of people. When "autistics," "hoarders," "the obese," or "paranoid schizophrenics" emerge as new kinds of people, new types of experts who then identify, assess, and treat them, also appear. Newly instituted organizations then develop, which are specifically set up to cater to these new kinds of people, or patients.

While it was possible to be a "paranoid schizophrenic" after this kind of person was *made up* by psychiatry in 1968, this is no longer an option after 2013. With the change of the "ecological niche," the conditions no longer exist for this specific diagnosis to thrive. It thus disappears, in what could be termed a process of "unmaking of people."[25]

The present study and its title, *Schizophrenia: An Unfinished History* envisions the *end* of this diagnosis, with the double meaning of *end* as both the purpose of a diagnosis, and its possible termination or demise. Modern psychiatry has moved from carving out categories of mental illnesses to delineating spectra of these disorders, which is considered a remarkable paradigm shift in its classification system. In this book, we will examine whether this shift from a *qualitative categorical* diagnosis (based on descriptive symptoms) to a spectrum-like, *dimensional* classification (based on biological or psychological dimensions and scales) is at least partly responsible for the effort of bringing an *end* to the diagnosis of schizophrenia.

Since the 1990s, epidemiologists, psychiatrists, historians, and journalists have all been asking if schizophrenia is disappearing as a medical diagnosis. An article in the Epidemiology section of *The Lancet*, titled "Is schizophrenia disappearing?" suggested a substantial decrease in the reported incidences of schizophrenia since the mid-1960s.[26] By the same token, a 2012 book titled *Schizophrenia Is a Misdiagnosis* criticized the validity of the diagnosis and announced its end.[27] Other articles appeared with titles such as "'Schizophrenia' does not exist,"[28] published in 2016 in the *British Medical Journal*, and "The concept of schizophrenia is coming to an end," published in *The Independent* in 2017. This latter piece stated that schizophrenia might face the same fate as *dementia praecox*, the very diagnosis it had historically come to replace.[29] Lastly, in the *Schizophrenia Bulletin*, a 2017 article suggested that the word might eventually be confined to history, not unlike the medical use of the term "dropsy."[30]

A Difference in Kind or in Degree?

Schizophrenia: An Unfinished History, then, aims to investigate two opposing ways of understanding mental health and its abnormalities, that have framed our perception from antiquity to the present day. Each of these views is *paradigmatic*, with different sets of shared commitments, practices, symbolic generalizations, models, and so-called exemplars.[31] The first, which we will call the *categorical view*, characterizes abnormal mental states and behaviors as *different in kind* from normal ones, just as elm trees are different from pine trees, and trees, more generally, are different from minerals or from animals. The second, the *clinical-dynamic view*, defines the difference between normal and disordered states as one of *degree*, placing it on a spectrum within a wider dimension of mental phenomena, in the same way that in medicine hypertension is different from hypotension.

These two intuitions (of a difference in natural kind – of given qualities, or essence, on the one hand – and in degree – of quantitative, scalar variations, on the other), have produced two very different ways of representing mental health and sickness. As distinct and, at times, irreconcilable ways of seeing and talking about mental illnesses, they rise and fall, in response to the different social and cultural milieu in which they are discussed, and intellectually or institutionally supported. One of the aims of this book is to ask whether we currently find ourselves in a milieu or climate that may provide the conditions for the disappearance of schizophrenia as a helpful critical and clinical term of diagnosis and treatment.

Several experts attribute the decline in the reported incidences of the diagnosis of schizophrenia to the growing availability of better psychopharmacological treatments, while others place more emphasis on reduced accessibility to the treatment centers that record these numbers, or even to higher rates of suicide. Still others argue that the underlying cause of this decline is not so much due to a reduction in the number of individuals who exhibit what psychiatrists came to define as symptoms of schizophrenia, but to a dramatic change in the *classification culture* of psychiatry as a medical professional discipline. The "twin pillars" of psychiatry's nosology (which provided the conditions for the birth of the term schizophrenia) are crumbling, some argue, and a new biomarker-based classification system should be reconstructed, brick by brick.[32]

It is important to keep in mind, however, that the vast majority of authors who criticize the diagnosis of schizophrenia agree that some individuals indeed *do* experience delusions, hallucinations, and disorganized speech that make them sound irrational. They admit that such individuals may also exhibit disorganized or catatonic behavior, flat affect, or the failure to maintain basic self-care. And yet, a growing number of authors maintain that, as a presumed disease entity – as an identifiable state, a natural kind – schizophrenia does not "exist." And while some claim that it could be considered and called an "end stage" of other untreated mental disorders (in the same way that heart failure is the terminal stage of various heart diseases), others won't even go that far, proposing instead to abolish the term schizophrenia altogether.[33]

To this day, the integrity of schizophrenia as a diagnosis is unproven, as there is no valid objective test for it. The failure to identify schizophrenia's biological markers, despite volumes of accumulated research data, has led professionals and laymen to propose discarding the label, both as a useful term, and as a biological or psychological category in its own right. Unsurprisingly, others have argued that to discard the concept and diagnosis of schizophrenia altogether would be premature and, hence, unwise and impractical. Indeed, it would represent a radical shift away from the current, predominantly *categorical disease model* of psychiatry, whose scientific and medical credentials (not to mention, institutional presence and prominence) are still largely unchallenged, forming a public and political reality to be reckoned with. As an alternative to the categorical method, the *dimensional model* still faces an uphill institutional battle to establish itself as a paradigm that carries similar weight in classifying mental illnesses. Yet, several examples and practices of this alternative model can already be found.

One such example is the diagnostic approach developed by the American National Institute of Mental Health (NIMH), the largest research organization in the world specializing in mental illness, whose mission is to study, understand, and treat mental illnesses – and thereby, to pave the way for prevention, recovery, and cure of these ailments. The NIMH's "Research Domain Criteria" (RDoC),[34] although intended as a research framework for new approaches to investigating mental disorders rather than a clinical diagnostic guide *per se*, aims to explain mental health and illness in terms of varying degrees of dysfunction in systems of emotion, cognition, motivation, and social behavior. The RDoC tries to identify basic *dimensions* of medical and psychological functioning that span the whole *range* of human behavior, from normal to abnormal. This shift (from distinct *categorical* diagnoses to a more *dimensional* approach) is arguably the result of what Richard Noll described as psychiatrists' increasing realization that "pouring muddy water from one jug into another" would not make it clearer. An alternative and, in their eyes, better "solution" would be "to break the jugs" instead.[35]

Another example of a dimensional system of evaluation is the "Hierarchical Taxonomy of Psychopathology" (HiTOP).[36] The HiTOP was developed by a group of psychologists and psychiatrists from several research centers, with the explicit purpose of offering an alternative to the neurobiologically oriented RDoC. The HiTOP regards mental health as a spectrum. It places mental health problems on a *continuum* between pathology and normality, in much the same way that we measure body weight or blood pressure. Just as human weight is measured on a numerical scale (from 1 to 250 kg) and blood pressure on a different scale (from, say, 40/70 to 100/190), according to the HiTOP, we can also find a *spectrum* ranging from normal to abnormal when it comes to memory, perception, attention, social communication, and the ability to regulate fear, loss, or rewards.

The old classification system of the DSM used a top-down approach, defining mental disorders on the basis of their symptoms and presuming underlying natural causes with their corresponding effects. In contrast, these recent models begin by defining the normal distribution of a given trait or characteristic. Only then do they consider what might cause a gradual dysregulation or dysfunction in these systems that might result in symptoms in need of eventual diagnosis and treatment. Instead of looking for delusions, hallucinations, thought disorders, disorganized speech or behavior (or any other symptom that supposedly "make up" schizophrenia as a given entity), they search for domains that span this *continuum* ranging from the normal to the pathological. In these domains, we find a host of phenomena, mental states, and episodes, which include fear, frustration, learning, perception, memory, language, attachment, communication, understanding of self and others. The aim is thus to avoid setting *arbitrary boundaries* between health and pathology, normal and abnormal, which in current systems run the risk of being taken as natural kinds. These alternative diagnostic models begin by looking for the basic building blocks of the psychopathological structure, and then work their way upwards to its highest level of generality (HiTOP). In sum, they presuppose that psychopathology is *dimensional* in nature, while still allowing for categorical diagnoses where these are useful for pragmatic treatment purposes – and, more specifically, to help patients secure disability benefits.

Suggestions for revising existing diagnostic practices have also been proposed by scholars outside of the mental health professions. For example, Nikolas Rose, a British sociologist, spent decades questioning the psychiatric enterprise and defending a move from "diagnosis" to "formulation." According to Rose's distinction, a complex story (one that includes the causes of the person's distress and that follows how their experiences might have penetrated "under their skin") would be just as appropriate in clinical practice as using a "name" to label a categorical diagnosis. Moreover, assessing the person's capabilities and impairments would be much more useful when planning their needs for receiving mental health services. The move from labels like "schizophrenia" to a story told about the person's overall situation and station in life, the biological, psychological, and social factors that have caused and shaped their ailment and suffering, and the identification of their required current care, would demand more listening on the part of everyone involved. Such listening, Rose argues "would be all to the good."[37]

Other voices in this larger conversation want to bring the diagnosis of schizophrenia to an *end* for very different reasons. Some psychiatrists, psychologists, social activists, survivors, ex-patients, and others have argued that the label "schizophrenic" is stigmatizing, due to the connotations of hopelessness, chronicity, and even dangerousness, that it carries. In response to this and to patients' suffering, they seek alternative, less discriminatory, and more appealing, diagnoses. "Extreme mental states," "voice-hearing," "non-ordinary states," or "diverse identities" are but a few of these suggested alternative designations.

Madness from Antiquity to the Present Day

This book proposes to tell the story of the possible *end* of schizophrenia as a diagnosis by shedding light on the early history and recent usage of this controversial term. While other medical or psychiatric terms that define abnormal mental states and behaviors – such as melancholia, mania, or "insanity" – date back to antiquity, schizophrenia is a relatively new technical term. That said, the perennial difficulty in characterizing abnormal mentalities and behaviors (either as *discrete* forms of human existence, or as part of a *continuum* between the normal and abnormal) goes all the way back to the Hebrew Bible and the New Testament, as the first chapter of this book explains.

As Hacking observed, the idea that it is impossible to retroactively diagnose individuals is a product of the "academically correct official history-of-medicine or philosophy-of-science teaching."[38] Nevertheless, if we set aside academic propriety and the potential self-righteousness it implies, we can follow Hacking and still carefully draw inferences from the way past cases were viewed by contemporary experts. The first chapter in this book thus uses foundational texts in Western culture, ranging from the Bible all the way up to Eugen Bleuler, to reconstruct the origins of the dispute on the relations between the normal and the abnormal (distinctness vs. continuity) when diagnosing individuals who suffer from a severe break in their perception of reality and withdraw from engagement with their social groups.

In Chapter 2, "The Birth of 'the Schizophrenias,'" we introduce the two major modern authorities on schizophrenia of the late nineteenth and early twentieth centuries, Emil Kraepelin and Eugen Bleuler. In their paradigmatic texts – Kraepelin's *Psychiatry: A Textbook for Students and Physicians* (1896) and Bleuler's *Dementia Praecox or the Group of Schizophrenias* (1911) – we will locate the crucial terminological change that appeared in the emergence of modern psychiatry's dispute over the nature of mental disorders, when the older category of *dementia praecox* was replaced with the new term, schizophrenia. As we will see, Kraepelin's and Bleuler's works can be considered as condensed forms of the two competing – categorical vs. dimensional – paradigms, which remain at the very heart of current debates on schizophrenia.

Chapter 3 then discusses these paradigms in the work of Sigmund Freud, the founding father of psychoanalysis. In his early works, Freud proposes that schizophrenic behavior lies on a continuum, running from neurosis to psychosis. In his later writing, however, Freud argues that schizophrenic behavior is different *in kind* from more typical behavior, even though he concedes it occurs *concurrently* with behaviors that are viewed as normal. As we will see, Freud's legacy of oscillating between these two structurally distinct paradigms continues to shape the discourse of psychoanalysis on schizophrenia and psychosis to this day.

Chapter 4, "A Moving Target," examines how the diagnosis of schizophrenia has changed over time. Tracing the definition of schizophrenia in the DSM from 1952 to 2013, this chapter analyzes the critiques and commentaries that professional task forces, activists, journalists, patients, and families have extended to every definition of schizophrenia proposed in the manual's seven different editions. It concludes with the DSM-5's declaration that it will systematically consider *ethical* questions and pragmatic matters in its efforts to revise the classification of psychiatric disorders.

In light of these ethical considerations, Chapter 5, "Hearing Voices," then discusses a relatively new form of protest against the diagnosis of schizophrenia. It discusses the example of the Hearing Voices Movement (HVM), which challenges the pathologization of voice-hearing and its systematic association with the diagnosis of schizophrenia. Indeed, while hearing voices was historically considered as one of the central symptoms of schizophrenia, the Hearing Voices Movement depicts it as a natural part of human experience, one that should not be relegated to a separate and abnormal domain. As we will suggest, this change in the interpretation of voice-hearing can be viewed as yet another incarnation of the dimensional model.

Chapter 6, "Stigma and the Problem of Naming," examines the decline of "schizophrenia" as a consequence of the stigma carried by the term itself, which, as some argue, leads to harmful discrimination.[39] This chapter explores the various calls for changing or dropping the name "schizophrenia" altogether around the world. As we will see, successful examples of name changes in Asian countries have provided both food for thought, and challenging inspiration, for Western attempts to reduce stigma and find alternative labels for the diagnosis.

The final chapter, "The Ethics of a Diagnosis," examines the rise and fall of schizophrenia in light of two competing philosophical models, that reveal the shifts in our understanding of a deeper, metaphysical structure. While the first model is open, continuous, inclusive, and dynamic, the other is closed, discontinuous, exclusive, and static. In light of these dual poles, the ethical implications distilled from the material discussed in the preceding chapters are evaluated.

As will become apparent throughout these chapters, this book ultimately explores the suggestion that the fundamentally eccentric nature of what we have come to call schizophrenia lends itself to contrasting interpretations, which reveal much deeper structural oppositions, between continuity and discontinuity, equilibrium and disequilibrium, and, ultimately, vitalism and mechanism. As these distinctions are unavoidable yet revisable, it is a critical and clinical imperative to use them provisionally and prudently. Scholars and theorists, psychiatrists and psychologists, psychoanalysts and mental health advocates, must all keep the pragmatic aim of healing patients firmly in mind when using classifications that are just that: "labels."

Instead of favoring one paradigm over the other, or slipping into relativism pure and simple, those who deal with mental illness must accept the paradox – even the aporia – of having two seemingly exclusive accounts of the disorder operating concurrently. Being "of two minds,"[40] they can then see a rabbit or a duck, in the full awareness that both are a case of "now you see it, now you don't," that present us with an incomplete sketch of what is, in "essence," a much more complex and intractable phenomenon.

Chapter 1
From the Bible to Bleuler

When reconstructing the history of schizophrenia as a diagnosis, a medical concept, and a condition that requires clinical treatment, it is important to keep the patient's view in mind.[1] As Roy Porter aptly instructed us, we ought to write the people's history of suffering as we try to understand what "schizophrenia" was for the person who was ill, diagnosed, and treated.[2] Here is one such narration, to begin with:

> I was diagnosed with schizophrenia on February 21, 1995, I was 22 years old, and my reaction was initially shock … the word "mad" surfaced in my mind. It was not just the word; my mind actually did a complete reversion to my childhood, particularly 2 stories: Alice in Wonderland and Dr Jekyll and Mr Hyde … The images of the [Mad] hatter, Mr Hyde, and those other famous characters made by the media … reinforce the notion of madness as something to instill comic relief or as fascinatingly dangerous: How can something that destroys families, relationships, and friendships be considered "funny." There is nothing laughable about losing one's direction in life. There is no joke in one's brain playing such vile tricks to take you to an anxiety point that may result in suicide. (Mark Ellerby, 2018)[3]

A common misconception exists in our society, inspired by the meaning of the word schizophrenia, in which those who are suffering, like Mr. Ellerby, are confusedly described as having simply a "split personality," what psychiatry termed "multiple personality disorder," or more recently "dissociative identity diffusion (DID)." Some mistake those who are diagnosed with the disorder as versions of Robert Louis Stevenson's characters in his 1886 novella *The Strange Case of Dr. Jekyll and Mr. Hyde*. And although the origin of the word schizophrenia does indeed come from the ancient Greek verb *schizô*, which means "to split, separate, dissociate," the more accurate image of schizophrenia that corresponds with the experience of "losing one's direction in life," to quote Ellerby's moving first-person account cited above, is rather that of "an orchestra without a conductor."[4]

The term schizophrenia emerged in twentieth-century Germany, when modern attempts to scientifically classify madness borrowed heavily from Greek dictionaries and created a series of neologisms (such as "phobia," "manic-depressive psychosis," or "paranoia") to add to ancient concepts defining abnormal mental states and unusual behavior (such as "melancholia" or "mania") the more generic notion of "madness." The schism or split, inevitably suggested by the modern name schizophrenia, meant not to denote a split *in two*, but rather to express the tearing apart of the psychological functioning, a peculiar destruction of the cohesiveness of the self, a dissociation of the unity of the personality to a point of complete disintegration of one's thoughts, emotions, and behavior.

Today, schizophrenia is a psychiatric diagnosis that is assigned mostly to individuals who suffer delusions, hallucinations, disorganized speech, and chaotic behavior, as well as diminished emotional expression, resulting in severe dysfunction in work, inter-personal relationships, and self-care. While naming the different symptomatic manifestations of what we call schizophrenia, we will refer to examples from experts by experience, such as Susan Weiner, whose first-person account conveys the experience of going mad.[5]

The most common symptom of schizophrenia is having delusions. The particular false and fixed beliefs that persist despite all the evidence to the contrary and are associated with the diagnosis of schizophrenia are: (1) *persecutory delusions*: "This evil dictator (as I called him) pursued me down the highways of the United States … [with the] initial intent to possess the whole of my country, transforming it into a slave state";[6] (2) *delusions of control*, such as the belief that one's thoughts or actions are being influenced and directed by external forces, accompanied by one's feelings of loss of control: "This time, awful misogynist language broke into my consciousness. 'Cunt,' 'Whore,' and similar curses were like a bell in my brain … I was completely unprepared for such an onslaught … sometimes later I would believe people could read my mind";[7] and (3) *delusions of reference*, where an ordinary neutral perception is believed to have a special and personal meaning for the individual, typified in assertions such as "I began to believe that coded messages were held for me in signs, billboards, and advertising … I soon began to wonder if the TV and films held messages that I was supposed to follow too." In addition, there are the (4) *grandiose delusions*: "In madness it was up to me to do my part in freeing the country from its stranglehold by a new and seemingly omnipotent potentate … I believe it was my duty to free each individual in the United States from the mental tyranny of the 'evil dictator'"; "I was a spy! I had a heroic place in the hidden world of war that most people didn't pay attention to"; (5) *erotomanic delusions*: "If something had a phallic shape I thought it was a romantic advance by hidden interlocutor"; (6) *nihilistic delusions*, exemplified by statements such as "I tried to face with courage experiences that felt like torture, with the spreading darkness that wanted to devour my nation and consumed its citizens"; and, finally, (7) *somatic delusions* that other sufferers conveyed such as "my heart is rotting."[8]

All of these latter mental phenomena are likewise seen as possible symptoms that call for a consideration of the schizophrenia diagnosis. Moreover, hallucinations that are typical of schizophrenia include the reported presence of negative and derogatory voices, as in "you are evil, you are a whore," "you are the reason your brother is dead, you should die" or, for that matter, voices that command the individual to act in certain ways: "you should burn this house," "you should jump off this bridge." Lastly, they consist in hearing voices that presumably converse about the individual in question, so that the voice of X would say: "he is going to take the knife now," followed by voice Y: "no, he isn't, he is a coward."

But beyond this list of symptoms, the most defining characteristic of an individual that would most likely be diagnosed as suffering from schizophrenia is the feeling that they provoke in the observer, of being incomprehensible and inaccessible. THE feeling the other person receives from them.

Schizophrenia is considered by many to be the paradigmatic, "most troubling" form of madness,[9] its "Far Side."[10] Most histories of this condition begin with Emil Kraepelin, the father of modern psychiatry, whose endeavor to classify mental illness in the late nineteenth century gave rise to the diagnosis of *dementia praecox*, the forerunner of the term schizophrenia. However, it seems that the "abnormal" kinds of behavior resembling those we have come to name schizophrenia were already identified, long before the term was first coined in the scholarly literature in 1911. Citing descriptions going back more than 3000 years (from

Ancient Mesopotamia through fourteenth-century BCE Ancient India, fifth- and fourth-centuries BCE Ancient Greece and Rome, all the way to the Middle Ages and fifteenth- through seventeenth-century Europe), some scholars contend that the phenomenon that now goes by that name schizophrenia is "probably very old."[11]

In this chapter, we will see how texts written long before the term appeared can teach us about how extreme forms of "madness" were viewed throughout history, both by those who experienced it firsthand and those who observed it in others. Although writers of every epoch insist on the uniqueness of their interpretation of the phenomenon, two trends can be identified across this history: one that places madness at the extreme end of a *spectrum* that includes the norm, and another that views it as a distinct and *categorical* "other."[12]

Terms such as "madness," "lunacy," or "insanity," together with descriptions of people who, in the eyes of their contemporaries, displayed disturbances in their habits and conduct that indicate the loss of a *shared* reality or *common* sense, can thus be used to write a history that predates the term schizophrenia. In other words, our story begins in the period well before the term schizophrenia was coined and its presumed "proper history" can be studied. The numerous (and often remarkable) ancient and medieval descriptions of the transformation of individuals who have "gone mad" show how previous eras dealt with the perennial difficulty of characterizing perceived deviant mentality and behavior, as being either at the extreme end of normal human experience or as a discrete form, to be diagnosed by experts and treated by specialists as isolated phenomena.

Yet, in studying the understanding of madness before modern psychiatry established the diagnosis of schizophrenia, we should avoid presentism and retrospective projections. Especially, we should not assume that "madness," "madmen," and "mad-doctors" (as they are described in these earlier texts) can be easily translated into the modern idioms of "schizophrenia," "schizophrenics," and "psychiatrists," respectively. Instead, the meaning and interpretation, the explanation and understanding of madness, depend on how the term is understood in its different historical, geographical, cultural, theological, and philosophical contexts. We would even contend that what constitutes "mad" people is determined by themselves and/or according to their contemporary witnesses and experts.

Prophets or Beasts? Madness in the Bible

> And the Spirit of God came upon him, and he prophesied among them. And it came to pass, when all that knew him beforetime saw that, behold, he prophesied among the prophets, then the people said one to another, what is this that is come unto the son of Kish? Is Saul also among the prophets? (1 Samuel 10:10–11)

Although schizophrenia is a diagnosis used in psychiatry, the term "madness" was not always understood, or used, as a medical concept. In fact, as Madalina Vârtejanu-Joubert, an expert on madness in Ancient Near East History and the Hebrew Bible, argues, when it comes to the early Hebrew tradition, madness is not part of the history of medicine but of political, religious, and legal anthropology.[13] In the Hebrew Bible, madmen are characterized either as human beings who have been degraded to the level of beasts, or as select individuals who are elevated towards the presence of the divine. In both cases, men who behave in strange ways seem incomprehensible to their fellow human beings, having become something *other* than merely recognizably human. Whether they belong to the animal kingdom or the divine realm, mad people are deemed to be, so it seems, of an entirely different, unique kind.

The first time the word "madness" appears in the Hebrew Bible, in the Book of Deuteronomy, it is presented as a form of divine punishment. As Moses delivers the Lord's words to the people of Israel (recounting all the blessings He shall grant them should they follow His words, and listing the numerous curses He will bring upon them should they not hearken to His voice), he says: "The Lord will smite you with *madness* and with blindness and with bewilderment of heart."[14] As Vârtejanu-Joubert shows, the Hebrew word for madness, "shigaon" resembles expressions with a similar root in other ancient Semitic languages, implying that to be mad is to be "like a *bear* with a sore head," or "to squeal like a *pig*."[15] In fact, in the later story of Nebuchadnezzar, the king of Babylon, who is punished with madness for his pride, we clearly see this degradation of the monarch to a bestial, lower form of life. Nebuchadnezzar's human heart (which was considered the seat of the higher faculties of reason, will, and judgment) is changed into that of an animal; he "eats grass as *oxen*, and his body is wet with the dew of heaven, until his hairs were grown like *eagles'* feathers, and his nails like *birds'* claws."[16]

Another depiction of madness as a degradation of the human spirit can be found in the gospels, in the New Testament. In Mark 5, Jesus is reported to visit the country of the Gerasenes and is confronted by "a man with an unclean spirit."[17] Here as well, the madman is compared to the *wolves* and the *dogs* that roam around naked, without shelter or clothing, screaming at the graveyard. The fearful villagers try to restrain the madman with chains and fetters, and feed him as if he were an animal. When Jesus is called to intervene and asks him for his name, the man replies: "My name is Legion; for we are many."[18] Jesus then sends the "legion," the "unclean spirits" into a passing herd of *swine* which, having been transformed, run into the water and drown. As a result of this miracle, the demoniac (the man who had been possessed by demons) conducts himself as a human once again, "sitting and clothed and in his right mind."[19]

In these early traditions, however, madness does not always involve changing into a lower form of life. The word "mad" or *meshuga* is also used to designate the transformation into a *higher* form of being, namely that of the prophet, the *navi*. For example, in the famous case of King Saul's bizarre gestures and nudity, the question arises of whether Saul should be counted "also among the prophets?"[20] Indeed, in Hebrew, "to behave like a prophet" can also mean "to rave," "to act like one who is beside himself," or "to behave in an uncontrolled manner."[21] People who displayed behavior such as King Saul's were seen as strange. As we saw in the words from 1 Samuel, cited in the epigraph to this section, those who knew him before noticed that he had changed:

> And he stripped off his clothes also, and prophesied before Samuel in like manner, and lay down naked all that day and all that night. (1 Samuel 19:24)

They thus had to ask themselves what had happened to him and, indeed, whether he had become a raving prophet, from then on belonging to a different category of humans.

Yet not only bystanders or contemporaries, who all too often mocked and isolated those who were thus afflicted, questioned the transformation of those who, in fact, behaved like prophets. The latter themselves also acknowledged their alteration. Such individuals clearly experienced themselves as being different from the rest of society, with its firmly established customs and well-circumscribed, sanctioned forms of conduct.

That said, the prophets of the Bible are depicted in ways that make it difficult, even for their contemporaries, to know whether they are divinely inspired or, on the contrary, gravely deluded. Indeed, the prophets claimed that when the divine spirit seized them, they had visions and could not help but behave strangely. As emissaries of the divine, Hebrew prophets such as Isaiah, Jeremiah, Elijah, and Ezekiel are said to conduct themselves in eccentric and irrational ways. In fact, Ezekiel, more than others, has been retroactively diagnosed as a schizophrenic.[22]

In these ancient depictions, madness is defined as a different spiritual *quality* that opposes the mad individual to those considered sane. Madness is seen as the result of possession (having an unclean spirit or being haunted by demons), as a consequence of "in-spiration" (that is, of being *in* the *spirit* of God that came "mightily upon" the individual in question) or as a departure of the good spirit, followed by torment by an evil substitute:[23]

> Now the spirit of the Lord departed from Saul, and an evil spirit from the Lord tormented him. (1 Samuel 16:14)

In Saul's story, madness is a matter of "another heart,"[24] while in the punishment of King Nebuchadnezzar, it is a change from a "man's heart" to a "beast's heart."[25] In these ancient texts, a *qualitative*, rather than *quantitative*, difference thus exists between the mad and the sane. If the work of the prophet is to communicate the word of God, who is so very different from humans, then it is possible that he, too, will be unintelligible. Since the work of God is seen as foreign or alien (in biblical Hebrew: "strange is his deed, and foreign is his act"), his messengers may very well be judged the same.[26] The seemingly "mad" conduct of prophets is the irruption of God's alterity into the world of humans, his strange otherness, which manifests itself in "deviant" and unexpected conduct and language.[27] Mad persons are considered and shown to be different and outlandish, precisely due to this otherness.

The representation of madness in late antiquity (notably in the Jewish tradition known as the Halacha and the Aggada) is consistent with the depiction of its "strangeness" and "alterity" in the Bible. In these texts too, if not divinely foreign, the madman is perceived as *other* than human: he is said to walk alone at night, roaming like a *dog* or a *wolf*, sleeping in cemeteries, tearing off his clothes.[28] The madman is also compared to an "*ox* goring another ox," a *camel*, or an *ass*.[29] And, indeed, more generally, in both the Old and New Testaments (the Hebrew Bible and the Christian gospels), as well as in later Jewish Talmudic writings and rabbinical commentaries, madness, even when it is considered to be a temporary condition, most often connotes a *categorically different* kind of existence, with its own distinct and unique pattern of conduct and mental qualities.

Unsacred Brains and Untamed Horses: Madness in Greco-Roman Texts

> I am about to discuss the disease called "sacred." It is not, in my opinion, any more divine or more sacred than other diseases, but has a natural cause, and its supposed divine origin is due to men's inexperience, and to their wonder at its peculiar character. (Hippocrates, *The Sacred Disease*)

While madness continued to be depicted as in the biblical sources as a supernaturally caused, categorically different, and "strange" phenomenon, the Greco-Roman tradition began to differentiate between madness as a form of possession, and madness as a natural affliction.

Caelius Aurelianus, a fifth century CE doctor, writes: "Plato, in the Phaedrus, declares that madness is twofold: one comes from a tension of the mind, having a cause in the body, the other is divine or sent down, and is inspired by Apollo; now we call this divination."[30] As discussed in the Introduction, in the *Phaedrus*, Plato's two types of madness correspond to the duality we now understand to be at the core of the human species, namely that of body and mind (or soul), of the physical and the metaphysical, the material and the spiritual.

As we saw previously, in explaining madness as inspiration by the gods, Plato suggests that prophetic madness is inspired by Apollo, as the gift of divination; mystic madness caused by Dionysus initiates one into mysteries; poetic madness is inspired by the Muses; and, finally, the madness of love is given to humans by Aphrodite and Eros.[31] Yet when madness, by contrast, is seen not as divine inspiration but as a bodily ailment, mad people are viewed as bad or shameful.[32] They are kept at home, out of view of wider society, and sometimes stoned to death.[33]

With the differentiation between divine, meaningful, or "good madness," on the one hand, and "bad madness" as a pathology of the mind and the body, on the other, Greco-Roman doctors parted from philosophers, marking an epistemological juncture where madness entered the history of medicine and its changing definitions of illnesses.

As Chiara Thumiger, a classicist and historian of ancient medicine and mental diseases, has argued, in Greco-Roman traditions, madness found a clear, albeit nuanced and differentiated, physiological explanation.[34] Indeed, a series of important innovations occurred during this period. First, a radically somatic interpretation of madness was offered. Second, madness became categorized as a bodily disease that is part of a more general classification of natural phenomena. And, finally, an approach to madness appeared that was both physiological *and* ethical. Indeed, according to the dominant view in this period of late Antiquity, mental health and soundness were thought to be achieved by maintaining a modicum of spiritual and ethical integrity.

In the medical corpus of Hippocratic texts from the fifth to fourth centuries BCE, madness is clearly framed not in divine or sacred but in naturalistic terms, as a manifestation of bodily dysfunction. At the time, the body's functions were believed to rely on the four so-called humors or fluids, and their associated qualities: blood (which is hot and wet), yellow bile or choler (which is hot and dry), black bile (which is cold and dry) and, finally, phlegm (which is cold and wet). The condition of the humors and their overall corporeal *balance* were thought to relate both to macrocosmic factors (such as the seasons or the position of the celestial bodies) and to microcosmic elements in each individual. According to this model, when the humors or fluids are in a good temperament, good mixture, or balance (*eukrasia*), this is conducive to good health. An imbalance (*dyskrasia*) or bad mixture of the humors, on the other hand, harms the wellbeing of humans and causes disease.

Health and illness were thus seen not as categorically distinct or different in kind, but as existing on a *spectrum*. They were understood as a function of relative states of greater or lesser equilibrium of the different building blocks that constituted not only the human organism, but also the whole universe. These extended beyond the humors, to the four elements (earth, air, fire, and water); the four seasons (summer, fall, winter, and spring); the four qualities (hot, cold, wet, and dry); and the four temperaments, or mental states (sanguine, choleric, melancholic, and phlegmatic). Since the body was deemed to be subject to numerous influences, it was thought to oscillate constantly between health and illness. This rationale for understanding human beings set sickness and health on a continuous scale, ranging between imbalance and balance, too much or too little, of the quantity of a substance and its power, rather than opposing them as two distinct categories. Maintaining the body's dynamic equilibrium (between extremes), keeping its internal substances in well-proportioned mixture, was considered an important part of people's daily routine. More specifically, while the management of health involved a constant recalibration of an ideal state of humoral balance, the treatment of disease was directed at restoring it.

Furthermore, as Roy Porter observed, Greek medicine postulated that health and illness were "organic" or "constitutional," deriving not from an external pathogen, but from inner processes. The inside of the body and the mind were seen as interconnected, so that the body affected the mind (e.g., fever causes delirium) and the mind affected the body. Intense emotions, for example, were thought to be responsible for a myriad of physical disorders, ranging from respiratory diseases to rheumatism, even death. A broken heart or a great fright, in this context, was seen as lethal.

Madness was thus seen as rooted in the individual, in the person's body and mind. For example, in *Hysteria in Virgins*, Hippocrates observes a young female patient and writes: "When these places are filled with blood, shivering sets in with fever … when this is the state of affairs, the girl goes crazy because of the violent inflammation."[35]

In this case, the afflicted girl is understood to have become murderous, fearful, distraught, and anxious because of the bad condition of her blood. She says dreadful things and has visions that tell her to kill herself, she has a desire for death "as if it was a form of good."[36] According to the Hippocratic texts, the *abundance* of blood, when it rushes up to the heart and to the lungs, is understood to create insanity in women. In this case, unlike other parts of the body (where the veins are straight and the blood flows quickly), the veins in the heart and the *phrenes* are slanted, and thus form "a critical place for insanity and suited for madness."[37]

The Hippocratic text *The Sacred Disease* also identifies the source of madness in the brain, mocking the idea that some forms of madness are divine.[38] Here, the brain is seen as responsible for emotions such as joy, delight, sorrow, grief, and despondency. It is also considered as the seat of intellect, wisdom, and knowledge. When the brain, which is dry and cold while healthy, becomes moist, it makes us "mad and delirious." In this case, it can inspire fear, sleeplessness, aimless anxieties, absent-mindedness, and "acts that are contrary to habit."[39]

The Hippocratic Corpus thus offers a coherent representation of mental disorders.[40] According to the Hippocratic doctors, mental disturbances are embodied and visible. Madness can be seen on patients' faces, in their movements, their postures and gestures, their eating behaviors, sleep, and sexuality. Madness is also diagnosed based on patients' reports about their disturbed sensations and perceptions. Finally, mental disturbance can be seen in the emotional responses of the patient, their ability to reason, and their – at times extraordinary – behavior.[41]

Although these early Hippocratic texts understand the differences between mental health and illness in terms of a humoral spectrum, they also contain attempts to categorize and differentiate the respective states of balance and imbalance. For example, *The Sacred Disease* offers the following differentiation between various kinds of madness: "Those who are mad through phlegm are quiet, and neither shout nor make a disturbance; those maddened through bile are noisy, evil-doers and restless, always doing something inopportune."[42] If the brain is chilled, "the patient suffers from causeless distress and anguish," but when the brain is suddenly heated, the patient "shouts and cries at night."[43]

While it differentiates these types of madness based on the various humors, the *Sacred Disease* suggests that these states could also be part of normal occurrences such as dreams. Like these nightly visions, they too are reversible. As the Hippocratic author explains, the heating of the brain (which is caused by an *abundance* of blood that rushes into it, and *boils* it) can also follow a fearful dream. When the person wakes up and regains his consciousness, the blood is dispersed into the veins once more, and the "mad" manifestations cease. The text also argues that the same phenomenon can occur in the waking state, when "the face is flushed, and the eyes are red, mostly when a man is afraid and his mind contemplates some evil act."[44]

The Romans, for their part, also recorded a variety of types of madness. The first known psychiatric taxonomy of antiquity in the Western tradition, *De Medicina*, was written by Cornelius Celsus.[45] In this work, Celsus distinguishes between "three types of madness" (*tria genera insaniae*), which are classified according to their duration: madness that is similar to the Greek *phrenitis* is an acute, quick furor; *mania* is a longer insanity without fever; and, lastly, *longissimum* corresponds to *melancholia*.[46] Thumiger finds three elements in this Roman text that are relevant to later discussions of madness: first, the distinction between the acute and the chronic; second, the identification of somatic causes (e.g., fever); and, finally, the division of madness into three types (in this case, *phrenitis*, *mania*, and *melancholia*). Interestingly, Celsus further adds the original idea that insanity can be treated not only by balancing the body's humors, but also by a form of psychotherapy, occupational therapy, cognitive exercises, and social activities.[47]

The most famous Greek doctor, however, is Galen of Pergamon (130–210 CE), whose work remained deeply influential among medical professionals and other scholars, until late into the seventeenth century. Significantly, Galen did not pay much attention to the classification of disorders, or to discussions of diseases or syndromes.[48] Instead, as was the case in the Hebrew Bible and the tradition of commentary standing on its shoulders, in *The Passions and Errors of the Soul*, Galen sees madness as the absence of the single defining human characteristic, that is, "the special gift of reason."[49]

In Galen's view, madness thus represents a lower kind of being (similar to that of a wild animal, a horse, or a dog, an "inferior man," i.e., a slave or a child), driven by the irrational forces of the soul.[50] Mad behavior, such as kicking and screaming, biting, ripping off one's clothes or hurting others, is more typical of a wild animal than a human being. However, Galen argues that this transformation into an inferior mode of being is not irreversible. In the spirit of Plato's metaphor of the soul as a charioteer, Galen writes, "untamed horses are useless but horsemen can in a short time make them submissive and manageable."[51] These wild beasts, which symbolize untamed and unreasonable forces, are of two kinds. The irascible force located in the heart, which generates emotions such as courage, anger, and joy, is compared to animals that can be domesticated, like horses or dogs, which can be disciplined. But as regards the concupiscible force that seeks bodily pleasures (such as erotic desire, carnal lust, gluttony, or drunkenness), the comparison is to goats or boars, which cannot be domesticated, only weakened. Galen thus creates distinct categories, distinguishing between those who practice reason, and those who are unreasonable. But at the same time, he also offers a spectrum, placing the reasonable wise man at one end, inferior men (such as children and slaves) in the middle, wild animals that can be tamed lower, and untamable animals at the very bottom.

Galen is also known to have emphasized what later became known as the "non-naturals"; six factors that affect the body and mind, but are not innate or part of the body itself. These six hygienic elements are the ambient air, food and drink, exercise and rest, sleep and wakefulness, excretion and retention, and the passions of the soul.[52] All of these, according to Galen, need to be regulated and regimented for one to attain, maintain, or restore mental health.

Just as he makes a distinction between animals that can be trained and those that cannot, Galen also differentiates between those whose madness is curable, and those that cannot be redeemed. As Thumiger shows, it is when Galen becomes "entirely materialistic and deterministic," that he proposes the radical suggestion of killing those whose mental disturbance is due to such a severe damage to the body that it deems them "beyond redemption or cure."[53]

From this limited selection of Greco-Roman texts on madness, one can already clearly infer that when madness is regarded as part of a spectrum, on which it differs only *quantitatively* or *relatively* from sanity (i.e., as a result of having either too much or too little of the humors, in the biological interpretation, or too little reason and determination, insofar as the mental capacities are evaluated in their own right), the madman can be restored to health in body and mind. By contrast, the opposite conception of madness, as being caused by "severe damage to one's bodily conditions" and affecting the very *qualitative* nature of one's being, leads to the near-inevitable conclusion that madness, as such, is incurable. This is what, in turn, leads to the idea that the irredeemably mad person must be contained or set apart, cast out at best, or eliminated at worst.

Holy and Unholy Madness in Medieval Times

> But whenever I was sick or depressed in my mind, the devil would begin to whisper that I would be damned because I had not confessed and been absolved of that secret sin. ... All the while I saw, as I thought, devils opening their mouths as if to swallow me alive, their insides full of fire. They would sometime grab at me or utter threats; they would pull me around in the daytime and at night throughout all this length of time. These devils would call out loud to me; they continually terrified me with their cries telling me to leave the church, deny my faith, abandon God, his mother, and all the saints in heaven. (Margery Kempe, *The Book of Margery Kempe,* 26)[54]

Being depressed in her mind, her body usurped, hearing voices, while deep down also terrified of being condemned to all-out damnation, Margery Kempe (1373–1458), whose personal account of her experience of madness opens this new segment of our cursory history, exemplifies the way madness was understood in the Middle Ages. Madness, we read here, is first and foremost a product of the multiple and diverse ways the connections between body, mind, and soul are individually and collectively experienced, culturally as well as theologically conceived of.

The close interplay of religion and medicine, the demonic and the natural, affected the variety of (at times, overlapping) treatments for madness, from physical restraint to medication, and from psychological diversion to plain brutality or neglect. Claire Trenery, an expert on the representation of madness in the Middle Ages, and Peregrine Horden, a scholar of medieval medicine, distill some of the more common reactions to cases of madness from the extraordinarily complex field of forces at play during this period.[55] The main signs of madness at the time were aberrations of thought, oddness of imagination, and suicidal behavior. The causes of madness were understood to be physiological (e.g., dietary), psychological (e.g., emanating from a morbid imagination), or belonging to the realm of the spirits (e.g., possession by a spirit, a demon, or divine providence). When contemporary experts of the period wrote about madness, many of them did not see these causes as mutually exclusive. According to them, the body could afflict the soul and the soul could damage the body, just as demons or God could use the body and soul to create a state of madness in mortals.

During the High Middle Ages, when the first universities were founded in Europe, many theological and practical medical manuscripts were composed and widely circulated. Hippocrates and Galen had been translated into Latin as early as the sixth century CE, but by 1000–1250 CE, they were being used as textbooks in emerging medical schools. One of the most famous circulating medical encyclopedias of the later Middle Ages was the *Canon of Medicine*, written by the Persian physician Ibn Sina (980–1037), better known by his Latinized name, Avicenna.

According to Ibn Sina, the brain is divided into three parts, each with a distinct function. The *imaginative* faculty is located at the front of the brain and processes the information received by the senses. This sensory data is then passed on to *rationality*, the central brain faculty, which forms it into concepts and judgments. Finally, *memories* are stored at the back of the brain, as images literally imprinted in its wet matter.[56] Mental illnesses, Ibn Sina concludes, are caused by humoral or anatomical abnormalities in one or more of these three areas.

As in the tradition that began with Celsus, in these medical texts, three main conditions were associated with madness: frenzy (*frenesis*), mania (*mania*), and melancholy (*melancholia*). Yet, few treatments were available for them. When the body was the target, the proposed treatment was based on the idea that opposites cure. Hence if madness was attributed to heating of the brain, coolness was prescribed. In such cases, shaving the head and drenching it in water or oil was a prescribed remedy. Cutting open the artery in the head for bloodletting was another.[57]

But in medieval times, madness was not always understood to be naturally caused by imbalance of the humors. When symptoms were bizarre – when the individual had hallucinations and delusions, or, for that matter, started to bark like a dog or crow like a rooster – doctors suspected the cause to be demonic, or in any case, supernatural.[58] While demons were not believed to be able to infiltrate the sacred, incorruptible soul, some medieval physicians accepted that they could manipulate the mind by entering the body surreptitiously. By producing erroneous images, demons could confuse the imagination and impair a person's reason, such that the affected individual was no longer able to correctly use the information provided by the senses.[59]

Based on the literature of the time, Trenery and Horden suggest that although "demoniacs" were associated with abnormal powers, convulsions, blaspheming, abhorrence of sacred objects, and aggression, distinctions were not always made between demonic possession, on the one hand, and other forms of madness, on the other. *Both* involved wild gestures, violence, twisted facial expressions, and shouting, that phenomenologically or descriptively speaking, remained indistinguishable or, at least, overlapped.

In *Nebuchadnezzar's Children: Conventions of Madness in Middle English Literature*, the late Canadian medievalist Penelope Doob divides popular literary portrayals of madness into three different classes: that of the "Mad Sinner," the "Unholy Wild Man," and the "Holy Wild Man."[60] All three, she argues, were influenced by the popular biblical figure of Nebuchadnezzar, who, as we saw, was punished by being degraded into bestial existence. Madness was a form of "otherness," which triggered various responses, including "fascination, fear, laughter, pity, and revulsion."[61] From the eleventh century onward, all those who were excluded from what came to be known as Christendom (including Jews, Saracens, and heretics) risked being accused of thinking and acting "differently." Any deviance was classified as a major defect, confusion, or madness. In fact, the vernacular, for the "other" was "maniac," "insane," or "*fol*" (i.e., madman, in French), among other terms.[62]

Medieval art, moreover, depicted the demoniac with disheveled hair and torn clothes, while the demon itself was often shown entering or leaving its victim through the mouth, in line with the New Testament story of the Gerasene demoniac, retold at the beginning of this chapter. As Sander Gilman claims in *Seeing the Insane*,[63] to be represented, this "otherness" of the mad required some form of physical marking or wild appearance, such as a lack of clothes, hairiness, a staff in the hand, or a hunched stance. These signs served to visually set the afflicted apart from the common people or the normal. *The Ship of Fools*, an image that was born in the Middle Ages, captures both the otherness and the isolation of the mad thus depicted and, *de facto*, cast out.[64]

A telling example of this "otherness" of medieval madness is the story of Margery Kempe, with which we opened this segment. Since the rediscovery of *The Book of Margery Kempe* in 1934, historians have been particularly interested in using this text to explore the medieval connections between madness, divine inspiration, and mysticism.[65] Kempe, who

Post Partum Depression

was born around 1373, describes how she "went out of her mind" after the birth of her first child. By her own account, for about eight months, the devil placed in her mind a terrifying fear of eternal damnation, as she saw and heard devils speak (or, rather, holler) with flamed tongues. She describes feeling herself to be a passive object intruded on by sinister spiritual forces, understanding everything she did or experienced from there on as being caused by these intruding external forces.

Her story

Margery Kempe continued to have visions and hallucinations for the rest of her life. She recalls that she "saw our Lady faint and fall down and lie still upon the ground" and, even more significantly, notes that she experienced herself to be "a madwoman, crying and roaring."[66] Her eccentric behavior was interpreted by her contemporaries either as a result of an "evil spirit" tormenting her body, or as the consequence of a "strange bodily affliction."[67] She describes others who suffered from similar conditions – crying loudly, being violent, hitting and biting to the point of being restrained and shackled – as being "deranged."[68]

This kind of unruly beastly behavior was also recorded much earlier, during the Byzantine period. As Trenery and Horden note, the emperor Justin II (r. 565–578) is described as having lost his reason, resembling an animal, and, therefore, being restrained.[69] Like in the earlier Greco-Roman or Hellenistic period, in Byzantium, madness was seen both in the Galenic medical humoral tradition (as an "illness coming from the cranium" and, hence, in natural terms) and in supernatural terms (as a result of possession by spirits). What distinguished the East more strongly from the West during this period was the different appreciation of the so-called "holy fool." Indeed, at the time, the madness of the holy fool was considered a form of piety distinct from insanity. These "mad" individuals radically avoided the attention of admirers of their "holiness," and instead served to "critique the corrupt norms of the society around them" in unique, if exemplary, ways.[70]

His story

Even though holy fools also existed in Medieval Islam[71] (and restraint or beating of the insane was not unusual there either), these supernaturalistic approaches coexisted with the heavy influence of Galenic learning, with its naturalistic, somatic, and ethical conceptions of mental illness. The latter involved an alternative treatment altogether, which relied on modulating the six non-naturals (air, food and drink, rest and exercise, sleep and waking, excretion and retention, and handling the emotions).

This kind of treatment also included creating relaxing surroundings for the afflicted individual, with soothing sounds and scents.

In earlier times, in the West and East, both under Christian and Muslim rule, the chronically mad were often placed in the same category as infants and, hence, were mainly cared for by their families or communities. However, during the Middle Ages, institutional social and medical care for the mad began to emerge. Treatments were based on humoral remedies, such as purging, to restore equilibrium, while sedation and confinement in cells were practiced with violent patients.

Throughout the period, whenever madness was defined as "otherness," that is, as a wholly separate category of being, possibly caused by demons and spirits, the treatment aimed at either "extracting" the madness – exorcising or expelling it – or at protecting its "holiness." In both scenarios, the question of the person's morality was central. By contrast, when the madness was seen as the result of a natural imbalance in the body, caused by either too much or too little of a particular substance or material quality – and, hence, not as the sign of a categorically different metaphysical condition or, alternatively, of a moral defect or, rather, perfection – treatments were meant simply to restore the original balance. That said, to unprepared modern-day eyes, some of the means to bring back such a state of natural equilibrium (e.g., by bloodletting, purging, or cupping) now seem objectionable, not to say torturous.

This "othering" of madness and of madmen would remain common practice throughout history, even up to our age. As such, it has become a cause and justification for a categorically different theorization of and engagement with those who happen to experience non-ordinary states of mind, hear voices, have visions or persecutory ideas, while exhibiting unusual behavior that expresses them or leads up to them.

Early Modern Madness: God, Satan, Witches, and Poison

One night, I said there was a great clap of Thunder like the shot of a Piece of Ordnance, came down directly over my Bed; and that the same night, a while after, I heard like the voice of two Young Men singing in the Yard, over against my Chamber; which I said were Devils in the likeness of Men, singing for joy that they overcome me; and in the morning as I was going to rise,

> the Scripture in the 10th. of *Heb.* And the last words of the 26th. Verse, was suggested to me from Heaven (as I thought) *There remains no more Sacrifice for sin*; and this delusion remained with me as an Oracle all along; that by this miracle of the Thunder, and the Voice and the Scripture, God revealed to me that I was Damned. (From A Narrative of God's Gracious Dealing with that Choice Christian Mrs. Hannah Allen, 1683)[72]

Traumatic experiences, bad dreams and suicide attempts, fear of enchantment and of witches stealing milk from breasts, were among the symptoms associated with madness in Europe between 1500 and 1700. As Elizabeth Mellyn, an expert on mental illness in early modern Italy, amply documents, at the time, Europe displayed extremely varied representations of madness.[73] Fools, melancholic artists, brooding scholars, obsessive lovers, mad prophets, and the divinely or demonically possessed were commonly described, in great detail. Based on extensive sources in legal archives, doctors' casebooks, and the first written records of Europe's first mental hospitals, Mellyn concludes that, while in early modern Europe madness was thought of as more somber and gloomy than in the Middle Ages, characterized mainly by anguish, sorrow, and torment (and perceived quite literally as dark, involving melancholia or *black* bile, the dark influence of Saturn, fears of darkness and perils of the night), institutional and therapeutic strategies to treat the insane remained more or less unchanged, geared toward restoring original harmony and a natural equilibrium. Although voyages to the New World led to interest in exotic drugs, the excitement about a chemical cure failed in challenging the authority of Galen's doctrine of the humors. It was still widely believed that both natural and supernatural forces had an impact on the human body and soul, so that madness could be caused by terrestrial as well as celestial, even demonic, spiritual factors. Thus, healers of insanity included university-trained physicians, but also priests, exorcists, alchemists, astrological or occult healers, remedy sellers, tooth drawers, snake charmers, and plain charlatans. Some early modern hospitals treated the severely disturbed, while monasteries and convents continued to offer hospitality to the insane, mainly to protect the material and spiritual integrity of their respective communities. For the criminally insane, prison, it seems, was the default option.

Most learned physicians treated their mentally disturbed patients by balancing the six non-naturals, prescribing therapeutic baths, as well as traditional remedies such as powerful emetics, purgatives, and bloodletting. The goal was not just to restore humoral balance in the body, it was also to create a harmony between the inner and outer worlds of those who suffered from madness.

In the cases treated by Richard Napier, the famous early modern physician, witches, demons, and spirits were believed to be the instigators of madness, alongside physical causes such as pathogenic diets and emotional distress in the form of sadness, fear, jealousy, loss of love, or of one's estate. When reporting on his observation and treatment of an insane woman, Napier notes:

> CASE 16959: Agnes Olny of Tebworth in Chalgrave, 38 years. Wednesday 19 May 1602, 9:45 am ... the husband for his furious and insane wife. Senseless. Has no use of her wits & light headed ... A frantic woman. Mad & laughs & misterms [i.e., uses the wrong words]. First had good motions & now worse & worse. About 3 years since delivered of a child which by means of an unskillful midwife perished & rent the woman that she ever after continued lame & could never since hold her water. Upon this day sennet [i.e., upon the seventh day] about 12 of the clock she began to wax mad when Sun and Moon came both to be in Gemini & Mercury dispositer [a technical term in astrology] of both the lights. A thick muddish water. [Treatment information, including Latin phrase meaning "God for this sick little woman, may Satan be crushed under Christ's feet, and may my medication be blessed, so that she may be freed from this distraction of mind and also be greatly and powerfully consoled, and with compassion and blessing."] (From Selected Cases in Full, From Simon Forman's and Richard Napier's Medical Record)[74]

Other medieval doctors operated in similar ways: when confronted with a young man who imagined himself to be a priest, delivering sermons to imaginary congregants, the Italian physician Bartolomeo Montagnana (*c.*1380–1452) diagnosed melancholy. In order to rid the man of his delusions (*corruptas imaginationes*), Montagnana prescribed conversation, music, and light entertainment, and for the rest, instructed him to avoid the company of monks (particularly those wearing black robes).[75]

A notable change in the way health and illness were understood at this time was further introduced by the Swiss-born physician Paracelsus (1493–1541), who was the first to refute the widely accepted Greek idea that diseases were caused by humoral imbalances. Paracelsus argued instead that diseases were caused by poisons, and cure could be delivered by powerful chemical agents.[76] Nonetheless, his innovative ideas took on only gradually, and in his work entitled *Diseases that Deprive Man of His Reason*, Paracelsus also attributed madness to witchcraft, astral influence, sinful imagination, and, once again, disordered humors.[77] Paracelsus' treatments included bloodletting based on the humoral theory, alongside chemical therapy in the form of powerful drugs, made of silver, iron, mercury, lead, gold, pearls, coral, sulfur, or sapphires. These were considered as toxins to be used to fight other toxins, following Paracelsus' famous idea that "All things are poison, and nothing is without poison; the dosage alone makes it a poison." Increasingly, opiates were deemed the most effective when treating mental disorders.[78]

Just as he was unable to fully liberate himself from the stronghold of Galen's humoral doctrine, Paracelsus also remained influenced by the ancient idea that celestial bodies (the planets and stars) exerted powerful forces on all terrestrial forces of nature, which could be harnessed to heal the body and mind. Furthermore, the ethical dimension that remained from Galenic medicine was still widely held, and the belief that immoral behavior led to an imbalance in the body, making it weak and penetrable by hostile forces, was popular. Preventive measures thus included both bodily and spiritual hygiene. In most cases, the physical body *and* the metaphysical soul were largely seen as treatable. While physicians aimed to restore balance in the body by manipulating the six non-naturals, the clergy used "soul remedies" like confession, communion, pilgrimage, and exorcism, the latter mostly as a remedy of last resort to balance out the disturbances of the soul.[79]

The early moderns thus understood madness as being either the result of an *imbalance* in the body, or as an *infiltration* by a foreign hostile force – whether in the natural form of a poison or in the supernatural guise of demons and evil spirits. The imbalance of humors and their qualities was further attributed to changes in the external, terrestrial, or celestial environment, and was at times seen as deriving from the mad person's unregimented behavior (such as disorganized diet, sleep, exercises, etc.). A disequilibrium of the body was itself considered a possible precondition for a qualitative change, caused by the invasion of the foreign agent that caused the madness in question. According to the first interpretation, sanity could be restored by reinstating quantitative balance. According to the second, the different quality – and the invasive, foreign element – needed to be expelled *in toto*.

Modern Madness: A Disease Entity, a Natural Kind

> Some of my unfortunate patients labored under the horrors of a most gloomy and desponding melancholy. Others were furious and subject to the influence of a perpetual delirium. Some appeared to possess a correct judgment upon most subjects, but were occasionally agitated by violent sallies of maniacal fury; while those of another class were sunk into a state of stupid idiotism and imbecility. Symptoms so different and all comprehended under the general title of insanity, required on my part, much study and discrimination. (Philippe Pinel, *A Treatise on Insanity*, 1806)[80]

Like other doctors working in hospitals and asylums during the mid-eighteenth century, Philippe Pinel, chief physician at the Salpêtrière, noticed the many different mental sufferings that were all classified under the broad title of insanity. Dissatisfied with the lack of discrimination between them, he writes:

> It is to be hoped, that our system of classification, independent of its methodical clearness and discrimination, will continue towards the establishment of proper rules for the internal government of lunatic hospitals and serve to discover or confirm some general indications of treatment, which in order to avoid empirical experiments, ought to be respectively adapted to *each species* and variety of mental derangement. (Philippe Pinel, *A Treatise on Insanity*, 1806)[81]

It was during this time, as the first "lunatic hospitals" emerged, that physicians tried to systematically "carve nature at its joints." This meant studying the genus of insanity and classifying its varied species, creating distinct categories of insanity based on their different symptoms, hoping to offer each distinct illness the treatment it required. As German

E. Berrios and Ivana S. Marková have amply documented, this process of demystifying madness may have had its roots in Enlightenment thought. Be that as it may, the weakness of its premises and procedure would quickly become all too clear. After all, if indeed madness is, first and foremost, a cultural object with a historical index, and as such not conducive to being framed or reframed as a natural kind, to be fixed and measured objectively (like gold, tree, or tiger, each of which could presumably be easily "carved at the joints"), then the aforementioned classificatory project never stood much of a chance and, in all likelihood, could never have been accomplished completely.[82]

As stated above, during the seventeenth century, the Galenic view, which considered madness as a functional disturbance of the body caused by an imbalance of the four humors or the six non-naturals, always existed side by side with spiritual and metaphysical explanations that conceived madness as the result of a foreign invasion (and, hence, proposed remedies to expel these very invaders). But, as the eighteenth century brought about a general secularization of thought and life, new questions regarding human beings and the nature they are part of (developments we now associate with the so-called "Scientific Revolution") dramatically changed the moderns' idea of madness overall.

According to Berrios and Marková, during this time, madness increasingly began to be viewed as a *natural kind.* Like plants, physical and mental diseases were now seen as sharing common, ontological features that can be used to classify them once and for all. During this period, most classifications applied the method devised by the father of modern taxonomy, the Swedish botanist, zoologist, and physician, Carl Linnaeus (1707–78). This classificatory method used a privileged set of features of the species and phenomena at hand to group both plants and diseases. In his 1759 work, *Genera Morborum* [*Classification of Diseases*], Linnaeus argued that the system that served the botanist might as well also serve the physician. By classifying diseases into classes, genera, and species, physicians can gain more clarity about disease: "Symptoms are to disease as leaves and stems are to plants."[83] Thus, for example, his Class V, *the Mentales* ("Diseases in which the Functions of the Mind are disturbed") contains "1. *Ideales*: those in which the Judgment is principally affected," among them Delirium, Mania, and Melancholia; "2. *Imaginarii*: those in which the Imagination is principally affected," such as Vertigo and Hypochondriasis;

and "3. *Pathetici*: those in which the Appetites and Passions are principally affected," such as Bulimia, Erotomania, and Nostalgia.[84]

Linnaeus' close friend and collaborator, François Boissier de Sauvages (1706–67), a professor at the medical school of Montpellier, was a vigorous classifier, who argued that medicine should follow the botanical model of classification by observable signs. He criticized the Galenic tradition, which classifies diseases according to imaginary anatomy and hypothetical causes, instructing his followers to stick to the testimony of their senses.

Unlike these botanical models, which were based on the observed characteristics of the disease, by the late eighteenth century, William Cullen (1710–90), an influential professor of medicine and physics at the University of Edinburgh, suggested diseases be classified according to their possible etiology, that is, according to the cause of their disorders and natural history. In his *First Lines of Physic*, Cullen gave the name *neurosis* to a class of diseases that, in his definition, included irritation of the "nerves," rather than focal lesions in the brain per se.[85] One of the four "orders" of the neuroses was a group of "insanities" or so-called "*vesaniae*," whose examples included *amentia* (idiotic insanity), *melancholia* (unsound mind in a sorrowful manner), *mania* (unsound mind in a furious manner), and *oneirodynia* (intense mental disturbance associated with dreaming).[86]

Another classification system was offered by the celebrated French physician Philippe Pinel (1745–1826), with whom we opened this section, who suggested turning back to detailed clinical observation, noting the course of disease, and incorporating the patient's life history. In his *Medico-Philosophical Treatise on Mental Alienation or Mania*, Pinel presented a classification of mental disorders that included four classes of insanity: maniacal insanity, melancholia, dementia, and idiocy.[87] Maniacal insanity, according to Pinel, was typically temporary – yet sometimes chronic – and frequently curable. Melancholia was defined by "a dreamy taciturn manner, touchy and suspicious, with a desire to be left alone."[88] Dementia was seen as gradually eroding the victim's thoughts and could not be cured. Finally, idiocy was the term used to describe a condition in which the intellect is not fully developed. These categories were still largely in use until the mid-nineteenth century, when hundreds of other psychiatric classifications were published across Europe.

The stage is now set for the historical and conceptual question that interests us here: what became of the category of schizophrenia when the term was coined, and what led to its diagnosis and definition in the first place?

During this modern Enlightenment period, the concept of mental disease as a cluster of mental symptoms was first introduced, theoretically delineated, and clinically applied. As Berrios notes, descriptive psychopathology was also soon introduced as a new language in the field of mental afflictions. Its method and technical idiom served a new profession, namely "alienism," which would become the precursor of "psychiatry," and which, as soon as it emerged, established itself as a trade, a science, and a medical practice.[89] During the rise of the asylum system, conflicts erupted between alienists, on the one hand, and legislatures, the clergy, and civil society, on the other.

The idea that complaints were signs of disease allowed mental symptoms to be thought of as smaller units of "mental disease," understood as a condition, a disorder, or, indeed, an illness. Whether the symptoms were mere exaggerations of "normal" mental functions on a wider *spectrum*, or whether, on the contrary, they were a *categorically* distinct new phenomenon was a much-debated question during the nineteenth century. Psychologists tended to argue for the former, and alienists for the latter.[90]

Most of the data collected on mental illness during this period came from the asylums. The deplorable sanitary conditions in these institutions – with their overcrowding, outbreaks of epidemics and infections, and downright neglect – led to high mortality rates among patients. In response to these conditions, physicians were legally obliged to be present in the asylums and keep records of their observations. The large cohorts of patients treated in the asylums were considered not as individual sufferers, but rather as inferior, pathological specimens.[91] Data collected from these patients then served as a foundation for the newly developed field of psychopathology.[92]

One important question for psychopathologists was to determine what differentiates normal from abnormal behavior and experience. And because no biological markers were available to answer this question, deviance from the proper, ethical, and acceptable social norms, together with patients' self-reports on their state of mind, became the defining criteria to determine mental illness. Indeed, the science of psychopathology, which started out from this "hybrid platform" due to an absence of clear biological markers and tests, has not changed much in its contrary ambition and inclination. To this day, clinicians still base their examinations both on the observed behavior and the subjective experience of the individuals they treat. The latter reveal two opposed aspects of a single phenomenon, which lead to contrasting paradigmatic explanations and self-understandings of the same symptoms (the objectively observed and recorded, on the one hand, and the subjectively experienced and reported, on the other).[93]

But the mere differentiation between the normal and the abnormal or the psychopathological, which determined who would be placed in the asylums, was never enough. "The Era of the Asylum,"[94] as Edward Shorter, a social historian specializing in the history of the insane, aptly names this period, saw an ever-increasing need to place the mentally ill also in different wings of these institutions. In its footsteps, a further differentiation among those committed to the asylum became necessary. Some criteria used to place patients in different areas of the building were completely unrelated to the person's illness (e.g., male or female), but some were based on their diagnosis (e.g., agitated or quiet, acute or chronic, rational or irrational, continent or incontinent, epileptic or non-epileptic, organic or functional, criminal or non-criminal).[95]

Psychiatry was in fact "a profession in reverse," writes the sociologist Andrew Abbott. It began with the establishment of its institutions, that is to say, the asylums, and only later developed its expert knowledge regarding the mental illnesses that the residents in these houses supposedly suffered from.[96] It was only after the asylums were established that the further professionalization of alienism (i.e., the study, understanding of, and caring for those who suffered from "mental alienation" in Europe and, in this respect, the precursor of psychiatry as a scientific discipline) took place through the development of local professional societies, textbooks, journals, training procedures, and examinations, and perhaps even more importantly, through largely unsuccessful efforts to establish a uniform systematic description of diseases, a so-called *nosographic lexicon*.[97] In the process, the asylums enabled "a minor epistemological revolution," and theories that assumed that madness was in the body became more and more prevalent.[98]

The insanities, during this period, were seen as disorders of the senses and of the movement of the nervous system, without fever or focal lesion. They were differentiated from conditions like Parkinson's disease and multiple sclerosis, for which clear lesions of the brain were indeed found. It was neurology, the other new profession that emerged during this time, that explicitly aimed to treat these latter conditions. Insanities such as hypochondriasis, hysteria, anxiety disorders, obsessive-compulsive disorder, and neurotic depressions were now named "psychoses," while the term "neuroses" was reserved for what was increasingly believed to be a psychological conflict.[99]

Not only were the "psychoses" contrasted with the "neuroses," in the nineteenth century the former term also came to replace the more general and colloquial concept of madness, together with the different symptoms that define it such as hallucinations, delusions, mental confusion, irrationality, and thought disorders. Aspiring to offer not merely a symptom-based classification system, but, as in the rest of medicine, a system that classifies different illnesses based on causation (as different diseases may exhibit similar symptoms but nonetheless have distinctive causes), the psychoses were further divided into more specific diagnostic groups during this period: "functional" versus "organic," "endogenous" or "exogenous," while "acute and chronic" cases were now also distinguished for the first time. Madness with no "known anatomical lesion" was named "functional psychosis," and included diagnoses such as *delirium hallucinatorium*, *mania*, *melancholia*, circular psychosis, paranoia, and acute dementia.[100] Forms of "organic psychoses," by contrast, were related to other physical diseases like syphilis, but also to diseases of the brain, such as brain tumors, and to those thought to arise from other nervous disorders, such as epilepsy.

As mentioned, yet another differentiation was created within the psychoses between forms of psychosis that were seen as caused by *external* agents, such as toxic substances, infections, syphilis, alcoholism, and brain infections. These were considered to be based on "exogenous" causes. Yet other forms of psychosis, such as neurasthenia, hysteria, epilepsy, and migraine were considered to arise from *internal* sources and were thus labeled "endogenous."[101]

In the nineteenth century, mental disorders thus came to be thought of as *classifiable* not unlike plants, animals, or minerals, according to either external features (i.e., their visible symptoms) or, as was common practice in other fields of medicine, based on their presumed causes.[102] It was precisely with such a classificatory zeal that mental illnesses were increasingly approached. What emerged was the understanding that there is a correspondence between the *causes* of different mental illnesses, some possible *visible damage* to the brain, various *observed symptoms*, and the *final outcome* of the condition. This growing insight enabled Emil Kraepelin (1856–1926), the main figure discussed in the next chapter, to group together several existing diagnoses into two large nosological entities, which would come to be known as "the twin pillars" of the modern classification of so-called psychiatric diseases: "manic-depressive insanity," on the one hand, and *dementia praecox*, the precursor of schizophrenia, on the other.

The criterion of "prognosis," or outcome, was central to Kraepelin's system of diagnosis, and was more precisely defined in terms of "curability" and "incurability." In Kraepelin's early writings, there were thus two groups of "madness": manic-depressive insanity, where the hope of "complete restoration" was possible, and *dementia praecox*, a steadily progressive kind of mental illness, whose inevitable outcome was deterioration and which resulted in dementia.

Psychiatric Classification and the Making of Schizophrenia

Western history, since its early depiction in the Old Testament, had shown two fundamental ways of conceiving madness. While the first implies that health and illness exist on a *spectrum* as relative states of greater or lesser *equilibrium*, the second view implies that mental illness is *categorically different* from mental health.

The diagnosis of *dementia praecox*, which later gave way to schizophrenia, was born in the nineteenth century, a period that in the history of madness, mad people, and mad institutions was characterized by attempts on the part of the medical profession to create *distinct categories* of so-called disease entities as *natural kinds*. Just as botanists had shown that, based on their natural properties, pine trees were similar to each other and different from elm trees, psychiatrists, doctors, and other clinicians hoped to reveal the exact nature of mental disorders, and to differentiate between their distinct natural kinds in the clearest of terms. Unlike some of the earlier views of mental disorders, which saw the body and mind as constantly oscillating between health and illness, and considered health as a form of humoral and moral equilibrium, the mainstream view of alienists in the nineteenth century was that mental disorders were completely different in *kind* from normal mental states.

Nineteenth-century European medicine, with its laboratories and hospitals, supported the notion that diseases are specific, objective, *physical entities* that exist outside their unique manifestation in a particular human being.[103] Regardless of the place or person in which they are located, disease entities were believed to have typical symptoms, to follow specific courses, produce particular outcomes, and obey an underlying biological mechanism. These disease units were viewed not only as different from health, but also as having *clear boundaries* that separated them from one another. It is in the framework of this *episteme*, to cite Michel Foucault's well-known term, that we see a general shift from "dis-ease" to diseases and from "*mal-aise*" (a state of discomfort) to *malaise* (an illness).[104] It is in the wake of this transformation of "dis-ease," experienced as discomfort, into a disease, seen as an externally diagnosed separate entity, that the downright pessimistic diagnosis of *dementia praecox*, with its grim prognosis, and in its wake that of schizophrenia, came into being.

Chapter 2

The Birth of "the Schizophrenias"

> Gentlemen, you have before you today a strongly-built and well-nourished man, aged twenty-one, who entered the hospital a few weeks ago ... [B]esides the emotional barrenness, there is also a high degree of weakness of judgment and flightiness, although the pure memory has suffered little, if at all. We have a mental and emotional infirmity to deal with ... [T]his infirmity is the incurable outcome of a very common history of disease, to which we will provisionally give the name dementia praecox. (Emil Kraepelin, *Lectures on Clinical Psychiatry*, 1904)[1]

Most histories of schizophrenia begin with the man who coined the term *dementia praecox*, the German psychiatrist Emil Kraepelin (1856–1926). Kraepelin began his training at the University of Leipzig before becoming a professor of psychiatry at the Imperial University of Dorpat in the Russian Empire, in 1882 (now Tartu, in Estonia). He was subsequently appointed to professorships in Heidelberg and at the University of Munich.

It has been suggested that Kraepelin found the presence of mad people personally overwhelming, and that his tireless effort at the psychiatric classification of mental illness were a way of avoiding direct clinical work with mentally ill patients. For instance, while working in a Munich mental asylum, he wrote:

> The first impressions of my new job were discouraging. The confusing throng of demented, sometimes unapproachable, sometimes obtrusive patients with their ridiculous or repellent, pitiable or dangerous oddities, the futility of the medical treatment, which was usually limited to salutations and the clumsiest bodily care, the complete helplessness against these types of insanity, for which there was no scientific explanation, made me feel the entire rigour of my chosen profession. As they had done in Wurzburg, the chaotic and repulsive pictures of the day's work also followed me into

> the nights and left me in doubt, whether I could really get used to this occupation.[2]

He was thus relieved when Wilhelm Wundt (1832–1920), the founding father of experimental psychology, offered him a chance to concentrate on his academic career and write his second doctoral thesis on the effects of psychoactive drugs. Kraepelin was also grateful for Wundt's invitation to publish a small *Kompendium der Psychiatrie* (*Compendium of Psychiatry*), which would allow him to earn some extra money. Over the next 30 years, this small publication (which by Kraepelin's admission offered nothing new in 1883) grew into a comprehensive, four-volume 2500-page textbook, entitled *Psychiatrie* (*Psychiatry*).[3]

In *American Madness*, his comprehensive book on the history of *dementia praecox* in America, Richard Noll considers the subsequent nine printed editions of Kraepelin's textbook to have fundamentally transformed the entire profession of psychiatry.[4] Indeed, Kraepelin was deeply dissatisfied with the field of psychiatry of his time, claiming that it lacked proper methods of classification and systematization. In his view, it failed to clearly differentiate between separate concepts, and lacked a sound somatic establishment of individual diseases. It became his lifelong ambition to completely restructure the technical vocabulary and, thereby, the clinical tools, of the emerging discipline of psychiatry.

Although he was the first to use the term *dementia praecox* to refer to conditions that were later baptized as schizophrenia, it is important to note, however, that Kraepelin was not the first to identify this special kind of psychiatric disorder. In Europe, a number of nineteenth-century psychiatrists had already described mental disorders with unknown causes, that mainly affected *young people* and were generally characterized by *progressive deterioration*. The French alienist Bénédict-Augustin Morel (1809–73), for instance, first used the term "*démence précoce*" to describe a small group of adolescent patients with severe disturbances in their expression of will and voluntary movement. The German neurologist and psychiatrist Wilhelm Griesinger (1817–68) used the term "dementia paralytica." Sir Thomas Smith Clouston (1840–1915), a Scottish psychiatrist, named a similar condition "adolescent insanity," while his German counterpart, Karl Ludwig Kahlbaum (1828–99), suggested it be described as a "catatonic syndrome." Kahlbaum's younger collaborator,

Ewald Hecker (1843–1909), named the syndrome *hebephrenia*, after the Greek goddess of youth, Hebe. Kraepelin's own contribution was to propose integrating all of these clinical descriptions into a single diagnostic term, called *dementia praecox* (see figure 2).

His motivation for doing so is described in a groundbreaking paper, which he read to the annual meeting of German psychiatrists in Heidelberg in September 1896, entitled "Ziele und Wege der klinischen

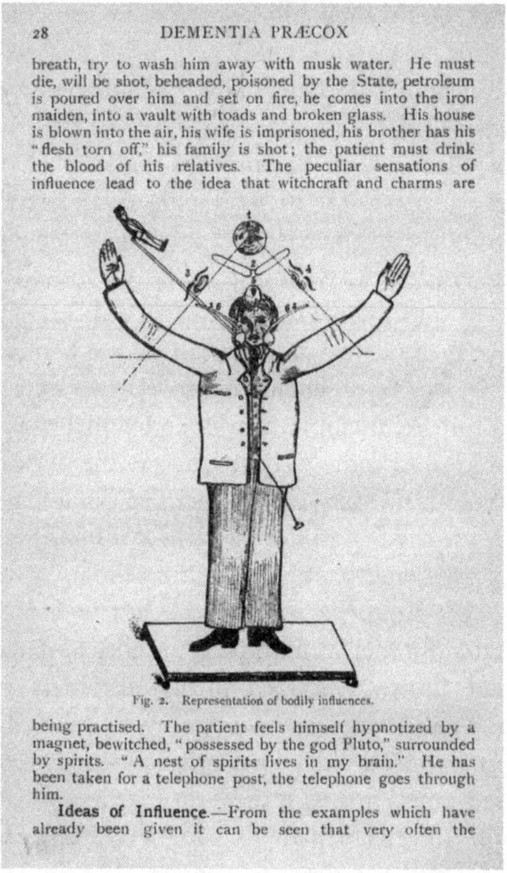

28 DEMENTIA PRÆCOX

breath, try to wash him away with musk water. He must die, will be shot, beheaded, poisoned by the State, petroleum is poured over him and set on fire, he comes into the iron maiden, into a vault with toads and broken glass. His house is blown into the air, his wife is imprisoned, his brother has his "flesh torn off," his family is shot; the patient must drink the blood of his relatives. The peculiar sensations of influence lead to the idea that witchcraft and charms are

Fig. 2. Representation of bodily influences.

being practised. The patient feels himself hypnotized by a magnet, bewitched, "possessed by the god Pluto," surrounded by spirits. "A nest of spirits lives in my brain." He has been taken for a telephone post, the telephone goes through him.

Ideas of Influence.—From the examples which have already been given it can be seen that very often the

Figure 2 Emil Kraepelin (1856–1926) was the first, in 1896, to regard *dementia praecox*, which was later renamed schizophrenia, as a distinct disease
Source: Emil Kraepelin, *Dementia praecox and paraphrenia* (Edinburgh: Livingstone, 1919). Courtesy of Oskar Diethelm Library, DeWitt Wallace Institute of Psychiatry: History, Policy, & the Arts, Weill Cornell Medical College

Psychiatrie [Aims and ways of clinical psychiatry]."[5] In this lecture, Kraepelin claimed that for psychiatry to become a genuine medical science, new theoretical formulations and clinical terms (which would correspond to the facts as they appeared in empirical reality) needed to be constructed and rigorously defined. The true meaning and significance of observed symptoms could only be ascertained if psychiatrists paid more attention to the actual *course*, and the possible *end*, of the disease that they studied and treated.

Kraepelin famously compiled hundreds of cards (his famous *Zählkarten*) with his patients' initials and their final diagnosis, which was made after they had been discharged, using follow-up observations. This led him to conclude that the decisive factor in grouping together patients with different diagnoses was the *final stage* of the disease, rather than the abnormalities encountered when a patient first appeared at the clinic.[6] As Jack Bohlen, the main protagonist of Philip Dick's 1964 novel *Martian Time Slip*, who emigrates to Mars to escape episodes of schizophrenia, aptly puts it:

> That's what they mean when they say schizophrenia isn't a diagnosis; it's a prognosis – it doesn't say anything about what you have, only about how you'll wind up. And I'm not going to wind up like that, he said to himself. Like Manfred Steiner, mute and in an institution.[7]

Building on ideas that were beginning to gain traction in his circle of colleagues (especially those featured in Kahlbaum's 1863 work, *The Classification of Mental Diseases and the Division of Psychic Disturbances*), Kraepelin became increasingly open to the idea of including the duration – the length, or itinerary – of the mental illness into his system of classification.[8] The idea that different disorders had different trajectories (and an individual, unique natural history) was accepted in other fields of medicine, but this was the first time that it had been applied to the various types of insanity.

Accurate diagnosis and effective prognosis thus began by taking into account the precise course of the disorder, the age of its onset, the duration of the illness, and its eventual outcome. The fourth edition of Kraepelin's *Psychiatry*, published in 1893, offered a psychiatric nomenclature (an elaborate system of precise names for a wide variety of psychiatric disorders) based on the conviction that, *over time*, some mental diseases led to *degeneration*. Chapter VIII of this revised, 700-page long volume was entitled "The Psychic Degeneration Processes."[9] In this text, among a host of other diseases characterized by the rapid development of a permanent state of psychological *weakness*, we find Kraepelin's first reference to *dementia praecox*. In the fifth edition, *dementia praecox* appears as an independent disease, separate from paraphrenia and paranoia, and in the sixth edition, Kraepelin added the *early age of onset and deteriorating clinical course*.

To go back to the patient Kraepelin described to his colleagues and to give a picture of what they were observing in these institutions, feeling increasingly that a new diagnosis was warranted, it may be helpful to further quote the inventor of *dementia praecox* more fully. Of his patient Kraepelin noted:

> He sits quietly looking in front of him, and does not raise his eyes when he is spoken to, but evidently understands all our questions very well, for he answers quite relevantly, though slowly and often only after repeated questioning … [I]t is all the same to him who appears or disappears where he is or who talks to him and takes care of him, and he does not even once ask their name. This peculiar and fundamental want of any strong feeling of the impressions of life, with unimpaired ability to understand and to remember, is really the diagnostic symptom of the disease we have before us.[10]

It was notably in the seventh edition of his *Lectures on Clinical Psychiatry* that Kraepelin collected all his observations and completed his synthesis. The term *dementia praecox* was used to describe a mental illness that afflicted young people (the term "*praecox*" pointing to the notion of precociousness). It was seen as a condition, which led to severe cognitive and behavioral decline ("dementia"), and was responsible for most admissions to insane institutions.[11]

Kraepelin separated *dementia praecox* from manic-depressive insanity on the basis of their supposed etiology, the progress of their symptoms, and their eventual prognosis. His differentiation between the two disorders created "the twin pillars" of modern psychiatry's classification system (which today we see collapsing[12]) and rightly earned him recognition as "psychiatry's Linnaeus,"[13] an honorary attribution he himself might not have fully agreed with.[14] Kraepelin's original contribution consisted in providing extensive data in support of this purported distinct and separate *disease unit*.[15] Indeed, the amount of data Kraepelin collected from a large number of cases over a long period of time was unprecedented. As a result of his wide-ranging documentation and research, Kraepelin concluded that mental illnesses are to be understood, first and foremost, as *natural disease entities* (*natürliche Krankheitseinheiten*), whose respective *prognoses* serve as their very organizing principle. Thus, Kraepelin offered alienists a new way of viewing the insane.

Indeed, in this new approach, the diagnosis of *dementia praecox* was based on the *end state* of the disease (i.e., dementia), the incurable and permanent disability that the affliction caused in young people. This prognosis-oriented diagnosis served to distinguish the curable from the incurable and was a reflection of the "triumph of institutional needs:"[16] once a prognosis of *dementia praecox* was made, the *incurables* could be transferred into different asylums, allowing new patients to be admitted. In other words, as Richard Noll argues, the psychiatric definition and clinical diagnosis of *dementia praecox* served both a medical *and* an administrative purpose.

That said, Kraepelin developed several reservations about his own nosology. These doubts he expressed as early as the second edition of his textbook. Kraepelin came to view his own hard-fought classifications as "necessarily provisional," that is, as empirically derived disease categories that were merely practical and didactical, but did not necessarily point to a clear-cut distinction in reality, in other words, in nature.[17] As Kraepelin put it, they could not aspire to be a "true classification" as their claim to general validity lacked "further scientific value."[18] It was in the seventh edition that Kraepelin completed the synthesis of *dementia praecox*, and where he acknowledged that, in some cases, the disease's onset might be late and that some patients might even recover.[19] In the eighth edition (1915), Kraepelin partially retreated from his previous assertion that the early age onset of *dementia praecox* and its universally bad prognosis were intrinsic to it.[20]

The disease entity named *dementia praecox*, then, emerged at a time when mental illnesses were viewed much in the same way as other medical disease categories. Even if their causes were not yet known, it was believed that biological research would ultimately prove that these categories revealed distinct and separate *natural kinds*.

And indeed, in addition to his achievements in nosology, Kraepelin is also known for his interest in the biology of insanity. Whether it was measuring the skulls of the insane or taking their pulses, he seemed on the lookout for *biological markers* that would yield a possible prognosis.[21] Some of his ideas were rejected by American and English alienists in particular. Among these was the speculation that *dementia praecox* is a metabolic disease in which substances produced in other areas of the body poison the brain, which then causes delusions, hallucinations, and cognitive deterioration. Despite this initial reticence, this aspect of Kraepelin's work in particular, gradually won international recognition.

Furthermore, Kraepelin's depiction of psychiatric disorders as "natural disease units" that could be studied in the laboratory – and of which *dementia praecox* would remain the first and best-known example – was by and large welcomed by the psychiatric establishment.[22] The wish to repeat psychiatry's triumphant story of the diagnosis of the so-called General Paralysis of the Insane (GPI), a devastating form of insanity responsible for a large percentage of asylum admissions, had never been given up. After all, once this form of insanity was reclassified as neurosyphilis, a "natural disease unit," a valid diagnosis by the Wassermann test[23] could easily be achieved and the suffering patient effectively treated with somatic therapy (with the introduction of penicillin, it was widely believed that this form of insanity, described in terms of GPI, would be abolished altogether).

While Kraepelin was not yet fully satisfied with his own delimitation of the mental illness's boundaries (or, indeed, with the further subdivisions he had created in the meantime), he *did* believe that his main thesis of the separate and definite character of *dementia praecox* had been largely substantiated by the existing scholarship.

For the scientists of the time, the idea that a single pathological organism and a disease could potentially explain a wide variety of symptoms was but the sound application of Occam's razor (the idea that the simplest explanation is the most plausible one) to the plethora of hypotheses and explanations that could be found in clinical medicine generally and in the emerging discipline of psychiatry in particular. In other words, they believed they were capable of explaining multiple symptoms at once, with a single tool.

Furthermore, the firm expectation that Kraepelin's systematic study of *dementia praecox* would, like GPI, yield a clear definition of a discrete disease entity, was a considerable motivating force for psychiatrists who worked in overcrowded and underfunded mental asylums, struggling to treat increasing numbers of "hopeless victims" of the disorder. As previously mentioned, Kraepelin's diagnosis served not just a medical need, but also a pragmatic administrative requirement. By marking off the "hopeless" and "incurable" from other patients, and transferring them to an asylum for long-term care, psychiatrists were able to free up the scarce institutional resources to which they had laid claim.

Kraepelin's endeavor to create an effective classification system for modern psychiatry was driven by a skeptical mindset. In its results, it was less dogmatic than that of the generation of so-called neo-Kraepelinians, who in the years leading up to the 1980 revision of the DSM, successfully lobbied to set the critical terms for the its formulation. In this sense, as Hannah Decker observes, Kraepelin may have been less of a Kraepelinian than were his most ardent followers.[24] Not surprisingly, new scholarship is re-envisioning Kraepelin, re-envealing him to be a much more creative and generative founding father of psychiatry than he was later made out to be.[25] As Kendler recently concluded, Kraepelin was a pragmatist – not a purist – in his nosological work. In other words, he was arguably more tentative about his conclusions than many who claimed to follow his lead.[26] Noll, too, argues that even though Kraepelin viewed *dementia praecox* as a *natural disease entity*, he did not believe that its etiology could be located in brain cells or otherwise be analyzed by placing biological specimens under a microscope. What made the disease stand out as a distinct entity was, in his view, the *psychological* deterioration that characterized especially the terminal phase of its clinical phenomenon.

This important caveat allowed Kraepelin to describe a variety of *dementia praecox* phenomena, *ranging from severe to very mild cases.* It also enabled him to distinguish the disease from three forms of "periodic insanity," namely the symptoms of manic, circular, and depressive mental episodes and afflictions, which did not have "deterioration to dementia" as their ultimate outcome.

Based on numerous observations of his patients' speech and behavior, Kraepelin thus demonstrated how *dementia praecox*, as a *qualitatively* different disease, progressed from an initial state where attention, will, and thought began to fail, via a deterioration expressed in inattentiveness, silliness, and delusion, all the way up to apathy, muteness, confusion, and incontinence. Even though he acknowledged that his research resulted in no known etiology or clear cause for the illness, Kraepelin described other shared characteristics of this disorder. For instance, he found that *dementia praecox* was far more common in male than in female patients, and observed that in more than half of all cases, there was an early onset, between the ages of 16 and 22. Finally, he noted that in most cases, not only did the disease reveal itself suddenly but also its general deterioration was rapid.

To give a telling example, in his 1920 article entitled "The manifestations of insanity," Kraepelin claimed mental disorders should be investigated more broadly, rather than merely symptomatically or pathologically.[27] As is well known, World War I led to massive psychiatric injuries in soldiers who, needless to say, were not hereditarily predisposed to mental illnesses, yet suffered from traumatic stress (similar to what we now call post-traumatic stress disorder, or PTSD) and related ailments.

After the war, Kraepelin could not easily deny the psychological causes of mental disorders. In fact, he ended up concluding that foundational mental states such as mood, thought, will, perception, and memory should also be considered when diagnosing mental disorders. He even proposed using methods of empathy and psychoanalysis, together with patients' own account of their suffering and distress, in order to understand the clinical phenomena more thoroughly.

When discussing a possible developmental outline of disease manifestations, Kraepelin admitted that in order to be successful in matters of clinical diagnosis and treatment, one needed to trace the manifestation of psychological lives to the roots in the psyche, not only of the young child, but also of primitive man, and even animals. He was hoping to discover to what extent certain illnesses reflected an eruption of emotions that were otherwise concealed by our more civilized selves.[28] In the end, Kraepelin was optimistic about the prospects of charting such new avenues of research, "despite the poverty of our current knowledge."[29]

However, it was his earlier and less informed work on the diagnosis of *dementia praecox* that migrated all over the world. As Noll points out, while the fifth edition of *Psychiatry* (1896) introduced the diagnosis of *dementia praecox* to American asylums, the textbook's sixth edition (1899) earned Kraepelin his global renown.[30] Alienists and psychologists from America, Russia, Sweden, the Netherlands, Italy, England, France, Japan, and Turkey paid attention, and many travelled to Germany to study with him.

One of the alienists who journeyed to Kraepelin's clinic in Heidelberg was Eugen Bleuler (1857–1939), the Swiss psychiatrist who would coin the term "schizophrenia" in 1908. Indeed, the term "schizophrenia" was introduced in a lecture given by Bleuler to the German Psychiatric Association in Berlin, on April 24, 1908, with the title, "Die Prognose der Dementia praecox (Schizophreniegruppe)," or "The diagnosis of Dementia praecox (The group of schizophrenias)."[31]

Although it was completed in 1908, Bleuler's well-known book *Dementia Praecox or the Group of Schizophrenias* was not published until 1911. It is thus very well possible that Kraepelin had read Bleuler's manuscript and assimilated relevant parts of it into the third volume of the eighth edition of his *Psychiatry*, published in 1915. According to Assen Jablensky, at this point, Kraepelin himself considered replacing the *categorical* disease notion of schizophrenia with a *dimensional* model.[32] While in the *categorical approach* schizophrenia is clearly separated from other mental illnesses (especially manic-depressive disorder) based on their course and prognosis, the *dimensional approach* implies a classification based on different functions (such as relation to reality, attention, will, psychosocial adaptation, and so on). Each of the latter reveals a continuum from, say, optimal reality testing to a complete break with reality or also: a span of attention ranging from charged activity to lack of interest in the world as a whole; from having a strong will to having no urge at all; or, indeed, from having no difficulty in psychosocial adaptation, on one end of the spectrum, to complete psychosocial disintegration, on the other. Bleuler, as we will discuss more fully in our next section, urged his readers to view schizophrenia in precisely such a dimensional framework, assuming a *continuum* that spanned many phenomena from the normal to the schizophrenic. In the history that we are tracing here, step by step, Bleuler not only significantly enriched the clinical picture of schizophrenic psychopathology, he also promoted an explanatory and interpretative model with which a broad *spectrum* of experiences, symptoms, and signs, stretching from the normal to the pathological, could be observed and accounted for.

More than a "Renamer": Paul Eugen Bleuler

> Unfortunately we could not shirk the uncomfortable duty of coining a new name for this disease. But the present one seems too awkward. It only designates the disease, not the diseased; moreover, it is impossible to derive from it an adjective denoting the characteristic of this illness. … I am well aware of the disadvantages of the proposed name, but I know of no better one. It is really quite impossible to find a perfect name for a concept which is still developing and changing. I call *dementia praecox* "schizophrenia" because (as I hope to demonstrate) the "splitting" of the different psychic functions is one of its most important characteristics. For the sake of convenience, I use the word in the singular although it is apparent that the group includes several diseases. (Bleuler, *Dementia Praecox or the Group of Schizophrenias*, 1911)[33]

While Emil Kraepelin was developing his ideas based mostly on his collection of cards (the *Zählkarten*, which he would also study during his weekends away from patients, at Lake Starnberg)[34] and focused on the cognitive disturbances of his asylum patients, Paul Eugen Bleuler (figure 3) was forming his own theories, drawing on his clinical encounters with patients at the Burghölzli hospital in Zurich. Unlike Kraepelin, who generally believed that the cause of madness would one day be found in the body, Bleuler mostly sought to explain his patients' symptoms in terms of their emotions and by identifying the psychogenetic causes of mental illness.

Bleuler's career ascent began in 1886, when he became Director of the Rheinau clinic. During the 13 years he spent there, he collected most of the cases cited in his 1911 monograph, *Dementia Praecox or the Group of Schizophrenias.* Not only did Bleuler listen to his patients, he also learned about them by participating in every aspect of their daily lives, from sharing meals to working with them on the hospital grounds. Immediately following his tenure at Rheinau, which ended in 1898, Bleuler was appointed to the most prominent position

Figure 3 Paul Eugen Bleuler (1857–1939)
Source: Wikimedia Commons

in academic psychiatry in Switzerland, the Chair of Psychiatry at the University of Zurich (in addition to his directorship of Burghölzli in the same city).

Like his predecessor, the psychiatrist Auguste Forel (1848–1931), Bleuler was trained in the natural sciences. Yet unlike Forel, he soon recognized that these sciences could not offer a full understanding of the human mind. His further encounters with psychiatric patients and his close observations of them during treatment allowed him to further broaden his concept of the disease, which he now decided to name "schizophrenia," despite his hesitation, as the above epigraph makes amply clear.

It is possible that Bleuler's more psychotherapeutic (rather than biological) attitude to schizophrenia was rooted in his experience with his sister, who was diagnosed with schizophrenia, and whom he took care of at the Burghölzli clinic after the death of their parents. During his tenure there (1898–1927), Bleuler initially lived alone, but was later joined by his wife and family in the apartment reserved for the director, on the first floor of the clinic's main building. Working with mentally ill patients while living on the premises of the clinic allowed him to constantly revisit, develop, and revise his ideas on schizophrenia. He penned a series of important articles on the subject that testify to this fact and to the fruitfulness of his approach. Moreover, not only did he publish six editions of his major textbook during his lifetime, his son Manfred Bleuler (1903–94), the Swiss psychiatrist, co-authored nine more editions of the same work after his death.

Although Bleuler was considered by some of his peers to be nothing more than a "renamer and continuator," the new name ("schizophrenia") he coined was the logical consequence of a far more fundamental redefinition of the pathology in question. Indeed, the change of name indicated a deeper shift that had led Bleuler to see the disease as a treatable, if complex, psychological process, rather than a biological process with an inescapable deteriorating course.

In the first mention of the term "schizophrenia" in his 1908 lecture, Bleuler went straight to the heart of the matter:

> I am taking the liberty of employing the word *schizophrenia* for revising the Kraepelinian concept. In my opinion, the breaking up or splitting of psychic functioning is an excellent symptom of the whole group.[35]

After observing his patients closely, Bleuler concluded that their condition and mental suffering were not due to a single disease. Rather, it was clear that there was a "whole group of schizophrenias"[36] that needed further attention and interpretation.[37] In his 1911 *magnum opus*, *Dementia Praecox or the Group of Schizophrenias* (see figure 4), Bleuler explained that the term "schizophrenia" designates a group of psychoses with different courses. Some of them are chronic, others are episodic; some can suddenly stop inflicting their harm, while others just keep on deteriorating. However, each of these psychoses, in Bleuler's eyes, shared a common feature: in all of them the personality loses its "unity."[38] The fragmentation of the personality's previously integrated mental faculties of thought, emotion, and will, together with the patient's own

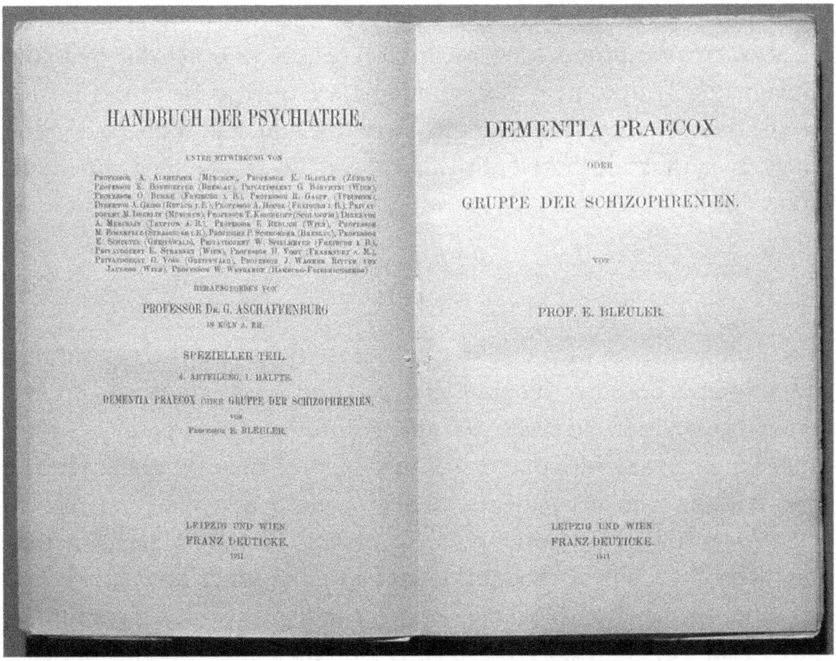

Figure 4 Title page of the first 1911 edition of Bleuler's *Dementia Praecox: The Group of Schizophrenias*
© Foto H.-P. Haack, via Wikimedia Commons
(https://commons.wikimedia.org/wiki/File:177_Eugen_Bleuler_1911.jpg)

subjective experience that the coherence of their self slips through their fingers, is at the core of these disorders. Moreover, they lead to confusion and withdrawal as the individual's thoughts, feelings and desires are no longer sensed as being connected to each other in recognizable and, more importantly, meaningful ways.

According to Bleuler, the ensuing alterations in thinking, feeling, volition, and relation to the external world are specific to this group of disorders. Bleuler considered "schizophrenia" to have four *fundamental symptoms*, that have come to be known as Bleuler's "four A's," namely: Associations, Affect, Ambivalence and Autism. He also suggested that schizophrenia included *accessory symptoms* or secondary disease manifestations, such as hallucinations and delusions that are "only episodes or exacerbations in the long, drawn-out course of the disease."[39] Because these symptoms make it difficult to keep patients at home, they also lead families to seek psychiatric help and hospitalization. But unlike the accessory symptoms (that might also feature in other diseases), the fundamental symptoms of schizophrenia are only to be found in this specific disease. They are present in every case and at every period of the illness. It is thus illustrative, in this context, to review them briefly in succession.

Associations

In schizophrenia, as Bleuler observed, associations lose their continuity and thinking becomes illogical and bizarre. Associations are created between two unrelated ideas that merge into one, with patients sometimes clinging to an idea that they return to, over and over again. Having conversations with his patients, Bleuler noticed that there was generally a "dearth of ideas to the point of monoideism."[40] Where one idea dominates the train of thought, disturbances of other associations can be found, such as the "blocking" of other thoughts, which gives further rise to a state of confusion. For Bleuler, two patients with schizophrenia can seem to be different, while sharing the same lack of purpose in their psychological associations. Among the many examples he gave is a letter written by a patient at the Burghölzli clinic:

> I am writing on a paper. The pen which I am using, is from a factory called "Perry & Co." This factory is in England. I assume this. Behind the name of Perry & Co. the city of London is inscribed; but not the city. The city of London is in England. I know this from my school-days. Then, I always liked geography. My last teacher in that subject was Professor August A. He was a man with black eyes. I also like black eyes. There are also blue and gray eyes and other sorts, too. I have heard it said that snakes have green eyes. All people have eyes. There are some, too, who are blind. These blind people are led about by a boy. It must be very terrible not to be able to see. There are people who can't see and, in addition, can't hear. I know some who hear too much. One can hear too much. There are many sick people in Burghölzli; they are called patients. One of them I like a great deal. His name is E. Sch. He taught me that in Burghölzli there are many kinds, patients, inmates, attendants. Then there are some who are not here at all. They are all peculiar people.[41]

The patient would fixate on certain things of previous sentences to continue on to the next sentence.

As we can see from the example Bleuler gave in his study, the patient who is writing a letter to her relative, cannot use the association between ideas effectively. Thus, her mode of communication, like her thinking, becomes scattered and meaningless. Although it is correct to associate London to the geography teacher, the black eye to blindness, to sick people, and, finally, to the hospital she is writing from – these associations do not form specific connections that would be sufficient for the patient to communicate a coherent message to her relative. Instead, her thoughts and speech are interrupted, and even if they are not entirely senseless, her words lose their purpose.

Based on observations such as this, Bleuler concluded that such disturbances of association occur on a *continuum*. Indeed, as he writes, "*All indicated disturbance may range from a maximum which corresponds to complete confusion, to a minimum which may be hardly noticeable.*"[42] For Bleuler, in cases of "cured" or "latent" *dementia praecox*, a disturbance of thinking can thus be detected. Whereas in normal thought processes, a number of images – actual and latent – determine each association, in schizophrenia, "*single images or whole combinations may be rendered ineffective, in an apparently haphazard fashion.*"[43] As a result, ideas and concepts tend to have very little connection in schizophrenic thinking, and, at times, have none at all. "*The result is that thinking becomes confused, bizarre, incorrect, abrupt.*"[44] While Bleuler claimed that "the emergence of an idea without any connection with [the] previous train of thought, or without any external stimulus, is so foreign to normal psychology," he also maintained that "connections with accidentally aroused ideas, condensation, clang associations, intermediate associations, and preservation of ideas are not foreign to the normal psyche."[45] While in the normal functioning of the psyche, they may seem exceptional or sporadic, in schizophrenia they are "*exaggerated* to the point of caricature."[46] The loosening of association is thus a prominent feature of schizophrenia. For Bleuler, the significance of the phenomenon was largely a result of the profound and lasting impression that his younger colleague, Carl Gustav Jung, and his experiments with association in schizophrenia patients, had made on him. Here, the central assumption was that the thought disorders seen in schizophrenia are not so much foreign to the normal psyche, but, rather, are merely an exaggerated form of some of its rare exceptions. This fundamentally contradicted Kraepelin's idea that the thought disorders of those with *dementia praecox* belong to a different category – and, hence, differ in kind rather than in degree, from "normal" psychical functioning.

Affectivity

The second "A" denotes the disappearance of affect, or emotions. Instead, we have a presentation of an all-pervading indifference. "I don't care the least, one way or the other," Bleuler cites one of Binswanger's patients. "I don't give a damn," as he further summarizes this emptied emotional world. These patients, Bleuler went on to explain, show no affect, they "sit about the institutions to which they are confined with expressionless faces ... like automatons, without any expression of satisfaction or dissatisfaction ... indifference to everything – to friends and relations, to vocation and enjoyment, to duties and rights, to good fortune or bad."[47] But for Bleuler, not all schizophrenics look alike: in *milder* cases, this indifference can be absent or disguised, and in some schizophrenics, notably those who are "never seen by a psychiatrist," among whom one finds "active writers, world improvers, health fanatics, founders of new religions," a very lively affect is at times displayed, "at least in certain directions."[48] Bleuler was therefore convinced that the psyche's capacity to produce affect did not disappear in schizophrenia.[49] Indeed, not all schizophrenics necessarily showed a defect in affect. Some were even ostensibly capable of parental love, sympathy for others, or even artistic empathy. Bleuler further emphasized the variety of the "schizophrenias" and believed that one could morally trust or distrust a schizophrenic just as little or as much as any other, "normal" person.[50] In other words, the character of the schizophrenic "is as manifold as that of the normal." Just as in any other group of people, Bleuler saw patients who remained loveable despite their disease, whereas he also incisively described people in the process of becoming "monsters of the most cruel, deceitful type."[51] Although this affective disturbance was often not felt as such by most patients, those who did register it sensed a growing feeling of emptiness. For example, one of Jung's patients, so Bleuler writes, could not pray because of the "hardening of her feelings," yet another felt he was "insensibilized."

Another common form of disordered affect was the unprovoked and inappropriate burst of laughter in inappropriate circumstances, for example, when a patient was told that a close family member had passed away.[52] Basing his work on a host of examples from his own clinical practice and drawing on patients' communications he received from his colleagues, Bleuler concluded that emotional disturbance was at the forefront of the clinical picture of schizophrenia. Yet, here too, the point was not to evoke or introduce biological or medical *categories*, presumed grounded in natural kinds, but, instead, a wide-ranging and continuous *spectrum*, stretching from mild to severe forms of illness, from curable to chronic symptoms of suffering.

Ambivalence

Ambivalence is the third fundamental symptom that Bleuler observed, even in mild cases of schizophrenia. In this process, the schizophrenic psyche simultaneously "endows" an object (a person, healthcare provider, or loved one) with both negative and positive indicators. Bleuler described several types of ambivalence, in some detail. The first, "affective ambivalence," occurs when patients hold opposite affects at the same time: for example, they perceive persons as angels and devils interchangeably, loving and hating them at the same time. Second, "ambivalence of will" occurs when the patient wants to do something and doesn't want to do it, at the very same moment – for example, if a patient wants to eat and brings a spoon to their mouth but then immediately withdraws it, so that the act of consuming food is never completed. Thirdly, in "intellectual ambivalence," a patient says something, then immediately contradicts or recants it – for example, in saying "I am a human being, I am not a human being." Bleuler also added the idea of "double-entry bookkeeping," to describe the mental state where the schizophrenic knows what is real yet holds on to what is false, thus stating one thing and its opposite, depending on the circumstances, as seems opportune.[53]

Autism

Autism, the last of the A's, denotes a "detachment from reality, together with the relative and absolute predominance of the inner life."[54] Even if the patient still operates in the external world, the significance of the outer reality is damaged and he or she remains indifferent to it. The patients in question try to resist any sensation or influence that comes from without, shutting themselves off whenever they can. The reality of their autistic world thus becomes stronger than any shared, external reality (the latter sometimes being experienced as an illusion). Yet as Bleuler asserted, autistic and realistic thinking can also exist side by side. Realistic thinking allows the patient to orient himself in reality, while autistic thinking is the source of delusion.[55]

The "fundamental symptoms" in this general rubric therefore overlap with each other, so that autism ends up containing aspects of affect, association, and ambivalence. As Manfred Bleuler would later explain, for his father, a decision to diagnose schizophrenia was based on multiple factors and, hence, was never based on "one or several individual symptoms."[56] It was only when a general failure of integrating one's self-experience and/or when one's ability to relate meaningfully to others was observed and reported by patients themselves that the diagnosis of schizophrenia seemed warranted.

Unlike Kraepelin, then, Bleuler pictured the psychic phenomena of mental illness on a *continuum*, depending on the severity of the "split," or the disintegration of the psyche. Thus, some interpreters consider Bleuler to be the originator of the concept of the so-called "schizophrenia-spectrum disorders," which we find in the latest edition of the manual of the psychiatric profession, the DSM-5 (2013). While his contemporaries kept on searching for *natural kinds*, Bleuler saw the heterogeneity of clinical pictures, from mild to severe, as well as their different outcomes. Hence, he spoke not just of a single disease entity, but rather of a "group of schizophrenias," a host of different manifestations of the diseases in question.

Although he was interested more in the psychology of schizophrenia than in its biology, Bleuler acknowledged that hereditary factors could also come into play. For example, he claimed that children of alcoholics are more prone to becoming schizophrenic, and further suggested that since hereditary factors cannot be excluded, marriage of such patients should be discouraged.[57] Next to this rather grim view of the disease, Bleuler ironically posited that the therapy of schizophrenia is one of the most rewarding works for "the physician who does not ascribe the results of the natural healing processes of psychosis to his own intervention."[58] In terms of treatment, he recommended interventions that can be traced back to the regimens of antiquity, such as balanced sleep, sensible nourishment, and controlled affect. He also recommended measures familiar from nineteenth-century moral treatment, such as engaging in regulated, non-demanding work. Farming and gardening, for example, could contribute to "healthy" thoughts, just as routine mechanical office work could support the organization of thoughts.[59] Occupational therapy, sports, recreational activities (such as dance and walks) were recommended by Bleuler as beneficial for schizophrenia. When the patient is highly agitated and these cannot be carried out, he advised the use of reasonable doses of sedatives. He made it clear that the "treatment of schizophrenia by medication does not exist," but that the principal rule is that "no patient must ever be completely given up. The doctor must always be prepared to take action and to offer the patient a chance to abandon his pathological way of thinking."[60]

Bleuler also warned against expensive therapies and discouraged somatic therapies that were tested but did not result in improvement, such as blood transfusion, saline infusions, fever therapies, and even turpentine injections. The latter treatment was based on the assumption that schizophrenia was an infectious disease, with turpentine raising the count of white blood cells, such that the body could more efficiently fight off the infection. Bleuler also harbored deep reservations with regard to special diets that were supposed to fatten the patients, not to mention with regard to sterilization of schizophrenics, among several other radical, severe, and, at times, lethal interventions. Moreover, Bleuler saw hospitalization as a last resort, to be considered only if and when the patient's behavior simply became too disturbing or dangerous.[61] And, if hospitalization was needed, as a rule, Bleuler recommended that patients be released sooner rather than later. He strongly criticized the overcrowded institutions that kept schizophrenics for long periods of time as *de facto* "work-slaves," and insisted that doctors should not wait for an ever unlikely complete "cure" before releasing patients back to their families.[62]

All in all, Bleuler was cautious regarding therapy, noting that "at present, we know of no measures, which will cure the disease, as such, or even bring it to a halt."[63] The only type of therapy that should be seriously considered, according to him, was the "psychic method," even if for lack of empirical evidence, "we are forced to grope in the dark."[64] The general task of the treatment is re-establishing the patient's contact with reality and combatting their autism.[65]

Whereas Kraepelin's ideas on *dementia praecox* were by and large influenced by the progress made in the natural sciences, Bleuler's revision was based on careful, close observations of – and conversations with – his suffering patients. Nonetheless, both agreed that there was something distinctive and typical about schizophrenia, a core – a "whatness," around which its symptoms all revolved. The Dutch psychiatrist Henricus Cornelius Rümke (1893–1967) even coined the term "Praecox Gefühl" or "praecox feeling," to indicate the experience of the clinician's reaction to this "whatness," a designation that was then part and parcel of the diagnosis of schizophrenia.

Even if Bleuler's views on the subject were at times contradictory, he distinguished between this essential core, which he located in the *fundamental* symptoms, the 4 A's (even if these were manifested on a continuous spectrum of severity), on the one hand, and the supplementary or *accessory* symptoms, including hallucinations, delusions, or catatonia (all part of what we might call "psychosis," but not specific to schizophrenia), on the other.

Bleuler's book represents the main source of his thinking on schizophrenia, especially in the renaming of *dementia praecox*. In his later writings, Bleuler pointed to the core phenomenon of schizophrenia as a psychological and behavioral detachment from reality and an ensuing withdrawal into a "world of one's own"; as the process that gives rise to a predominance of the inner life and to the loss of cohesion of the bounded self.

The name Bleuler would give to this disturbance keenly captured the resulting *split* within what ought to have been felt and perceived as a *unity*. As a diagnosis and by its very name, schizophrenia addressed the very nature of this disturbance that Bleuler observed in the structure of the self. Through the loosening of the associations that would normally hold the different parts and functions of the psyche together, the individual's fundamental identity was compromised. Unlike hallucinations and delusions, however, the core symptoms of schizophrenia could also be found in less severe forms of the disorder, as the mental states, episodes or events that formed part – and took place on – the gliding scale of a "schizophrenic spectrum."

The Birth of the Schizophrenias

Kraepelin's early attempts at creating a classification system of psychiatric diseases, with its emphasis on prognosis and on the standing possibility of disease degeneration, were based mainly on the thousands of cards with information *about* patients that had eventually given birth to the single diagnosis of *dementia praecox* (premised as it remained, in Kraepelin's case, on a categorical model). By contrast, Bleuler's face-to-face daily encounters and conversations *with* living and suffering patients delivered the diagnosis of "the schizophrenias," conceived of as plural in essence.

Although Bleuler embraced many of Kraepelin's clinical observations and accepted the general assumption that mental illness might have a physiological basis, he agreed with Freud and Jung on the idea that understanding schizophrenia also required the study of unconscious psychological processes.

While others studied its underlying brain mechanisms, Bleuler wished to explore schizophrenia neither through biological methods, nor on the basis of postmortem investigations – under a microscope, as it were. Rather, he opted for the method of dynamic psychiatry, which derives its knowledge from listening to a patient's communications and uncovering the complexes and conflicts operating in their *mind*.

In this framework, schizophrenia was conceived not as a unitary phenomenon, caused by one degenerative disease, but rather was understood as covering a range of "schizophrenias" that existed on a *continuum* with normal states, as well as with the neuroses and other psychological disturbances. As Bleuler put it, "differentiation from the functional neuroses is so vague, that a mild schizophrenic may give the impression of a hysteric. … Furthermore, practically all schizophrenic manifestations may appear to represent merely *exaggerations* of well-known neurotic symptoms."[66]

Bleuler's understanding of the symptoms of schizophrenia was deeply influenced by Freud's theories regarding the working of the mind. While most academic psychiatrists outright dismissed the emerging science of psychoanalysis as it was being developed at roughly the same time in

Vienna, by Freud himself and his immediate circle, Bleuler was the first university professor who introduced psychoanalytic research, theory, and practice in an academic clinic with hospitalized patients. This is not to deny or forget that Bleuler's relationship with Freud was marked and marred by profound ambivalence. Bleuler notably rejected the centrality Freud assigned to Eros or to infantile sexuality.[67] Nonetheless, under Bleuler's directorship, the Burghölzli clinic was willing to seriously consider and further explore psychoanalytic ideas.

As a clear sign of this interest and investment in psychoanalysis, Bleuler asked Jung, when he arrived at the clinic in 1900 to take up his very first professional post,[68] to give a presentation on Freud's *Interpretation of Dreams* (which had appeared that same year) to the hospital's staff. Jung had already used some of Freud's insights in his dissertation,[69] and in his famous monograph *The Psychology of Dementia Praecox*, he generously acknowledged his personal debt to the latter's "brilliant discoveries."[70] Jung's own experiments with word associations, which would later come to inform Bleuler's overall understanding of schizophrenia (including the first of the fundamental symptoms, the 4 A's discussed above), applied dynamic psychiatry to the explanation of the abnormal thought processes of the disease.[71]

Bleuler's own most significant work, where he questioned the early onset and dire prognosis of *dementia praecox* (proposing, as we have seen, a different nomenclature, namely that of the group of schizophrenias), was likewise influenced by Freud. From the latter, Bleuler adopted the more general idea of a continuum between normal and pathological states. In the preface to his book on the schizophrenias, Bleuler would thus write: "An important aspect of the attempt to advance and enlarge the concepts of psychopathology is nothing less than an application of Freud's ideas to dementia praecox."[72] He also added that, surely, his informed readers would quickly realize how greatly his own understanding of the disease was indebted to Freud, even if he did not mention his name in his discussions of the contemporary literature on the subject.[73] In fact, although Bleuler did not mention Freud in any of the chapters of his book, he nonetheless applied the very same mechanisms to psychosis that Freud had observed in himself, in his interpretation of dreams and self-analysis, and in his clinical practice, among his neurotic patients. Whether it was his understanding of the disturbance of associations in schizophrenia in terms of Freud's normal dream-work mechanisms of displacement, condensation, and symbolization, or his ideas that the fundamental schizophrenic symptoms could be understood in terms of the inevitable conflict between wish fulfillments, fears, and defense mechanisms that Freud observed in neurotic patients,[74] Bleuler's understanding of schizophrenic symptoms was very much inspired by the latter's early work. Like Jung, Bleuler picked up on the motif of the continuum that Freud's demonstration laid bare – the insight that the same mental mechanisms were at work both in dreams of normal people and in the symptom formation of neurotic patients – and extended it well beyond the domain Freud had covered, thus including the psychoses in it as well.

Freud himself had little interest in psychotic disorders. But in 1911 (the year Bleuler's *Dementia Praecox or the Group of Schizophrenias* was published), his famous discussion of a case of "paraphrenia" (Freud's own term for schizophrenia) came out in print.[75] Since Freud had not worked in an asylum and had no prolonged clinical encounters with patients diagnosed with "the schizophrenias," his case study and analysis were based on an indirect source, namely the memoirs of the now famous judge, Daniel Paul Schreber (1842–1911).[76] Freud's analysis of Schreber, to which we will return in our next chapter, was similar to the ongoing efforts at the Burghölzli clinic, striving to understand the psychology of schizophrenia. However, while Bleuler accepted the wider psychoanalytic idea that understanding schizophrenia required the study of unconscious psychological processes, he rejected much of Freud's analysis in his own 1912 review of Schreber's case. That said, Bleuler continued to insist that Freud's work inspires us to ask questions regarding psychological depths that no one before had truly fathomed, just as he encourages us to wander down sinuous tracks that few had dared to enter upon. In this respect, Bleuler insisted that Freud's contribution remained invaluable.[77]

Many of the physicians who visited or worked under Bleuler at the Burghölzli clinic, and whom Bleuler mentions in his book on the schizophrenias as co-workers who contributed ideas and observations to his understanding of that pathology, were deeply interested in psychoanalysis. Among them were Karl Abraham (1877–1925), who had come from Berlin and was influential in studying the more primitive mechanisms of psychosis; the Swiss psychiatrist Franz Riklin (1878–1938), who collaborated with Jung on word association and became the first secretary of the International Psychoanalytic Association; the Belarusian-German psychiatrist Max Eitingon (1881–1943), who was the founder of the psychoanalytic training model; and the Polish-born American psychiatrist A. A. Brill (1874–1948), who translated Freud into English and was one of his most enthusiastic proponents in the United States. Many of the other physicians on the staff of the Burghölzli, who mainly treated and studied schizophrenia in hospital settings, likewise contributed not only to the further understanding of the disease, but also provided insights and theories they developed in the process to the growing science of psychoanalysis.

Among the critics of Freud and the Zurich school was the psychiatrist and philosopher Karl Jaspers (1883–1969), who at first welcomed the new science as a viable alternative to the somatic medicine that viewed all psychological studies as unscientific, subjective, and useless. Yet Jaspers was also deeply suspicious of the psychoanalytic ambition to solve the puzzle of schizophrenic speech by deciphering meaning in what seemed otherwise inaccessible and unintelligible communications. In other words, Jaspers was uncomfortable with the transposition of the method of study, guided by theoretical and clinical concepts, from the analysis of neurotic patients, on the one hand, to the understanding of schizophrenia, on the other. More specifically, against the continuum model that Bleuler and Jung borrowed from Freud, Jaspers insisted on a *radical difference*, which, he believed, existed between hysteria and schizophrenic processes, a difference that could not be translated without losing sight of the unique experience of the patient.[78]

As we shall discuss in the next chapter, even though it was on the basis of Freud's theoretical and clinical concepts, developed in his studies of the neuroses, that the concept of schizophrenia was born at the Burghölzli clinic, psychoanalytic thinking about schizophrenia was – and would remain – far from uniform, much less coherent. Psychoanalysis radically departed from biological psychiatry's attempts at classifying different – categorically distinct – disease units according to their symptoms, course, and outcome, under a microscope in a lab, as it were. Instead, Freud, Jung, and Bleuler pointed towards the *shared* psychic mechanisms across a continuum, spectrum, or wider dimension, of the normal and the pathological. But when it came to interpreting the far edges of experience, that is, to schizophrenia, the psychoanalytic school of thought and clinical praxis was, and still is, deeply divided, with a lingering major question looming large. Does the spectrum extend as far as the psychoses, schizophrenia being its paradigmatic form, or do patients, diagnosed in these technical terms, fall over the edge of this continuum, such that their psyche must be considered fundamentally different from normal states and the mild neuroses that most of us suffer from? And if the latter, what makes such patients radically – perhaps, categorically – different in the end?

Chapter 3
Psychoanalysis and Schizophrenia

> 16 August 1887
> Dear Sir,
> Unfortunately I cannot make it possible for you to appreciate the sad conditions which have obtruded themselves. Once again I call your attention to the simple fact that you should discharge me without further delay, as I suffer all by myself from the novelties and if you were convinced of it you would surely discharge me immediately, because I have suffered from the beginning since I came here and am totally at the end of my health; I want an immediate discharge. It gets better immediately I am away from Zurich in another atmosphere where the horrors are no longer in evidence, etc. (Jung, *The Psychology of Dementia Praecox*, 1907)

Carl Jung, who was the recipient of the above letter from a patient at the Burghölzli, thought that psychiatry, because it lacked the microscope that "shows the dreaded bacillus" and was not equipped with the surgeon's knife that "halts at no difficulty and gives us glimpses of most inaccessible organs of vital importance," was at best a "stepchild" of the established discipline of medicine. While he believed that psychiatry's organ was the brain, he also insisted that for psychiatrists what really mattered was to be found in what lay beyond that material substance. The beyond, namely the mind, he conceived of as indefinable, "eluding all explanation, no matter how ingenious." Unlike any other branches of medicine that applied the scientific method, psychiatry, as "the art of healing the soul," on Jung's view, stood "ever at the door seeking in vain to weigh and measure as in the other departments of science."[1]

Nonetheless, he chose to train as a psychiatrist and joined the Burghölzli clinic in December 1900 (see figure 5). He lived on the clinic's grounds and experimented with severely disturbed hospitalized patients, treating them on a daily basis for many years. Unlike most asylum physicians, Jung and his colleagues at the Burghölzli were interested in the

Figure 5 The Burghölzli Clinic, where Bleuler coined the term schizophrenia and where most followers of Freud interested in mental illnesses came from during these years
Source: Zentralbibliothek Zürich, Graphische Sammlung und Fotoarchiv

psychology of insanity and, more specifically, in the histories and stories of their patients, most of them diagnosed with *dementia praecox*. On observing the 42-year-old dressmaker, with whose letter we opened this chapter, Jung noted:

> The patient was admitted in 1887 and since then has remained permanently in the asylum. She has a severe hereditary taint. Before admission she had, for several years, heard voices that slandered her. For a time, she contemplated suicide by drowning. She explained the voices as invisible telephones. They called out to her that she was a woman of doubtful character, that her child had been found in a toilet, that she had stolen a pair of scissors in order to poke out a child's eyes ... Now and then she used peculiar expressions, and in general spoke in a somewhat pretentious manner. ... The patient produced vivid delusional ideas: she had a fortune of millions, at night her bed was stuck full of needles. ... Pains in the back are caused by substances going through the walls covered with magnetism. ... The delusional ideas became more and more absurd. A large but incomprehensible role was played by the words "banknote monopoly." In 1892, the patient became "Queen of the Orphans"

> and "proprietress of Burghölzli Asylum" ... in 1897 she relates that Dr. D recently came out of her mouth, "tiny little Dr. D., the son of the emperor of Barbarossa" ... in 1899 patient is tormented at night by thousands of snakes. (Jung, *The Psychology of Dementia Praecox*, 1907)

Like his direct superior, Eugen Bleuler, Jung was a major figure in the Zurich school, which experimented with a large number of severely ill inpatients diagnosed with *dementia praecox* or (as the disease would later be baptized in that very institution) schizophrenia. Visitors from all over the world came to study at the Burghölzli, which became one of the great psychiatric hospitals in Europe. Jung's pioneering work, *Über die Psychologie der Dementia Praecox* (*Psychology of Dementia Praecox*), published in 1907, together with a series of nine papers based on lectures he gave to psychiatrists between 1914 and 1958, made him an expert on a diagnosis he did not even like much: "D. pr. [i.e., *dementia praecox*] is a most unfortunate term!" he wrote to Freud in a letter dated January 8, 1907, only to add: "From your standpoint, my D. pr. case could just as well be described as paranoia, which was in fact done in former times."[2]

Jung (who was Bleuler's first assistant at the Burghölzli) and Freud were already in contact with each other well before Freud began his correspondence with Bleuler in 1908. By the time he began writing his groundbreaking book on the psychology of *dementia praecox*,[3] Jung was internationally renowned for his studies in word associations.

Although both Jung and Bleuler fundamentally held on to what might be called – quite literally – a *toxic* theory of the mental disturbance in question, as they assumed that a natural substance or "toxin" was responsible for causing the symptoms of schizophrenia, Jung declared that he and his colleagues had "entirely abandoned the anatomical approach in our Zurich clinic" and, as consequence, "turned to the psychological investigation of mental disease."[4]

Under Bleuler's directorship, the Burghölzli clinic became a center of psychological experimentation. Using a "word association test" as a diagnostic tool, Jung and his colleagues asked patients to respond to a given word with the first word that came to mind. The list included 100 words, among them "lamp," "tree," and "bird," as well as "angry," "to abuse," and "to quarrel." Patients' response time (RT) was recorded, as well as their emotional and physiological responses. If the response time was particularly long, or the associated word was uncommon, nonsense, not remembered on recall, or accompanied by particular emotions, Jung considered this a "complex indicator," that is, a sign of an underlying unconscious psychological conflict. A "complex," according to Jung, meant an unconscious set of memories, associations, fantasies, expectations, and patterns of behavior, organized around a core element that provoked strong emotional responses. Complexes were believed to derive from early developmental experiences, related to unresolved needs from childhood, and traumas. Although Jung argued that, "every human mind contains much that is unacknowledged and hence unconscious as such; and no one can boast that he stands completely above his complexes,"[5] Bleuler hoped that at the Burghölzli, the test could be used to *diagnose*, and perhaps even classify, *dementia praecox*.[6] In his famous experiments, Jung noticed that when schizophrenic patients responded to the word association test, their complexes tended to predominate for a much longer time, and they would often get a burst of auditory hallucinations when they hit responses.

Freud, who was Jung's mentor in every other respect, first learned about the possible uses of psychoanalysis in the study and treatment of *dementia praecox* or schizophrenia from his Swiss disciple. While Jung was seeing schizophrenic patients on a daily basis at the Burghölzli clinic, Freud treated psychotic inpatients only for a brief period at the Vienna General Hospital, when he was studying psychiatry under Theodor Meynert, in 1883. As Freud readily admitted, "My experience in this field is meager";[7] "I see cases of dementia praecox only very rarely."[8] In a letter to Jung dated June 21, 1908, Freud further wrote, using the disease's common abbreviation: "Unfortunately I know too little about the mechanism of Dem. pr. or paranoia as compared with hysteria or obsessional neurosis. I have long wished for a strong impression in this field. The need to make a living and the requirements of therapy stand in the way."[9]

These "impressions" of schizophrenia were finally delivered to Freud by those very psychiatrists who, like Bleuler and Jung, soon came to be known as the "Zurichers."[10] As we saw in chapter 2, Bleuler and Jung were dissatisfied with the dire prognosis implied by the very term *dementia praecox*, which seemed to suggest that an inescapable and irreparable outcome had been diagnosed all-too conclusively in young patients. In reaction, Jung was active in the efforts to replace the all-determining diagnosis with the term "schizophrenia," which, given its etymology, seemed to be premised on a more ambiguous state or process, one of "two-mindedness," as it were. With Bleuler, Jung insisted that the term schizophrenia represented a dramatic shift of focus – away from both the prognosis of *dementia* as an endpoint, and the disease's early onset (*praecox*) – in what seemed a more nuanced and open-minded diagnosis of a *schism* in the personality, that is, a split, a dissociation, a fragmentation, and a separation from others.

Nevertheless, it is possible that this seemingly novel emphasis was, in fact, not as original as it had been made out to be. The Austrian psychoanalyst Otto Gross, for example, accused the "Bleuler-Jung School" of stealing his term "*dementia sejunctiva*," whereby the adjective *sejunctiva* translated the literal motif of "splitting" that the competing word "schizophrenia" nominally put front and center. Yet, in the short-lasting controversy that ensued, Freud himself was not impressed by Gross's claim, dismissing it as a "trifling matter of terminology."[11]

Jung's discontent with the term "*dementia praecox*" was most probably based on his own encounters with patients, as well as on the records of 647 other patients with the same diagnosis that he studied during these years. Together with his more psychoanalytically inspired colleagues at the Burghölzli, he disputed Kraepelin's notion that the abnormality they treated was an incurable condition that led to early dementia. The records they investigated showed that over a period of eight years, some of these patients were, on the contrary, able to return to their community and even resume their roles in the workforce.[12]

This different outcome was not the only finding that paved the way for the alternative to the term *dementia praecox*. Although they would become increasingly disenchanted with psychoanalysis as a theoretical project and practical method, both Jung and Bleuler remained deeply interested, not just in the appearance of the symptoms of the disorder in question, but also in interpreting the *meaning* of what patients themselves were communicating through, at times, inaccessible language and incomprehensible actions. As a new science of the mind, with its elaborate method of interpreting psychological symptoms in the same way that symbols were decoded in dreams, psychoanalysis provided a depth psychology to investigate these intractable phenomena. As the titles of both Bleuler's 1906 paper, "On Freudian mechanisms in the symptomatology of the psychoses,"[13] and Jung's famous 1907 monograph, *Psychology of*

Dementia Praecox[14] imply, it was in psychoanalysis and in-depth psychology that a definitive alternative to the Kraepelinian empirical framework, which stayed on the surface by merely recording the symptoms and course of the illness, could perhaps be found.

Jung's monograph was only the beginning of his exploration of the psychopathology now known as schizophrenia. Inspired by the work of French associationists such as Pierre Janet, Jung's word association test was designed to study the *disintegration* of the thought processes in the patients he treated and studied. Jung considered the name "schizophrenia" more suitable, not only because it did not include a fatal prognosis but also, relatedly, because it emphasized the *schism*, the splitting and fragmentation of the self, and, thereby, a failure of the integrative functions of the mind.

It was through the theories of his mentor Freud, that Jung discovered a radical challenge to the all too simple, binary division between the normal and the pathological. Freud's work on dreams, sexuality, symptoms, and the psychopathology of everyday life (to use the title of his book from 1905), put forward a different conception of selfhood. In this conception, internal conflicts are inevitable, universal, and are part and parcel of the human condition. Occupying a body, which has desires yet is situated in a confined external reality, infused with restrictive moral values and norms, humans are torn between the pleasure principle and the reality principle. Their mental structure is composed of three different agencies – namely the drives (the so-called id), the mediator between internal and external reality (the role played by the ego), and the insistence of critical conscience (or, as Freud called it, the superego) – each of them with its own dynamics and agenda. Conflicts between these modes of psychological and unconscious agency result in anxiety, which in turn activates so-called defense mechanisms (i.e., repression, projection, denial, displacement, etc.) that keep the "forbidden" material out of consciousness and decrease the stress. The difference between everyday pathologies (like Freudian slips or other parapraxes), milder pathologies (like neuroses) and more severe abnormalities (like psychoses) lies in the ability to keep the different parts of the mind integrated while finding good compromises between the three distinguished agencies.

Jung's close clinical experience with patients diagnosed with *dementia praecox* showed that the distinction between the different pathologies (between, say, neuroses and psychoses) was, in fact, far more fluid than was often claimed. In a letter to Freud on April 11, 1907, Jung wrote:

> An excellent analysis I recently made of a Dementia praec. patient has recalled to my mind many of the things we talked about together. I would like to put one question before you, which I am quite particularly racking my brains over. The structure of the case was altogether "hysteriform" so much so that during the analysis I lost all consciousness of talking with a Dem. praec. patient. The rapport (transference) was excellent, so that I got the whole story out of her in *one hour* ... Insight into the nature and origin of the illness became quite clear to her during the analysis, so that one might have expected considerable improvement.[15]

In his notes about this particular case, Jung reported that the connection with the patient was so excellent that the differences between *dementia praecox* (i.e., schizophrenia), on the one hand, and the less severe form of mental disorder, namely hysteria (i.e., neurosis), on the other, were unclear, and more generally these differences are becoming increasingly and "suspiciously blurred,"[16] once he starts analyzing them.

A year later, in 1908, while Jung was still observing fundamental similarities between both conditions, the differences between them were also becoming more and more pronounced. Asking to discuss with Freud the concept of what he now called "dementia praecox *sive* schizophrenia *sive* paranoia," Jung explicitly argued that the *only* differences he could discern between the severe pathology of schizophrenia and the milder form of hysteria consisted in the more infantile ways of thinking and associating.[17] In other words, the distinction between the two was that of a shift or varied gradation on a continuous developmental spectrum. Yet at the same time, still troubled by the question of similarity and difference between both diagnoses, he confessed that in treating "highly educated hysterics," he could also now clearly see "the *absolute difference* between dementia praecox and hysteria."[18]

While Jung was trying to elaborate a clearer classification that would succeed in differentiating the neuroses from the psychoses, Freud was generally unimpressed by psychiatric nosology as a scientific enterprise overall. He expressed his reservations most adamantly with regard to the diagnosis of schizophrenia in which Jung had invested so much thought and effort. Yet, in a 1926 letter to the Swiss Lutheran minister Oskar Pfister,[19] discussing a patient named A.B. whom he had been seeing for three months, Freud confessed a change of mind that had led him reluctantly to a diagnosis of schizophrenia in a patient. However, he immediately added, the diagnosis was based not so much on the combination of the latter's manifest symptoms. Rather, in this particular case, Freud wrote, "[w]henever he [the patient] succumbs to resistance, I tell myself that it is a case of schizophrenia after all."[20] In other words, it was the patient's unconscious opposition to the psychoanalytic process, his persistence in using his old compromises instead of developing new knowledge about himself, that earned him the diagnosis of schizophrenia according to Freud. The story of Freud's patient A.B. was retold by David Lynn, a psychiatrist who worked at the McLean hospital in Boston where much of the patient's records were found, and it merits retelling.[21]

A.B. was born to a wealthy American family and as a child already looked different from others. Precocious intellectually but also deeply fearful, A.B. was a loner, uninvolved in social activities or sports, who instead chose to spend his time in solitude. He was strange and aloof during high school and college, and was never employed after graduation. His strange beliefs began in adolescence, when after ejaculation he would become obsessed with fears that he had committed mass murder on his sperm (to which he attributed the name "spermanimalcules"), anxious that he might have killed a baby. He started experiencing paranoid delusions in his early twenties and began analysis after graduating college. He subsequently travelled to Switzerland, where Oskar Pfister took him into treatment. Pfister was alarmed by A.B.'s psychotic symptoms and consulted with Bleuler, who diagnosed the young man with "mild schizophrenia." Bleuler believed that this was an early stage of the illness and that psychoanalysis, especially if it focused on A.B.'s early life and education, could still be useful. Pfister, who referred the young man to Freud's treatment, received a letter from his mentor reassuring him not to worry "about your young American. The man can be helped."[22] In a letter to A.B.'s mother, dated July 1928, Freud wrote: "I have no right to keep from you that the diagnosis in your son's case is Paranoid Schizophrenia. However, you have a right to emphasize that such a diagnosis means little and does not help us penetrate the uncertainty about his future. Even Rousseau was such a case, not less abnormal."[23] As this letter reconfirms,

Freud was unimpressed with diagnoses of this kind. Indeed, as he wrote soon thereafter to Pfister: "I propose to leave aside the academic question of diagnosis and go on working with the living material."[24]

Yet, like Bleuler and Jung, it should be noted that Freud expressed his dissatisfaction not only with diagnoses in general but more specifically with the term *dementia praecox*. In a letter to Jung, he criticized the psychiatric term quite clearly: "I write paranoia and not *dementia praecox* because I regard the former as a good clinical type and the latter as a poor nosographical term."[25] In an earlier letter to Karl Abraham, Freud pointed out the "misleading use of the term" *dementia* in *dementia praecox* by psychiatrists, as he believed that "*dementia* in *dementia praecox* must be different from that of the senile, epileptic, etc." Nevertheless, he saw this use as a "matter of no concern."[26] Although he continued to use *dementia praecox* and "schizophrenia" interchangeably, Freud coined an alternative term, "paraphrenia," to replace these idioms, which now seemed dated and too imprecise. However, in doing so, his main goal was to make paranoia central to the abnormality in question. Indeed, Freud's most famous work on a case of schizophrenia is an essay from 1911 with the telling title, "Psycho-analytic notes on an autobiographical account of a case of paranoia (dementia paranoides)."[27]

It was Jung who led Freud to study Judge Daniel Paul Schreber's 1903 *Denkwürdigkeiten eines Nervenkranken* (*Memoirs of My Nervous Illness*).[28] Freud described the case – and person – of the psychotic Schreber as "wonderful." Schreber's memoir served as the basis not only for Freud's theory of schizophrenia, but also his more general libido theory (where he posited a form of mental "energy" which could be invested, discharged or damned up, and could thus cause pleasure, pain, and symptoms); his ideas on narcissism (or self-love as a stage before the development of love for others); and finally his ideas on object relations (the psychic structures that are created during infancy and determine the ways a person relates to others). All of these ideas and theories that were evoked by his work on Schreber's memoir were further developed in his later writings and played a crucial role in the development of psychoanalysis as the new science of the unconscious. And yet, as enthusiastic as he was about Schreber's memoir, Freud opened his written account of the case with a cautious disclaimer, as if to downplay expectations as to what he, for his part, might add in terms of insight – not to mention, treatment – in similar cases:

> The analytic investigation of paranoia presents difficulties of a peculiar nature to physicians who, like myself, are not attached to public institutions. We cannot accept patients suffering from this complaint, or at all events, we cannot keep them for long since we cannot offer treatment unless there is some prospect of therapeutic success.[29]

Although Freud had started analyzing patients while Schreber was fighting his first bouts of psychosis, and while he even believed Schreber to be still alive when his analysis of the memoir was published, for all we know, he never so much as considered meeting the judge in person.[30] Nor did he ever correspond with him. At the time, Freud did not believe that psychoanalysis could effectively help patients with schizophrenia. Psychoanalysis required the ability of the patient to form transference, in other words, to invest his or her libido, that is, love, in the figure of the doctor. Patients with schizophrenia, however, were believed to lack precisely that capacity. The "autism" attributed to them, to use one of Bleuler's fundamental A's (or, in other words, their general withdrawal from reality and away from people into their own world), would, it was assumed, not allow for transference to take place. As a result, the analyst was not in a position to offer even so much as "some prospect of therapeutic success."

While Freud remained deeply interested in the psychical mechanism that operated in psychosis and believed that just as psychoanalysis could learn from neurotic patients about our multifarious sexual desires (or the id), psychosis, he thought, could teach psychoanalysis about the constitution and functioning of the agency that is experienced as the I (or the self) and that integrates the inner world with the external reality (i.e., the ego). But since the clinical technique that psychoanalysis applied to neurotics was deemed not useful in this extreme case of pathology, Freud found it more productive to consult Schreber's memoir rather than meeting Schreber, the patient. Indeed, all the necessary, detailed insights about the protracted ways the psyche actually operates was in the text, from which Freud quotes extensively. It is based on Schreber's own account of his illness that Freud offered his psychoanalytic theory of schizophrenia, and it is this famous and controversial account to which we will now turn.

To begin with, Freud relies on Schreber's understanding of his first psychotic illness as being precipitated by "mental overstrain," when the judge stood for election at the Reichstag in 1884. After recovering from his first illness, Schreber spent eight happy years with his wife, and the only pain he reports is their inability to have children. A "very heavy burden of work" nevertheless prompted Schreber's second illness in 1893, when he acquired his new responsibilities as *Senatspräsident* in Dresden.[31] As Freud notes, between his first and second illness, Schreber had a few disturbing dreams. Notably, in a state between sleeping and waking, he had the thought "that after all it really must be very nice to be a woman submitting to the act of copulation," an idea that proved intolerable when he was awake.[32] Freud continues with the description of Schreber's second psychotic illness, which started with a "torturing bout of sleeplessness," emphasizing once more the triggering function of mental overload and its effects on the psyche as a whole.[33]

Schreber's condition worsened at Paul Flechsig's university clinic in Leipzig. In Schreber's delusional retelling, Flechsig had become nothing short of a "soul murderer."[34] Schreber was subsequently transferred to an institution in Coswig and eventually to the Sonnenstein Asylum, at Pirna, where he kept complaining of a softening of the brain, and later, of the distinct feeling he was in fact dead while his body was decomposing. More specifically, Schreber believed his body was being tortured in various ways, all this in the service of a higher, holy good.[35] The pain, assumes Freud, was so unbearable that Schreber tried to kill himself.

The religious character of Schreber's delusions included the idea that he was in direct communication with God, but also that he was the plaything of devils. In addition, he claimed to witness miraculous apparitions, to hear holy music, and to be living in a different universe. And, indeed, Freud sees Schreber as "full of ideas of pathological origin, that are inaccessible to correction by means of any objective appreciation and judgment of the external facts."[36]

But Schreber was not the typical sufferer of *dementia praecox*, as his psychiatrist, Dr. Weber had noted:

> Dr. Schreber shows no signs of confusion or of psychical inhibition, nor is his intelligence noticeably impaired. His mind is collected, his memory is excellent, he has at his disposal a very considerable store of knowledge (not merely upon legal questions, but in many other fields), and he is able to reproduce it

> in a connected train of thought. He takes an interest in following events in the world of politics, science and art, etc., and is constantly occupied with such matters … and an observer who was uninstructed upon his general condition would scarcely notice anything peculiar in these directions.[37]

Even when he believed that he had "a mission to redeem the world and to restore it to its lost state of bliss," even when he firmly believed that he could only achieve this by transforming from a man into a woman, Schreber was reportedly coherent enough to be eventually released from his confinement in the mental hospital and had his civil rights fully restored.[38]

Like the prophets described in chapter 1, Schreber considered himself to be a mouthpiece of God, conveying a message that, just as in biblical times, would fatefully fall on deaf ears. He knew he would not be understood, precisely because he was "touching on matters which human speech is scarcely, if at all, capable of expressing … since they lie entirely outside the scope of human experience and, indeed, [had] been revealed to him alone."[39]

Freud's Analysis of Schreber: Strangeness Made Familiar

> Dementia Praecox was a particular unhappy name to choose for it. The designation chosen by Bleuler for the same group of forms – "schizophrenia" – is also open to objection that the name appears appropriate only so long as we forget its literal meaning, i.e., split mind … since it is based on a characteristic of the disease … which does not belong exclusively to that disease … and cannot be regarded as the essential one. However, it is not on the whole of very great importance what names we give to clinical pictures. (Freud, "Psychoanalytic notes on an autobiographical account of a case of paranoia," 1911)

Before beginning his analysis of this particular case, Freud sets himself in sharp opposition to the clinical tradition of practically oriented psychiatrists, like Weber or Kraepelin. For Freud, these professionals were mostly interested in how patients' delusions influence their *strange* behavior, which their treatment immediately sought to mitigate, if not overcome. This perspective, however, fails to produce a deeper and fuller understanding of the psychopathological causes and symptoms of patients' behavior. The psychoanalyst, on the other hand, takes cumulative experience from the "talking cure," addressing the patients' speech and positing that even their strangest ideas are ultimately derived from "the *most general* and *comprehensible* impulses of the human mind."[40] In other words, psychoanalysts are interested in discovering the motives of such observed transformations, keeping track of the sinuous history of their development in the patient's life and treatment.

Freud then comments on the *familiarity* of the "redeemer phantasy" in which Schreber believes he is the son of God, and destined to save the world from its suffering or destruction, especially as it is presented in religion. He also describes the ways in which Schreber's delusion of transforming into a woman diverges from it. In doing so, Freud observes the *general* and *universal* traits of the phantasy, just as he points out the *peculiar* and *specific* elements that set this case apart. And while he remains convinced that there is a deeper meaning in Schreber's elaborate delusions, Freud also tellingly writes that "it requires more than a little faith to persist in the belief that *there is nevertheless 'method' in his 'madness'*."[41]

Moreover, as he deciphers and dives into the details of Schreber's mad world, Freud is struck by its "astonishing mixture of the *commonplace* and the clever, of what has been borrowed and what is *original*."[42]

In Freud's attempts to interpret the Schreber case, he refers to Jung's interpretation of a case of *dementia praecox*, which was "far more severe" and "exhibited symptoms far more remote from the normal."[43] Yet Freud sees his task predominantly as an effort in "*translation of the paranoic mode of expression into the normal one*" and, in this pursuit, admits that Schreber "not infrequently presses the key into our hands."[44] Unlike the psychiatrists of his time, Freud was concerned not only with diagnosing the pathological idea, but, first and foremost, with "the meaning and origin of this pathological idea."[45] For him, this hidden meaning made perfect sense once it was "translated" into the "normal" language of psychological development.[46] Freud even suggested that, notably from Schreber's writings and self-observation, psychiatrists might finally learn not to confuse "the world of the unconscious with the world of reality."[47] Moreover, the world of the unconscious, according to Freud, was to be found *neither* in biological toxins *nor* in the brain, but rather in theater plays, literary texts (whether novels or poetry) and world religions, all of whose motifs and references abound in Schreber's memoir. Concluding that the basis of Schreber's illness was the outburst of a homosexual impulse – which was, after all, a normal developmental stage of the sexual drive/libido according to psychoanalytic theory – Freud succinctly summed up his argument regarding the different phases of sexual development, on the one hand, and the even more remarkable *continuity* between the normal and the pathological, on the other:

> Generally speaking, every human being *oscillates* all through his life between heterosexual and homosexual feelings, and any frustration or disappointment in the one direction is apt to drive him over into the other.[48]

In discussing the role of Schreber's longing for his dead father and brother, his transformation of his doctor into a God, and of himself into a woman who could bear God's children, Freud differentiates the way psychoanalysis works with delusions from the textbook methods of his contemporaries in the field of psychiatry. He argues, for example, that we don't know the origin of megalomania, including Schreber's. Humbled in the face of these extravagant delusions, Freud writes, "[w]e are bound to admit that any attempt at throwing light upon the transformation in his delusion brings us up against extraordinary difficulties."[49] The only clues, he insists, that one could possibly find to solve these interpretative difficulties are to be found nowhere but in the memoir itself.

Following the idea that the schism is a major component of schizophrenia, Freud also explores the *splitting* processes revealed in Schreber's delusions. For example, in Schreber's writing, one finds splitting between the "upper" and "middle" Flechsig, the "lower" and "upper" God, and numerous other types of division or *de-composition* that are characteristic of the process of fracturing in the psyche.

Taking the lead from Jung's intuition, Freud explains this growing incapacity of the psyche to contain itself as a defensive mechanism, which serves to water down the all too powerful impressions suffered in childhood and repeated thereafter. Although he sees the conflict of the schizophrenic patient as similar to the neurotic (as emanating from the same love–hate ambivalence toward significant people in the patient's early life), he also notices a major *qualitative difference* between schizophrenic patients and neurotics. Indeed, neurotic patients exhibit an altogether different "class" of transference (that is, the ability to invest the libido, the drive, and "hold on" to a person/object in the world), which is lacking in schizophrenics.[50]

Moreover, Freud claimed, somewhat sarcastically, that the schizophrenic's pathological way of *generalizing*, opposed as it was to the *specific* transference experienced by neurotics toward their doctor, could also be found at the heart of the psychiatric profession. After all, psychiatry, likewise, tended to overlook the specific – or, rather, *special* – individual human being and its unique relation to treatment or therapy, focusing instead on its generic shell, that is, on the patient's body, by means of a medical – and, in this respect, scientific and *general* – diagnosis. To hammer home this point, Freud highlighted Schreber's idea that Dr. Flechsig was simply "incapable of learning anything by experience, and did not understand *living men* because he only knew how to deal with corpses."[51]

When Freud, for his part, compares the absurdity in Schreber's delusions with the absurdity we encounter in dreams (recalling that "absurdity in dreams expresses ridicule and derision"), he finds striking *similarities* between the creation of pathological delusions (since absurdity is, as he puts it, "used for the same purposes in paranoia") and the normal dream work of which his 1900 *Die Traumdeutung* (*The Interpretation of Dreams*) offers a classical analysis. In sum, Freud treats Schreber's delusional world as he would a dream, attempting to interpret its different details in order to arrive at its meaning. As in dream work, Freud identifies "condensations" and looks for the key that is "already in our hands."[52] Following Schreber's "clues" very closely, he asks whether it is possible that, for example, "the *anterior* realms of God and the fore-courts of Heaven," parts of Schreber's fantastic world, should "be regarded as a symbol of what is female," and "the *posterior* realms of God" that Schreber delineates, "as a symbol of what is male."[53]

To give yet another example, Freud's interest in Schreber's relationship with the sun – or "solar myth"[54] – further allows him to see *pathological* delusions as *normal* dreams, or instances of collective myths. The sun is nothing but a *symbol* for the father, Freud concludes, on the basis of examples taken from neurotic patients, from the writings of Nietzsche, and from the account of a child's life.[55] Freud thus explores the strange content of the schizophrenic's delusions, finding remarkable *parallels* with the content of normal dreams, collective myths, creative writing, and infantile mentality.

In fact, these cross-references allow him to regard schizophrenia as being *not* a different kind at all, let alone traceable to some identifiable natural essence or biological marker. On the contrary, in the case of Schreber, as Freud writes, "we find ourselves *once again* on the *familiar ground* of the father-complex."[56] It is the *universal, familiar* "infantile material" that Freud tries to reach, "translating the paranoic into the normal," nothing more, nothing less.

Similarly, in his interpretation of Schreber's delusion of turning into a woman (a "receptacle of God"), Freud chooses the same terminology with which he identifies *normal* mental phenomena, referring to this particular motif as that of a "feminine wishful phantasy."[57] Just as he understands children's play, dreams, and neurosis, here as well, Freud merely searches for the frustration (the "privation in real life") that gives rise to such a "wishful phantasy."[58] Here, he finds this "frustration" in the fact that Schreber and his wife were unable to have children, as all her pregnancies had resulted in stillbirths.[59]

Freud's discussion of schizophrenia's similarities to and differences from neurosis and the normal is extensive and contradictory. At times he writes that "there is *nothing characteristic of the form of disease* known as paranoia" that might not be found in other kinds of neuroses,[60] and claims that the defenses used in this condition are a totally "*normal* proceeding."[61] But at other times he is interested in what he names the "choice of neurosis"[62] or the *relative difference* between *singular* pathologies.

Jung, for his part, was also trying to find a clearer, categorical difference between the milder cases of mental suffering (i.e., the neuroses) and the more severe pathologies (i.e., the schizophrenias). In so doing, he conjectured that the difference between *dementia praecox* and hysteria might very well have its roots in the effect of the whole complex of the psychological unconscious conflict on the brain. While this complex in hysteria produced reparable symptoms, the affect in *dementia praecox*, Jung surmised, created a toxin, which might injure the brain in irreparable ways.[63] A change in metabolism, such as offered by Kraepelin with his more physical, biological explanation, was certainly possible according to Jung, who could even imagine that the "hypothetical X," that is, the highly toxic substance, lead to "debraining,"[64] a disturbance that was, perhaps, at the root of so-called schizophrenic "automatism."

In an apparent attempt to appease Freud (echoing his psychosexual theory of development), Jung for a moment even suggested that the sex glands might be a possible source of the toxins in question. However, he also added a telling disclaimer: "I have no proof of this, so I dropped the conjecture."[65] As a matter of fact, he said, "[w]e still know far too little, in fact nothing about the innermost nature of D. pr."[66] Yet Freud, for his part (and in spite of this gesture), remained deeply skeptical of the main direction that Jung's research and theorizing was taking. As he sarcastically wrote to Jung in 1908, hinting at psychiatrists searching for a biological/somatic cause for schizophrenia, believing that they could thus "carve nature at its joints:"

> I believe that if they [biological psychiatrists] were analyzed, it would turn out that they are still waiting for the discovery of the bacillus or protozoon of hysteria as for the messiah who must after all come someday to all true believers. When that happens a differential diagnosis from Dem. pr. ought to be a simple matter, since the hysteria parasite will no doubt have only one stiff whiplike appendage, while that of Dem. pr. will regularly show two and also take a different stain. Then we shall be able to leave psychology to the poets![67]

But Jung could not let go of the idea that what made *dementia praecox* different was a somatic factor, even as he tried to placate Freud:

> I think very many cases of Dem. praec. are due exclusively to purely psychological conflicts. But besides these, there are undoubtedly not a few cases where a physical weakness of some kind precipitates the psychosis. The secret of the constitution will hardly be unveiled from the psychological side alone.[68]

Freud was not happy with the proposed idea that some pathologies were different in kind and caused by toxins, while others were deemed to be a variation on a spectrum and, hence, should be placed on a continuum with the neuroses. Accordingly, he responded to Jung in the strongest of terms: "That is not very well possible. Entirely or not at all. ... As you know, so far no one knows anything about the supposed other kind of hysteria, dementia praecox, etc. *There is only our kind or else nothing at all is known.*"[69]

"Freud's kind" was supported by the Berlin psychiatrist Karl Abraham, one of Jung's assistants at the Burghölzli, who later became a key figure in the psychoanalytic movement, especially when it ventured into the field of the psychoses (see figure 6). Abraham, who worked as a clinician with patients diagnosed as schizophrenic at the clinic, suggested that there were more *analogies* than *differences* between normality and abnormality, and likewise, between the different "kinds" of abnormality. In his words, Freud's work "demonstrated the importance of infantile psychic activity for the dream and for hysteria"; and as he adds, "I can confirm that the same holds good for cases of dementia praecox, and so establish a new analogy between the dream, hysteria, and dementia praecox."[70]

Figure 6 Karl Abraham (1877–1925)
Source: Wikimedia Commons

While he was not able to convince Bleuler and Jung of the relevance of his "libido theory" to a better understanding of schizophrenia, Abraham became Freud's ambassador at the Burghölzli. Even after his return to Berlin where he set up his private practice, Freud encouraged him to continue exploring "the borderlines between *dementia praecox* and hysteria,"[71] and "the differences ... between hysteria and *dementia praecox*."[72] Abraham's training in the Zurich school under Bleuler and Jung made his clinical exposure, and knowledge of schizophrenia, credible. He quickly became a vocal substitute for Bleuler and Jung, who had begun to express increasing dissatisfaction with Freud's psychoanalysis in their own work with those they diagnosed as inpatient schizophrenics.[73]

At the Salzburg Congress of Psychoanalysis, held in 1908, Abraham read a paper in which he tried to find a *differential* diagnosis that would allow one to distinguish between pathologies that show similar symptoms, and more specifically, between *dementia praecox*, hysteria, and the obsessional neuroses.[74] On the one hand, he suggested that hysteria and *dementia praecox* shared a *common* set of causes that are rooted in the sexual development of the person (that is, from the early stage at which one gains satisfaction and pleasure from one's own body, by sucking a thumb, for example, to the later phase in which one develops fulfilling relationships with other persons). On the other hand, Abraham also emphasized the important *difference* between the two diagnoses. In his eyes, this difference lay precisely in the fact that unlike hysteria, *dementia praecox* involves patients completely withdrawing from the world shared with other human beings into their isolated selves, gaining satisfaction from their own body (in an autoerotic way) alone.[75]

With this idea, Abraham departed from his mentors' approach at Burghölzli, and resolutely applied Freud's psychosexual theory to the understanding of the neuroses *and* the psychoses. More importantly, not unlike Freud, Abraham also started assuming a continuity – rather than a difference in kind – between these two groups of abnormalities. In doing so, he posited a continuity between normalcy and pathology overall. Abraham thereby soundly disputed the theories of his fellow psychiatrists (in the Zurich school and beyond), according to which the difference between these abnormalities lay in their natural, biological, and causal determination (e.g., the idea that schizophrenia involved a pathogenic agent or somatic toxin, while neurosis did not).[76]

It was Jung's insistence on an *absolute difference* between schizophrenia and hysteria that eventually led to the inevitable break between the Zurich school with its Burghölzli clinic and its severely disturbed hospitalized patients, on the one hand, and the therapeutic practices and clientele of Freudian psychoanalysis, on the other.[77]

Despite his disappointment with Jung, however, Freud was undeterred. He continued to use the case of Schreber as the exemplification of his libido and psychosexual theories. The latter, he believed, explained not only normal development and the neuroses, but also the pathological phenomena associated with *dementia praecox*, paranoia, or schizophrenia. Moreover, for Freud, Schreber's extreme delusion of the great catastrophe of the end of the world was, likewise, absolutely crucial to his analysis of schizophrenia:

> Voices told him that the work of the past 14,000 years had now come to nothing, and that the earth's allotted span was only 212 years more. … He himself was "the only real man left alive," and the few human shapes that he still saw – the doctor, the attendants, the other patients – he explained as being "miracled up, cursorily improvised men."[78]

Whether the imagined catastrophe would be caused by glaciation (owing to the obfuscation of the sun), by an earthquake, or by the magic done by his doctor (who presumably spread general nervous disorders), Schreber's delusion of the end of the world could ultimately be explained, according to Freud, by the increasing withdrawal of the patient's love (or libido) from the world as a whole.[79]

Interpreting Schreber's repeated return to these motifs, Freud would therefore write: "everything has become indifferent and irrelevant to him … The end of the world is the projection of this internal catastrophe; his subjective world has come to an end since his withdrawal of his love from it."[80] Yet, following this delusional "destruction" of the world, Freud also imagined a rebuilding phase, one that leads to a no less strange, different delusional world, "not more splendid, it is true," but nonetheless such that, "at least," the judge can "once more live in it."[81]

Based on this analysis, Freud highlighted the only possible conclusion: "the delusional formation, which we take to be the pathological product, is in reality an attempt at recovery, a process of reconstruction."[82] In

Schreber's own words, the reconstruction of the ruins after the catastrophe leads to a "profound internal change" in that same world. Relationships with people and things in the world, which used to be affectionate, become strange and hostile. In itself, this delusional realization – or idealization – may seem to offer little solace to the patient in question, but at least for Schreber, there was now a world where previously a vacuum existed.

Freud's libido theory thus outlined a *spectrum* of development that runs from auto-erotism, via narcissism, to object love. The severity of the pathology in question would be merely "a measure of the amount of *regression*."[83] In "normal mental life," whenever the investment of love is released from one person (after a loss, for example), this naturally leads to a search for a substitute. In other words, the ability to hold onto objects by means of one's love can remain in place, until a new love object, substituting for the previous one, is found. In hysteria, by contrast, when this love is no longer invested in an object, the liberated energy/libido is transformed into anxiety or converted into physical symptoms. And, finally, according to Freud's schema, in the psychoses, the freed-up love or libidinal energy is invested solely in the patient's own ego. Withdrawn from the external world, this newly invested energy – projected onto the self – results, as a rule, in feelings of megalomania and hypochondria.

In sum, Freud's theory resists explaining paranoia/schizophrenia as well as other mental diseases as fundamentally different from one another, just as it prevents seeing them as fixed entities. Unlike lesions in the brain, or irreversible damage such as "debraining," libidinal energy can shift back and forth from the ego to the world. This insight challenged the therapeutic nihilism that characterized the Kraepelinian psychiatric model, but also that of the Zurich school to which Bleuler and Jung belonged (and from which Abraham and Freud slowly but steadily distanced themselves).

That said, Freud also acknowledged the possibility that the disturbance in the investment of love/libido – which put schizophrenia on a spectrum with normal and neurotic psychological phenomena – might very well be accompanied by severe and abnormal changes in the ego, which may set this illness apart. In other words, alongside the default interpretation of a primarily *quantitative* difference between the normal, on the one hand, and different pathologies, on the other, with more or less libidinal energy invested in the patient's ego or in the latter's external world, Freud surmised that there might nonetheless well be a *qualitative* distinction grounded in original or structural defects in the mental apparatus itself.

More specifically, as Freud reconstructed motifs from Schreber's memoir, it appeared to him that this patient's withdrawal from the external world might not have been complete, and, hence, that it differed greatly from the so-called *organic* psychoses. After all, the latter meant an irreversible change in the brain as was found, for example, in "Meynert's amentia," where the relationship with the external world ended up being *fully severed* and, in that sense, irrevocably lost.[84] Yet this, Freud insisted, was not the case for Schreber.

Freud agreed with Kraepelin that a different pathology of the libido, such as the one found in Schreber's case, merited its own diagnosis, but argued against his contemporary's hopeless picture of the condition: "'dementia praecox' was a particularly unhappy name to choose for it."[85] By the same token, Freud was convinced that Bleuler's chosen terminology for this group of systems was inadequate as well. Instead, Freud firmly believed that "schizophrenia" could only be an appropriate term as long as we forgot "its literal meaning." Indeed, the very motif and etymological root of "splitting" (i.e., the *schism*) implied in the word was neither exclusive to Schreber's particular disease nor an essential part of it.

Consequently, Freud went on to suggest renaming *dementia praecox* and using the term "paraphrenia" instead. His argument for doing so was simple. The proposed new term "has no special connotation" and, moreover, not only indicates a clear link to the old diagnosis of paranoia, but also to the more recent (and, in his eyes, far more relevant) nomenclature of *hebephrenia*. Terminological precision, however, quickly gave way to pragmatics. Indeed, as mentioned earlier, Freud did not follow his own suggestions and, in subsequent writings and correspondences, continued to use both the terms *dementia praecox* and "schizophrenia" to describe the peculiar kind of psychosis that the new idiom was deemed to render more faithfully.

Notwithstanding the name that Freud gave to the phenomenon, namely "paraphrenia," or his lack of consistency in subsequently using it, the distinguishing feature of schizophrenia or *dementia praecox* was, in his view, a general withdrawal of the patient's love from the world and everything in it. This withdrawal was a return to earlier ways of being, before the ability to relate to the world and invest one's love in people had developed; a way of being in which the effort to relieve the self of pain and to avail it of pleasure was perennially sought in the patient's own psyche and/or body.

Indeed, as we saw earlier, unlike the psychiatrists of his time, Freud considered that *mythology* was an important way of understanding a patient's peculiarities. He referred to Jung's assertion that the mythopoetic forces of mankind are not extinct and still have the same indirect and overall effect as they did in long-forgotten times in faraway places. Furthermore, Freud asserted that ontogenesis (the coming into being and further development of the individual) repeats the phylogenesis (the emergence and evolution of the species), such that not only in primitive man, but also in dreams of normal individuals and in people with their neuroses, we come upon the generic qualities of "the *child* and the peculiarities which characterize his modes of thought and his emotional life."[86] By extension and extrapolation, Freud found the child, the primitive mind, and the "abnormal" to be part of the normal adult mind, which even in its most "civilized" state, echoes and mimics immemorial strata of meaning and, indeed, mythmaking. In other words, Freud did not see primitive and modern man, normal and abnormal, child and grownup as *different in kind*, but rather as *differing on a spectrum* that stretches from prehistory to the present day, from infancy to old age. In 1913, he noted that even "the craziest speeches and the queerest poses and attitudes" displayed by schizophrenic patients become intelligible if approached in this spirit, by psychoanalysis.[87]

Psychoanalytic research, Freud went on to suggest, shows that "the most heterogeneous forms of mental disorder" are the result of processes that are "at bottom *identical* and which can be understood and described by means of psychological concepts."[88] The psychic continuum between the normal and the pathological (and between the conscious and the unconscious), shares the same mechanics and dynamics as dreams, which according to Freud, are paradigmatic and "are also to be found everywhere."[89] The only reasons for the manifestation of *different* clinical pictures (and distinct concepts to capture them) are the multiplicity of psychological defenses and the great variety of developmental fixations in which they are rooted. As Freud concluded, this is precisely why psychoanalysis "reveals an unexpected amount of affective disturbance and blinding of the intellect in normal no less than in sick people."[90]

Beyond the Schreber Case

Freud continued to discuss the question of paranoia and schizophrenia well after his famous notes on Schreber. In two 1915 essays, he filled in a significant gap in his theory by explaining the processes that underlay schizophrenic thinking, as he saw it.[91] In this particular context, Freud proposed the classification of two different forms of neurosis: on the one hand, the *transference neuroses* (which include anxiety hysteria, conversion hysteria, and obsessional neurosis) and, on the other, the *narcissistic neuroses*, that cover what Kraepelin had termed *dementia praecox* and what Bleuler had called schizophrenia. While in the first case, the capacity for transference (for investing love or libido in the analyst and the analysis) remains fully intact, "in the case of schizophrenia," the libido is withdrawn from the world and retreats into the ego.[92]

According to Freud, what makes the patient with schizophrenia so incomprehensible and his speech so nonsensical is his fundamental investment in the "word representation," rather than in the represented object itself. This leads patients to treat words as if they were the objects themselves.[93] To illustrate this idea, Freud offers the example of a case study by Victor Tausk.[94] In this case, after a quarrel with her lover, a female patient complains that "*her eyes were not right, they were twisted.*"[95] Indeed, as she explains:

> She could not understand him at all, he looked different every time; he was a hypocrite, *an eye-twister*, he had twisted her eyes; now she had twisted eyes; they were not her eyes anymore; now she saw the world with different eyes.

For Freud, such unintelligible remarks become meaningful when they are carefully analyzed: "Here the schizophrenic utterance exhibits a hypochondriac trait: it has become '*organ-speech.*'"[96] In fact, as Freud argued, in schizophrenia, words are subjected to the very same processes that produce dream-images out of latent dream-thoughts: "A single word ... takes over the representation of a whole train of thought." The dream-work, a normal process, likewise treats words like things, and thereby already creates what, strictly speaking, are none other than "'schizophrenic' utterances or neologisms."[97]

But, once again, Freud did not merely look for obvious similarities. He also sought out what distinguishes the "formation of substitutes" in schizophrenia, hysteria, and obsessional neurosis, respectively. Indeed, as he concluded, these yield very "subtle distinctions … which nevertheless make a strange impression."[98]

What is this strangeness, that makes schizophrenia and its terminological analogues stand out from other pathologies, and from the neuroses? Freud suggested that the oddness of the schizophrenic symptoms comes precisely from this "predominance of what has to do with words over what has to do with things."[99] Doubting whether the defense mechanisms he observed in the neuroses have anything in common with those taking place in schizophrenia, Freud concluded that the attempt at flight from the world and its reality "nevertheless remains a factor *common* [to the two classes of neurosis]."[100] The difference is merely that in schizophrenia, the flight of the ego is *much more* radical and profound.[101]

The peculiarity of schizophrenia is rooted, then, not in the detachment from reality, but in the effort to re-establish a world that has been lost, due to the withdrawal of the person's investment in it. However, being invested in words themselves, instead of in what they represent in the world, is not just a risk for schizophrenics, as Freud explained. "When we think in abstractions," he confessed, "the expression and content of our philosophizing then begins to acquire an unwelcome resemblance to the mode of operation of schizophrenics."[102]

Freud further discussed schizophrenia in 1923, in his seminal paper "The ego and the id," and in two subsequent articles in 1924: "Neurosis and psychosis" and "Loss of reality in neurosis and psychosis." In these latter articles, he argued that the *degree* of pathology depends on how well the ego navigates the outside world, and is able to silence the drives of the id. As Freud wrote, "in a neurosis the ego, in its dependence on reality, suppresses a piece of the id (of instinctual life), whereas in a psychosis, this same ego, in the service of the id, withdraws from a piece of reality."[103]

However, in his 1927 article "Fetishism," Freud expressed dissatisfaction with his 1924 analysis. He tried to reformulate the difference between neurosis and psychosis by reintroducing the idea of *splitting* or schism, the very process that gave schizophrenia its name. In this paper, he suggested that two contradictory positions exist simultaneously in the psyche: one responding to urges and desires, and the other responding to reality. This split, he observed, much like denial and disavowal, is often used as a defense by the schizophrenic ego.[104]

In 1937, towards the end of his life, Freud published two articles, "Analysis terminable and interminable" and "Constructions in analysis," where he reemphasized the overarching similarities between the normal and the schizophrenic. On the subject of delusional thinking in schizophrenia, he asserted, "the essence of it is that there is not only method in madness, as the poet has already perceived, but also a fragment of historic truth."[105] In addition, he noted that it might be worthwhile to analyze historical instances of the disease, to test assumptions about its management and treatment:

> The vain effort would be abandoned of convincing the patient of the error of his delusion and of its contradiction of reality; and, on the contrary, the recognition of its kernel of truth would afford common ground upon which the therapeutic process could develop … I believe that we should gain a great deal of valuable knowledge from work of this kind upon psychotics even if it led to no therapeutic success.[106]

A year later, in his book, *An Outline of Psycho-Analysis* (1938), he wrote: "Even in a state so far removed from the reality of the external world as one of hallucinatory confusion, one learns from patients after their recovery that at the time in some corner of their mind (as they put it) there was a normal person hidden, who, like a detached spectator, watched the hubbub of illness go past him."[107] In *Moses and Monotheism* (1939), finally, Freud described "a state within a state," where the inaccessible, psychotic part of the personality overwhelms the "normal" part, forcing it into its service.

As we have amply verified, Freud thus often characterizes psychotic and schizophrenic patients as *qualitatively similar* to neurotic ones, differing only in the *quantitative* nature of behavioral deviations (on a common sliding scale, as it were).

Preeminent in the scholarship examining this oscillation – if not blatant inconsistency – in Freud's writings, is Nathaniel London, analyst and past president of the Western New England Psychoanalytic Society.

London proposes that Freud, in fact, put forward *two* complex, if at times contradictory, theories of schizophrenia: the "unitary theory" on the one hand, and the "specific theory," on the other.[108] The unitary theory sought to create a single formula to explain and account for all mental phenomena. The same formula would thus apply to understanding both psychosis and neurosis. According to the latter, an internal conflict arises (among the agencies of the mental structure, which Freud calls the id, ego, and superego), resulting in anxiety (which activates defense mechanisms that keep the material out of consciousness). This anxiety, in turn, creates a defensive struggle whose aim is to reduce anxiety. This struggle culminates in regression to the point of fixation on one of the different stages of development of the libido (that is, on auto-erotism, narcissism, or on the oedipal level, where love is invested not so much in the self but rather in the very objects and persons that count as "not-me"). The difference between psychosis and neurosis, on this account, is in the fixation point and in the degree of regression in terms of the development of the libido: schizophrenics regress to earlier stages of development than neurotics, and revert to more primitive defense mechanisms. For example, whereas the neurotic *converts* a psychic conflict over masturbatory fantasies into an itch on the skin, the psychotic *projects* the guilt over these very same fantasies onto an imaginary god, who might well command him to cut off his hands.

The *unitary* theory of schizophrenia rests on two assumptions. (1) Schizophrenic behavior lies on a continuum, a spectrum that stretches from the neurotic to the psychotic. More precisely, although schizophrenic behavior is considered to be *more* severe than neurotic behavior, it is actually the polarized manifestation of the *same* behavior. (2) The theory of schizophrenia is part of the theory of unconscious conflict and defenses. Schizophrenia, too, is thus motivated by unconscious processes. Although traumatic factors are significant in the development of both neuroses and psychoses, in schizophrenia the unconscious trauma tends to be *more* significant, *more* pronounced, and, usually, occurs *earlier* in life.

According to this theory and its two premises, every person possesses the potential to develop schizophrenia, if they reach a certain threshold of internal conflict without resolution (or as Freud calls it, without "catharsis"). Delusional thinking, hallucinations, increased preoccupation with the body, and narcissism (all common symptoms of schizophrenia) can be explained by the theory, it is claimed, in terms of conflict and defense. The *severity* of schizophrenic symptoms can be viewed as stemming either from ego weakness and regressed ego functioning, or from an *excess* of aggressive/destructive internal conflicts, which differ from the libidinal/erotic conflicts that tend to lead to neuroses.[109]

Freud's *specific* theory of schizophrenia, by contrast, sees schizophrenia as an illness of a *different kind.* It includes the following two related assertions: (1) Schizophrenic behavior is *unique* and *qualitatively different* from more usual behaviors. This is the case even though schizophrenic behaviors do occur concurrently with these latter behaviors, and thus cannot easily be delineated or demarcated from them. (2) Of the clinical features considered to be unique to schizophrenia, the schizophrenic's inability to engage in transference is the primary reason why the psychoanalyst is so often unsuccessful in analyzing the patient. Every manifestation of schizophrenia, on this account, is understood as a withdrawal of the patient's love from the representations of external people/objects. Schizophrenic behavior is conceptualized as a reaction to an *internal* catastrophe, resulting in a relative – and, at times, absolute – loss of connection to reality. As a consequence, London explains, Freud sees schizophrenic symptomatology (expressed in forms of mental distress such as delusions and hallucinations) as the result of patients' attempts to compensate for psychological *deficiency* states, that is, for the disengagement from the world caused by this withdrawal.[110]

Although London never specifies whether Freud himself explicitly favored one of these two theories over the other, he does argue that Freud must have believed the specific theory to be superior. Indeed, he argues, the idea of a continuum of behavior from neuroses to schizophrenia would have been harder for Freud to embrace, especially as it applied to clinical treatment.[111] He holds that deep down, Freud believed that the psychotics' thought disturbances and complicated relations with people prevented them from associating freely or effectively, much less develop transferential relationships, love, or even rapport with the analyst. Without this "transference neurosis," which is the artificial illness that allows the patient to invest his love in the analyst, as if it were a parental figure, and with the analyst interpreting, making sense of this experience, the psychoanalytic cure was not possible.

That said, when Freud communicated with analysts who were ready to work analytically with psychotic patients, he was more optimistic about the analyzability of schizophrenic patients. In a letter to Abraham, dated October 21, 1907, after he made the distinction between dementia, which is clearly related to the ageing of the sick brain (senile dementia and epilepsy), and the so-called "dementia" in *dementia praecox*, Freud wrote: "Dementia Praecox must therefore be (*virtute*!) resolvable, must so to speak be a functional dementia."[112] Later Freud even supported Ernest Simmel, the Berlin psychoanalyst and founder of the first psychoanalytic sanatorium at Schloss Tegel, in his efforts to establish a psychoanalytic sanatorium in Los Angeles for these patients.[113]

Freud's Dual Legacy

This ambiguous legacy of Freud, according to which schizophrenia is perceived either as a matter of conflict and defense (similar to normalcy and neurosis, but involving a fixation in an earlier psychosexual stage) or as the result of a defect in the ego, was partly responsible for the emergence of two separate and irreconcilable psychoanalytic theories of schizophrenia. It also led to the emergence of two outspoken, if not self-proclaimed, schools of psychoanalysis.

On the one hand, the "ego defect school" holds that schizophrenia is a different *kind* of phenomenon, that differs *qualitatively* from the normal psyche and the neuroses. In this view, schizophrenia is the result of a constitutional defect in the ego, an inborn error or a deficit, caused by an early damaging object relation. This "defect" is characterized by the inability to invest libido (love or psychic energy) in the world and the people who populate it. It also involves a failure to perform other ego functions that are related to our shared reality.

On the other hand, the "conflict school" believes that schizophrenia is not a unique kind of disease, but rather that it is the result of a conflict between drives and defenses. This school posits a fundamental similarity between the normal, the neurotic, and the psychotic. In this paradigm, the difference is a *quantitative* one: in schizophrenia, the fixation simply occurs earlier in life, and the defenses are far *more primitive*, than in the neuroses. The fateful result is that the psyche's capacity for "reality-testing" is compromised, just as other symptomatology tends to be more *severe*.

James Grotstein, the late prominent psychoanalyst based in Los Angeles, argued that "rescuing" schizophrenia from the concept of "ego defect" would allow classical psychoanalytic techniques to be used effectively with patients who are diagnosed as schizophrenics.[114] Yet authors and clinicians of the ego-defect school, who assume schizophrenia is of a different kind, argue against what they consider an excessively "optimistic 'Pollyanna' approach," which in their view, "does violence to the severe *qualitative differences* between schizophrenia and neurosis."[115]

What to make, then, of this duality, and of Freud's position vis-à-vis its apparent theoretical and clinical impasse in the treatment of the psychoses? After all, Freud may have contributed to this impasse to no small extent, since he made fairly strong claims while he arguably treated no schizophrenic patients, and was further convinced that psychoanalysis might have little to offer in the most severe cases.

This much is certain: the concept of *schizophrenia* reflected Freud's understanding more than it did Kraepelin's. Psychological processes that were split could, in theory, be reintegrated. Psychotherapeutic interventions were thus possible and welcomed. For all of Freud's pessimism in the matter, the inclusion of psychotherapy and hope of healing were nested within the concept itself. Patients who had been diagnosed with schizophrenia could, with the right psychological treatment, be healed of the schism in the psyche and thus return to life and society. While Kraepelin's diagnosis of *dementia praecox* offered no such immediate therapeutic hope, the term schizophrenia, in Freud's outlook, presented both patients and their doctors with a more positive outlook.

Freud's legacy of oscillating between two paradigms – two structurally distinct, if not mutually exclusive, frameworks of understanding – continued to shape the discourse of psychoanalysis on schizophrenia and psychosis for years to come. Some psychoanalysts adopted the model of schizophrenia as a *discrete disease* and, in some cases, were ready to discuss it in natural, essential terms, as a disease of the brain. Others, on the contrary, held on to the *continuum* model, arguing that psychotic and non-psychotic elements existed in *all* individuals, regardless of their diagnosis or lack thereof. In other words, the only difference between those diagnosed as schizophrenic and those who are not would, therefore, be quantitative alone, that is, a matter of degree, not a distinction in kind.

In the early years of psychoanalysis, American psychoanalysts who adopted the psychodynamic model of schizophrenia interpreted Bleuler's basic symptoms as being on a continuum with normality. By and large, they were also prone to seeing just "a touch of schizophrenia" in many of their more troubled patients.[116] For them, schizophrenia was clearly a more severe psychological maladjustment than other personality or neurotic manifestations, but not, for that reason, out of the range of the ordinary ailments that psychoanalysts trusted they could treat. Less severe manifestations of schizophrenia, such as "ambulatory schizophrenia," "pseudoneurotic schizophrenia," and "borderline states," in their view still reflected the psychoanalytic or psychodynamic assumption of an overall continuum.[117]

In this context, the so-called "vulnerability hypothesis" entailed that all humans are subject to the possibility of a schizophrenic breakdown.[118] With sufficient stress or the right degree of vulnerability, the line between sanity and psychosis, it was claimed, was easily crossed. Proponents of this theory argued that some individuals traversed this boundary with little stress, while others only did so after experiencing a significant amount of psychic trauma. This interpretative model was based on the reported experiences of soldiers without schizoid predispositions, who had broken down during World War II as a result of war trauma. It was found that these soldiers and war victims demonstrated severe schizophrenic reactions, including delusions, hallucinations, and confusion, but also that all of their symptoms almost completely subsided once they had withdrawn from the battlefield.

Another example of thinkers who saw more continuity than discontinuity between schizophrenic symptoms and "normal" psychical activity can be found in the work of Harry Stack Sullivan, the American psychiatrist whose famous saying in the context of schizophrenia was: "we are all much more human than otherwise, be we happy and successful, contented and detached, miserable and mentally disordered or whatever."[119] Sullivan's words: "I believe the psychiatrist would agree that the schizophrenic is the most disorganized of the functional mental illnesses – *a continuation* of very much that is simply human,"[120] were a testimony to this. In other words, people with schizophrenia were like everyone else, but more so. Sullivan did not, thereby, intend to pathologize everyday experiences, but merely to highlight the continuity that, in his view, existed between the normal and the ordinary, on the one hand, and what was regarded as pathological, on the other. The aim was to resist and fundamentally question the all-too-rigid categorical difference, the sharp lines of demarcation that other psychiatrists had been drawing, without sufficient clinical data or theoretical analysis to back up their claims.

Likewise, Silvano Arieti, the Italian-born American psychiatrist, best known for his work on schizophrenia, found that not only was it hard to trace the exact boundaries of schizophrenia, but also that the concept was broad enough to include the pre-psychotic phases that he defined as "schizoid personality" and the "stormy personality," as well as some forms of paranoia, anorexia nervosa, and childhood schizophrenia.

Melanie Klein and Her Legacy

> The patient had been ill for three years when I saw him first. He suffered from hallucinations and was confused and at times violent. He had had altogether 90 insulin comas and many electric shocks. The superintendent of the mental hospital where the patient was living described him as one of the worst cases of schizophrenia he had had to deal with. He was said to be dangerously impulsive, withdrawn, and at times almost mute. Neither doctors nor nurses had been able to make contact with him. However, when two analytic colleagues saw him for consultation, they were able to make some contact, and they felt that psychoanalysis could be attempted … [T]he most important and striking feature in the analysis of this apparently entirely unapproachable and withdrawn patient was the interest he was able to show from the first moment in the analyst and the analytical procedure. (Herbert Rosenfeld, "Transference phenomena and transference-analysis in an acute catatonic schizophrenic patient," 1952)[121]

Another important psychoanalytic model that allows for the understanding of schizophrenia was developed in the United Kingdom by the Vienna-born British psychoanalyst Melanie Klein (figure 7), an analysand of Karl Abraham, and her followers, among them Herbert Rosenfeld with whom we opened this section. Klein inspired her pupils to continue Abraham's project, dating back to his days at the Burghölzli, to think about schizophrenia in psychoanalytic terms and offer psychoanalytically informed therapy to sufferers, including the most disturbed

Figure 7 Melanie Klein (1882–1960)
Source: Wikimedia Commons

ones among them. Klein made the "schism" or splits at the root of the diagnosis in question central to her theory of the mind, and recorded the developmentally essential processes of splitting that occur in *every* human psyche. She further explored how these processes predispose *all* human beings to splits of the self that – only at their most extreme – would come to manifest in the illness we now call schizophrenia.

Klein was deeply informed by Freud's theory of the Life and Death drives, formulated late in his career, which analyzed two mutually opposing forces whose actions were deemed to explain "the phenomena of life." *Eros* (or the libido) was defined by Freud as the force that drives the individual to join ever larger units (putting together individual and love object, family, community, etc.), while *Thanatos* (the death drive) sought to "dissolve those units and bring them back to their primaeval, inorganic state."[122] Klein, who was a firm advocate of the existence of such forces in the human psyche, argued that, as infants, we *all* suffer intense anxiety due to pressure of the death drive. Infants are extremely anxious following the trauma of birth and due to feelings of hunger and other painful frustrations. At a very early age, they experience these feelings as threats of annihilation. According to Klein, a very primitive ego exists at birth, which sets up early defenses to counter these terrible anxieties.

One of these earliest defensive mechanisms (which Klein considers as a phantasy) is that of *splitting*. In Klein's technical terminology, the *paranoid-schizoid position* refers to a constellation of anxieties (*paranoid*, that someone would harm me), defenses (*schizoid*, that is of splitting), and object relations (relationships with others, both internal and external) that characterize the first three months of life. Splitting of the self and of objects into "good" and "bad," loved and hated, is, in Klein's view, the main defense mechanism of the paranoid-schizoid position, with which the psyche combats this annihilation anxiety. According to her, this position continues to be operative in children and adults thereafter, *to a greater or lesser degree*.

Indeed, as Klein argues, this "binary" world is absolutely essential for the infant's development. By *splitting* the good from the bad, a "good internal object," or a sense of "goodness," is created, which then becomes the core of the ego, the center of the psyche, that serves as a nebula for other fragments of experience. This "core goodness" allows for the further integration of more complicated experiences of self and objects around it. This binary splitting is therefore an indispensable part of the development of the psyche, and leads to what can be envisioned as an eventual integration of self and of object. It also allows the integration of "goodness" and "badness," which creates a self and a world that are richer than "black" and "white," or other binary options. But while splitting is a "normal" process, *excessive* splitting can lead to "fragmentation" and cause severe disturbances, such as schizophrenia.

It is useful to recall, in light of what we discussed above, that in an appendix to one of her most influential papers on the matter, entitled "Notes on some schizoid mechanisms," Klein refers back to the Schreber case and Freud's analysis of it.[123] In this context, Klein foregrounds the splitting processes, especially in Schreber's description of the excessive splitting of his physician's soul. Indeed, for Schreber, Flechsig's "soul divisions" added up to as many as 46 subdivisions. As Klein writes: "These souls having multiplied till they became a 'nuisance,' and so 'God made a raid on them.' The result was that Flechsig's soul survived in 'only one or two shapes.'"[124] Klein also shows how the excessive splitting, epitomized by the division of Flechsig's soul, brought about a gradual loss of the doctor's intelligence and power. Yet, as Klein argues in clear contrast with Freud, not only was Flechsig's soul *split* into many components, Schreber's own ego was also fragmented, in turn.

In her own interpretation, Klein sees God and Flechsig as representing parts of Schreber's own self. By extension, she considers the conflict between Schreber and Flechsig (which, we recall, Freud saw as central to the end-of-the-world delusion of schizophrenia) a result of God's raid on Flechsig's 46 souls. "In my view," Klein writes, "this raid represents the annihilation by one part of the self of the other parts – which, as I contend, is a *schizoid* mechanism."[125]

Klein believes that schizophrenia is a result of the work of the death drive, where the *split* involves "one part of the ego annihilating other parts."[126] Schreber's world-catastrophe phantasy (which, again, is also the delusion of God's attack on Flechsig's many souls), would, in this interpretation, imply an overall "*preponderance* of the destructive impulse over the libido," of hate over love, nothing more, nothing less.[127] The difference between the binary splitting in the neuroses, on the one hand, and the schizophrenic fragmentation in the psychoses, on the other, is thus seen as being caused by an *excessive* death drive.

In other words, Klein does not see schizophrenia as a different natural kind or disease entity. On the contrary, in her view, the anxiety and defenses that characterize the condition are, in fact, an essential part of normal development, as it exhibits itself very early on in life. Klein's idea is that the "paranoid-schizoid position" takes place in the first three months of the child's life, and is fundamentally shaped by a paranoid anxiety of annihilation. The defense mechanisms that aim to relieve this infantile anxiety by *splitting* (schizoid) internal and external objects, emotions, and the ego into "good" and "bad," are thus "part of normal development and at the same time form the basis for later schizophrenic illness."[128] For her, *this very possibility of splitting is universal.* No human being is immune to it, biologically, psychologically, or, more broadly, existentially. Whether a person becomes schizophrenic depends on both constitutional factors (namely the intensity of the life and death drives they were born with) and environmental factors (such as the quality of the mother's mitigation of the anxiety at issue). In the normal development of the child and of the psyche, different anxieties and more mature defenses replace paranoid anxieties and schizoid defenses and do so gradually, if not irreversibly.

The second, more mature, position that Klein discerns in the development of the psyche is the "depressive position." Here, the main anxiety is that of the "loss of the object," and the adaptive defense is that of "reparation." It is important to note, however, that for Klein, the paranoid-schizoid ways of experiencing the world and relating to objects are never fully outgrown. Instead, our minds keep *oscillating* between both positions, each of them with their respective paths and outcomes. The anxieties and defenses found in schizophrenia are thus, again, not of a *different kind* but are part of the normal development and functioning of every human being. As one commentator aptly summarizes:

> To bring the argument full circle, the proposition is that in schizophrenia we are dealing with behavioral patterns common to, and potential in, all human beings. Each of us is capable of using schizoid mechanisms in our social relationships and, given sufficient amounts of stress, we are all capable of breaking down as well.[129]

Klein's ideas about early infantile anxieties and her novel ways of approaching the more primitive layers of the mind thus opened up possibilities for considering even the most disturbed patients in psychiatric wards as both understandable and treatable. In the Schreber case, Klein saw the ego attempting to heal itself by integrating the many souls of Flechsig into one or two, allowing them to at least regain their intelligence and power.

Klein (and those who would soon follow in her footsteps, notably in Britain and in the United States) offered a novel understanding of the early stages of the development of the non-verbal infant. These developments enabled psychoanalysts who had trained mostly in talking therapies to find their bearings, even when symbolization processes were delayed and the common use of words was no longer available as the main means of communicating with the patient.

As Françoise Davoine, a renowned psychiatrist and psychoanalyst who greatly contributed to our understanding of the psychoses, explained in clear terms, the very concept of symbolization was derived from the Greek word *symbolon*, which was linked to the ideas of "throwing together," "uniting," "connecting," and "integrating."[130] In its original sense, the term referred to the ritual of breaking an object in two, which, when put back together, bears witness to an original relationship between friends, parents, and children, and later, between any two parties in a contract. The opposite of *symbolon* was *diabolos*, which goes back to the words for "throwing apart," "disconnecting," or, indeed, "splitting."[131] The *diabolos*, or devil, is the name of the one who creates schisms, who severs and divides.

As we saw in the previous chapter, in coining the term "schizophrenia," Bleuler had referred to this very idea of a schism or split. In fact, when he first introduced the concept in his 1908 lecture, he said: "I believe that the tearing apart ('*Zerreissung*') or splitting ('*Spaltung*') of the psychic functions is a prominent symptom of the whole group."[132] Three years later, in his classic book *Dementia Praecox and the Group of Schizophrenias*, he added, we recall: "I call dementia praecox 'schizophrenia' because (as I hope to demonstrate) the 'splitting' of the different psychic functions is one of its most important characteristics."[133]

Despite Klein's findings about the importance of symbol formation in the development of the ego – and notwithstanding the progress she witnessed as a psychoanalyst working with children suffering from severe psychosis[134] – she was very cautious when it came to the *symbolum* (the Latinized rendition of the Greek *symbolon*). To put it differently, she was skeptical of the psychoanalytic process of "putting together the pieces" when treating those diagnosed with schizophrenia. Indeed, she claimed that although her work did shed light on the relevance of the emotional experiences of early childhood to the fixation points for adult psychosis, psychoanalytic work with schizophrenic patients needed to be explored much further before it could make more far-reaching claims.

In "The Psycho-Analytic Play Technique: Its History and Significance," Klein would also assert that the work of psychoanalysts who treated schizophrenic patients *in psychiatric settings* seemed "to justify hopes for the future."[135] Many of her writings refer to psychiatrists (that is, medical doctors, unlike herself), such as Hanna Segal, Herbert Rosenfeld, and

Wilfred Bion, as the new generation of promising – and soon to be very influential – psychoanalysts who, by working with schizophrenic patients in hospital settings and by having constantly in mind that splitting and integration are the central processes in the life of the mind, significantly enriched the psychoanalytic knowledge of early anxieties and defenses and thereby provided future tools and prospects for their successful treatment.

Among the psychoanalysts mentioned by Klein, Hanna Segal (who worked at Long Grove Hospital in Surrey, UK, notably with Polish soldiers suffering from extreme mental states) developed important concepts regarding the concrete way of thinking and communicating that characterizes patients with schizophrenia. In the same vein, Herbert Rosenfeld, with whose case we opened this section, worked at Maudsley Hospital in South London, which was widely known for its psychoanalytic approach. Rosenfeld presented detailed cases of psychoanalytic treatment of severely disturbed patients with schizophrenia, emphasizing the destructive processes that led both to deep confusion and to an increasingly debilitating feeling of fragmentation. Finally, Wilfred Bion, who worked in army hospitals such as Northfield and Birmingham, created a psychoanalytic theory of thinking, based on his understanding of early mental states, encountered in cases of schizophrenia. All three were deeply invested in the rigorous psychoanalytic exploration and treatment of the disease and its symptoms. They observed and theorized the dynamic of schisms and repairs and offered psychoanalytic therapy as a possible way of integrating the ruptures.

Because she lacked medical training, Klein did not work in hospital settings and thus had to trust that these psychiatrically trained psychoanalysts would, where possible, apply her psychoanalytic thoughts and techniques faithfully, in order to judge the unique benefits of psychoanalysis for patients suffering from schizophrenia.

Psychoanalysis in Psychiatric Hospitals

Deborah, the heroine of Joanne Greenberg's famous novel, *I Never Promised You a Rose Garden*, was diagnosed as schizophrenic and treated in the most famous psychoanalytically informed psychiatric hospital in America, Chestnut Lodge, in Rockville, Maryland. As the novel relates:

> The kingdom of Yr had a kind of neutral place which was called the fourth level. It was achieved only by accident and could not be reached by formula or an act of will. At the fourth level there was no emotion to endure, no past or future to grind against. There was no memory or possession of any self, nothing except dead facts which came unbidden when she needed them and which had no feeling attached to them … In the world where she was most alive, the sun split in the sky, the earth erupted, her body was torn to pieces, her teeth and bones crazed and broken to fragments. In the other place where the ghosts and shadows lived, a car turned into a side drive and down a road to where an old red-brick building stood. It was Victorian, a little run down and surrounded by trees. Very good façade for a madhouse. (Joanne Greenberg, *I Never Promised You a Rose Garden*, 1964)

Although American psychiatrists had already been experimenting with psychoanalysis even before Jewish émigré analysts arrived on their shores, the neo-somatic revolution I described in my earlier book, *Psychosis, Psychoanalysis and Psychiatry in Postwar America: On the Borderland of Madness*, went hand in hand with an exodus of psychoanalysts from psychiatric hospitals. Analysts left severely ill hospitalized patients, mainly suffering from schizophrenia, in favor of the "worried well," whom they now treated primarily in their private practices and through psychoanalytic institutes.[136]

That said, the fact that, in America, only physicians were allowed to practice psychoanalysis also paradoxically gave psychoanalysts direct access to influential roles in psychiatric hospitals. Many, especially those practicing in the Washington-Baltimore area, increasingly devoted themselves to patients suffering from schizophrenia. Interestingly, most of them defined their work as a form of dynamic psychiatry that was more eclectic than traditional psychoanalysis, and more psychologically oriented than traditional psychiatry.

Often, the central facets of psychoanalysis (such as the key role of the "transference" or of the drives in the patient's inner world) were deemed incompatible with this kind of framework, which tended to emphasize the interpersonal relationship between the patient and his or her direct environment. The most significant and strikingly independent work in this spirit was done by psychoanalysts at the Chestnut Lodge hospital.

Some of the most representative texts and case studies about schizophrenia stemmed from this generation of pioneering psychoanalysts, such as Harold Searles' 1960 *The Non-Human Environment in Normal Development and in Schizophrenia*, and his *Collected Papers on Schizophrenia and Related Subjects* from 1965. Frieda Fromm-Reichmann's 1960 *Principles of Intensive Psychotherapy* also deserves mentioning in this context, even though, while it refers to severely ill hospitalized patients, it barely mentions the word "schizophrenia." In fact, when and where it is mentioned, it mostly resists the presumed dire prognosis associated with *dementia praecox*. In any case, the Chestnut Lodge group was an exception to the general pattern of medicalizing and naturalizing patients.

Viewing schizophrenia within psychoanalysis as a "different kind" (that is, as a "defect" in the ego) mostly led clinical theoreticians and practitioners, in these years, to adopt predominantly *materialistic* theories about a dysfunctional or damaged brain. This conception was especially found among more "medicalized" psychoanalysts. It was more common in the United States than in Europe, where psychoanalysis did not become medicalized in the same way for a host of historical, cultural, and institutional reasons, and many of its practitioners were not medical doctors and did not work in psychiatric hospitals. By contrast, the blurring of the boundaries between dynamic psychiatry and psychiatry as a medical field in the United States largely resulted in the "neo-somatic" model. This model gained such hegemony that most of the writings about schizophrenia by American psychoanalysts that received traction tended to focus on the biological factors that caused schizophrenia and made it a distinct class of mental disorders. These psychoanalysts supported a neurobiological approach, in the spirit of Kraepelin, arguing that schizophrenia was the result of an abnormality in the brain, hence, a phenomenon of a natural kind of its own.

Unlike Freud, who near the end of his life argued that mankind as a whole "developed delusions which are inaccessible to logical criticism and which contradict reality,"[137] these psychoanalysts distanced themselves from patients diagnosed with schizophrenia. Unlike the founding father of their discipline, who seemed to have noticed, early on, that delusions were lurking all around him – and who, later in life, would not even exclude psychoanalysis from the potential risk of being afflicted by thought disorders that resembled these very same abnormalities – many of his followers chose to see schizophrenia as a separate disease entity, distinct from other abnormalities; in other words, as the Other of the "normal."

In the history of psychiatric classifications that aimed at defining schizophrenia and other disorders, as we will see in our next chapter, Freud and Kraepelin came to be seen as the most representative proponents of two opposing paradigms. While Freud's psychodynamic work was used as the model for the presumed continuity between the normal and the pathological, Kraepelin was the adopted father of a new generation of psychiatrists that searched for a clearer classification of disorders. The neo-Kraepelinians, as they were named, tried to rid their influential diagnostic manual (the DSM) of what were, in their eyes, lingering Freudian legacies that blurred boundaries between the normal and the pathological. Instead, they hoped to reestablish sharply defined diagnostic categories, allowing psychiatrists and clinicians to clearly differentiate between the sane and the insane, in the first place, and between the different pathologies, in the second place. In fact, as we will discuss in chapter 4, the dualism – or split – between the paradigms that Freud and Kraepelin and their respective followers established and exemplified[138] continues to define and haunt psychiatry to this day as it struggles to diagnose, treat, and prevent mental illness across an ever-broader spectrum of phenomena, the utmost extreme of which (not least in terms of suffering) is labeled as schizophrenia.

Chapter 4
A Moving Target

> The line between creativity and madness can be *razor thin* … experiencing the world in a different way can lead to sharp and fruitful insights … The DSM [the *Diagnostic and Statistical Manual of Mental Disorders*] makes a *rough distinction* between disorders of thought and disorders of mood. Schizophrenia is an example of ader that affects thinking, and so it is referred to as a thought disorder. (Elyn R. Saks, *The Center Cannot Hold*, 2007)[1]

The DSM is one of the most influential books in psychiatry. Alongside the International Classification of Diseases (ICD), which is published by the World Health Organization (WHO) and covers a wide array of pathologies, including physical ones, the DSM classifies mental disorders. Sometimes referred to as the "Bible" of psychiatry, it is considered the main classification system of mental disorders in the United States and around the world. It defines, names, and differentiates mental disorders, which influences how they are diagnosed and treated by doctors, and has impact on insurance coverage, pharmaceutical funding, and clinical trials. It is used not only by mental health professionals and healthcare institutions, but also by the lay public. Its categories feature in legislation and in the guidelines of many bureaucratic agencies.

The DSM has been revised several times, from its creation in the 1950s to its fifth edition in 2013, growing in size and complexity with each revision. Each version of the manual has seen additions, deletions, and revisions that have dramatically changed both individual disorders and the concept of mental illness itself.[2] Throughout the DSM's history, the boundaries of specific mental disorders have shifted, producing different definitions of the disorders and variations in the criteria that allow them to be diagnosed. In this chapter, we will focus on the condition we now call "schizophrenia," retracing the evolution of its diagnosis in the DSM, showing how it changed, narrowed, and expanded over time. As we will see, "being a schizophrenic," "having schizophrenia," or "being on the schizophrenia spectrum" are not fixed or stable labels, but rather, their meaning and use have evolved over the years, and will perhaps continue to do so.

A good starting point for our discussion here is the celebrated autobiography of Elyn R. Saks, a professor of psychiatry who was diagnosed with, and treated for, schizophrenia, and whose observations opened this chapter. In her book, Dr. Saks asks the question we strive to answer, historicize, and contextualize in these pages: "what is schizophrenia?" In formulating her thoughtful reply, she frames things from the perspective of the institution of modern psychiatry, which defines schizophrenia as a thought disorder:

> The DSM places schizophrenia among thought disorders characterized by psychosis. Psychosis is broadly defined as being out of touch with reality – what one of my professors at Yale once referred to as "nuts." The disorganized thinking I suffer is also a core feature of schizophrenia.[3]

The definition and set of criteria used to diagnose the "thought disorder" of schizophrenia have changed over the years with the different revisions of the DSM. To use Saks' own phrasing, it might well be that the DSM makes an all too "rough distinction" where a "razor thin" line in fact exists. And, indeed, as we will verify, the evolution of the diagnosis of schizophrenia throughout the revisions of the DSM shows that psychiatry strived, and at times struggled, to come up with a stable definition of the condition, or collection of "symptoms," that compose the broad range of phenomena we learn to identify as "schizophrenia."

Tracing the evolution of the diagnosis of schizophrenia in the five editions of the DSM will allow us to verify and exemplify Hacking's fundamental idea that it is, historically and conceptually speaking, a "moving target,"[4] perhaps even a "transient" mental disease that appears at a time and in a place, and later "fades away."[5] As we shall see, the debates surrounding the publication of the different editions of the DSM demonstrate how the diagnosis of schizophrenia has changed over time. Indeed, from a diagnosis that initially placed psychological reactions on a normal-to-pathological continuum, it shifted toward isolating a distinct disorder with clear sub-categories (paranoid, disorganized, residual, etc.), before finally diagnosing its phenomena on a spectrum of similar – if less severe – states, with different markers. Strictly speaking, then, there is no such thing as a single, stable object that corresponds to the word "schizophrenia." Rather, there is a complex description that has evolved through time (and does so to this very day), which has nonetheless failed, thus far, to pinpoint the exact characteristics, boundaries, and causes of the condition, and is unlikely to determine these features once and for all.

The Psychiatric Bible

The first edition of the manual, known as the DSM-I (1952), and its second edition, the DSM-II (1968), were strongly influenced by the psychoanalytic, psychodynamic models that were developed in the Swiss Burghölzli school. The Swiss school of psychoanalysis found a foothold in American psychiatry through a Swiss-born neurologist named Adolf Meyer (1866–1950), who moved to Chicago in 1892 and became one of the most influential American psychiatrists of the twentieth century. At the opening of the Henry Phipps Psychiatric Clinic of Johns Hopkins University in 1913, which Meyer directed from 1909 until his retirement in 1940, Bleuler, the coiner of the term schizophrenia, was one of the distinguished speakers.[6] It was also in the same clinic that the first patient in the United States diagnosed with schizophrenia (as opposed to *dementia praecox*) was admitted.[7]

Faced with the limitations of his Swiss mentors and of Freudian psychoanalysis in understanding his patients, Meyer developed his own particular approach to psychiatric illnesses. He opposed Kraepelin's idea of "dementia" and chronicity, based on his own observation that there were "enough instances of recovery."[8] He argued that psychiatry, which was born out of the study of insanity based on autopsies in the asylums (a study preoccupied with descriptions and classifications), developed into a science which dealt with *living beings* in a dynamic way. He named his approach "psychobiology," and defined psychiatry as a study of the responses of individuals to the events of their lives.[9] This shift allowed him to distance himself not only from the existing science of psychiatry, as he saw it, but also from Freudian psychoanalysis, while holding on to the psychodynamic conception of mental phenomena, according to which the "normal" and the "disordered" are situated on a continuum.

All disorders, Meyer claimed, were to be considered as complex reactions to different forms and degrees of environmental stress. Therefore, there is absolutely no reason to draw all-too-sharp distinctions between them, as if they sprang from entities or states that were different in kind. According to Susan Lamb, who studied the founding of the Phipps Clinic and the early history of Meyer's treatment methods, this conceptual shift from insanity to maladjustment represented the "new psychiatry" which resonated loudly in an age inspired by hopes of social progress.[10]

Meyer did not believe that a patient contracted a disease called "schizophrenia" any more than he or she became "a schizophrenic."[11] For him, schizophrenia was not an ontological entity distinct from the person; it was not the result of an attack on the organism from within or without, but instead developed as part of the individual's *adaptive* performance, a *reaction* to difficult life events or to environmental stresses at a given phase of their development.

Instead of "schizophrenia," Meyer therefore proposed the term "schizophrenic reaction-type," which was consistent with his more general plan to remake psychiatry as a clinical science. He hoped that "typing" (that is, suggesting types of reactions) as opposed to classifying (based on presumed anatomical lesions, toxins, hereditary degeneration, etc.), would satisfy psychiatry's medical expectations and diagnostic needs.[12] Indeed, the first edition of the DSM issued to psychiatrists across the United States, only two years after Meyer's death, catalogued different schizophrenic reaction types rather than focusing on its putative biological markers.

The preference for Bleuler's term and approach, at least until after World War II, was arguably due to the rise of psychoanalysis in American psychiatry at the time. With psychoanalytic theory and technique as the conceptual and clinical framework, psychodynamic psychiatrists, who believed mental disorders were a response to life events, concluded that the only difference between a schizophrenic patient in the asylum and a neurotic outpatient in private practice was that the first had a *severe* reaction to an adverse life event, whereas the latter had a *milder* response to it. Symptoms were seen as part of a *continuum* with normal mentality and behavior. Some psychiatrists even went so far as to claim that there was "a touch of schizophrenia" in their otherwise "normal" patients.[13]

As explained in previous chapters, unlike *dementia praecox* (conceived as a single, differentiated disease entity, with a clear, negative prognosis), schizophrenia was originally seen as "a group" of disorders. Indeed, Bleuler's famous book title, *Dementia Praecox or the Group of Schizophrenias*, indicated as much.[14] According to Bleuler, this group of "schizophrenias" included melancholic and manic patients, those with hallucinatory confusion, paranoids, patients with incurable hypochondria or compulsion, and even, according to his 1924 list, some "nervous people."[15] Bleuler's more explicit psychological orientation, together with Freud's ultimate idea of a continuum between normality and pathology, and Meyer's notion of mental illnesses as a set of reactions to unfavorable life experiences, took hold in the United States over time. In its wake, schizophrenia was perceived as a set of *more severe* psychological maladjustments found in some patients, compared to the *milder* neurotic manifestations affecting most others.

In this psychoanalytic spirit of diagnosis, the two early editions of the DSM were organized and formulated. Again, the psychoses were seen as *severe* mental disorders characterized by a significant break with reality, hallucinations, delusions, and illogical thinking. The neuroses, by contrast, were defined as *milder* mental disorders, characterized by some distortions of reality, but not a severe break with it. As we will see, it was only in the third edition of DSM, published in 1980, that this framework, based on the continuum model, was resolutely abandoned.

With the DSM-III, an alternative – indeed, opposing – medical paradigm, introducing a clear distinction between the normal and the abnormal – and between different disorders – was adopted. This major shift in paradigms occurred in the wake of and as part of the "neo-Kraepelinian" revolution in psychiatry in the 1970s (to which we will return soon). But it was also a consequence of the controversies surrounding the validity of diagnostic criteria in general in the previous versions of the DSM, just as it reflected a growing need to narrow down the particular criteria for schizophrenia, as it became obvious that, notably in the United States, the condition was being diagnosed much more frequently than, for instance, in the United Kingdom. Based on the idea that psychiatric disorders are natural kinds that can be classified along *razor-thin* lines, American psychiatry aimed to deliver *clear-cut* diagnoses of mental illnesses, including schizophrenia.

However, the limits of this attempt to carve nature at its joints resurfaced several decades later, when a dimensional model was reintroduced into the DSM. In the years leading up to its latest edition in 2013, the DSM, once again, revisited, redescribed, and redefined schizophrenia – along with other psychoses – as a group of disorders that were not very neatly differentiated, but rather ought to be placed on a continuum, that is, on a spectrum, with varying degrees of severity. Although this reversal of the original demarcation between normal and pathological symptoms could well have been seen as a straightforward return to the so-called "continuum view" within psychoanalysis, it was seen, rather, as an attempted leap forward toward defining mental disorders in terms of natural kinds. In the same way that fir trees are distinguished from elms and pines, and as clearly as gold is differentiated from tigers and bears, mental illnesses, it was claimed, could be put into various natural or categorial rubrics. With an emphasis on those newly postulated distinctions – differences in kind, whose foundation was deemed to rely on clear and discrete criteria and constitutive factors (ranging from genes to cells, elements of brain circuitry, and the like) – an alternative kind of continuity between the normal and the pathological was once again constructed.

In what follows, we will look at the intricate and complex evolution of the diagnosis of schizophrenia in the various editions of the DSM. As we will discover and analyze, the mental condition in question turned out to be a "moving target" of sorts, one that changed over time and illustrated, once more, the ongoing alternation between the categorical and dimensional models of explanation and interpretation that we have been consistently tracking in its different historical phases.

DSM-I (1952): Schizophrenic Reactions

The diagnosis or definition of the term schizophrenia itself makes no appearance yet in the first edition of the DSM. The manual only spoke of a "schizophrenic reaction" to life stressors and traumas that are not portrayed and explained as resulting from intrinsic natural or organic causes but call for a different, more complex and imaginative, indeed, contextualized kind of interpretation. A telling and relevant case is presented in the following vignette:

> *Patient B:* This 31-year-old, divorced male was brought to the hospital by the police on the complaint of disturbing the peace. On admission, the patient

> was confused, bewildered, and stated that he heard voices, which told him that his "wife" was in danger. He had been married but his wife left him after two months of marriage. He also believed that he could communicate with others through telepathy. ... During the patient's adolescence, his father committed suicide. The patient then left school in order to support the family; he later enlisted in the Navy, serving for six years. After discharge, the patient re-entered and graduated from high school. Since then, he has been employed as a machinist and is regarded as an excellent worker by his employer. The patient states that his interest in autofellatio began while reading either the Bible or Shakespeare. He read a quotation to the effect that, "A man should drink from his own springs"; upon reading this, he felt a spark jump from the page to him. He interpreted this as meaning that a man should drink the semen from his penis. He was extremely reluctant to discuss any other deviant behavior. The psychiatric diagnosis was *Schizophrenic Reaction Catatonic Type*.[16]

Patient B was diagnosed in 1954 as suffering from a "*schizophrenic reaction*," based on the DSM-I that was published in 1952. In *reaction* to his divorce, he experienced a severe disturbance in his reality testing (he heard ominous voices that did not exist in reality, he believed his thoughts could be communicated, and he felt forced to drink his own semen). Indeed, in the DSM-I, the patient's "strong tendency to retreat from reality," his "emotional disharmony, unpredictable disturbance in the stream of thought, and regressive behavior," all of which were criteria for the diagnosis in question, were understood as a *schizophrenic reaction* to life events. This not only held true for his response to the immediate departure of his wife, but also echoed the childhood trauma related to the loss of his father to suicide. *Schizophrenic reactions*, listed among the psychotic disorders, were considered part of a broader category called the "functional psychoses," a terminology that referred to mental disorders with a *psychogenic* origin (as opposed to an organic one, one that was found in the body), and without clear physical causes or changes in the brain.[17]

It is generally argued that the DSM-I was fundamentally psychoanalytically or psychodynamically inspired.[18] Even though some have challenged this long-held view,[19] in the case of schizophrenia, Meyer's aforementioned psychodynamic ideas (explaining both the psychoses and the neuroses as *reactions* to adverse life events) and Freud's general idea (that the difference between the psychoses and the neuroses is located in the *intensity* of a person's withdrawal from reality and the extent of the resulting regression) clearly made their imprint on the first published edition of the manual, which emphasized the *reactive*, rather than organic, nature of schizophrenia.[20]

Furthermore, even though the authors of the DSM-I claimed that the group of "schizophrenic reactions" was synonymous to "the formerly used *dementia praecox*," the dire prognosis that was attached to this latter, distinctly Kraepelinian, diagnosis was somewhat mitigated.[21] In the DSM-I, the tendency toward further mental "deterioration" was now claimed to be relevant to *some*, yet not all, of these psychological reactions.

The authors of the DSM-I strove to make clear distinctions and classifications. They differentiated the schizophrenic reactions from other types of reactions, such as "affective reactions," "paranoid reactions," and, finally, from "psychotic reactions, without clearly defined structural change." *All* schizophrenic reactions involved fundamental disorders in the person's relationship to reality and ability to form concepts, which led to "affective, behavioral, and intellectual disturbances in varying degrees and mixtures." The schizophrenic reactions were then divided into different subtypes, which could be summarized as follows:

1. The "simple" type of schizophrenic reaction involves mainly a withdrawal: a reduced interest and attachment to the external world, and an "impoverishment of human relationships." The general level of functioning is low and the patient is apathetic and indifferent.[22] Delusions or hallucinations are on the whole very rare.
2. The "hebephrenic" type of schizophrenic reaction is characterized by shallow and inappropriate affect. Patients can giggle unpredictably, or behave in a silly way, and show mannerism. They report delusions of a somatic nature, hallucinations, and generally present regressive behavior.[23]
3. The "catatonic" schizophrenic reaction is related to motor behavior, which becomes inhibited to the point of stupor or, on the contrary, excessive and excited.
4. The "paranoid" type is characterized by autistic, unrealistic thinking, that is, by delusions of persecution and/or grandeur, implausible ideas of reference (when the patient gets the impression that everything

refers back to them), and bouts of hostility, aggression, or unpredictable behavior.

5. In the "schizoaffective" type of reaction, patients experience elated affect or depression accompanying a predominantly schizophrenic content.
6. Schizophrenic reactions may also occur before puberty, and in this case, belong to the "childhood" type. These reactions include psychotic episodes, manifesting themselves primarily in autism.
7. Lastly, schizophrenic reactions of the "residual" type apply to patients who only show residual disturbance of thinking, affectivity, and/or behavior, once they have improved significantly from a psychotic schizophrenic reaction.

Alongside these relatively sharply defined schizophrenic reactions, the DSM-I also lists an "acute undifferentiated" type of reaction. This subtype describes individuals who manifest a wide variety of schizophrenic symptoms that mostly disappear in a matter of weeks. In this group, we find patients with "latent," "incipient," and "pre-psychotic" reactions, who don't show a full schizophrenic reaction, but merely present a *more severe* picture of schizoid personality.[24] Therefore, although the DSM-I tries, in the spirit of Kraepelin, to create clear and distinct, differentiated groups, it also presents a *spectrum*-like alternative, where the "undifferentiated" type of reaction describes a state that ventures "beyond" the milder schizoid personality disorder and yet is not as *severe* as schizophrenic reactions themselves.[25]

It is the grim prognosis, together with the patient's strong tendency to retreat from reality, the "emotional disharmony," unpredictable disturbances in stream of thought, and regressive behavior, that mark the ultimate differentiation between the milder picture of a personality disorder, on the one hand, and the severe manifestation of the schizophrenic reaction, on the other.

DSM-II (1968): From Reaction to Disease

The publication of the second edition of the psychiatric manual was in response to what its authors saw as the fact that "the people of all nations live in one world" and as a way to collaborate with the World Health

Organization (WHO), which promoted a uniform system of classification of disorders. "The rapid integration of psychiatry with the rest of medicine," so the authors of the new manual wrote, created a need for a psychiatric nomenclature and classification systems like those used by other medical professionals.[26] As we can see from the "case" that follows, the DSM-II hoped to offer a further refinement of the conceptual and clinical tools of the diagnosis. As we can see in the example that follows, by changing the diagnosis of "schizophrenic reaction" to "schizophrenia," the authors hoped to provide a definitive *name* for the disease, just as other fields of medicine labeled theirs, and in accordance with international developments:

> The subject is a 56-year-old divorced male, a high school graduate, trained tool and die maker … Through his 33-some years of treatment, the patient has been consistently diagnosed as a chronic schizophrenic, paranoid type (DSM-II: 295.3). He manifests classic symptoms of this diagnostic category, that is, auditory hallucinations, inappropriate affect, anxiety, complex persecutory delusions, autistic and magical thinking, and preservative and stereotyped behavior. His judgment and insight are found poor, while his memory for recent events and orientation to time, place and person generally show no impairment.[27]

The patient described above was diagnosed as a "Chronic Schizophrenic, Paranoid Type," with the DSM-II numerical code, 295.3. Published in 1968, the DSM-II was based on the ICD-8 of the WHO, alongside a glossary of definitions offered by American contributors. Given the growing exodus of psychiatrists from psychiatric hospitals during these years, in its introduction, the DSM-II redefined the possible uses of the suggested nomenclature in classifying the illnesses which were diagnosed and treated in mental hospitals, but *also* in psychiatric clinics, office practices, general hospitals, community mental health centers, and during consultations in courts or industrial health services.[28]

Due to the broadening of the field, the members of the committee suggested terms that would "facilitate maximum communication" within the profession and reduce confusion and ambiguity to a minimum.[29] In so doing, they acknowledged that the use of "different names for the same thing implied different attitudes and concepts."[30] They also stated that their goal was to avoid using terms which suggested a particular view about the nature of the disorder or its causes. To explain their attitude toward diagnostic categories that, in their eyes, were controversial, they applied their new suggested term "schizophrenia" to diagnose the condition that the first edition of the DSM classified as "schizophrenic reaction."[31]

However, the committee members claimed that the "change of label has not changed the nature of the disorder," and that they did not wish to discourage a continuing debate about the *nature* or *causes* of schizophrenia. In fact, the committee itself could not agree on "*what this disorder is*," in its very origin and nature, so to speak, but only on "*what to call it*."[32] That said, removing the term "reaction" from the diagnoses listed by DSM-I was in all likelihood a direct response to the mounting pressures to de-psychologize and re-medicalize psychiatry. This tendency led to a perceived desire (or need) to diagnose "actual diseases," rather than mere "reactions," just like other medical specialists did.

Comes from a need for answers

Generally speaking, the DSM-II divides mental disorders into two classes: the first is the psychoses and the second refers to the neuroses, personality disorders, and other nonpsychotic mental disorders.[33] The psychoses are disorders in which mental functioning is impaired to a *degree* that interferes with the patient's ability to meet the ordinary demands of life and recognize reality.[34] According to the DSM-II, schizophrenia belongs to the kind of psychoses that are "not attributed to physical conditions."[35] It is described as a *group* of disorders, "the schizophrenias," all manifesting a disturbance of "thinking, mood and behavior," and primarily defined as a *severe* form of thought disorder.[36] These "schizophrenias" are to be distinguished from the "affective psychoses," which are dominated by mood disorders, and from "paranoid states," where the distortion of reality is *not as severe*, and from which other psychotic symptoms are largely absent.[37]

The number of subtypes of the schizophrenias rose from nine different schizophrenic reactions in the DSM-I, to 13 types in the DSM-II.[38] With its more differentiated list of diagnoses, DSM-II aimed at a greater accuracy in "carving" the perceived "nature" of psychiatric disorders "at the joints." Interestingly, in the years between the publication of the DSM-II in 1968 and the DSM-III in 1980, it was the diagnosis of schizophrenia itself that made the biggest headlines and prompted the major revision and paradigm shift that came with the issuing of the manual's third iteration. Indeed, schizophrenia became the first and most prominent target in a concerted attempt to correct the gravest omissions in diagnostic reliability in the psychiatric profession.

The first major study on schizophrenia that was executed during this time by the WHO was "The International Pilot Study of Schizophrenia" (IPSS).[39] This transcultural psychiatric study of schizophrenia was carried out between 1966 and 1973 in nine countries, and demonstrated that it was possible to reliably diagnose schizophrenia, even across countries that were economically and socioculturally very different. The study concluded that (1) syndromes of schizophrenia occurred in all investigated cultures and geographical areas; (2) the rate of incidence was similar in different populations; and, finally, in a 5-year follow-up study, (3) that while the course and prognosis were extremely variable, the outcome was significantly better in developing countries such as India and Nigeria.[40] This "better outcome" axiom was challenged based on a number of other longitudinal studies of schizophrenia, in 11 low- and middle-income countries, undertaken by other institutions,[41] a challenge that was itself criticized as well.[42]

The second major study on the diagnosis of schizophrenia was more specifically critical of the DSM. The "US/UK International Diagnostic Project," published in 1971 by Robert Kendell and his colleagues, pointed out the lack of, and much-needed, reliable description of symptoms and precise definition of schizophrenia (and other psychiatric disorders) in the DSM.[43] An expert on the classification of mental disorders and author of the psychiatric classic *The Role of Diagnosis in Psychiatry* (1975), Kendell conducted a comparative study where psychiatric diagnoses were given, based on eight videotaped diagnostic interviews with patients. Major disagreements occurred between large audiences of American and British psychiatrists, which led to the conclusion that the American concept of schizophrenia was much broader than its British counterpart or, in other words, that schizophrenia was being diagnosed a lot more in the United States than in the United Kingdom. Indeed, the American notion and treatment of schizophrenia often included what British psychiatrists generally considered to be symptoms of less severe psychiatric diagnoses, such as depressive illness, manic illness, neurotic illness, and personality disorder.

In their comments about the findings of this study, Kendell et al. argued that "though one may discuss whose concept of schizophrenia is more useful, or closer to Bleuler's original description, one cannot meaningfully discuss which is right, for we have no external criterion to appeal to – no morbid anatomy, no etiological agent, no biochemical or physiological anomaly."[44] In other words, there are no underlying biological markers to help identify schizophrenia and distinguish it from other diseases by using physiological criteria. Kendell and his co-authors also hypothesized that the main reason for the Anglo-American discrepancies had to do with the distinct authority of psychoanalysis and psychoanalysts in North America, which they described as being probably "more important than any factual discoveries."[45] The authors further stressed that "no concept of schizophrenia can be either right or wrong," and that the diagnosis was made much more freely on the US East Coast than anywhere else. As a result, they submitted, the term schizophrenia was "losing much of its original meaning," and was "approaching the point" where it had become a mere "synonym for functional mental illness,"[46] that is, for a disease not caused by some organic dysfunction.

Comparing it with the evolution of the diagnosis of mania, Kendell and his co-authors believed that, over time, the concept of schizophrenia would radically change due to therapeutic innovations and biochemical or physiological discoveries. For instance, as they noted, mania was a diagnosis that was about to disappear but was reinstituted when lithium was introduced as an effective medication to prevent manic episodes. Patients who were regarded as schizophrenics were reassigned a diagnosis of manic depression, "in order that they may be given lithium salts."[47] In the same spirit, schizophrenia might also make its comeback, insofar as where there is a therapy, there is a diagnosis. Although approximately four years later the dopamine hypothesis of schizophrenia (DHS) appeared (based on the effect of the first generation of antipsychotic drugs on so-called schizophrenic symptoms),[48] the speculation that a single neurotransmitter could account for all that was observed in schizophrenia, as Kendler and Schaffner argued, turned out to be "a will-o'-the-wisp" which ended "with a whimper."[49] If it truly aspired to mature as a science, it was argued, then psychiatry would need a much better theoretical account of its object of study and of the subjects in its care.

Going back to the famous UK/US study of the 1970s, the authors agreed that the title of their 1971 article "Diagnostic criteria of American and British psychiatrists" might be somewhat misleading. Indeed, the article proposed to compare the theoretical and clinical work of American and British psychiatrists that led to the overextension of the concept of schizophrenia. However, at the time of the study, they only sampled American psychiatrists from New York, who were mostly psychoanalytically oriented.

While in the spirit of Freud, the latter tended to view a continuity between the normal and the pathological, a very different group of psychiatrists working at Washington University in St. Louis (who soon came to be known as the "neo-Kraepelinians"), assumed instead that a clear categorical difference existed, not only between normalcy and pathology, but also between the different mental disorders.[50] Urged by US psychiatrist John Feighner, a discussion group led by Eli Robins and colleagues developed a new set of diagnostic criteria for 15 mental disorders, with the aim of improving the reliability of psychiatric diagnoses. Published in 1972, these so-called "Feighner criteria" formed the basis for the development of the Research Diagnostic Criteria (RDC), which in turn, were central to the later writing and rewording of DSM-III.[51]

In their pursuit to re-medicalize psychiatry, the neo-Kraepelinians aimed to create and professionally enshrine specific disease categories. The group was clear about basing psychiatric diagnoses on "data" rather than "opinion or tradition," as was shown in their 1972 "Diagnostic criteria for use in psychiatric research."[52] They firmly believed that there existed fixed, natural categories of mental disorders, among which were schizophrenia, manic-depressive disorder, homosexuality, and hysteria. They argued that these categories were not only reliable, they were also *valid*. In other words, these categories mapped onto real differences that existed in nature.

But a year later, in 1973, a third major study on schizophrenia was published in the renowned journal *Science* asking: "If sanity and insanity exist, how shall we know them?," and famously concluding that "it is clear that we cannot distinguish the sane from the insane in psychiatric hospitals."[53] This challenge to psychiatry led the neo-Kraepelinians to become even more galvanized in trying to place psychiatry on a firmer medical footing.

In the provocative *Science* article entitled "On being sane in insane places" and based on a study that has since been seriously contested, the author David Rosenhan, a Stanford professor, challenged psychiatry's very ability to successfully diagnose mental disorders. Rosenhan's study, which is considered a game changer in the revisions that would lead up to the publication of DSM-III, took the diagnosis of schizophrenia as its point of departure and line of attack on the psychiatric establishment's ability to differentiate and classify mental disorders.

In the experiment, designed, executed, and reported by Rosenhan himself, eight "pseudopatients" (one psychology graduate student in his twenties and seven older subjects – three psychologists, a pediatrician, a painter, a housewife, and Rosenhan himself), were directed to admit themselves into 12 psychiatric hospitals, complaining that they heard unfamiliar voices saying "empty," "hollow," and "thud."[54] Upon admission, so the experiment required, the pseudopatients were to stop simulating any symptoms of psychiatric illness and were instructed to behave normally – except for writing their observations – a fact that was later corroborated by the staff reports of the different hospitals, which uniformly described them as "friendly," "cooperative," and exhibiting "no abnormal indications."[55]

According to Rosenhan, out of the 12 members of the group, 11 were diagnosed as schizophrenics and one (despite his identical, agreed-upon symptomatology) as suffering from a manic-depressive psychosis. Rosenhan further reports that they were all discharged with a diagnosis of "paranoid schizophrenia in remission," even though, as Rosenhan clearly claimed, they were all perfectly "sane" and had claimed no more than hearing a voice saying three simple words when admitted to the hospital.

Rosenhan's experiment is important as it challenged the "reliability, utility, and meaning of such terms as 'sanity,' 'insanity,' 'mental illness,' and 'schizophrenia'." The experiment also called into question the more general claim of psychiatry to be able to accurately differentiate between normality and abnormality, and between their respective guiding notions and concepts.[56]

Although Rosenhan's experiment was recently discredited by Susannah Cahalan, who was able to locate his private files along with the medical records of three of the pseudopatients,[57] his 1973 publication made a

Is psychiatry accurate? who can say who is sane and insane

deep and lasting impression on psychiatry, which never fully managed to recover and clear the apparent stain left on its public respectability.

Debates stimulated by this article touched on issues of the tentative nature of psychiatric diagnoses. That is, they raised the issues of how labeling and stigma contribute to feelings and experiences of powerlessness and depersonalization in psychiatric hospitals. Needless to say, this resonated with the sentiments of antipsychiatry, whether from radical left activists and Marxists (such as David Cooper, who coined the term "antipsychiatry," R. D. Laing, who, together with Aaron Esterson, wrote *Sanity, Madness and the Family*, Michel Foucault in his *The History of Madness in the Age of Reason*, or Erving Goffman in his *Asylums* and *Stigma*), or from far-right libertarians such as Thomas Szasz (with his famous *The Myth of Mental Illness*).[58] Although antipsychiatry was never a cohesive movement with an agreed-upon manifesto, most of these authors believed the idea that psychiatric diagnoses were problematic, to say the least, and that psychiatry strongly differed from other medical specialties. Hence, when it was published, Rosenhan's study raised the poignant and embarrassing question as to whether psychiatric taxonomy was possible at all. More specifically, it was now inquired what methodologies could be responsibly used in studying and treating mental disorders and what, if any, was the validity of psychiatric diagnoses?

When Robert Spitzer, the Columbia University psychiatrist and major architect of the DSM-III, managed to obtain Rosenhan's own pseudopatient records from the Haverford psychiatric hospital, he found that "Lurie" (the name under which Rosenhan had checked himself in as a patient) had feigned more severe symptoms than those he reported in the *Science* article. These symptoms included alleged suicidal thoughts, provoked by the voices he claimed to hear. In 1975, Spitzer published his methodological critique of Rosenhan's study, yet did not expose the author personally. Instead, he used his findings to mobilize the support of the American Psychiatric Association and to recruit psychiatrists who, like himself, were interested in promoting the medical model in psychiatry, to construct clear categorical diagnoses, ideally based on biology, as was the case with different diseases in other fields of medicine.

While, like Freud, psychodynamic psychiatrists had seen no need to create strict medical taxonomies of mental illness (assuming a universal and psychological, rather than organic, cause of mental disorders), the neo-Kraepelinians, led by Spitzer, focused on the *manifest* symptoms of patients, rather than on depth psychology. "True schizophrenia" was seen as a syndrome that inevitably and irrevocably resulted in severe deterioration of the patient's functioning, as shown already by Kraepelin. Accordingly, whenever patients showed remission, it was questioned whether the initial diagnosis had been valid and whether they had schizophrenia in the first place.[59]

In retrospect, it can be concluded that Rosenhan's questionable but provocative article, and the US/UK diagnostic criteria research from the early 1970s, exposed not only specific faults within the diagnosis of schizophrenia, but also a general dissatisfaction with the overly broad, nonspecific, diagnostic definitions offered by the DSM-II. The editors of DSM-III thus sought to correct the clear embarrassments revealed by these publications. Specifically, they strove to set up a better classification system to solve the obvious problems in determining the reliability and validity of psychiatric diagnoses. By "reliability," the editors of the DSM-III meant a diagnosis that involved two or more separate interviewers. By "validity," they meant that the diagnosis also had to be accurate.

Armed with the proper razor-sharp knives, skillful butchers would be better equipped to "carve nature at its joints." Similarly, patients could be treated more effectively if their diagnosis and prognosis were based on a more precise reading of their condition. The overall result of the neo-Kraepelinian efforts in the new DSM, was that of an extensive, checklist approach. This new outlook accommodated psychiatry's scientific and clinical ambition to offer more clarification and standardization, as it entered the last two decades of the twentieth century.

DSM-III (1980): Narrowing Down the Concept of Schizophrenia

The DSM-III is often remembered for its important innovations and is said to have revolutionized psychiatric classifications and diagnoses by proposing more precise, symptom-based definitions of mental disorders as well as explicit and reliable diagnostic criteria, guided by scientific principles and evidence. In comparison to the DSM-II, in the third edition of the manual, schizophrenia comprises a more homogeneous group of disorders with a poor prognosis, as we can see in the following vignette:

> Ben, single, white, 21 years old, entered Chestnut Lodge in the early 1960s. His overt psychiatric illness began while he was attending college in his hometown, and followed two losses: his girlfriend Amy died mysteriously …, and the maternal grandmother died shortly thereafter. … Ben's mother sent him on an errand. He never returned … According to his mother's version, he knocked on a stranger's door and announced he had cancer and syphilis. The frightened stranger called the police, who detained Ben for observation and then sent him to a nearby general hospital … the hospital record version said Ben attempted suicide by inhaling carbon monoxide from a running car following a bout of heavy drinking during which he was frightened when a man made homosexual advances. … [B]y all accounts it seems that Ben suffered an acute psychosis … [which] included hallucinations and delusions. … Ben's psychosis appeared to be a "first break": that is, an acute psychotic breakdown which, until it lasts long enough, is labeled "brief reactive psychosis" or "schizophreniform psychosis" in DSM-III. By the time Ben came to Chestnut Lodge, he had been actively ill for six months, long enough to be labeled schizophrenic by DSM-III criteria.[60]

As this illustration shows, schizophrenia as a target had "moved" again. After 1980, differentiating between schizophrenia and other types of less severe psychoses was based on the *duration* of the condition. Indeed, as we see in the above case, the emphasis is on the "six months" during which Ben suffered from psychotic symptoms, a period which is deemed "long enough" for him to be considered schizophrenic according to the DSM-III.

Although the DSM-III's initial aim was to align the DSM nomenclature with that of the International Classification of Diseases (ICD), its architects took pride in improving the reliability and validity of psychiatric diagnoses. However, when we take a closer look at the opening pages of the new manual, we see that it is more nuanced than one might expect. Indeed, despite its vast ambitions, the DSM-III opens with a proviso and disclaimer that suggests methodological modesty, if nothing else. As the editors stipulate, "in DSM-III there is no assumption that each mental disorder is *a discrete entity with sharp boundaries* (discontinuity) between it and other mental disorders, as well as between it and 'No Mental Disorder.'"[61] In other words, neither the longstanding controversy regarding the presumed continuity or discontinuity between diagnostic entities, nor the directly related question of whether some disorders differed from each other *qualitatively* (implying discontinuity between the symptoms and causes at issue) or *quantitatively* (confirming differences merely on a continuum of severity), would be solved by the third edition of the manual. At least, this was not its avowed ambition.

When justifying the preference for separate categories, in specific cases, the authors of the DSM-III cautiously argued for the "clinical usefulness of the distinction," instead of overconfidently proclaiming "a resolution of the controversy as to whether or not these conditions are in fact quantitatively or qualitatively different."[62] In what was in all likelihood an indirect response to the antipsychiatric critique of the 1960s and 1970s, the authors of the DSM-III stressed that they did not categorize or classify individuals, thus avoiding the problem of "spoiled identities."[63] Rather, their aim was merely to classify the "disorders that individuals have."[64] They thus refrained from using terms and expressions such as "a schizophrenic" and, instead, encouraged the use of phrases such as "an individual with schizophrenia." In addition, the editors declared that although individuals with the same mental disorder "show at least the defining features of the disorder," the clinical management and outcome of that disorder may well be very different.[65] In other words, while two individuals may share the core features of a mental illness and have the same diagnosis, the way in which the illness plays out in their actual lives may differ greatly.

The authors of the DSM-III strove to remain atheoretical, that is, to stay neutral when it came to explaining the causes of mental illnesses or psychopathologies. One of the most important innovations of the third edition of the manual was the new definition of the general concept of "mental disorder." Mental disorders, the authors claimed, exhibit a "clinically significant behavioral or psychological syndrome or pattern that occurs in an individual and that is typically associated with either a *painful* symptom (distress) or *impairment* in one or more important areas of functioning (disability)."[66] The dysfunction, they inferred, is behavioral, psychological, or biological. What had still been possible within the terms of the DSM-I and II was now no longer an option. The observed and theorized dysfunction, DSM-III concluded, is *not* located solely in the interaction between the individual and society but, instead, has a primary intrinsic psychic and natural basis.

More specifically, the DSM-III presented an innovative "multi-axial" approach to mental illness: it required that every patient be evaluated along five "axes," each of which referred to a different class of information. While "Axis I" would record clinical syndromes, "Axis II" would cover personality disorders and specific developmental disorders. "Axis III" would document *physical* disorders and conditions, with the explicit disclaimer that "mental" and "physical" disturbances might change "as our understanding of the pathophysiology of these disorders increases"; in other words, one day, mental disorders might very well prove to be physical disorders. "Axis IV" would register the severity of psychosocial stressors, and "Axis V" would capture the highest level of adaptive functioning of the patient during the past year. The rationale behind this overall change of perspective on mental illness was to ensure that attention was given to the "types of disorders, aspects of the environment, and areas of functioning that might be overlooked if the focus were on assessing a single presenting problem."[67]

The manual gives an example of what a multi-axial diagnosis might look like in the case of schizophrenia. It offers a schema of determining features in certain patients, with the code numbers included in the abbreviated description:

Axis I: 295.92 Schizophrenia, Undifferentiated Type, Chronic
V62.89 Borderline Intellectual Functioning (Provisional)
Axis II: V71.08 No diagnosis on Axis II
Axis III: Late effects of viral encephalitis
Axis IV: Psychosocial stressors: death of mother Severity: 6 – Extreme
Axis V: Highest level of adaptive functioning past year: 6 – Very poor.

This technical medical idiom (whose function, according to Charles Rosenberg, is to act as a password and facilitate communication between administrative apparatuses) uses abbreviated codes to describe hypothetical patients whose sufferings can be rendered – even humanized – in more elaborate and personalized narrative terms. This aspect can be seen in the opening of this section, in the description of Ben by his doctors.

This is not to suggest that mental health professionals would ever mistake their patients for nothing more than a "295.92." However, the patient in question would not be covered by insurance or receive proper treatment in relevant institutional settings were it not for the profiling of this psychological algorithm, as the concrete life of the patient would be of no further interest to the bureaucratic-medicalized system as such.

The diagnosis of schizophrenia thus changed significantly in this third edition of the DSM. Belonging on Axis I, schizophrenia now appeared as part of a new category, of so-called "schizophrenic disorders." It no longer belonged under the rubric of "psychoses not attributed to physical conditions," as it did in the DSM-II. Furthermore, there was a new acknowledgment that this "group of disorders" included mental illnesses and symptoms that most likely had very different causes. As a consequence, while the common usage continued to refer to "schizophrenia," the technically more accurate description, it was now held, was that of "schizophrenic disorders."[68]

As we see, the spectral debate between Kraepelin and Bleuler continued to haunt the DSM-III. Indeed, DSM-III *either* emphasized the tendency toward a deteriorating course, as Kraepelin had professed, *or* gave more weight to the underlying psychological disturbances, as Bleuler, inspired by Freud, had suggested.

Nevertheless, a new figure was also introduced to this legacy, a psychiatrist, who, as we will see in the next chapter, became a much more significant voice in the debates on schizophrenia than he intended to be. Kurt Schneider (1887–1967), a German psychiatrist, was the first to identify the so-called "first rank symptoms"[69] of schizophrenia as early as 1939. These "first rank symptoms" were all severe and ended up making psychotic features central to the diagnosis of schizophrenia. Indeed, with his list of clear symptoms required for the diagnosis, Schneider was seen as a major inspiration to the authors of the DSM-III, who sought to reliably differentiate the disorder from the other psychotic disorders which they listed and described.[70] Due to their severity and because they came to be the defining features of schizophrenia according to the DSM-III, Schneider's first-rank symptoms were and are still held responsible, by some clinicians and commentators, for the general assumption or misconception according to which schizophrenic patients are "mad" or "crazy." Schizophrenia was now associated with symptoms including auditory hallucinations and delusions, thought withdrawal (i.e., believing that one's thoughts can be removed from one's mind), thought insertion (i.e., believing that they can be inserted into one's mind), thought interruption (i.e., believing they can be interrupted from the outside or by someone else), and thought broadcasting (believing one's thoughts can be heard by other people). All of these elements further added a sense of strangeness to the picture painted by the diagnosis of schizophrenia.

By highlighting the delusions, hallucinations, and disorganization involved in schizophrenia and giving them a central role in diagnosing the condition, the DSM-III hoped to exclude disorders that had previously fallen under the definition of schizophrenia, but were not considered as *truly severe* (such as "latent schizophrenia," "borderline schizophrenia," and "simple schizophrenia"). In the DSM-III, these milder disorders were labeled as mere "personality disorders," of which the "schizotypal personality disorder" was a common example.

As we witnessed in Ben's example, the third edition of the manual added the further diagnostic criterion of a minimal duration of six months of the symptoms in question, to differentiate schizophrenia from the less severe mental disorders, whose sufferings extended over relatively brief intervals. A further restrictive criterion was added, that of the patient's age at the onset of schizophrenia. Indeed, unless the patient was less than 45 years old, the given diagnosis could not be that of schizophrenia. Anyone over 45 would be diagnosed with "atypical psychosis."

Although the authors of the DSM-III declared that, unlike Kraepelin's *dementia praecox*, their use of the concept of schizophrenia was not limited to illnesses with a deteriorating course, they nonetheless admitted that it "*always* involve[d] deterioration from a previous level of functioning … in such areas as work, social relations, and self-care."[71] It was this deterioration that led to the common observation, among family members and friends, that the person suffering seemed, in many respects, simply "not the same."[72]

As Elyn Saks writes in the passage with which we opened this chapter, throughout modern history, schizophrenia was mainly seen as a thought disorder. How, then, was this presumed disorderly thinking of the schizophrenic concretely described?

First, with Schneider as its major guide, the DSM-III defined schizophrenia as a disorder that affects both the *content* and *form* of a person's *thoughts*. Delusions are the most famous example of disordered *thought content* in schizophrenia. One common kind of delusion is of a persecutory kind, which is in place when, for example, the person feels spied on, or as one patient describes, it feels as if other persons are conspiring to harm them in particular: "I believed that there were persons in the world who were out to get me in some way. I then further deduced that my doctor's diagnosis was a part of this conspiracy."[73] Another type of delusion is that of reference. In the latter, otherwise insignificant events or objects are given particular, unusual significance or seen as carrying messages addressed to the patient. This might occur when a television commentator is experienced as mocking the patient's discourse or demeanor, to give a well-known example. Further examples include the delusion of "thought broadcasting," mentioned earlier, and somatic, grandiose, religious, as well as nihilistic delusions, although these are less common. For example, Ben, the suicidal patient described in the vignette with which we opened this section, suffered from persecutory and grandiose delusions, believing others felt he was "stupid," that his therapist "would either kill him or seduce him," and "worry[ing] intensely about being homosexual."[74]

Disordered thought *content* persists even when the patient is exposed to evidence that their delusions are "false." As author Kevin Alan Lee describes, referring to his own case: "In some of my delusions, I believed that people were speaking to me as if I was God. I maintained this belief even after experiencing other perceptions that would lead me to believe the contrary … Even though I was partially aware of this conflict in identity, I never really acknowledged the fact that they contradicted each other."[75]

By the same token, disorder in the *form* of the person's thoughts is also indicative of schizophrenia. For instance, Lee describes an occasion in which his thought process became illogical and difficult to penetrate from the outside:

> I remember asking one of the nurses at the inpatient unit about my score in a math competition that I had competed in, during my high school years. These thoughts somehow connected my participation in this math competition to the very reason for my stay at the inpatient unit. This seemingly illogical conclusion of mine illustrates how racing thoughts can link two random and distinct thoughts, into a single and cohesive conception.[76]

Incoherent and incomprehensible speech also falls under this category of disorders in the *form of thought*. Bleuler's "loosening of associations" is a case in point. Indeed, the speech of patients with schizophrenia disorders was deemed to be impoverished, vague, overly abstract or inordinately concrete, and in any case, repetitive and stereotyped.[77] Neologisms (the invention of new words), perseveration (excessive repetition of words or sounds), clanging (patterns of speech based on puns and rhymes rather than meaning), and blocking (interrupting one's speech while ostensibly in pursuit of a goal) were also mentioned as typical examples of the schizophrenic's formal thought disorders. An example of such disturbances could already be found in the description of the 56-year-old patient invoked in our discussion of the DSM-II above. In fact, this patient was said to use schizophrenic neologisms, unusual words, and peculiarities of syntax and morphology:

> the subject's use of the noun *war* as a verb (*a black Korean wared me*), associations based on homonymity (e.g., *Canada look for peace and piece of ass*), any of the bizarre usages, which resemble deliberate figures of speech, *medical punishment, death wages* ... occur in phrases such as *four thrillion dollars* ... *Judist* (i.e., lover of Judaism).[78]

However, experiences regarding the disruption in the content and form of one's thoughts and speech were not the only elements that would lead someone to be diagnosed with schizophrenia according to the directives of the DSM-III. The *second* major disorder, according to this edition of the manual, was found in the area of perception, that is, in the form of hallucinations, notably auditory ones, such as *hearing voices*, as we will see in more detail in chapter 5. These auditory hallucinations were seen as particularly characteristic of the illness.[79] For instance, patients might hear voices speaking directly to them, insulting them, or commenting on their behavior. Ben, to return to his case once more, repeatedly heard his name being called out. Similarly, Norma MacDonald, a patient who wrote about her own schizophrenic condition in the 1960s, described her voices as being authoritative, even persecutory:

> I could eat and sleep very little because of voices telling me I mustn't. I was "forced" by voices to walk miles and miles about the city until my feet were

> blistered and bleeding, and then I was persuaded to do an increasing number of senseless things.[80]

Tactile or somatic hallucinations – the experience of spontaneous bodily sensations, for example – were considered much less frequent. In fact, not only were hallucinations related to vision, taste, or smells considered rarer in schizophrenia, whenever and wherever they did appear, the authors of the manual surmised, they might instead indicate a wholly different, *organic* disorder.

Thirdly, disturbed affect was also central to the DSM-III's diagnostic criteria for schizophrenia. Reduced intensity of affective (i.e., emotional) expression was seen as yet another symptom of the disorder.[81] In *The Split Mind*, for example, Kevin Alan Lee describes how his own flattened affect led to interpersonal difficulties and trouble communicating with others. Indeed, as he describes, the reduction in the range and intensity of his emotional responses affected his facial expressions and eye contact, which became problematic during his college years and professional life, since employers and professors felt disturbed by the "intense and glaring look on [his] face" and assumed that they were being "stared down" by him when in fact they were not.[82] According to the DSM-III, while these pathological emotional responses could be considered a sign of schizophrenia itself, they were also a possible side effect of the antipsychotic drugs that became the treatment of choice for schizophrenia in the mid-1950s and replaced harsher treatments such as lobotomies and a variety of shock therapies.[83]

A disturbance in the sense of self is also characterized by DSM-III as being experienced by patients with schizophrenia. This element, which continued to be discussed in psychoanalytic terms, was described as the "loss of ego boundaries." Likewise, "ambivalence," one of Bleuler's 4 A's, which could eventually lead to a total cessation of activity, was still part of the clinical picture of schizophrenia. Withdrawal from the external world, as observed by Freud in the case of Schreber, together with the "egocentric and illogical ideas and fantasies in which objective facts are obscured, distorted, or excluded," were judged to be a further characteristic of the schizophrenic disturbance, disrupting the patient's relations with the external world.[84] For example, Lee also describes his own experience of feeling withdrawn from the world and its goal-oriented requirements: "On one occasion, I was performing usher duties at my cousin's wedding. At times, I would forget my role in that wedding, and I would then stand aimlessly. During those states of confusion, I found it extremely difficult to be fully aware within my environment. Subsequently I did not really fulfill my role at that wedding party."[85]

This long list of criteria, however, is far from complete. Disturbance in psychomotor behavior (such as catatonic stupor, rigidity, or excitement) as well as all sorts of mannerisms, grimacing, or waxy flexibility, were all part of the extended concept of schizophrenia according to the DSM-III. Nevertheless, a few general traits quickly emerge from this summary picture.[86] For one thing, the diagnosis of the schizophrenic disorders, the authors posited, requires a change in the personality of the individual, for the duration of at least six months. For another, with the specter of the diagnosis of *dementia praecox* and *hebephrenia* hovering over its pages, the DSM-III further indicated the deficiencies that schizophrenia causes in the routines of the patients' daily functioning, work, social relations, and self-care. As a consequence of their cognitive impairment, poor judgment, and psychotic behavior, it was argued, individuals who suffer from schizophrenia are thus said to need care and, depending on the level of their inability to deal with everyday life, require either direct supervision or institutionalization. All the more so, according to the authors of the DSM-III, as the very concept of schizophrenia contains the risk that patients pose to others (e.g., due to violent behavior) and to themselves (e.g., due to increased suicidality or owing to their deprived and impoverished environment).

Paradoxically, while aiming at creating ever clearer, increasingly differentiated, categories and criteria, the authors of the DSM-III also identified a "premorbid personality" that could eventually develop into schizophrenia, sowing the very seed for a classification that no longer "carves nature at its joint" but rather establishes a spectrum, a gliding scale, a continuum, and, thereby, gives a dimensional account of the illness. A suspicious, introverted, withdrawn, or eccentric personality that might have met the criteria for paranoid, schizoid, schizotypal, or borderline personality disorder, was thus seen as sharing much in common with a type of personality on the verge of developing a schizophrenic disorder.

Lastly, alongside these predisposing personality traits, the DSM-III clearly indicated that schizophrenia also had social determinants or factors, appearing "more commonly among the lower socioeconomic groups." The authors were less convinced about the causes or reasons for this sociological finding, however. Had the person "drifted downward," or could they simply not move upward due to their debilitating condition? Or perhaps it sufficed to say that there were simply more causes for higher stress levels among the disadvantaged socioeconomic groups.[87]

The manual also discussed the respective rates, in various populations, of those that fit its diagnostic description. While in Europe and Asia they saw a narrower percentage of schizophrenic patients (about 0.2–1% of the general population), the rate in the United States was deemed slightly higher. By contrast, they noted, the diagnosis was equally distributed among males and females. They also reported on the findings from twin studies, concluding that genetic factors played as important a role as nongenetic ones.

A long list of criteria was therefore put forth in the DSM-III, in order to allow diagnosticians to carve at nature's joints, differentiating between schizophrenia and other disorders more skillfully. And yet, paradoxically, in the process it became more and more apparent that schizophrenia was hard to distinguish, not only from many other pathologies, but also from those behaviors that are otherwise considered normal. In fact, as the manual itself concludes, "beliefs or experiences of members of religious or other subcultural groups may be difficult to distinguish from delusions or hallucinations." It is the fact that they are "shared and accepted" by a larger group that distinguishes them from what is, strictly speaking, psychosis.

Since part of the criticism surrounding the American diagnosis of schizophrenia was that its framework was too broad, the main goal of the authors of the DSM-III was to narrow it down.[88] Thus, in addition to setting the minimum duration (of six months), and the age of onset (before 45), the number of subtypes of the illness also shrunk to a total of only five ("disorganized type," "catatonic type," "paranoid type," "undifferentiated type," and "residual type").

Part of Spitzer's attempts to narrow down the concept of schizophrenia with the aim of avoiding what were, in his eyes, unwarranted diagnoses, was based on his claim that there was no such thing as a "mild" case of schizophrenia. He therefore proposed to subsume diagnoses like "latent schizophrenia," "borderline schizophrenia," or "simple schizophrenia" under the label "schizotypal personality disorder," a designation that still contained some of the oddities of schizophrenia, but nonetheless captured something *less severe* than schizophrenia proper.[89]

The concept of schizophrenia used by DSM-III was inspired by the neo-Kraepelinian belief that formal diagnostic criteria should be based, not simply upon the judgment and experience of clinicians, but on the empirical findings of scientific research. The so-called "Feighner criteria" were formulated to produce more homogeneous and "valid" diagnoses, informed not only by signs and symptoms, but also by specific data regarding the patient, including their age at the onset of the illness, their sex, and their race.[90] Such data stemmed from laboratory studies and provided specific exclusion criteria for each kind of diagnosis.

As Spitzer had claimed, the definition of schizophrenia proposed by the DSM-III also aimed to improve reliability. Hence it needed to reflect the results from the most recent research data. Only this, Spitzer was convinced, would allow psychiatrists and clinicians to relate the diagnosis more closely to the eventual prognosis and treatment. It would further help to minimize the stigma of labeling, and achieve clinical acceptability, while reducing differences in interpretation and validation that existed between American and European colleagues.[91] In sum, the manual's mission was to present psychiatry as a medical, scientific field, endowed with a diagnostic system of symptom-based descriptions, of discretely constructed disease entities. In its very rigor and accuracy, it would thus be compatible with the biological model that explains physical diseases or bodily abnormalities.[92] The mission proved successful. Given its wide reception, distribution, and broad acceptance, the US government, together with pharmaceutical companies, allocated major funds for psychopharmacological research with respect to mental disorders. As Richard Noll argued, where once eclecticism reigned in psychiatry, the DSM-III pushed for – and accomplished – nothing short of a biological takeover of psychiatry.[93]

Some of the criticism of the DSM-III diagnosis of the schizophrenic disorders, especially coming from the camp of psychotherapeutic psychiatrists, was motivated by the suspicion that the new version of the manual was not inherently better at diagnosing schizophrenia than either

DSM-I or DSM-II had been. The objection was that the manual's classificatory approach was ultimately arbitrary and, hence, that it should be accepted as just "one system, among many."[94] Even if DSM-III's set of criteria was generally reliable and valuable in terms of research, it did not provide or construct strict "validity," the critics countered. Rather, it merely identified "the most chronic schizophrenics."[95] In addition, the manual's atheoretical impetus offered neither genetic nor psychodynamic understandings, and its identification of schizophrenia as "severe weakness" seemed to lead to a kind of therapeutic nihilism, that is, to giving up hope that treatment could contribute to cure or recovery of these patients. "At the present time," objectors concluded, "when evaluating a patient for schizophrenia, DSM-III should be considered, but clearly not as the final word."[96]

DSM-III-R (1987): Schizophrenia, in the Singular

Seven years of research, following the publication of DSM-III, culminated in a revision of the manual, now entitled DSM-III-R with R standing for revision. DSM-III-R contributed a further cleanup, by accepting only one category of "schizophrenia" in the singular, as opposed to the five subtypes of schizophrenia delineated in the DSM-III.[97]

Although at first glance the criteria for schizophrenia might look very similar to those found in the third edition of the manual, in the DSM-III-R, an undeniable further narrowing of the concept and diagnosis of schizophrenia took place. Criterion A that included the most characteristic symptoms of the disorder (three types of delusion, two types of hallucinations, and incoherent thought, speech or behavior) now required a duration of one week at a minimum and only "bizarre delusions" were included as somatic delusions. In other words, grandiose, religious, nihilistic delusions as well as delusions with persecutory or jealous content were completely absent from the revised manual. Moreover, the criterion that required onset before the age of 45 was dropped.[98] Finally, a history of autistic disorder was now allowed for the additional diagnosis of schizophrenia, if and only if there were prominent delusions and hallucinations.[99]

Through the Feighner criteria, the DSM-III had successfully narrowed down the concept of "schizophrenia." By requiring even stricter measures, the DSM-III-R further reduced the number of people diagnosed with schizophrenia by 10%.[100] Yet the narrowing of the definition could not in itself form a substitute for finding a real biological variable that might be consistently associated with schizophrenia.[101] Psychiatrists who had set out to narrow down the heterogeneity of the many schizophrenias resorted to criteria and diagnoses that would subsequently have to be sorted out according to their different causes, responses to treatment, family history, neurophysiologic dysfunction, or, indeed, recognized biologic markers.[102] The definitional process and ever-subtler differentiation led to a slippery slope, that of the "death of a thousand qualifications."[103] It was no coincidence, then, that the American Psychiatric Association (APA) was soon cautioned that if it continued to change its "standard" definition too often and drastically, it would open up an ever-greater chasm – and, hence, a discontinuity – between the insights and results drawn from its present and past pursuits of scientific and medical, scholarly and clinical, research. "Research progress," it was wisely observed, "will be impeded if we are forced to rediscover the wheel every 7 to 10 years."[104]

DSM-IV (1994): Broadening the Concept of Schizophrenia

The DSM-IV was published only seven years after the DSM-III-R and promised to rely less on experts' opinions and more heavily on objective, empirical data when reworking its classificatory categories. Based on these developments, the patient, in this following vignette, was diagnosed as a schizophrenic, by a doctor who recorded the following:

> A pale, stooped woman of 39 years … referred for a psychiatric evaluation for possible hospitalization by her family doctor, who was concerned about her low level of functioning. Her only complaint to him was, "I have a decline in self-care and low life level." Her mother reports that there has indeed been a decline, but that it has been over many years.

The mother reported that in the last few months the patient had remained in her room, mute and still. From the history of the patient, we learn that 12 years earlier, she was a supervisor in the occupational therapy department of a large hospital, living in her own apartment, and engaged to a young man.

> The man broke the engagement, and she became increasingly disorganized, wandering aimlessly in the street, wearing mismatched clothing. She was fired from her job, and eventually the police were called to hospitalize her. They broke into her apartment, which was in shambles, filled with papers, food, and broken objects.

After her discharge from the hospital, the patient's family hoped that she would "gather herself together and embark again on a real life," yet the report continues that

> Over the years she became more withdrawn and less functional. Most of the time she has been watching TV and cooking. Her cooking consisted of mixing a bizarre combination of ingredients, such as broccoli and cake mix, cooking them and then eating them alone because no one else in the family would eat her meals. … She stopped bathing and brushing her hair or teeth. She ate less and less, although she denied loss of appetite, and over a period of several years lost 20 pounds. She would sleep at all hours. Eventually she became an erratic, wetting her bed frequently and filling the room with a pounding odor of urine.

The patient was admitted again to a psychiatric hospital where she

> sat with her hands tightly clasped in her lap and avoided looking at the doctor who interviewed her. She answered questions readily and did not appear suspicious or guarded but her affect was shallow. She denied depressed mood, delusions, or hallucinations. However, her answers became increasingly idiosyncratic and irrelevant as the interview progressed. In response to a question about her strange cooking habits, she replied that she did not wish to discuss recent events in Russia.[105] (DSM-IV casebook, 32–3)

The authors of the DSM-IV note that it would be a stretch, using the DSM-III or DSM-III-R, to diagnose the patient as a schizophrenic. The DSM-IV, however, includes additional negative symptoms, such as alogia (i.e., a low amount of speech, or speech with poor content) and avolition (i.e., an inability to persist in goal-directed activities) that allowed them to assign her the diagnosis.[106]

DSM addition

While the DSM-III had narrowed its ambitions in defining schizophrenia, the authors of the DSM-IV, on the contrary, announced their plans to significantly *broaden* the concept of schizophrenia once more. Indeed, in the final wording of the DSM-IV, the diagnosis of schizophrenia would now include also "other psychotic disorders" that had psychotic symptoms as their defining feature.

The new edition of the manual introduced a novel distinction, namely between the "positive" and "negative" symptoms of schizophrenia, which were placed on a *spectrum* with normality. In this context, "positive symptoms," which included delusions, hallucinations, disorganized speech and behavior were described in terms of "an *excess* or distortion of normal functions," while "negative symptoms" were characterized in terms of "a *diminution* or loss of normal functions" (so-called flattened affect being a case in point).[107]

Symptoms are first described, therefore, in this fourth edition, in terms of the *normal* functions of the psyche, and only subsequently – in parentheses – as the *pathological* manifestation of a deviance in mental functioning. All the psychological functions that are disturbed in schizophrenia are exhaustively listed, only to be contrasted and confronted with their dysfunction.[108] For example, "perception" is followed by "hallucinations," again, in parentheses.[109] With the "negative symptoms," likewise, the pathology is first defined in relation to its normal counterpart and only subsequently as a symptom of illness. Consequently, in the words of the authors, negative symptoms are fundamentally "restrictions in the *range* and intensity of emotional expression (affective flattening), in the fluency and productivity of thought and speech (alogia), and in the initiation of goal-directed behavior (avolition)."[110] As the authors of the DSM-IV adamantly posited: "although quite ubiquitous in schizophrenia, negative symptoms are difficult to evaluate because *they occur on a continuum with normality*, are nonspecific, and may be due to a variety of other factors."[111] These factors, they further specified, include "environmental under-stimulation and demoralization."[112]

In the DSM-IV, "bizarre delusions" were deemed crucial in the definition of schizophrenia, and could qualify as *the single most important symptom* to satisfy the first criterion for the diagnosis (which would otherwise require two symptoms of the first criterion). The manual specifies that "bizarre" delusions are "clearly implausible and not understandable and do not derive from ordinary life experiences."[113] As an example, they offer the following hypothetical case: if a person believes that a stranger has removed their internal organs and replaced them with someone else's without leaving any wounds or scars, this clearly qualifies as a bizarre delusion. What would *not* be bizarre would be the alternative scenario – a delusion, which under the circumstances is, in fact, entirely plausible – where the individual believes that they are under police surveillance.

However, the DSM-IV also seems to suggest that the line that divides the normal from the pathological might be more blurred than it seems. In fact, as the authors go on to note, delusions can be understood as erroneous beliefs, and the distinction between a delusion and a *normal,* but strongly held, idea "is sometimes difficult to make and depends on the *degree* of conviction with which the belief is held despite clear contradictory evidence."[114] While one of the special characteristics of schizophrenic delusions is their bizarreness, the authors also admit that "bizarreness" may be quite difficult to discern and judge, especially since its meaning and impact might well depend on the different cultural contexts in which it is manifested.

In the same way that not all delusions would warrant a diagnosis of schizophrenia in DSM-IV, some hallucinations were also viewed as part of a *broader spectrum*, with those on a "range of normal experience," such as hallucinations occurring while falling asleep (called hypnagogic), and those the patient perceives while waking up (called hypnopompic). On this spectrum, the authors conclude, hallucinations can also be "a normal part of religious experience in certain cultural contexts."[115]

Thought disorders, as we saw, were the third symptom to classify schizophrenia and were what Bleuler considered "the single most important feature of schizophrenia." In the fourth edition of the manual, however, these were replaced by "disorganized speech." As part of their effort to rely exclusively on empirical observation (and because thoughts cannot be seen), the authors introduced disorganized speech as the outward, visible and audible symptom of the illness in question. From "derailment of speech" to speech that is "so *severely* disorganized that it is nearly incomprehensible and resembles receptive aphasia" (i.e., "word salad," as Bleuler called it), the DSM-IV paints a spectrum on which *mildly* disorganized speech is common and not specific to schizophrenia, but *severe* disorganized speech, which impairs effective communication, is.[116]

more spectrum

The fourth major symptom of schizophrenia, according to the manual, is disorganized behavior, which is at the core of the patient's difficulties in performing everyday activities. Here too, the idea of *range* is decisive, "from childlike silliness to unpredictable agitation."[117] As the manual states, disorganized behavior must be "*gross*" to qualify as a distinctive criterion. In other words, the individual's behavior needs to be unintelligible to fit the diagnosis of schizophrenia. The historical image of the madman, as "markedly disheveled" and displaying inappropriate behavior such as masturbating in public, shouting, or swearing, finds its place under this rubric and, for all purposes, counts as schizophrenic. That said, the authors also caution not to apply this criterion "too broadly," and make sure the behavior is in fact "grossly disorganized." In any case, Criterion B for schizophrenia involves dysfunction in one or more major areas of everyday functioning: interpersonal relations, work, education, or self-care. Individuals with schizophrenia are said to be less likely to complete their education, hold jobs, get married, or sustain social contacts.[118]

Following their agenda of producing a classification based on empirical research data, the authors of DSM-IV admitted that there were, as of yet, no laboratory findings that could identify schizophrenia. Nevertheless, they immediately added that structural abnormalities in the brain "have consistently been demonstrated in individuals with schizophrenia."[119] Using structural and functional imaging techniques, they claimed, had convincingly shown a host of possible indicators, such as the "enlargement of the ventricular system and prominent sulci in the cortex," "decreased temporal and hippocampal size, increased size of the basal ganglia, decreased cerebral size," "abnormal cerebral blood flow or glucose utilization in specific brain regions," especially in the prefrontal cortex.[120] Until the publication of their edition, brain abnormalities had only been reported with regard to organic disorders, but here, they surmised, "neurological soft signs" (i.e., neurological abnormalities that are not related to a specific area of the brain) could be observed in patients who are "physically awkward" or have poor coordination, and might be meaningfully cited as somehow associated with schizophrenia. Other physical anomalies that were introduced in the fourth edition were likewise based on physical characteristics, like having a "highly arched palate, narrow- or wide-set eyes or subtle malformations of the ears."[121]

The DSM-IV also urged clinicians to consider socioeconomic or cultural situations that differed from their own, both nationally and internationally. For example, while catatonic behavior was reported as relatively uncommon among those diagnosed with schizophrenia in the United States, it was common in non-Western countries. Furthermore, in developing countries, it was observed, individuals with schizophrenia had a more acute course of their mental illness, but also had a better outcome than those diagnosed in industrialized nations.

The importance attributed to the early onset of symptoms, which gave the name to *hebephrenia* or *dementia praecox*, was still relevant in the DSM-IV, a hundred years after it was first introduced. So was the case for the insistence on schizophrenia as a disorder with a dire prognosis. Complete remission was said to be rare, and while some cases might show a relatively stable course, others manifested a "progressive worsening associated with severe disability."[122] Although they tended toward biomedical and genetic factors in their classification of schizophrenia, the authors of the fourth edition of the manual also used a host of twin studies to confirm the importance of environmental factors.[123]

The DSM was further used for research purposes. Using the diagnostic criteria of the DSM-IV, research conducted in Australia, India, and Sarawak (Malaysia) underlined the individual and cultural variations linked to the diagnosis across the globe. For example, Indian individuals with schizophrenia were found to report negative symptoms far more frequently than in other places, whereas individuals from Sarawak, Malaysia, often made more claims of disorganized symptoms. In addition, "Schneiderian delusions" of control and thought broadcast, insertion or withdrawal (named after Kurt Schneider) were less frequent in Sarawak than in Australia. Curiously, a subgroup of 20 Indian individuals with schizophrenia reported no lifetime delusions or hallucinations whatsoever. These findings potentially challenged the long-held view in modern psychiatry that the general symptoms of schizophrenia were fundamentally similar across cultural groups, while the only difference could presumably be found in the content of the respective psychotic symptoms.

Cultural differences w/ Schizo symptoms and diagnoses.

Transition Toward the Spectrum of Schizophrenia

To summarize, the new definition of "schizophrenia" in the fourth manual required a one-month minimum of active-phase symptoms such as delusions, hallucinations, disorganized behavior, and speech (this was much longer than the DSM-III-R, which merely required one week). It stipulated that two or more of the following five symptoms needed to be present: delusions, hallucinations, disorganized speech, grossly disorganized or catatonic behavior, and negative symptoms. Moreover, a new categorization of symptoms was created that offered a broad spectrum of sorts, with "positive symptoms" (an excess or distortion of normal functions) and "negative symptoms" (a diminution or loss of normal functions).

Strikingly, according to the DSM-IV, there were 114 ways to be a schizophrenic (provided the person displays at least two elements out of the following: again, hallucinations, disorganized speech, grossly disorganized or catatonic behavior, negative symptoms or at least one element among bizarre delusions, running commentary voice, or two or more voices conversing). It was assumed that these were all associated with the same causes and could benefit from the same treatment.[124]

Between the publication of the DSM-IV in 1994 and DSM-5 in 2013, not much happened in terms of the different classifications in psychiatry. Similarly, the DSM-IV-TR ("TR" standing for Text Revised) introduced no major novelties. Nonetheless, in the ongoing scholarship on psychiatric classifications, diagnoses, and schizophrenia, the theoretical and clinical debates were rather lively. Scholars, philosophers, psychologists, and psychiatrists, among them Ian Hacking,[125] Nick Haslam,[126] Rachel Cooper,[127] John Sadler,[128] Kenneth Kendler,[129] and Peter Zachar,[130] incisively asked what kind of "things" psychiatric disorders actually *are*?[131] Do they exist in nature, and how can we come to know them? Indeed, were medical doctors and other clinicians using sociopolitical, practical, or scientific concepts to discuss schizophrenia and other mental disturbances? And how, if at all, could one classify mental disorders?

In fact, a chasm seemed to have opened up, between two extreme positions, that this book strives to make apparent. On the one hand, the "naive-realists" or "objectivists" (as they were called) saw mental disorders as definable, essence-based, and objective entities in nature.

They believed these were discoverable by carving psychiatric nature at its joints, as we saw. On the other hand, the opposed camp defended a dimensional perspective, viewing mental disorders as belonging on a *continuum*, a spectrum, along which people differ by degrees only. These scholars and scientists introduced alternative concepts, such as "practical kinds," "fuzzy kinds," "interactive kinds," "indifferent kinds," or simply "diagnostic kinds," to name just a few. They investigated the roles of different *values* which had implicitly been at play in the modern making of psychiatric classifications.[132] By contrast, others in this line of thought developed statistical techniques to examine diagnostic constructs.[133]

Some, like Nick Haslam, an Australian professor of psychology, suggested that, like other fields of medicine, psychiatry might adopt a plurality of diagnostic labels, some of which would amount to "practical kinds," while others would rely on the assumption of natural kinds. According to this interpretation, some mental disorders would be better suited to classifications made following a dimensional model, while others, on the contrary, would benefit far more from being viewed in terms of discrete kinds.

Alongside these scholarly critiques, the National Institute of Mental Health (NIMH) continued to push a research agenda aiming to examine the underlying systems that contribute to psychopathology by investigating what role genetics, epidemiological factors, cognitive psychological elements, or sociological features played in the onset of mental illnesses. Their researchers began developing a robust alternative for the DSM categories, and a radically new way of classifying psychopathology that might help to identify the causal mechanisms underlying (or cross-cutting) the syndromes listed in the latest DSM. As we noted in the introduction, by 2010, this latter project was baptized as the Research Domain Criteria (RDoC).[134]

The new project was supposed to base its efforts not only on manifest symptoms (the so-called "laundry lists"), but also on multiple levels of analysis, from the molecular to the social. Although the RDoC relied on the analysis of a wide variety of factors (such as fear, memory, attention, social communication, etc.), it was particularly focused on trying to discover the neural circuitry of psychopathology, using research methodologies drawn mainly from genetics and neuroscience.

An additional line of research was devoted not so much to rearranging the "forest" or discussing isolated "trees," to use Hacking's metaphor, but rather, to exploring the multiple ways in which clinicians and patients reacted to the classifications at hand.[135] For example, when asked about their application of the DSM-IV's criteria, clinicians admitted that they first tended to differentiate between organic and nonorganic disorders, and only then, between psychotic and neurotic disorders, just as the early editions of the DSM required.[136] Indeed, different generations of professionals believed that mental disorders found their origin and nature in *weaker essences*, that they were not as "real" or "natural" as organic disorders. Many held, furthermore, that these disorders had no single underlying cause.[137]

Using the criteria offered by the DSM-IV-TR, a study on the personal experience of those diagnosed with schizophrenia revealed striking differences with the more formal – at times, caricatured, and stereotyped – depictions in the DSM.[138] Although the personal experience of individuals revealed shared similarities among the cases covered by the DSM's five diagnostic criteria (delusions, hallucinations, disorganized speech, disorganized behavior, and negative symptoms), it also went well beyond what the manual stipulated. Participants in the study described strong emotional reactions to their symptoms – feelings unforeseen by the different editions of the DSM – such as fear, sadness, embarrassment, and alienation. In contradistinction with the common view, which characterizes schizophrenic patients as being generally indifferent, the study described the patients' intense interest in accomplishing personal goals, while highlighting their painful realization that engrossing, confusing, and distracting hallucinations were a serious obstacle in this process. For example, in his memoir *The Day the Voices Stopped*, Ken Steele describes the emotional turmoil caused by the announcement of an upcoming reunion with his parents, together with his growing worry that his condition would prevent him from interacting with them adequately:

> I should have been delighted by the news, but I was in turmoil. Past history became caught up in present expectations as I tried to deal with a multitude of emotions: anger, guilt, failure, sadness, excitement, expectation, rejection, acceptance, betrayal, and hope all at the same time … I was terrified that I

> might suffer a serious setback in my illness and desperately wanted to turn to my therapist for help.[139]

In its recommendations, the study concluded that the DSM-IV-TR criteria would greatly benefit from incorporating patients' personal experiences in its assessment – and proposed treatment – of schizophrenia.

Initially, the categories suggested by previous editions of the manual were meant to refer to syndromes and define disease entities for clinicians and researchers to use in their diagnosis of patients. However, through an almost inevitable process of reification, these categories and criteria then came to be perceived as reflecting natural disease entities, whose causes, treatments, and outcomes were roughly similar in all cases. Yet, although the categories and criteria were important in establishing – and enabling – professional communication about psychiatric entities, they also imposed arbitrary boundaries where, at best, only "fuzzy" lines of demarcation were to be found. In other words, it became increasingly apparent that in psychological and psychiatric matters, there was no such thing as a single, given "nature" to be carved at its joints.

As the planning of DSM-5 was already underway, a special issue of *Schizophrenia Bulletin* presented a selection of articles documenting the proceedings of a conference under the title "Deconstructing psychosis."[140] The conference belonged to a series devoted to "The Future of Psychiatric Diagnosis: Refining the Research Agenda," convened by the APA, in collaboration with the WHO and the US National Institutes of Health (NIH), with extensive funding provided by the latter. The journal issue's editorial was tellingly titled "Time for a fresh start? Rethinking psychosis in DSM-V."[141] Its guest editors were Carol Tamminga, a psychiatrist with specific interest in brain pathology in serious mental illnesses, and Jim van Os (a well-known advocate for the abolition of the diagnosis of schizophrenia and author of the 2016 article "Schizophrenia does not exist," to which we return in chapter 6).

"Deconstructing psychosis" focused on processing the massive scientific and clinical evidence that had been accumulated by a variety of research programs in diverse areas. For five years, scientists and clinicians from all over the world were asked to summarize evidence from their respective disciplines that could be relevant to diagnose psychotic disorders, including schizophrenia. They were also encouraged to consider the data in relation to the more general question of the representation of psychosis, in either categorical terms, or in a dimensional depiction of the phenomena on a continuous scale.

The aim of "Deconstructing psychosis" was not to provide quick recommendations or spell out which criteria to use for which categories in the future DSM-5. Rather, it attempted to assess to what degree current diagnostic practice was still in agreement with data gathered in clinical and basic research.

The conclusion of "Deconstructing psychosis" was that "although our diagnostic classification systems are reliable and useful, they have limited validity in defining biological entities because these are unknown for most mental illnesses."[142] The authors further claimed that "the existence of diagnostic labels with limited validity in psychiatry needs to be tackled and improved with each subsequent version" of their diagnostic systems. The mounting sense, in short, was that this could best be done by incorporating dimensional approaches into psychiatry's current categorical systems of diagnosis and classification. It is this task that the DSM-5 would set for itself. The shift from the bulky Roman numeral system to Arabic numbers was explained as the authors' intention for the manual to be "a living document," which could be easily revised and updated (such that we would see DSM-5.1 followed by DSM-5.2, etc.), based on the latest empirical and clinical evidence. In other words, it was clearly understood that psychiatry's targets would in all likelihood continue to move.

DSM-5 (2013): Shifting the Paradigm, the Schizophrenia Spectrum and Other Psychotic Disorders

The authors of the DSM-5, seeking to move away from categorical diagnoses, developing instead a dimensional approach to psychiatric diagnoses, included in the next edition of the manual the newly termed schizophrenia spectrum disorders. One of the cases with which they hoped to exemplify the new diagnosis was that of Ms. Allen:

> Felicia Allen was a 32-year-old woman brought to the ER by police after she apparently tried to steal a bus. ... According to the psychiatrist, Ms. Allen had received a diagnosis of "childhood-onset, treatment-resistant, paranoid schizophrenia." She had started hearing voices by age 5. Big, strong, intrusive,

> and psychotic, she had been hospitalized almost constantly since age 11. Her auditory hallucinations generally consisted of a critical voice commenting on her behavior. Her thinking was concrete, but when relaxed she could be self-reflective … She had spent almost no period of life developing normally and so had very little experience with the real world. Ms. Allen had been taking clozapine for 1 year, with good resolution of her auditory hallucinations. She had gained 35 pounds during that time, but she had less trouble getting out of bed in the morning, was hoping that she could eventually get a job and live more independently, and had insisted on continuing to take the clozapine. The bus trip to the shopping mall was intended to be a step in that direction. Diagnosis: Schizophrenia, multiple episodes, currently in active phase.[143]

The discussion of Ms. Allen, in the "clinical cases" section of the DSM-5, explains that schizophrenia was a heterogeneous disorder and that it affected a variety of *domains*. In fact, the vignette assumes that "it is likely that there are multiple schizophrenias, differentiated by as yet unknown markers."[144] The abandonment of categories in the new manual, it is further suggested, was due to insufficient evidence regarding their validity. Ms. Allen was thus diagnosed based on the activity and chronicity of her symptoms, as well as on grounds of the severity of the five core symptoms of schizophrenia, using a scale from 0 to 4.[145]

As we have seen, the debates that erupted between the publication of the DSM-IV and DSM-5 led to the inclusion of such dimensionality – the continuity of the spectrum – into the depiction of some disorders.[146] And, indeed, a major shift occurred as the authors of the DSM-5 expressly admitted, in their introduction to the new manual, that "we have come to recognize that *the boundaries between disorders are more porous than originally perceived.*"[147] As they explain, even though some mental disorders may have "well-defined boundaries around symptom clusters," scientific evidence now suggests that many disorders should be "placed on a spectrum with closely related disorders" with which they share symptoms, genetic and environmental risk factors, and possibly even neural substrates.[148] In explaining their dimensional approach to diagnosis, the authors further added:

> Because the previous DSM approach considered each diagnosis as categorically separate from health and from other diagnoses, it did not capture the

> widespread sharing of symptoms and risk factors across many disorders that is apparent in studies of comorbidity.[149]

As we saw, the earlier manuals produced narrow diagnostic categories that failed to capture the clinical reality where symptoms within the *same* mental disorders varied significantly. They were also unable to account for the substantial overlapping of these symptoms across *different* disorders. "Like most common human ills," as the authors of the DSM-5 note, "mental disorders are heterogeneous at many levels, ranging from genetic risk factors to symptoms." In the chapter discussing the actual use of the new manual, they therefore advised that until the exact causes of specific disorders were identified, allowing them to fully validate their diagnoses, the most important standard for the DSM-5 disorder criteria would remain their *clinical utility*, that is, their usefulness in determining the clinical course and treatment response of individuals grouped together by a given set of diagnostic criteria.[150]

In terms of the checklists of the disorders, the language of the DSM-5 is strikingly similar to that of DSM-IV. On a conceptual level, however, many radical changes clearly appear.[151]

The first is the disappearance of the multi-axial approach to diagnosis, which reflects a shift to a narrower, biomedical approach to mental disorders, as opposed to a model that also took psychological and social factors into account. This shift was justified as an attempt to shape the manual's diagnostic system in ways that matched the rest of medicine.[152]

The second major revision is the downplaying of harm in the general definition of mental disorders. The new definition merely states: "Mental disorders are *usually* associated with significant distress or disability in social, occupational, or other important activities."[153] As a result, under the DSM-5, individuals with symptoms indicative of schizophrenia, who were for the rest not harmed by their condition (or at risk of harming others), could still receive a diagnosis of schizophrenia. For example, if the person heard voices but was not harmed by them, then he or she would most likely still be diagnosed with schizophrenia.[154]

The third major innovation is the distinct neurological and genetical direction taken by the new manual. Although DSM-5 states that a diagnosis does not carry any necessary implications as to the causes of the individual's mental disorder, its revised chapter structure is deeply informed by "recent research in neuroscience" and by "emerging genetic linkages between diagnostic groups."[155] This new structure, it is argued, should improve clinicians' ability to "identify" a diagnosis in a *disorder spectrum*, "based on common neurocircuitry, genetic vulnerability, and environmental exposures."[156] Without the laboratory tests needed to determine the validity of their diagnoses, the authors of DSM-5 thus struggled anew to understand the relationship of various psychiatric disorders to each other, on the one hand, and to normal states (such as normal fantasy play in children, a normal part of religious experience, or a normal part of wake-sleep cycles), on the other.

Diagnoses needed to be backed by tests or at least a neurologic answer.

In fact, in preparation for the new manual, the so-called "Psychotic Disorders Work Group" proposed the new category of a very wide spectrum of schizophrenia and psychotic disorders. Accordingly, the members of the DSM-5 Task Force claimed that "the boundaries between many disorder 'categories' are more fluid over the life course than DSM-IV recognized."[157]

By the same token, the chapter on schizophrenia in the DSM-5 is organized along a "*gradient of psychopathology*." This dimensional model begins with conditions that "do not reach full criteria for a psychotic disorder or are limited to one domain of psychopathology." We subsequently find further conditions whose characteristics do reach full criteria, but are limited in time. Only then, in the manual, do we finally arrive at the diagnosis of a "schizophrenia spectrum disorder." This new broad group of symptoms ends up including "schizophrenia" on one end of the spectrum, and "schizotypal (personality) disorder" on the other. The word "personality" is given in parentheses – indicating a general indecisiveness on the part of the authors to locate symptoms in specific rubrics – as this same disorder was already (and still is) part of the chapters on personality disorders (including the schizotypal, schizoid, and paranoid types).

Disorders in the *broader spectrum* are, again, defined by abnormalities in one or more of the following five domains: delusions, hallucinations, disorganized thinking (speech), grossly disorganized or abnormal motor behavior (including catatonia), and negative symptoms.[158] To be diagnosed with the disorder, the patient needs to suffer from two out of five positive symptoms (belonging to the first three domains), provided one of these is having delusions, hallucinations, or disorganized thinking. The special attribution of bizarre delusions and Schneiderian first-rank auditory hallucinations (e.g., two or more voices conversing) were eliminated, as they were seen as unspecific and not reliable enough to distinguish bizarre from non-bizarre delusions. In the same way, the different subtypes of schizophrenia were removed from this edition due to their limited diagnostic stability, low reliability, and poor validity.[159] As we saw in the introduction to this book, Tony could not have been diagnosed as a "paranoid schizophrenic" *after* 2013, that is, after the publication of DSM-5.

In contrast to the tradition of seemingly endless subtyping, DSM-5 introduced an alternative explanatory and interpretative tool, that identifies *psychopathological dimensions.* These, it is now assumed, reveal the heterogeneity of schizophrenic symptoms in a manner that is both theoretically valid and – more importantly – clinically useful.[160] Indeed, the authors of the DSM-5 admit that the characteristic symptoms of schizophrenia involve a *range* of cognitive, behavioral, and emotional dysfunctions, with various degrees of severity.[161] They consider that individuals with the disorder will vary substantially with regard to most of these features, which shows that schizophrenia is increasingly seen as "a heterogeneous clinical syndrome."[162]

Interestingly, in a chapter entitled "Conditions for further study," the new manual discusses the highly controversial term "attenuated psychosis syndrome" (APS), to draw a less severe clinical picture than that of full-blown psychosis. APS is a diagnosis offered for individuals who are at *high risk* for psychosis. A subject of enormous controversy, APS was placed within the wide category of "other specified schizophrenia spectrum and psychotic disorders." Most of the individuals who would qualify for an APS diagnosis showed identifiable symptomology of anxiety, depression, or substance abuse. The fact that they often requested help for these symptoms was used as an argument to justify the symptomatic treatment they received, and to avoid assigning them "the more *traumatic diagnosis of schizophrenia.*"[163]

All these efforts to diagnose cases on the milder end of the spectrum would soon be criticized, partly because they included variants of normal behavior.[164] Although Thomas Insel, the head of the NIMH when the DSM-5 was published, concluded that psychiatry was lagging behind when it came to prevention (precisely because it failed to identify milder cases), his proposal meant to move psychiatry from "mental" or "behavioral" disorders, to disorders in the neurocircuitry in the brain, thus finding the milder cases in otherwise normal populations. The proliferation of the prefix *neuro-* in the new edition of the DSM (which even led some to argue it deserved to be renamed the NeuroDSM)[165] gave rise to concerns that social and psychological research, together with such early interventions, might be progressively – and fatally – excluded. Worries were voiced that the unholy "marriage of convenience" between psychiatry and psychopharmaceutical companies would end up using the newly suggested continuum model to dubious ends.

Indeed, the DSM-5 allowed the increasing diagnosis of less severe cases on the spectrum of schizophrenia, which would potentially lead to drug treatment as a preventive measure of choice, even for very mild cases. As Barnaby Nelson, an Australian clinical psychologist, cautioned in his report, "Don't jump the gun,"[166] prevention based on this kind of spectrum meant that individuals who were merely "at risk" for the disorder, might all of a sudden have to carry the stigmatizing diagnosis of a severe mental disorder. Worse, they might even be inappropriately prescribed heavy – and at times debilitating – anti-psychotic drugs.[167]

These fears were especially justified in the United States, as Patrick McGorry, a pioneer in high-risk mental states research and a member of the Australian group, pointed out. Indeed, McGorry underlined the urgent need to break "the nexus in the US that drug treatment is the main or only form of intervention for patients – a nexus reinforced by the hard neurobiological reductionism that took over American psychiatry from the 1980s."[168]

Enthusiastic as they were about the prospect of *preventing* cases of severe schizophrenia, those in the research field of patients at high risk quickly voiced their concerns. This "cautionary note" included calls for paying more attention to the "powerful peripheral forces, such as economic imperatives (managed care) or ideological policies (deinstitutionalization)," that could pose "great risk to patient care."[169] These policies, they warned, might inadvertently become the "new clouds to shut out the preventive sunshine."[170]

As we can see, not only did the DSM-5 receive ample criticism from the "realist, essentialist," that is, biomedically oriented psychiatrists (who were worried by the lack of biological markers, physiological risk factors, and genetic results required to determine mental illnesses).[171] Psychiatrists, more deeply invested in the opposed, psychosocial model, who were concerned that the DSM-5 heedlessly tilted in the direction of biological reductionism, also decried it.

A Moving Target

As Kieran McNally argues, schizophrenia has never been a stable object that remained identical, much less identifiable, throughout history.[172] In this chapter, we traced its instability and variance through the laborious and ingenious maze of the various editions of the DSM. Although many clinicians would admit that they "know a schizophrenic when they see one" (as private communications with them will quickly attest), the strict definition of schizophrenia has remained an elusive target. Similarly, the presumed boundaries between the normal and pathological – with which it stands and falls – have remained imprecisely demarcated, at any rate, seemingly impossible to draw with exactitude.

As we will demonstrate in chapter 6, schizophrenia had become a derogatory designation. An understandable demand was thus put on the members of the APA, asking that more recent studies, geared towards minimizing the stigma associated with the diagnoses, be considered in the next revision of the DSM.[173] And, indeed, the classification's own potential to produce harm – by facilitating stigma, overtreatment, and so on – is, for the first time, considered in the manual's latest adjustments and updates.

The DSM-5 openly acknowledges cases in which "the adoption of the proposed diagnosis exceed[ed] the benefit that would accrue to affected individuals."[174] False positives and their mistreatment, the legal and bureaucratic consequences of a given diagnosis, and the medicalization of "normal" individuals were considered as possible harmful consequences, alongside stigmatization and self-stigmatization. The aim, in short, was to ensure that diagnoses based on the manual would do more good than harm, and that proposals for eventual name changes should be considered with this in mind.

In our next two chapters, we will therefore discuss the efforts of patients, doctors, and advocates to demedicalize and depathologize hearing voices – a phenomenon that, as we saw in this chapter, became for diagnostic purposes a "first rank symptom" of schizophrenia, and was responsible for what some might call "false positives." We will also examine current debates and proposals to abolish the term "schizophrenia" altogether and rename the disorder. Indeed, as some advocates argued, due to the stigma it carries, the diagnosis of schizophrenia itself poses a serious challenge to the Hippocratic oath, which requires practitioners to "first do no harm."

Chapter 5
Hearing Voices

> I was sobbing uncontrollably when I felt a presence very near to me; I believed it was Jesus. I could speak with him, and he consoled me. Then I heard the voices of the Father of Heaven and Mary, the Blessed Virgin. Jesus' voice faded for the most part, and the voices of Mary and our Father remained with me during my odyssey into the depths of schizophrenia. I had crossed the line of faith into the evil world of schizophrenia. (Valerie Fox, "First person account: A glimpse of schizophrenia," 2002)[1]

Hearing voices – or "auditory verbal hallucinations" (AVH[2]) – was only an "accessory" symptom in the original definition of schizophrenia according to Bleuler, who coined the term. But since the publication of DSM-III, it has become one of the most defining symptoms of schizophrenia. Numerous patients diagnosed with schizophrenia report hearing voices. As Kevin Alan Lee describes in his book, *A Split Mind*:

> During my youth, I would hear voices only for a short duration of time and mainly at random. However, while in a deeply psychotic state, I would hear voices throughout much of the day ... The voices I heard would usually be speaking to me, as if I was having a telepathic conversation with them. These voices would sometimes encourage me to believe in certain things, act in a certain way, or perform a specific action ... While severely ill, I eventually concluded that these voices were communicating through a state-of-the-art microchip that was implanted into my head. I probably got this idea from my paranoid state of mind, in combination with something that I may have seen on television or in a movie.[3]

Voice-hearing can be experienced in a variety of ways by patients, ranging from benevolent messages to traumatizing persecution. Nevertheless, it seems that, at least from the perspective of the medical profession, voice-hearing is systematically considered as a sign of pathology, testifying to a discrete disease entity, as a symptom to be alleviated rather than a possible sign of human difference or a personal reaction to life's stresses. Some advocates have spoken up to counteract this perspective on voice-hearing. More specifically, the Hearing Voices Movement (HVM), a user-led, social movement, which appeared in the late 1980s in the Netherlands, has since then significantly challenged biomedical and naturalistic understandings of voice-hearing, particularly the link between auditory hallucinations and schizophrenia.

As the example of the Hearing Voices Movement will reveal, and as Simon McCarthy-Jones argues in his compelling book, *Hearing Voices: The Histories, Causes and Meanings of Auditory Verbal Hallucinations*, two "jostling discourses" of hearing voices have always existed side by side: the biomedical, pathological story, and the spiritual or otherwise meaningful story.[4] While the former understands voice-hearing as a sign of mental illness, the latter regards it as a potentially "significant, and (spiritually or psychologically) meaningful" human experience, as part of a continuum of human experience, rather than the sign of a distinct pathology. This tension between a medicalized and a more personal, if not thereby necessarily spiritual or religious, understanding of voice-hearing matches the broader, dual tension that we have been teasing out and highlighting in this book. According to the latter tension, the defining features of schizophrenia can be understood in terms of categorically different marks of a distinct illness, on the one hand, and as part of a continuous, wider spectrum that includes the normal as one of its dimensions, on the other.

A genealogical inquiry into voice-hearing teaches us that the medical discourse on this phenomenon can be traced far back in history, to antiquity and possibly even to ancient Egyptian and Mesopotamian times. In fact, throughout the history of voice-hearing, our dual paradigm can be found to re-emerge again and again, with a biological discourse considering it as a sign of pathology (possibly even of a damaged brain) and another conceiving of it as a natural capacity, available to all humans. According to the latter view, in some individuals (depending on life circumstances and other non-purely biological factors), such capacity can lead to distress, difficulty in coping, or overwhelming intensity, without this necessarily meaning that the individual in question is "sick," "unhealthy," or "abnormal."

The growth of the HVM, which situates voice-hearing on a spectrum that connects the normal and the "abnormal" and fights for the destigmatization and depathologization of auditory verbal hallucinations, went hand in hand with other professional and public efforts to abolish the diagnosis of schizophrenia. Indeed, the word "schizophrenia" itself was seen by the movement's founders as a harmful label that led to silenced patients and sufferers.

Although the history of hearing voices shows how the phenomenon became associated with insanity, it also reveals that, throughout, people have tried to liberate it from madness.[5] In fact, as McCarthy-Jones argues, in the West, the very concept of "hallucination" was invented during the mid-seventeenth century, when Church authorities sought to invalidate people's claims to having direct communications with the divine.[6] The medicalization of the discourse around voice-hearing thus appeared as part of a specific, well-circumscribed, and documented process that attempted to control, punish, and regulate those who claimed to possess mystical abilities of discerning the voice of God.

As with the very concept of schizophrenia, one must be cautious, therefore, when speaking of "auditory verbal hallucinations" (AVH), not to apply the concept to historical periods and societies that would not have described their experiences in these terms.[7] This is especially the case as the concept of AVH implies an objective, ontological existence of a pathological phenomenon, that is, something that exists "out there, independently of the psychiatric discourses and practices that attempt to define and to treat it."[8] In what follows, we will thus keep in mind psychiatric discourse's ability to create specific realities when it makes diagnoses, and the potential influence it has over the material that it claims to merely describe.[9] The example of hearing voices is particularly suited to make this clear. As Christopher Cook, in his 2019 book *Hearing Voices, Demonic and Divine*, argues, whereas psychiatry traditionally regarded schizophrenia and other diagnostic categories of psychosis as "categorically and qualitatively different" from normality, in recent years, psychotic-like experiences in the general population are increasingly seen as "being on a quantitative continuum" with mental illness.[10]

Hearing Voices in the Ancient World

> And when the Lord saw that he turned aside to see, God called unto him out of the midst of the bush, and said Moses, Moses. And he said, Here am I. (Exodus 3:4)

> Also I heard the voice of the Lord, saying, Whom shall I send, and who will go for us? Then said I, Here am I; send me. (Isaiah 6:8)

Voice-hearing is hardly a recent phenomenon and can be traced back to the earliest scriptures of the Hebrew Bible. Cook, whom we cited above, recalls how God was heard by Adam and Eve, as well as by Cain, Noah, Abraham, Isaac, Rebekah, and Jacob, all of whom are described as having substantial conversations with the Lord. In the book of Genesis, humans also hear the voice of a serpent (in the case of Eve), as well as those of angels (in the case of Hagar, Abraham, and Sarah and Lot). However, in the subsequent books of the Torah, the Prophets, and Writings (also known as the Old Testament), the Lord gradually "speaks less and less" to humans. As Richard Friedman argues, in the early chapters of Genesis,[11] God spoke to humans in familiar conversation, but from then on, mostly speaks through the intermediary of an angel.[12] And when at Mount Sinai the Israelites hear the voice of God, they are so terrified that they ask Moses to speak, pleading "let not God speak with us lest we die."[13] Friedman sees this shift as the beginning of prophecy.

The prophets of the Old Testament, whom we encountered in chapter 1, heard the voice of God. While God answered Moses "in thunder," Elijah heard a "sound of sheer silence," and the major prophets, notably Isaiah (as we saw in the epigraph to this section), Jeremiah, and Ezekiel, received revelations through visions, auditions, thoughts, and ideas. In either case, Cook argues, the receptive part of this process is regarded as "an act of speech on the part of God, and in this sense, we can say that God 'has spoken.'"[14] Though we cannot know the experience of the prophet, we do know that hearing voices played an important part in it. And not all voices were benign. Indeed, the Judeo-Christian scriptures contain voices that incited genocide, including the murder of innocent infants and children. In sum, Hebrew prophecy seems to have been an experience of both hearing and conveying voices, but not all those who claimed to hear voices were prophets. There were those who falsely claimed to hear voices (liars, or those who simply said what people wanted to hear, each often motivated by gain), but also those who genuinely heard voices, that were not necessarily inspired or authoritative. That said, in principle, there was no reason to believe that someone who was mentally ill could not also be a prophet.[15]

During Greek Antiquity, ample records of the phenomenon of voice-hearing can, likewise, be found. In *The Greeks and the Irrational,* E. R. Dodds explains that the most common type of hallucination in Ancient Greece was that of individuals experiencing visions of gods or hearing divine voices during the waking state, mostly conveying a message, which "commands or forbids the performance of certain acts."[16] One of the most famous examples of voice-hearing in Ancient Greece is that of Socrates (469–399 BCE), who famously heard the voice of his "daemon" address him since childhood. As Socrates describes it, the voice "always deters me from the course of action I was intending to engage in, but it never gives me positive advice."[17] The voice thus appeared, as A. A. Long puts it, "in moments when he found himself seriously divided over the right course of action to follow."[18] Nevertheless, although it provided valuable moral guidance, if only negatively, the question of Socrates' voice was raised at his trial where he was condemned to death for introducing new divinities into the Polis. As M. L. McPherran argues, Socrates' ability to hear a divine voice without going to the temple (that is, his intimate relationship with the divine) produced "envy, hatred and slander" in others, because his voice had not been "licensed by the state."[19] Indeed, in this ancient polytheistic society, only "priests, necromancers and oracles" were supposed to experience voices, but "ordinary persons ... did not ... expect to hear the voice of a divinity."[20]

Aristotle (384–322 BCE), the empirically minded Ancient Greek philosopher, introduced a more naturalistic perspective, explaining voice-hearing as "internally arising voice-traces" being mistaken by the person for coming from without.[21] Indeed, according to Aristotle, sensory perception of external objects created physical changes in the body that left traces behind of the perception or image (called "phantasms," which were important for exercising the faculty of imagination). Yet these "phantasms" can sometimes be mistaken for external perceptions, which creates what we now call hallucinations. In Aristotle's own words, "even when the external object of perception has departed, the impressions it has made persist and are themselves objects of perception: and let us assume, besides, that we are easily deceived respecting the operations of sense-perception when we are excited by emotion."[22]

During Roman Antiquity, biological explanations of voice-hearing appeared for the first time, as more specific instances of the naturalizing accounts of madness, which we described in chapter 1. These types of accounts mostly explain voice-hearing as an excess of black bile in the body, even though a socially acceptable framework for voice-hearing was also prevalent at the time. McCarthy-Jones cites the example of the festival of Parentalia during which good spirits were honored.[23] During the second century CE, Aurelius Cornelius Celsus, whom we met in chapter 1, distinguished between hallucinations, which occur in *phrenesis* (the acute delirium that arises with a fever), in melancholia (which lasts longer and occurs in the absence of fever), or in the class of madness that seems to emerge without a cause.[24] Celsus further differentiated between hallucinations with a "gloomy" nature and those with a "cheerful" outlook and mood. This type of biological conception led to a primarily physical treatment of hallucinations, based on humoral theory. Purging or using hellebore, for example, were prescribed to rid the individual from the excess of black bile.[25]

In the New Testament, by contrast, hearing voices was an indication of external supernatural communication, whether with the divine, or with demons. Although there are relatively few accounts of hearing voices in Christian scripture, those that are identifiable as such are deeply significant, according to Cook.[26] Voices experienced as an encounter with the divine could be attributed to angels, as in the case of Mary being visited by the angel Gabriel. By the same token, the birth of Jesus was announced to the shepherds by the angel, which implies that a voice was heard.[27] Other examples abound, and include a voice from heaven being heard at Jesus' baptism, and later on, Jesus being tempted in the wilderness and hearing the voice of Satan.[28] Saul (who will become Paul) also heard a voice at his conversion, reported in the Acts of the Apostles,[29] and the New Testament concludes with an apocalyptic visionary panorama, which includes many voices, in the Revelation of John.[30]

As McCarthy-Jones argues, one of the central effects Christianity had on voice-hearing in later centuries was to modify the deeper meaning attributed to the events of our inner lives: "thoughts become moralized, and this needs to be monitored: 'You were now morally responsible for what happened in your head.'"[31] From then on, although they were not necessarily seen as pathological signs *per se*, voice-hearing experiences were nevertheless treated suspiciously, with the looming influence of the devil deemed "ever-present."[32]

An important author in this respect, who wrote extensively about voices in the Christian era, was St. Augustine (354–450). Augustine proposed a tripartite model of Man, whose being he divided into body, soul, and spirit. While the soul[33] was a living thing equipped with reason and created by God to rule the body, the spirit[34] was the deepest part of "inner man" and the site of communication, if not communion, with God.[35] This tripartite model created a structure where the self is open to divine and demonic intrusions alike. Augustine further distinguished between three different types of visions: corporeal, imaginative, and spiritual/intellectual. This distinction applied directly to the auditory experiences of voice-hearing, or "locutions," as they were called at the time.

On the one hand, "corporeal locutions" were perceived through the body, via the senses. Indeed, the exterior voice appears to be "speaking externally" to the subject and to be heard by the "outward ear," as would be the case when we hear natural speech.[36] "Imaginative locutions," on the other hand, were experienced as a "distinct" interior voice, which speaks clearly but is recognized to be inside one's mind.[37] These, for Augustine, are caused by memories, or "fictitious images, fashioned by the power of thought."[38] In "spiritual/intellectual locutions" however, a voice is heard, but "without any sound or words." It is directly "imprinted" – that is, it leaves an indelible impression – on the spirit via the intellect, without involving the senses.[39] As it happens, such an "inarticulate voice"[40] leaves "more of an impression" than actual, definite words.[41]

Christianity assigned different spiritual value to these three kinds of voices: while "imaginative" locutions were treated suspiciously by the Church, not least because their precision made them more difficult to "resist,"[42] and since "corporeal" ones were always already regarded with "suspicion and dislike,"[43] it fell to "spiritual/intellectual" locutions to be granted the highest status among them. And, while corporeal and imaginative locutions were far more likely to stem from demonic forces, voices heard without any sound or words (spiritual/intellectual locutions) were considered more uniquely suited to come from a possibly divine source. At the same time, and for the same reasons, "visionaries" – that is, individuals who experienced visual, rather than merely auditory, hallucinations – were held in much higher esteem than voice-hearers (including those experiencing "spiritual/intellectual" locutions), in great part because the eyes were believed to be the window to the soul, "making it the desired form of divine communication."[44]

Women and Voice-Hearing in Medieval Times

> And behold! In the forty-third year of my earthly course, as I was gazing with great fear and trembling attention at a heavenly vision, I saw a great splendor in which resounded a voice from Heaven, saying to me, "O fragile human, ashes of ashes, and filth of filth! Say and write what you see and hear." (Hildegard of Bingen, *Scivias*, 1990)[45]

Women's accounts of hearing divine voices began to appear in late medieval and early modern Europe. Hildegard of Bingen (1098–1179), for example, often considered the first medieval female mystic, claimed to have visions and hear the voice of God (see figure 8). As she wrote, "I heard the voice from Heaven saying to Me, 'Speak therefore of these wonders' ... Again I heard a voice from Heaven saying to me, 'Cry out and write!'"[46] Although the Church authenticated Hildegard's voices as being of divine origin, religious authorities often struggled to silence women's accounts of voice-hearing throughout the medieval and early modern period.[47]

In the twelfth century, a new understanding of possession emerged. The phenomenon was now conceived as capable of occurring without any bodily manifestations, that is, in a purely spiritual – or, put anachronistically, in a strictly psychological – way.[48] While in late medieval times, women who exhibited "spiritual uniqueness" would come to be seen and accepted as "prophetesses, visionaries, divine guides and saints," by the early sixteenth century, the Church's theological and institutional anxieties led to them being regarded primarily as "witches, victims of possession or fakes."[49]

One key medieval author, who took great care to separate individuals who were merely "mad" from those who actually experienced divine

Figure 8 Hildegard von Bingen (1098–1179)
Source: Wikimedia Commons

communication, was Thomas Aquinas (1225–74). In his central theological opus, the *Summa Theologiae*, Aquinas followed Aristotle (or, as he called him, "the Philosopher") in his explanation of voice-hearing, claiming that the same type of activity of the humors that occurs when dreaming, could also occur during the waking state. As Aquinas writes, "the commotion of the spirits and humors may be so great that such appearances may even occur to those who are awake, as is seen in mad people and the like."[50] In these latter cases, the cause of "madness" or *phrenesis* is to be found in the body. And yet, Aquinas acknowledges that those individuals who experienced "naturally occurring" hallucinations (as opposed to those of supernatural origin) are still often thought to be prophets. Although Aquinas believed that angels could carry divine messages and induce voices by moving "the spirits and humors from within"[51] (just as he claimed that "the devil sometimes utters what is false," but "the Holy Ghost never"[52]), individuals who experienced "naturally" occurring hallucinations were, in his view, "foolish and mad ... not true but false prophets"; after all, "they speak a vision of their own heart, and not out of the mouth of the Lord."[53]

Aquinas was also keen to understand exactly how God could communicate with finite humans. Being the direct recipient of voices, he noted, was not enough to make one a prophet; rather, one also needed to correctly interpret the voices. As McCarthy-Jones summarizes, for Aquinas, the ability to interpret the meaning of such experiences was said to occur "through the bestowing of a divine prophetic light (*lumen propheticum*) on the individual."[54] That said, during medieval times, the Christian Church remained extremely cautious in its willingness to acknowledge or sanctify those individuals that could rightly have claimed to have heard supernatural voices. As McCarthy-Jones notes, before, after, and during the Middle Ages, the established Church did not automatically assume that an individual who heard voices was possessed or being spoken to by God or the Devil.[55] Indeed, Christian thinkers had a wide arsenal of both naturalistic and supernatural explanations for the phenomenon of hearing voices, with biology entering into both types of accounts.[56]

In response to scholastic approaches such as those of Aquinas, at the time, the idea of a personal relation with the divine (or with Christ) re-emerged and asserted its authority. This led to the emergence of a mode of thinking (and of agency) that would soon take the spiritual and practical form of "a prominent mysticism," based on emotion and personal introspection.[57] During the fourteenth century especially, numerous mystics, many of whom were women, experienced visions and heard voices. Some of these, such as St. Birgitta of Sweden (1303–73), who heard the voice of the Virgin Mary, or St. Catherine of Siena (1347–80), who, like St. Birgitta, militated to convince Pope Gregory XI to move the papacy from Avignon back to Rome,[58] played important political roles due to the authority granted to them by their divine voice-hearing. This power given to women was resented and resisted by some. A case in point is the theologian Jean Gerson, who suspected that Gregory XI had been "seduced" by female visionaries, accusing St. Birgitta and St. Catherine of having caused the Great Western Schism (the period in the Roman Catholic Church, from 1378 to 1417, when there were two, then three rival popes, each with his own following, his own Cardinals, and his own administrative offices).[59] Indeed, political opponents attacked both women,[60] in a tense historical situation, where many deemed the Great Schism "a satanic means to increase confusion," making it all the more urgent to discern between divine and demonic voices.[61]

But some of the female mystics of the time, such as Julian of Norwich (1342–1416), whose hearing of voices occurred during a near-fatal illness, could clearly discern between what they experienced as the graceful heavenly words received directly from God and those troublesome words that were diabolic. While God revealed his words to Julian "very gently, voicelessly, and without opening his lips," telling her "you shall not be overcome," and while Jesus famously said to her "all shall be well, and all shall be well, and all manner of things shall be well,"[62] the devil's voices were in fact quite different:

> After this the devil came back with his heat and stench and preoccupied me … I could also hear an audible jabbering and a talking, as though it were two people, and both to my way of thinking were jabbering at once, as if they were busily debating something; and it was all low muttering I understood nothing they said, but I thought all this was to drive me to despair. (Julian of Norwich, *Revelations of Divine Love*, 2015 [1675])[63]

Margery Kempe (1373–1438), who visited Julian and was encouraged by the anchorite to continue on her spiritual path, heard the voices of devils, saints, and of Jesus. She could discern which was frightening, which ones she heard "with her physical ears," and which voice was that of the Lord, who spoke directly to her:

> And soon the merciful Lord, present everywhere, said to her, comforting His unworthy servant "Daughter, it is more pleasing to me that you suffer humiliation and scorn, injustice and distresses, than if your head was chopped off three times a day, every day for seven years."[64]

Among women who claimed to have heard voices during this historical period, Joan of Arc (*c.*1412–31) was probably the most famous example. Her life and fate also exemplified how risky revelations of this nature truly were. As is well known, Joan was burnt at the stake at the age of 19.

On the second day of her trial, on February 22, 1431, she confessed: "I was thirteen when I had a Voice from God for my help and guidance. The first time that I heard this voice, I was very much frightened."[65] The archangel Michael admonished her to be pure and holy and religious. She also heard St. Catherine the Virgin and St. Margaret who told her to go into France to relieve Orléans.[66] Until the end of her life, Joan of Arc insisted that her voices came from God and were not meant to deceive her but to guide her. But since voices perceived as emanating from an external source were considered the lowest form, her voice-hearing was viewed with suspicion by ecclesial authorities. Moreover, the voices were speaking French (the language of the masses) rather than Latin (the language of the clergy), which made them lack authority from the moment they were uttered and heard. In sum, then, since layperson and female testimonies of voice-hearing were perceived as active threats to religious authorities, they were increasingly pathologized and persecuted.

What was the proper response to hearing voices, then, and what was the right way of discerning and dealing with them? If any such extraordinary revelations should happen to an individual person, then he or she, so the Church reasoned, should reject them with holy, humble, and diffident modesty. Such a person should, first of all, think of such matters as resulting from an injured or dysfunctional imagination (as a distinctive function of a faculty of the soul to conceive things) and, hence, should worry about being ill, in the very same way that insane, manic, or depressive people were.[67] How many among those who were exposed to these phenomena felt compelled to follow these instructions rather than suffer the consequences? And how much of the Church's invectives and condemnations were internalized by whole systems of knowledge and learning – medicine and psychiatry included – in subsequent centuries, to this very day?

As they have done with Julian of Norwich and Margery Kempe, who were retrospectively diagnosed as suffering from various psychiatric disorders, modern scholars have assigned psychiatric labels to Joan of Arc, ranging from multiple personality disorder[68] to psychopathy,[69] and even schizophrenia.[70] Yet, as Cook shows, others chose a more cautious approach and placed the voice-hearing in its specific, religious, historical, and cultural context.[71] Doing so has led to more nuanced pictures and portraits of these respective figures. Indeed, notwithstanding the significance of the three aforementioned women and the voices they claimed to have heard, many witnesses and authoritative writers throughout the late medieval period expressed serious concern about the phenomena in question. Walter Hilton (*c.*1340–96), an English Augustinian canon, is a case in point. Hilton made a distinction between "true" voice-hearing, that was based on inner spiritual virtues and reflected "true knowledge and perception of God and spiritual things," on the one hand, and a less trusted array of voices, visions, and other sensible experiences, "whether of sound, taste, smell, or of warmth felt like a glowing fire in the breast or in other parts of the body," on the other.[72] Hilton argued that true contemplation consisted in a "spiritual feeling," that is, an awareness of God that occurred within the soul and the mind, as opposed to bodily sensations and perceptions. Only the genuine mystic, who lived a life of virtue, would eventually be able to hear the "hidden voice of Jesus" within.[73]

The Renaissance and Onward to the Protestant Reformation

From the Renaissance onwards, voices were increasingly viewed as intrusive thoughts rather than as external, that is, "spiritual" visitations. To give one example, Johann Weyer's (1515–88) work *De prestigiis daemonum et incantationibus ac venefiis* ("On demonic manifestations, incantations and magicians"), published in 1563, claimed that witches were not directly or externally affected by the devil, but merely suffered from hallucinations caused by melancholy, that is, from a disease with internal, physical causes.[74]

The printing revolution of the 1540s, and the numerous copies of the Bible that were subsequently disseminated, caused a significant increase in the already growing questioning of the clergy's interpretation of religious scripture, including its efforts at moderating or punitively disciplining marginal figures and movements, female mystics and women's orders among them.[75] In 1517, the flame of the Protestant Reformation was lit, so the legend goes, when Martin Luther – who at the time was still a small-town monk – nailed the "Ninety-Five Theses on the Power and Efficacy of Indulgences" to the door of Wittenberg Cathedral.[76] The upheavals that ensued and the protestation against the doctrines and practices of the Roman Catholic Church went hand in hand with a radical change in the understanding of voice-hearing.

Protestantism, as a doctrine that values the individual's – rather than the clergy's or tradition's – interpretation of scripture, put forth a general conception where anyone should be able to interpret their own religious experience, their reading of particular passages, and their relation to God, independently; provided that such hermeneutics remained in line with the overall tenet of the Bible's insistence on "justification by grace and faith alone." By extension, the Reformers also resisted the purely medical explanations of phenomena such as voice-hearing. Luther, who was faced with many self-proclaimed "prophets" that claimed to be in direct contact with the voice of God, even without the mediation of scripture, famously concluded that a simple maxim allowed the separation of the wheat from the chaff: one could hear from God, but if it contradicted scripture, it was not God speaking.[77]

Accordingly, on grounds of principle, Luther resisted the medicalization of religious voice-hearing, further criticizing the tendency of physicians to overwrite spiritual explanations with proto-medical ones. In fact, Luther explicitly remarked that medical doctors "draw conclusions about the nature of the constitution of the blood or the whole body" of the voice-hearer, rather than acknowledging the possible divine nature of the voices thus communicated.[78] As he observed, such physicians "say that one's complexion or melancholy is to blame, or the heavenly planets, or they invent some other natural cause," for the seemingly inexplicable, but potentially spiritual, phenomena in question.[79] Against these medical approaches, Luther argued that divine visions and voices were not necessarily "melancholy dreams that have no bearing on reality," but should be seriously examined as eventual signs of God speaking to the individual.[80] Yet, just as there was a putative "decline of magic" in modern religion, as Keith Thomas showed in his massive study *Religion and the Decline of Magic*,[81] there also was a decline in credibility, it seems, of spiritual communication – whether direct or indirect – through the mediation of supranatural voices.

By the mid-eighteenth century, the medicalization of hearing voices had progressed even further, and the educated elite now largely tended to believe that "people who claimed to have divine inspirations or devilish afflictions were insane."[82] In his 1758 *Treatise on Madness*, for instance, William Battie maintained that someone who is "fully and unalterably persuaded of the existence or of the appearance of any thing, which either does not exist or does not actually appear to him, and who behaves according to such erroneous persuasion," is "properly mad."[83]

As McCarthy-Jones argues, the new sense of self that began to develop in the West from the sixteenth century onwards was fundamentally "antithetical" to the experience of hearing voices.[84] The Reformation had given voice-hearers a chance to attribute their own meaning to their most intimate religious experience, and sixteenth-century Spanish mystics such as St. Teresa of Ávila (1515–82), who, when she first heard the voice of the Lord was reported to be terrified, later developed her own theory of "these spiritual voices."[85] During this time, St. John of the Cross (1542–91), too, elaborated his detailed "phenomenological analysis" of voices and was especially wary of voices perceived by way of bodily hearing: the more exterior and corporeal these things are, the less certain is their divine origin, he wrote in *The Ascent to Mount Carmel*.[86] But not only was the risk of deception extensively commented upon during this period, in England, the Anglican Church also "unleash[ed]" medicine onto voice-hearers.[87] This inevitably led the tradition of voice-hearing to lose some of its earlier force and radiance, and, indeed, much of its deeper and richer meaning, as its manifestations became increasingly pathologized in official circles.

That said, while educated elites accepted the new, reductive medical theories, the lay population, by contrast, remained much less convinced, which was in part due to medicine's inability to efficiently relieve voice-hearers from their distress.[88] During the seventeenth century, the authority to discriminate between the true and false was transferred from theological discourses and ecclesial bodies to their medical counterparts, which further led to the pathologization of voice-hearing in religious dissenters, women, and marginal groups. At the beginning of the nineteenth century, however, the medical establishment had "full authority" over the matter in question.[89] This victory and hegemony paved the way for the idea that hallucinations, as was commonplace around the *fin-de-siècle*, were considered as being, in fact, signs of mental illness. In this context, the developing scientific psychiatric discourse and practice of the time was presented as the only adequate theoretical and clinical, interpretative and therapeutic framework, to both understand and treat them successfully.[90]

Hearing Voices and Modern Psychiatry

> It speaks to me all the time, said one of them, it told me that it is necessary to go and ask the Pope for a pardon. – Do you know who speaks to you? – No, I don't recognize it, it is not the voice of anybody. – The voice is it far or near? – It is neither far nor near, one would say that it is in my chest. – Is it like a voice? – Not really, it is not a voice, I do not hear anything, I sense I am spoken to. (Pierre Janet, *L'automatisme psychologique*, 1973 [1889])

In *Mysticism*, her famous book from 1911, Evelyn Underhill, an English philosopher and a mystic, writes that "pathology and religion have both been over-hasty in their eagerness to snatch" at the complex phenomenon of voice-hearing, and have done so mostly "for their own purposes."[91] At the end of the nineteenth century, as testified by the epigraph of this section, medical doctors, such as the French psychiatrist Pierre Janet, studied altered states of consciousness and, more specifically, the phenomenon of voice-hearing, which they understood as a manifestation of the *disrupted* integration of psychological functioning. Medicine and psychiatry increasingly took over from the Church, thus preparing the overwhelming tendency to pathologize and culturally depreciate the various forms of voice-hearing that define the default prejudice against its manifestation to this very day.

At first, the phenomenon of hearing voices was categorized as merely a symptom of mental disorders in nineteenth-century asylums.[92] With the rise of scientific medicine, doctors in asylums sought to explain even more singular, unfamiliar, and abnormal psychological phenomena in scientific terms. From there on, they invoked and used the technical term "delusions" to describe the mental state of patients who heard voices. Even when patients invoked their auditory experiences in expressly religious terms (including the conviction that they were sinners if they heard such voices in the first place), physicians did not hesitate and, in the same medical and psychiatric register, labeled their experiences as "religious delusions," that is, as pathologies.

In an 1846 article published in the medical journal *The Lancet*, John Conolly, the superintendent at the Hanwell asylum who served on the national Lunacy Commission to oversee county asylums in England and Wales, wrote accordingly: "Delusive impressions as to sound are very troublesome to many patients; they hear voices, and hold conversations and arguments; and they fancy their relatives are imprisoned, or that persons are allowed to persecute them."[93] Case studies from asylums show a 28-year-old female patient who, it was reported, "sees individuals who are not present, such as Louis Philippe & the Pope," and added that "she hears persons under her bed."[94] Yet another woman was said to suffer "various delusions such as hearing voices in the night and fancying that horses are being changed into men." Nevertheless, so-called "hallucinations of hearing" were not yet considered as symptoms of any *particular* type of insanity. They could be experienced, it was widely held, by patients diagnosed with melancholia, mania, dementia, and general paralysis, as well as "alcoholic insanity."

A professional interest in the scientific classification of voice-hearing, which began with Janet, who distinguished between "verbal hallucinations" (involving language, including writing, and the feeling of being addressed via a linguistic medium), on the one hand, and "hallucinations of the sense of hearing" (notably of external voices), on the other, was also prevalent among German-speaking psychiatrists. The German neurologist, Richard von Krafft-Ebing, for his part, tried not only to classify different kinds of hallucinations and to discover the order underlying them, but was especially interested in establishing the different biological etiologies that would shed light on their genesis. "Voices," in Krafft-Ebing's categorization, were accordingly to be distinguished from different kinds of "ordinary sense perceptions."[95]

Like Janet and Krafft-Ebing, Kraepelin (who, as we saw in chapter 2, had coined the term *dementia praecox* to differentiate a peculiar set of symptoms from those of manic-depressive insanity) was also interested in what he called a "special type of disturbance of hearing" that included "inner voices," as well as "whisperings," "telephoning," and "telegraphing."[96] Although Kraepelin was primarily interested in the biological causality of these symptoms, in the second chapter of his *Dementia Praecox and Paraphrenia*, he nonetheless invoked a form of *agitated dementia praecox*, whose victims he vividly depicted as being typically marked by the experience of voice-hearing:

> What the voices say is, as a rule, unpleasant and disturbing. "The voices rushed in on me at all times as burning lions," said a patient. The patient is

> everywhere made a fool of and teased, mocked, grossly abused, and threatened. People speak about him; everyone is occupied with him; the whole workshop screams; "there is a petty espionage," "like legal proceedings"; he hears voices, "as one reads of them in stories of murder and Indians." Someone calls out: Rascal, vagrant, miserable scoundrel, "incendiary, parricide," "good for nothing," "anarchist, rogue, thieving murderer," "filthy fellow, filthy blockhead, filthy beast," "vagabond," "scamp," "swine," "filthy swine," ... "town whore," ... "criminal, criminal," "offended, offended." ... [T]he patient is threatened with having his ears cut off, his feet chopped off, with being sawn asunder, with being beheaded; there is a command from the government to stab him.[97]

Kraepelin reported that patients heard, among other things, cocks crowing, shooting, birds chirping, bees humming, murmurings, screaming, scolding, voices from the cellar. The voices, moreover, mostly aggressively insulted the patient.

Yet voice-hearing was hardly the central characteristic of Kraepelin's broader diagnosis of *dementia praecox*, his signature concept. Bleuler's introduction of the term schizophrenia even further minimized the significance of hearing voices in the emerging pathological picture of the disorder. In 1911, Bleuler proposed that auditory verbal hallucinations (AVH) merely belonged to the accessory symptoms of schizophrenia. For him, they were merely a by-product of the patient's "loosened associations," as we will recall, one of the four fundamental symptoms of the disease.[98] As we discussed in chapter 2, Bleuler also intimated that the content of the voices might be understood in specifically psychological terms. While Kraepelin still associated voice-hearing with the excitation of *sensory* centers, Bleuler felt that this characterization of the phenomenon failed to "do sufficient justice to the fact that hallucinations express entire strivings."[99] In Bleuler's own view, then, one could surely find "wishes and fears, strivings and their obstacles," hidden underneath or within the voices, that served as expressions of "thoughts, fears and drives."[100] Bleuler even added that "[i]n part (possibly entirely) the overt symptomatology certainly represents the expression of a more or less unsuccessful attempt to find a way out of an intolerable situation,"[101] thus emphasizing the psychological dimension that, as we will see below, would eventually become a basic tenet of the Hearing Voices Movement's own understanding of the phenomenon.

Jung's ideas, which we examined in chapter 3, would also resurface among the central ideas governing the HVM, from its foundation to this very day. Jung believed the hearing of voices consisted in meaningful experiences. Even when he viewed it as part of schizophrenia, he concluded that there was "no symptom which could be described as psychologically groundless and meaningless."[102] Keeping up with the psychodynamic view of health and illness, Jung rejected the reduction of voices to a mere "disease of the brain cells."[103] He linked voice-hearing to normal phenomena such as dream production and repressed complexes that force themselves "across the threshold of consciousness."[104]

However, despite these psychodynamic approaches to voice-hearing, during the mid-twentieth century, the meaning of the phenomenon was still undergoing critical debate within the discipline of psychiatry. Numerous key psychiatric figures (such as the American psychiatrist Karl Menninger) maintained that voices in "normal" people were rare and that when they did occur, they were "typically signs of psychosis."[105] Others, on the contrary, argued that voices could also be found in sane people. In other words, the question of whether voice-hearing should be understood as symptomatic of a kind of pathology or as an extreme mental state on a single continuum of psychological phenomena was far from being resolved at the time. Although voice-hearing does not appear in the text of DSM-I, and only appears once in the DSM-II, hallucinations increasingly became associated with psychosis, in general, and with schizophrenia, in particular. As we can see in the first-person account that follows, the experience of hearing voices was tied to the fear of being medically diagnosed as insane:

> "You're alone," an insidious voice told me. "You're going to get what's coming to you" … "You're going down there," a voice that sounded like Joy's hissed at me. "You wait until you see what I'm going to do to you." No one moved or looked startled. It was just me hearing the voice. I tried not to answer it. Better to ignore the voice, repress it, and soldier on, I thought. … I did not want to look mad, like them. Any symptoms of hearing voices would go on medical case notes, be raised as proof of insanity and keep me locked up in the hell of the ward away from family and friends and what seemed

> like a long-distant normal life. (Benjamin Gray, "Hidden demons: A personal account of hearing voices and the alternative of the Hearing Voices Movement," 2008)[106]

While the first three major scholarly authorities on the diagnosis of schizophrenia – namely Kraepelin, Bleuler, and Jung – included the phenomenon of voice-hearing in the array of symptoms making up the disorder, none gave it such a central role as did the German psychiatrist Kurt Schneider (1887–1967), whom we met in the previous chapter. From a mere "accessory symptom," to use Bleuler's term, Schneider, as it were, upgraded the voice-hearing phenomenon by placing it among the "first rank symptoms" of schizophrenia. Among the seven suggested types of hallucinations and delusions pertaining to these symptoms, he included audible thoughts, voices arguing and/or discussing, voices commenting, somatic passivity experience, thought withdrawal/influenced thought, thought broadcasting, and delusional perceptions. Although some decades later, these hallucinations and delusions would be named after him – namely Schneiderian symptoms – he was cautious and modest in his assessment of their role. Schneider first published his ideas about them not in a scholarly article, but in a "brochure for general practitioners," entitled *Psychischer Befund und psychiatrische Diagnose.*[107] There, he wrote: "If they are present without a doubt and no underlying physical disease can be identified, then we clinically speak in all modesty of schizophrenia."[108] As Heinz Katschnig has argued, Schneider did not conceive of the latter as a "disease entity in the medical sense," but rather, characterized the diagnosis in terms of a "psychopathological type."[109]

As an admirer of Karl Jaspers, who himself had offered a wide variety of phenomenological descriptions of abnormal psychological phenomena, Schneider did not believe in the existence of separate psychiatric disease entities, as Kraepelin had done. He also advocated "[Freeing] psychiatry from the slavery of neurology."[110] As Katschnig explains, Schneider considered himself a phenomenologist and a psychopathologist, following in Jaspers' footsteps. He searched the inner psychological experiences of his patients for interpretative clues, with the explicit aim of discovering a broad range of "types of human reactions," rather than separate disease entities. More specifically, his goal was to assist the general practitioner, without formal psychiatric training, in learning how to detect schizophrenia, aided by the description of what he called "practical types."[111] Indeed, in a letter written by Schneider to Jaspers as early as 1923, the former emphasized the need to be pragmatic in one's diagnostic efforts. As he aptly put it: "Methodological subtleties are not enough, one also has to show that it is useful for something."[112]

Nevertheless, Schneider was well aware of the remaining complexities in negotiating the boundaries between what he called "pure" psychiatry, on the one hand, and "symptomatic" psychiatry, on the other. As an independent discipline, the former was to study and deal with "the varieties, types, and reactive forms of the human being," without any reference to presumed "disease entities." The latter, by contrast, started out by explaining mental symptoms as the effects of causes, understood in terms of bodily or brain diseases, whose proper comprehension was relegated to neurology. Yet, interestingly, according to Schneider, there was a host of phenomena, often of a psychotic nature, that could not (yet) be entrusted to either one of these two opposed fields of inquiry.[113]

Partially due to the ominous year of publication of his aforementioned brochure, in 1939, Schneider's ideas went mostly unnoticed. Another reason for this, it has been argued, was that he put very little effort in disseminating them in professional circles beyond the general practitioners who formed his intended audience.[114] In fact, on the occasion of the publication of the third edition of his well-received – and much-debated – volume *Clinical Psychopathology*, he looked back to the early, ill-fated brochure that first introduced the idea of auditory hallucinations as "first rank symptoms" of schizophrenia, and wrote to a friend that he no longer believed in the correctness of the ideas propounded there. In the same context, he voiced his deeper and broader concern that "Psychopathology plays only a modest role nowadays, in some hospitals no role at all."[115]

By introducing the idea of "first rank symptoms," Schneider had aimed to help general practitioners to "cut to the chase," rather than assist fellow psychiatrists in further "carving nature at its joints." For him, schizophrenia should not be conceived of as a disease entity in the medical sense of the term, but rather as a "psychopathological type," or in other words a "practical kind." In a 1968 obituary, it was correctly emphasized that Schneider never exhibited interest in any of the "short- or long-lived clinical entities which are so popular with psychiatrists," such as the ones previously defined by Kraepelin or, much later, classified in the DSM-III.[116] The tragic irony, however, is that his "first rank symptoms," published below the disciplinary radar, so to speak, and on the verge of World War II, would nonetheless be mined to "carve out" such distinct entities, and were adopted by the psychiatrists spearheading the neo-Kraepelinian revolution, in preparation for the publication of DSM-III in 1980.

As we discussed in our previous chapter, the explicit goal of the DSM-III's architects was to offer reliability and validity to psychiatric diagnoses, by introducing the assumption of discrete psychiatric disease entities. Schneider's "first rank symptoms," which, in his own prescient words "might also be of interest to psychiatrists," became the most prominent criteria for the diagnosis of schizophrenia, more than 40 years after the fact; which is to say, long after they had been submitted to an audience and readership of general practitioners for pragmatic purposes alone.[117] This belated rise to prominence of the Schneiderian symptoms in the field of psychiatry (and its most authoritative document) has at least in part been attributed to the successes of the antipsychotic drugs that had been introduced during the 1950s to alleviate the effect of hallucinations and delusions.[118] In this sense, then, one might argue that a "psychotic" symptom such as that of hearing voices had become recognized as a key symptom of schizophrenia at least in part as a consequence of the evolution in psychopharmacology.

While Kraepelin was more interested in the course of *dementia praecox*, and Bleuler, in his diagnostic efforts, had considered hallucinations and delusions accessory symptoms, and while both emphasized schizophrenic withdrawal and inactivity – symptoms that were, in fact, often only worsened by the first generation of neuroleptics (i.e., anti-psychotics) – the success of the new drugs might have contributed to a renewed interest among psychiatrists in those symptoms that could now be medicated and treated this way.

The other possible reason for the stronger link between "first rank symptoms" (and, among them, hearing voices) and schizophrenia in the DSM-III was related to other problems of reliability that the manual was seeking to resolve. Assessing the presence or absence of hallucinations and delusions was easier to agree upon, and since, as we discussed in the previous chapter, Rosenhan's experiment continued to haunt psychiatry and its failure to diagnose schizophrenia achieving reliability and possibly validity remained psychiatry's most cherished goals.

Not everyone was pleased with this new emphasis on Schneiderian symptoms, however. Seymour Kety, for example, the first scientific director of the National Institute of Mental Health, and a strong advocate of a genetic theory of schizophrenia, quickly protested.[119] According to him, although "first rank symptoms" were more easily perceived and described – or, for that matter, comfortably "put into checklists and fed into computers" – and although they covered a prevalent syndrome that did not come with the dire prognosis of schizophrenia, just as they might even be more responsive to the treatments psychiatry had on offer, a simple and sobering truth had to prevail: the phenomena in question, telling as they might be, were not the thing itself, that is, they were "not schizophrenia."[120]

It was in the DSM-III, as we demonstrated, that voice-hearing was first mentioned explicitly and specifically in relation to the psychotic disorders. In this context, AVHs were mainly linked to schizophrenia, but were also discussed in relation to other disorders, such as "alcoholic hallucinosis" or "multiple personality disorder." As the DSM-III explains, while hallucinations are common in the schizophrenic disorders, auditory hallucinations, where the individual hears voices coming from outside the head, are the most common. Especially characteristic are those voices that speak directly to the patient, comment on their behavior, issue commands, or insult them.[121]

Although, according to the DSM-III, auditory hallucinations could also be identified in manic episodes ("God's voice explaining that the individual has a special mission") or in major depressive episodes (e.g., berating the individual for their shortcomings or sins), it was notably the hearing of very specific voices that was considered significant enough to warrant the diagnoses of schizophrenic disorders.[122] Such was the case especially with auditory hallucinations in which either a voice keeps up a "running commentary" on the individual's behavior or thoughts, or two or more voices converse with each other.[123]

As we noted, in the DSM IV-TR, the Schneiderian symptoms were somewhat toned down, as the manual stated the increasing need to contextualize symptoms: visual or auditory hallucinations with a religious content might now be a "normal part of religious experience" (e.g., seeing the Virgin Mary or hearing God's voice).[124] A voice-hearer suffering from serious "social/occupational impairment" would be considered as suffering from a mental disorder, but in the absence of such impairment, the diagnosis in question did not seem justified. This would be the case even if the voice-hearing experience in itself was exactly the same in both cases.[125]

While during the four successive stages of its neo-somatic revolution (completed with the "decade of the brain" in the 1990s),[126] psychiatry took a decisively biomedical turn in its approach to voice-hearing, some psychologists began moving away from psychiatric diagnoses and towards a focus on voices in their own right, with the so-called "complaint-based approach."[127] As we will see below, this tension between personal and medical discourse, with their contrasting interpretations of voice-hearing, would continue to play itself out in the later opposition between the emerging grassroots and consumer-led movements (such as the HVM), which took these phenomena to be meaningful, on the one hand, and the official psychiatric discourse, which merely viewed them as symptoms to be alleviated, on the other. While the latter tended to consider voice-hearing as expressive of a disease entity, the former implicitly adopted the continuum model, as it took voice-hearing to be part of the full scale and broad spectrum of human diversity.[128]

For proponents of the biomedical model, "auditory verbal hallucinations," then, were seen as one of the illness's distinct and differentiating features of a "natural kind." In one article, for example, Massoud Stephane and colleagues described AVHs as a symptom of brain disease, "just like blindness or hemiplegia."[129] Similarly, in a comparative study of mental health professional staff in Saudi Arabia and the UK, Saeed Wahass from the Department of Psychiatry at King Fahd Hospital of King Faisal University, in Riyadh, and Gerry Kent from the Department of Psychology, at the University of Sheffield in the UK, found that while psychiatric staff in both Saudi Arabia and the UK agreed that hallucinations can be indications of schizophrenia, Saudi Arabian staff members, who tended to take a more "medical" view of auditory hallucinations, were less likely to consider non-medical causes, and finally had more confidence in medical interventions. It is interesting to note that these mental health professionals reported keeping more social distance from patients who hear voices than the staff in the UK, who overall believed that hallucinations could be due to a variety of causes, other than biochemical disturbances, namely "not only biological causes such as heredity and brain damage, but also environmental factors such as bad childhood experiences and stressful life events."[130] Wahass and Kent further note that "social distance issues are consistent with the stigma associated with mental health problems in SA, and such cultural views might also contribute to the medicalization of the difficulties associated with auditory hallucinations."[131]

At the other end of the spectrum, however, there emerged another view, that rejected the stigmatizing – social and clinical – consequences of labeling voice-hearing as a symptom of schizophrenia. This alternative view associated voice-hearing not with illness directly, but only when coupled with an inability to cope with everyday life.

This emancipating insight into the powers of de-medicalization was central to the successful efforts of the Hearing Voices Movement and its founders, Marius Romme (a professor of community psychiatry), his wife Sandra Escher (a researcher and journalist), and Patsy Hague (one of Romme's patients who reported hearing voices), to make themselves and the patients they represented heard, loudly and clearly. The movement articulated a clear, alternative, anti-biopsychiatric way of understanding voice-hearing that will occupy us in the next section of this chapter. Today, this movement has grown considerably, with numerous collaborators and researchers, experts "by experience" (i.e., voice-hearers or their family members) as well as experts "by training" (such as academics and clinicians) joining their ranks.

Before delving into the theoretical and clinical ideas of the HVM, it is important to note that not all affected individuals dealing with these phenomena struggled – or, at present, struggle – to cope with voice-hearing in the exact same way, or to the same degree. Indeed, anthropologists and social scientists have underlined that responses to voice-hearing vary tremendously across cultures, time, and place. In what follows, we will thus make a brief detour through the question of the impact of cultural variation on the experience of voice-hearing, which will allow us to better understand the unique arguments of the HVM and its proponents, and the significant shift in the understanding of voice-hearing that they introduced during the last few decades of the twentieth century; a shift that, as we will see, eventually became one of the driving forces behind the gradual decline of schizophrenia as a distinct diagnosis, grounded in nature.

The Role of Culture

Anthropologist Tanya Luhrmann, who also received training in psychology, offers some valuable insights in her study of how culture affects the experiences of people with auditory hallucinations. She studied the differences in voice-hearing experiences in Ghana, India, and the United States, arguing that too often, psychiatrists overlook the important role played by culture in the understanding of psychiatric illness in general, and auditory hallucinations in particular. Luhrmann claims that the experience of voice-hearing is in fact complex and mutable, varying both among individuals and across time and place. In one important qualitative study, Luhrmann and her colleagues, notably R. Padmavati and Hema Tharoor, collaborators at the Schizophrenia Research Foundation (SCARF) in Chennai, India, together with Akwasi Osei from the Accra General Psychiatric Hospital in Accra, Ghana, compared the experience of auditory hallucinations in people across three different cultures.[132] They interviewed three groups of 20 adults, who had been diagnosed with schizophrenia, about their subjective experiences with voice-hearing and the meaning they attributed to it. These subjects were selected from a group of patients at the San Mateo County Psychiatric Hospital, in California, among the inpatients at the Accra General Psychiatric Hospital, and at the Schizophrenia Research Foundation. As Luhrmann and her colleagues found, the voice-hearing experiences in all three settings shared numerous similarities. The main difference they noted was in the quality of the voice-hearing experience, especially in terms of the relationship that the individual had with the voices.[133] As the authors point out, unlike the participants from Ghana and India, those from the United States all used known diagnostic labels to describe their experience, and tended to pathologize the phenomena under consideration. They seemed to have a more difficult relationship to their voices, who often emitted violent commands and addressed them with harsh, hateful, or persecutory speech. In contrast, people in India and Ghana were more likely to describe richer relationships with their voices. In fact, "many participants" in the Chennai and Accra samples described their predominant experience of the voices as positive, whereas "not one American did so."[134]

Instead, subjects from the United States described their voices as a "bombardment"[135] and as symptoms of a brain disease caused by genetics or trauma.[136] They did not feel they had a personal relationship with the voices. Most of the time, they did not even report knowing who was addressing them. By contrast, many in the Chennai and Accra samples seemed to experience their voices as people, such as a brother, a neighbor, or a "human-like spirit" known to the participant.[137] Not only did these respondents have "real human relationships"[138] with the voices in question, they did not experience them as being threatening. For example, more than 50 percent of the individuals in Chennai experienced their voices as coming from direct family members or their kin, instructing them to accomplish various tasks: "They talk as if elder people advising younger people, one subject said."[139] In Accra, where it was culturally accepted that "disembodied spirits can talk,"[140] only a few subjects described voices in terms of brain disease. The majority recounted the experience as being predominantly positive and some claimed to hear God speaking to them. As Luhrmann reports, the voices were often experienced as sources of valuable advice or of moral guidance:

> "Mostly, the voices are good," one participant remarked ... A man, admitted for the first time in 2007, said: "They just tell me to do the right thing. If I hadn't had these voices I would have been dead long ago."[141]

By contrast, for US participants, the voices were often experienced as intrusions into their mind, as violations or disruptions of their own, private world.[142] Most importantly, the meaning of what the voices said was often written off as irrelevant and, hence, not experienced as a meaningful personal interaction. One participant stated, for instance: "I don't think there's anything there or anything. I think it's just the way my mind works."[143] Conversely, the participants from Chennai and Accra interpreted their hearing of voices as genuine relationships, not as the sign and suffering of a violated or dysfunctional mind.[144]

For Luhrmann, these cultural variations can be explained by the fact that the Western world fosters individual-centered frameworks of experience, meaning, and interpretation, whereas the Indian subcontinent and the continent of Africa do not. Indeed, Europeans and Americans imagine themselves as autonomous individuals, Luhrmann writes, who live in a clinical culture where patients "have the right to know, and should know, their diagnosis," and where unusual auditory events are understood as symptoms, rather than people or spirits.[145] Outside of Western culture, she continues, the self is seen as being fundamentally constituted through relationships with others, and interdependence is more strongly emphasized.[146] Therefore, cultural variation, both on the part of patients and of their medical doctors, can have a tremendous impact on the effects and understanding of voice-hearing from both an existential and a clinical perspective. In fact, it seems that the way people pay attention to their voices may alter the meaning, even the very content, of what the voices actually say. As Luhrmann and her colleagues argue, just as culture and context matter, even specific therapies themselves may also alter what patients hear their voices say.[147]

These observations lead to an important conclusion: it seems that the experience of hearing voices is shaped in decisive ways by social environment and local culture, and the latter might have notable clinical implications as well. As Luhrmann surmises, schizophrenia, thus contextualized, might have "a more variable outcome than once was thought," given that the patients' environment "affects not only the severity but also the rate of illness."[148] In other words, the finding that schizophrenia has a more benign course and outcome outside the West "remains robust," and, moreover, the harsh, violent voices heard in the West may not be an "inevitable" feature of schizophrenia.[149] It is precisely this insight, namely that is possible for a person or patient to entertain a different kind of relationship with the heard voices, and that improving the latter reduces the voice's "caustic quality," that lies at the heart of the Hearing Voices Movement's innovative conception of voice-hearing;[150] a conception, it will be clear, that originated in the West even though it resonates with the voices from other regions and cultures that Luhrmann et al. studied in detail.

Listening to the Voices

> Sometimes I hear voices at night before I go to bed. This voice might be telling me that there is someone outside my front door, or there is someone messing with my car in the parking lot. When this happens, I have learned to check the evidence to reassure myself by looking through my front door's peep hole, or even opening my front door to find nothing and no one is there … Even though I take my medication regularly, I still hear some voices. The difference is most of the time I can manage them. … I have also learned that if the voices are getting really negative, I can call someone in my support system, perhaps my parents, and talk to them about what the voices are saying … I don't know if a person with schizophrenia can ever be totally free of voices, but it is possible to survive the voices and lead a much more normal life, even with them playing in the background of your life. (Jason Jepson, "Surviving the Voices," 2018)[151]

Throughout history, voice-hearers have often found themselves in a marginal position, similar to that of women, children, disabled, and non-white people, whose voices and opinions have been dismissed as unreliable.[152] In addition, as we saw above, the predominantly medical model and increased biologization of mental illness in the West has subjected the modern experience of hearing voices to the technical "expertise" of psychiatric discourse. Indeed, the latter has ended up in the role of "spokesperson" for voice-hearers, translating, if not explaining or ventriloquizing, their most intimate experiences. Both historical and cultural, social and intellectual tendencies have left little space for voice-hearers themselves to make sense of – and attribute their own meaning to – what they hear. As we can see in Jepson's account, the voices even in his subjective experience are part of his schizophrenia, to be medicated, managed, and ideally silenced.

In direct reaction to these dominant practices and discourses of discrimination and subjugation, as sociologist Arthur Frank notes in his book *The Wounded Storyteller*, the second half of the twentieth century has seen patients of all stripes, "expert[s] by experience" in their own right, adamantly reclaim their own narratives and self-understanding.[153] As Frank writes, "those who have been the objects of others' reports are now telling their own stories. In doing so, they define the ethic of our times: an ethic of voice, affording each a right to speak her own truth, in her own words."[154] Similarly, in a 2002 article, Dillon and May argue that "clinical language has colonized experiences of distress and alienation," and that, conversely, recovery "seems to be about a decolonizing process, a reclaiming of experience."[155]

It is in this general context of critical responses to the silencing of certain minoritarian voices that voice-hearers too, began to tell their own truths, shifting the emphasis toward more personal accounts, the psycho-social aspects, and the meaning of their experiences. Their counter-narrative has moved increasingly away from the essentialist, naturalistic, biological, and medical models, that had hitherto constituted the main explanation and dominant interpretation of these experiences and the phenomena they attest to.[156] This fundamental shift of perspectives – and, indeed, of paradigms – so it seems would not have been possible without the appearance of the Hearing Voices Movement at the end of the 1980s, followed by the dissemination of their ideas on an international scale, which directly challenged the association between voice-hearing and schizophrenia.

The Hearing Voices Movement emerged in Maastricht, the Netherlands, in 1987 from a meeting between Marius Romme and his patient, Patsy Hague, who had been diagnosed with schizophrenia and had come to consult Romme because she heard voices.[157] After being hospitalized and prescribed antipsychotics that did not alleviate her symptoms, Hague had become increasingly suicidal. However, her realization that, throughout parts of ancient, medieval, and modern history, voice-hearing had not always been condemned or pathologized – and, indeed, had been greatly valued at times – provided Hague with a reassuring perspective, leading to a shift in her self-understanding and an effort to destigmatize her own experiences. As Hague herself noted, "those of us who still hear voices are therefore probably living in the wrong century."[158]

Following her initial encounter with Romme, meetings were organized with other voice-hearers who identified with Hague's experience and encountered similar existential and institutional difficulties in coping with the voices they heard. On Dutch national television, Romme called for voice-hearers in the Netherlands to come forward; he received some 450 responses, out of which 150 had never before had any contact with psychiatric institutions.[159] Among these, Romme collected the insights of 20 non-patient respondents who were able to successfully cope with their experience. These voice-hearers were then invited to speak at a conference in the city of Utrecht, in the heart of the Netherlands. The findings were published by Romme and Escher in the *Schizophrenia Bulletin*, in 1989, in the very first paper to articulate the ideas and sketch out the practices of the new HVM.[160] From there on, an international community for voice-hearing (now coordinated by INTERVOICE, the acronym for the International Network for Training, Education and Research into Hearing Voices, formed in 1997) was created, while further support groups and voice-hearing networks emerged, many of which quickly spread to other countries.[161] Thus, while HVM originated in the collaborative research undertaken by Romme, Escher and Hague, it soon became apparent that its growing prominence and influence went hand in hand with its further organizational development and impact, as a primarily user-led and, importantly, "survivor-led," movement.[162]

The Hearing Voices Movement has by now become a powerful international social network, with active chapters throughout Europe, North America, Australia, and New Zealand, as well as emerging offshoots in Latin America, Africa, and Asia. Among the members of the Hearing Voices support groups, it appeared that numerous individuals had acquired coping skills that allowed them to live with their voices, and, hence, had no need to resort to medical or psychiatric assistance.[163]

At the heart of the HVM's ideas is an understanding of recovery. For the members of the movement, hearing voices should be understood as a meaningful, if uncommon, human feature, rather than a symptom that sets voice-hearers apart from "normal" individuals. Voice-hearing, in this sense, is interpreted and appreciated as an aspect of *diversity*.[164] Rather than being seen and feared or, worse, condemned as "abnormal or aberrant," it is conceptualized as an intelligible and effective response to emotional and interpersonal, psychological and social, circumstances. In other words, the experience of hearing voices forms part of a continuum or spectrum of mental phenomena, and, importantly, is also shared by individuals who do not have the specific symptoms that might lead to a medical diagnosis of mental illness. In fact, it turns out that a non-negligible portion (between 2 and 6 percent) of the general population claims to hear or to have heard voices, without being troubled by them in any significant way.[165]

The movement insists that the phenomenon of voice-hearing should be understood and destigmatized, rather than pathologized and medicalized in a vain or fatal attempt to suppress its "symptoms." It advocates for empowerment and acceptance, as well as the rights of individuals who hear voices, arguing that it is not voice-hearing *per se*, but only the relationship the individual entertains with his or her voices, that may cause distress and other difficulties in the pursuits of everyday life.[166]

Recovery thus mainly involves learning how to cope with – rather than get rid of – the voices, the hearing of which is in itself not seen as a sign of mental illness, much less of schizophrenia.[167] Importantly, being able and allowed to narrate one's personal understanding of the experience of voice-hearing (as well as the possible trauma underlying it) and, hence, to talk openly about it in a shared or public – at any rate, destigmatized – setting, are considered key components of the recovery process in question.[168] The movement affirms that voices not only could, but as a matter of fact should be explained by the person's recounted life history, including its suffered traumas, rather than by one or the other biological factor, presumably responsible for the person having a "broken brain."[169] Voices, they argue, should be explored in their deeper and wider meaning, rather than written off as insignificant or reduced to mere biological or brain dysfunction, a sign of psychiatric illness in need of serious medication. Valuing this process of exploration also leads Hearing Voices groups to emphasize the importance of social support and belonging among peers, as opposed to the medical professional establishment's – or larger society's – obsession with "cures," "therapies," or "treatments" of the "symptoms" accompanying the voice-hearers' experience.

Contrary to the early vision of schizophrenia, with its dire prognosis, Romme and his colleagues believe in restoration. In *Living with Voices: 50 Stories of Recovery*, they lay out nine central aspects of the coping process.[170] Among these, one finds elements such as encountering an individual who "takes an interest in the voice-hearer," "giving hope by showing a way out and *normalizing* the experience," "meeting people who accept the voices as real," "being accepted as a voice-hearer by others, but also by oneself," "making choices" (i.e., choosing to stay alive, making friends, choosing a career, pursuing self-development, etc.). Most importantly, recovery is contingent on working with the voices, that is, on establishing an enduring and, in this sense, manageable, livable, relationship with them. As McCarthy-Jones specifies, when the voices are felt to belong to the voice-hearers, because what they say "clearly applies to them,"[171] treatment focuses on improving relations with these voices in everyday life, "recognizing social disempowerment, rebuilding social networks and achieving independence."[172]

The HVM has indeed enabled numerous individuals to achieve a sense of empowerment and improved coping skills. It allowed the characterization of voice-hearers to shift from being psychiatric patients, presumably with very few chances of recovery, to becoming "experts by experience," taking the role of much-needed "advocates, activists or researchers." Yet although these ideas have been "tentatively accepted" by a few professionals in the mental health system,[173] several psychiatrists have argued that the claims made by the HVM need further substantiation by empirical research. In short, the medical field has by and large required the movement to produce formal testing with more "rigorous designs," if its ambition is to represent "more than an ideology."[174]

It is fair to say that the movement has fundamentally challenged the authority of mainstream psychiatry and its diagnostic categories, proposing an alternative to the traditional disease model and its modern institutionalization. Because it requires "full participation of experts by experience at all stages" and follows a "nothing about us without us" approach, HVM's model has been described as entertaining an uneasy relationship with the research methods traditionally used within the medical and social sciences.[175]

In the model adopted by the HVM, the reference to trauma, rather than to naturalistic or biomedical means of explanation, is most often used to highlight the causes of the voices. This understanding requires that the content, and the deeper or wider meaning of the voices, be taken seriously and addressed in ways that are almost never – or very rarely – found in more conventional institutionalized psychiatric settings. By contrast, in the HVM recovery paradigm, the individual works with the voices themselves and, in so doing, following their lead, as it were, explores distressing life events and traumatic episodes in relation to – or, dare one say, in conversation with – them. All this entails taking into consideration the person's complete life history, as it coheres or lays itself bare in the "symptom." Bleuler and Jung had already advocated as much. Tools such as the "Maastricht Hearing Voices Interview" (a questionnaire that gathers information about the history, content, and meaning of the voice-hearer's experience, information that can also be used for eventual treatment planning) and the "Construct" that was derived from it (a tool with the help of which the interviewer and the voice-hearer collaborate to produce an understanding of the purpose of the voices and what problems the voices might represent) can be used to explore, and even attempt to resolve, the latent conflicts that may underlie the voices' presence.[176] This offers an alternative to voice-hearers, now able to identify themselves as such, even as they are still being told by medical professionals that the "real" cause of their experience (mere "symptoms," so the argument goes) is that of a brain disease.

Developing its theory in direct partnership with voice-hearers themselves, the HVM proposes a non-naturalistic, psychological understanding of the phenomenon, whose meaning is ultimately determined by the individuals themselves in relation to the integrality of their life history, including its traumas.[177] It is also important to note that the HVM clearly values diversity of opinion in the matters close to its heart. Its members, theorists and practitioners alike, are far from adopting a radical anti-medication stance. That this is the case, even though medication as a means to alleviate or eradicate the role played by the voices is considered as a potential obstacle to working out their psychological or biographical significance, should give us pause for reflection. After all, what this means is that medication, such as the prescription and use of anti-psychotics, is viewed as being merely "one of many available strategies," in a broader effort of encouraging individuals to "make their own decisions about their treatment and have the necessary information to make an informed choice."[178]

According to Romme, the goal of recovery is therefore not cure, but rather, the emancipation of the individual who hears voices. In other words, "getting rid of voices is neither necessary, nor that important," as the latter are not in and of themselves seen as pathological symptoms.[179] On the contrary, in the very same way that homosexuality used to be a psychiatric diagnosis, a human variation that was pathologized and stigmatized, voice-hearing, it is claimed, needs to be met with acceptance.

Both the presence and meaningful resource of the heard voices themselves and, thereby, a destigmatized and full acceptance of voice-hearers more generally, are what matters here. One can hear voices and not be schizophrenic. In and of itself, so the movement urges, this should caution against the tendency to systematically medicalize individuals with unique experiences, to directly or indirectly force them to change into what they are not (i.e., non-voice-hearers), often with the full weight of psychiatric, medical, and even political institutions backing these questionable efforts.[180]

A New Identity: The Voice-Hearer

The experience of voice-hearing, at least in the West, has dramatically shifted over time. After being socially valued throughout much of its history, it subsequently became increasingly pathologized and stigmatized. This was notably the case when hearing voices became a first-rank symptom of schizophrenia and thereby the main sign of an apparent brain disease.

At the pinnacle of this shift in understanding or rather explaining the hearing-voices phenomenon, notably in the DSM-IV, only one out of the list of five so-called "criterion A symptoms" (i.e., delusions, hallucinations, disorganized speech, catatonic behavior, and negative symptoms) was required to justify the diagnosis of schizophrenia, if and only if the voices comprised a running commentary on a person's thoughts or behavior and/or two or more voices were conversing. Before the DSM-IV, two of these criteria had been necessary to diagnose schizophrenia, but in the wake of the fourth edition of the manual, the sheer presence of such auditory symptoms (again, a running commentary on one's thoughts or the presence of two voices in conversation) was enough, it was claimed, to warrant the diagnosis. While the DSM-5 removed this exception and affirmed instead that, in theory, a person could be diagnosed with schizophrenia *without* having auditory hallucinations (e.g., if they suffered delusions and manifested disorganized speech), the phenomenon of hearing voices remained one of the first and most prominent symptoms to justify a diagnosis of schizophrenia.

The Hearing Voices Movement argued against this more recent decision and posited once again that voice-hearing should not automatically be associated with schizophrenia. For the HVM, the term "schizophrenia" was not only socially stigmatizing but also – theoretically and clinically speaking – fundamentally flawed. In its view, it was a label without any scientific validity, randomly and often brutally applied without any reference to, much less relevance for, an individual's life experiences, good or bad. Furthermore, it was claimed that "schizophrenia" was a diagnosis that completely ignored the existing connections between such life experiences, on the one hand, and core illness experiences by which the subject or patient might be stricken, on the other. Rather than ostracize and silence people who hear voices, the HVM sought to create space for their narratives, stories, voices, personal thoughts, and experiences, all of which, it was believed, would lead to far more humane – phenomenologically rich and, indeed, holistic – approaches of understanding and treating mental illness, in the present and foreseeable future.

This meant that psychiatry and mental health workers, rather than doing things "to" or "for" people in patronizing ways, ought to begin to work *democratically*, "with" them. The latter ambition is evinced particularly in Romme's groundbreaking oeuvre. One example, found in his writings and clinical practice, was the solemn conviction that a more democratic psychiatry would use advance agreements or so-called "directives," according to which people with mental health problems could agree (or, indeed, disagree) with the recommendations made by the mental health team, notably when they were well and stable. Such agreements and directives might also lay out what future treatments patients should receive when, instead, they were considered unwell, unstable, and suffering from mental health problems, including those evidenced by hearing voices. Details and differences in theoretical premises and clinical practices aside, it would become increasingly clear that the HVM and the experiential content of voice-hearers needed a seat at the table and, indeed, to be fully and conscientiously considered by psychiatrists and mental health professionals. In any case, doing so would begin the necessary – beneficial, productive and perhaps even more salutary – process of opening up the field and institutions for mental health and beyond, in the direction of a more democratic partnership between sufferers and healers, patients and doctors.

The shift we observed and broadly reconstructed in this chapter occurred at a moment when, to use Michel Foucault's formula, the minority's perspective found itself more and more in opposition to dominating social norms, values, and beliefs.[181] In an effort to help the pendulum swing further back, from the late 1980s onwards, the Hearing Voices Movement opened up the discussion of madness to people by appealing to a wide range of experiences, while articulating a different and strikingly original set of theoretical premises and clinical perspectives. Its core values, however, remained rooted in the so-called *continuum model*. The HVM depicted voice-hearing as a part of normal human experience, implying that the potential for hearing voices was inherent in each and every one of us. Interestingly, this claim would find ample support in later epidemiological studies, which suggested that "a significant minority of the population have had an experience of hearing voices at least once in their life."[182] While proponents of the disease-based understanding of hearing voices considered hallucinations to be a main characteristic of schizophrenic pathology, advocates of the continuum paradigm fought against this tendency to consider such experiences as part of a separate and abnormal domain of psychological suffering. For the latter group, voice-hearing should be understood as part of a broader spectrum of human experience, a continuum on which the symptoms of schizophrenia, such as auditory hallucinations, were but an extreme pole. In other words, according to this view, such phenomena should not be misunderstood as revealing a difference of a natural (i.e., biological or genetic) kind.

Nevertheless, to this day, psychiatric discourse remains by and large attached to the naturalizing, biomedical conception of voice-hearing, despite the wider acceptance facilitated by the international dissemination of HVM's ideas. Indeed, as McCarthy-Jones concludes with an eye to the present, a "somewhat uneasy" relationship currently exists between psychiatry and the movement, due to the association of voice-hearing and brain disease in psychiatry, to the debate over the validity of the concept of schizophrenia, and to "professional interests" being threatened.[183]

Despite this unease and uncertain outcome, HVM advocates, with the movement's emancipatory philosophy and ongoing emphasis on psychosocial causal explanations of the phenomenon on their side, claim that the change from demoting voice-hearing to a symptom to seeing it as a meaningful experience in itself, represented a radical shift of paradigms. In fact, as we have suggested and will further demonstrate, the shift – or pendulum swing – back, toward a less stigmatizing conception of voice-hearing that animated theoretical discourses and spiritual practices in the past, has wide-ranging implications for the way in which voice-hearers could assume new, more socially accepted and liberating, collective identities. As A. Woods puts it:

> Twenty-five years after the Hearing Voices Movement first created the space for people to discuss voices, "the voicehearer" has become established as an identity people can adopt, inhabit, and mobilize in order to lay claim to a view of voice-hearing as meaningful in the context of people's lives. The challenge, perhaps, for the next quarter century is for the mental health professions fully to recognize this claim and its potentially radical implications.[184]

By arguing that the experience of voice-hearing appears to extend into the general population, the research findings and advocacy work of the HVM suggests that, if anything, "prevailing views in Western society of voices as inevitable signs of psychiatric disturbance need to be reevaluated."[185] Indeed, one radical interpretation of the phenomenon would go as far as stating that: "If we really listen, voices may be heard to tell us more about broken societies than broken brains."[186] In any case, by recognizing the importance of personal narrative in recovery and by bringing to the fore the problems linked to a lifelong and fateful diagnosis such as schizophrenia, the HVM conducted important work in reducing the stigma associated with it. As we saw in chapter 4, from DSM-5 onward, not only did psychiatrists become more aware of the stigmatizing effect of the diagnosis of schizophrenia, many other advocates and peer support groups of patients pushed for the omission of "schizophrenia" altogether, demanding a name change at the very least. It is to this pivotal and detrimental role of psychological and social stigma, its repercussions for both patients and medical professionals seeking to treat and heal them, that we will devote the next chapter.

Chapter 6
Stigma and the Problem of Naming

> I received an actual diagnosis: "Chronic paranoid schizophrenia with acute exacerbation." My prognosis, I was told, was listed as "Grave." … Here it was in writing: The Diagnosis. What did it mean? … I'd always been optimistic that when and if the mystery of me was solved, it could be fixed; now I was being told that whatever had gone wrong with inside my head was permanent and, from all indications, unfixable … it felt more like a death sentence than a medical diagnosis. (Elyn R. Saks, *The Center Cannot Hold*, 2007)

Stressing the undeniable given that once a medical term has been firmly established, it becomes extremely difficult to ever change it, in its recommendations regarding the process of naming new human infectious diseases, the WHO has been explicit about avoiding nomenclature that would "incite undue fear."[1] As we pointed out in chapter 4, for the first time in its history, the fifth revision of the DSM explicitly addressed the dangerous potential of psychiatric classifications to become such "fear-inciting" terms.

Indeed, it was claimed, psychiatric diagnoses can cause harm due to their inadvertent contribution to stigmatization, both of the patient's self and of his or her social persona. In *Our Most Troubling Madness*, Johanne Eliacin gives the example of a patient named Violet, who refused to refer to herself as "schizophrenic" or as having schizophrenia. Rather, Violet referred to her struggles simply as "the illness," as a neutral term for her condition. Significantly, she "avoided the term schizophrenia not because she didn't know it but because it meant too much."[2] Although patients and their families have been campaigning since the 1970s to rename schizophrenia for such reasons,[3] numerous doctors, who took the Hippocratic Oath of *primum non nocere*, joined efforts in the years leading up to the publication of the DSM-5, and continued to do so after the manual was published. With their own eyes, they saw – and, indeed, conscientiously studied – the personal and social damage resulting from both self-stigmatization and its public equivalent, noting that the very diagnosis of schizophrenia involves the attribution of a negative, depreciating label. They also investigated and published extensive research on patients' and laypersons' reactions to available or proposed alternative names.[4]

In this chapter, we will examine some of the more recent discussions that link resistance to the diagnosis of schizophrenia, the push for its abolition, and the increasing realization of its potentially damaging effects. These conversations and, at times, ensuing controversies, have prompted a series of dramatic changes throughout the world, as patients and doctors alike strive to find ways of reducing the negative, stigma-inducing connotations of the label itself. Indeed, as we shall see, some writers have come to view the term "schizophrenia" as an anachronistic and harmful misnomer, that has very little to do with – and sheds virtually no light on – the deeper and, all too often, harmful causes of an individual's mental suffering and resulting isolation. They demand an end to its use, due to its connotations of hopelessness, chronicity, and dangerousness. These deeply ingrained associations, they claim, perpetuate negative representations of patients, create artificial social distance between the "normal" and the "sick," and may even diminish chances of recovery. For proponents of dropping the term altogether, the simple acknowledgment of patients' suffering, based on the stigma associated with "schizophrenia," is what ultimately prompts the quest to find alternative, less stigmatizing, diagnoses.

One of the ideas at the core of the "name change" debate is that being mentally ill is not just a matter of coping with symptoms. As one study showed, mentally ill patients struggle not only with the symptoms of their disorder – such as hallucinations, delusions, confusion, reduced affect, and similar sufferings – but also with stigma, which affects "multiple dimensions of their everyday life and functioning."[5] Indeed, in addition to clinical symptoms, patients are often the targets of negative social labels and attitudes that lead to stigma, both in Western countries and across the world.[6] A 2004 survey among the German population, for example, revealed that the opinion that schizophrenic persons are "unpredictable and incompetent" was, surprisingly, "most frequently endorsed by the public," a judgment to which "perceived dangerousness"[7] was also added. Another 2004 study found that Moroccan families of patients with schizophrenia also suffered from stigma. In fact, 86.7 percent of those interviewed reported they had hard lives because of the stigma created by the illness. The study further found similar results in other European, North American, and some Arab and Islamic countries. As the authors showed, "despite the belief that traditional societies are more supportive of the weak and the sick, stigma is a major burden in addition to that of the illness."[8] Thus, while it was obvious that the nature of the stigma varied across different geographical regions, peoples, and nations, it remained at its core a constant and, all too often, enduring social response to individuals suffering from mental symptoms, irrespective of the existing or apparent differences between their cultural traditions.

As Gil Dov Hoftman, an American psychiatrist, defined the problem, stigma can be considered a form of "social injustice" that affects patients in a variety of ways. It may contribute to the onset of psychotic episodes, but, more generally, it also "delays treatment attainment, promotes social isolation, stress, and maladaptive coping behaviors, and places individuals with schizophrenia at higher risk for a more severe illness course."[9] In fact, since 2001, the WHO has considered the stigma of mental illness a global health problem in its own right, one that has direct repercussions on the quality of life of individuals, precisely by negatively affecting their self-understanding (see figure 9).[10]

It is important to underscore, at this point, that the phenomenon of stigma should not be reduced to its outwardly observable effects and expressions, such as negative social attitudes or actions. Rather, stigma has several components, none of which are easily measurable or identifiable. To begin with, language itself can inaugurate, carry and convey, disseminate and solidify, social stigma. Through its very meaning, use, and force, it can become an important "source and sign" of stigmatization. Although one reason for renaming the term *dementia praecox* as "schizophrenia" was the former's inability to be used as an adjective, while the latter makes this possible (as in "schizophrenic"), it has been observed that the latter linguistic differentiation and its indiscriminate use becomes, in itself – if often inadvertently – an integral part of the difficulties experienced by the person who suffers. While with physical illness (as in the case of diabetes, for example) "the person afflicted" remains one of "us" with what is perceived as an added attribute, the

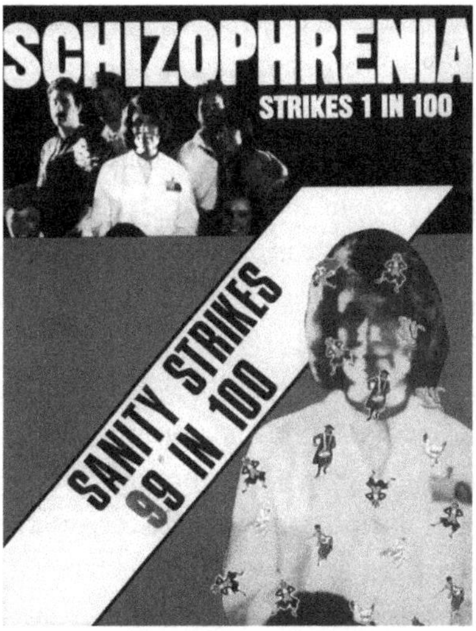

Figure 9 Breaking the stigma
Source: Dunn, Tim and Heller, Liane. (1986, June). Schizophrenia strikes 1 in 100. *Phoenix Rising*, 6(1), 2. Courtesy of Oskar Diethelm Library, DeWitt Wallace Institute of Psychiatry: History, Policy, & the Arts, Weill Cornell Medical College

"schizophrenic," by contrast, "becomes one of 'them' and *is* the label we affix to them."[11] As Steve Colori writes in his first-person account of schizophrenia: "Having schizophrenia means living undercover because it's not considered socially acceptable. Every single day I am out in public there are people using stigmatic words like psycho, schizo, crazy, psychotic, schizophrenic, and a slew of others." As a consequence, when Colori meets new people, he has to ensure that he creates a reaction "that makes them think I am just like them … I can't afford for people I work with and interact with daily to know I have schizoaffective disorder. I'm concerned they would disparage me, be afraid of me, treat me differently, or completely avoid me."[12]

As we have seen, the DSM-III tried to mitigate this possible damage caused by its own nomenclature, clearly stressing that its terms did not *intend* to categorize or classify individuals as such, in their very nature, but rather merely offered labels, not themselves descriptions, of the very "disorders that individuals have."[13] In the process, the DSM-III ended up encouraging professionals to refrain from using expressions such as "a schizophrenic." In their place, it was suggested that more "wordy" phrases, such as "an individual with schizophrenia," might be more appropriate and less prone to misunderstanding and/or abuse.

In what follows, we will examine the stigmatizing consequences of the schizophrenia diagnosis for patients, and look at a series of proposed anti-stigmatizing solutions. We will retrace the debates around the diagnosis's name change, exploring how dropping the name "schizophrenia" might lead to further changes, both in our attitudes *towards* and our *understanding of* the disorder itself.

Yet, firstly, we need to understand how stigma works. Even when it involves a single trait, such as suffering from schizophrenia, the stigmatizing process itself involves several components. To begin, stigmatizing involves labeling socially important differences, such as hearing voices or having delusions. It further involves linking labeled people with negative stereotypes, for instance when some individuals believe that people with schizophrenia are violent or unpredictable. People thus become subsequently categorized as "psychotic" or "schizophrenic," for example, which creates additional social exclusion. Finally, negative consequences, such as status loss and discrimination, tend to follow. Thus, stigmatized individuals may suffer from employment and health care inequalities, incarceration, homelessness, and retaliatory violence, among others.[14] As one patient explained: "With diabetes, there is no stigma ... Diabetes patients can even tell an employer about their disease, whereas schizoaffective patients would be most unwise to."[15]

Furthermore, there are several types of stigma. Usually, three core aspects or dimensions of stigma are differentiated, namely institutional stigma, social stigma, and self-stigma (or internalized stigma). It will be helpful to describe these respective features in some further detail.

The first type of stigma linked to schizophrenia, namely "institutional stigma," can be felt in the various kinds of structural discrimination that patients suffer from, each of them with negative effects on their own lives and, importantly, also those of their families. This can manifest itself in the policies of both public and private institutions that restrict opportunities for people with mental illnesses, and can lead to discrimination in employment, wages, mortgages, housing, and education.[16] For example, a 25-year-old patient named Anne, who had been hospitalized several times with acute symptoms of schizophrenia, had a relapse after having been symptom-free, living on her own, and working in a local tourist information office for several months. Once she had recovered from her relapse and was ready to return to work, her employer fired her, believing that she might have a dangerous outburst in the office due to her mental illness. Despite a successful recovery from her symptoms, Anne ended up losing her job, her apartment, and her friends in the month following her discharge from the hospital. As her case shows, the effects of institutional stigma can snowball into disastrous material consequences, whereas it is generally acknowledged that "a person with diabetes is unlikely to encounter comparably consequential public stigma related to her illness."[17]

This explains why institutionalized stigma often goes hand in hand with a reluctance to disclose one's diagnosis. Patients rightly worry that making their illness public will "decrease job opportunities and social status, cause shame, and lead to involuntary hospitalization," all of which, in turn, may result in "delayed treatment seeking and worse clinical outcomes."[18] Even psychology students, as Ron Bassman points out, are reluctant to reveal their mental health issues. "Stung by the insensitivity and misinformation perpetuated in their programs," they prefer to hide their past and suffer silently, knowing that "it is not in their best interest to disclose their histories if they expect to succeed."[19] Institutional stigma also comes in a variety of other ways, which negatively impact the lives of suffering individuals. For example, patients with mental illness (including schizophrenia) receive "the least amount of funding per disability-adjusted life-years," despite having one of the largest disease burdens worldwide.[20] To make matters worse, treatment facilities for schizophrenia are often located in "isolated, disadvantaged, or otherwise limited-access areas."[21]

The second type of stigma is called "social stigma," an expression that refers to the negative effects caused by widely circulating misconceptions about the mentally ill. Studies from Canada, England, and Germany have helped to identify various factors that come into play in these negative prejudices, that can lead to discriminatory practices, such as *fear and exclusion* ("persons with severe mental illness are to be feared and, therefore, kept out of communities"); *authoritarianism* ("persons with severe mental illness are irresponsible, so their life decisions should be made by others"); and, finally, *benevolence* ("persons with severe mental illness are childlike and need to be cared for").[22] In the case of schizophrenia, social stigma often associates the condition with an image of violence and dangerousness. For example, in 2004, psychologist Amy Watson found in a vignette study that Chicago police officers were much more likely to ascribe violent intent to "minimally violent" perpetrators if they were labeled as schizophrenics.[23] And yet, as Jonathan Metzl writes, "the actual number of violent acts committed by persons diagnosed with the illness are equal to, and in some cases lower than, rates of violence committed by everyone else."[24] In fact, those diagnosed with schizophrenia are victimized between 65 and 130 percent more than the general population.[25] Large-scale studies in the United States have even shown that an individual diagnosed with schizophrenia has an exponentially greater risk of being assaulted by others, rather than the other way around.[26] As Mark Ellerby, who was diagnosed with schizophrenia, writes, if we want to overcome the stigma for those who are diagnosed, we should put ourselves in the shoes of those who suffer. Ellerby, for his part, refutes the association of schizophrenia with dangerous psychopathy – reflected, as we have seen, in the misconception of schizophrenia as a condition resembling the split personalities of Dr. Jekyll and Mr. Hyde – insisting instead that, if anything, as a patient suffering from schizophrenic symptoms, he felt *more* responsible towards others. In his words: "my brain tended to feel responsible for the entire world around me; even issues that had nothing to do with me would prompt me to think that I was responsible."[27]

In a similar vein, Kevin Alan Lee, who was diagnosed with schizophrenia at age 20, opens his book, *The Split Mind: Schizophrenia from an Insider's Point of View*, by observing that "persons suffering from a mental illness are not lesser human beings. We are similar to the average person except for the fact that we have poor health."[28] The social stigma linked to schizophrenia has gotten much worse in recent decades. One study found that in 1996, a representative sample of the general population in the United States was 2.5 times more likely to perceive mentally ill people as potentially "violent and frightening" than when a similar sample was studied in 1950.[29] In Germany, too, a 2005 study found that there was an increase in stigmatizing attitudes towards people with schizophrenia.[30]

The third type of stigma is called self-stigma and refers to the process of identity transformation that occurs when individuals internalize and endorse a mental illness stigma, which leads to a diminished sense of self-esteem and self-efficacy.[31] Their previously held or desired identities are thus "spoiled," to use one Erving Goffman's term, borrowed from the subtitle of his famous 1963 book, *Stigma: Notes on the Management of Spoiled Identity*. As Goffman points out, for the stigmatized individual, shame becomes a "central possibility, arising from the individual's perception of one of his own attributes as being a defiling thing to possess, and one he can readily see himself as not possessing."[32] As one patient aptly puts it, shortly after being diagnosed with schizophrenia: "When I realized I had a mental illness, I was very ashamed of myself for several months. I had always thought I was a smart person. How could I become mentally ill?"[33]

Whether social, institutional, or internalized, stigma creates a negative snowball effect, which justifies the urgency of anti-stigma efforts and campaigns, including those that seek to rename the diagnosis of schizophrenia. As we will see in this chapter, the preconceptions and prejudice associated with schizophrenia are damaging not only to patients' overall lives but also to the clinical or therapeutic outcomes of the treatment they receive. It is important to understand that the discussion about changing the name "schizophrenia" is not just a matter of reducing its *social* stigma. More to the point, it aims to reduce *all* types of stigma, including so-called "iatrogenic stigma" (i.e., the stigma caused by medicine itself) and the whole complex of harmful, often indirect effects caused by the diagnosis on patients' lives. Some claim that replacing the name "schizophrenia" should, first and foremost, be considered an attempt to change the stigma caused by psychiatry as it uses "misleading, mystifying and, ultimately, stigma-inducing terminology."[34] After all, the term "schizophrenia" can be stigma-inducing precisely because "it confusingly and mystifyingly refers to a disease that is characterized by a split mind, a psychological state that the public cannot personally relate to," as it can with depression, for instance, with which numerous individuals can identify and are familiar, at least to some degree. The term schizophrenia, by contrast, as Jim van Os, one of the main proponents of the growing effort to drop the label altogether argues, simply does not match "any *generally known human experience*," which explains why it is much more likely to "induce fear and exclusion."[35] In fact, this author concludes, the potential for new forms of stigmatization of any replacement term for the label "schizophrenia" would be "inversely proportional" to the degree in which the general public recognizes the term as an integral part of its own ways of thinking and is able to translate it into its own modes of experience.[36] In other words, it is the confrontation with the "otherness" of a relatively small class of unfortunate patients to which an illness of an altogether different kind is attributed (as is historically and still largely the case with the diagnosis of schizophrenia) that Van Os sees as the source of the stigma and harm.

Schizophrenia as "Life Unworthy of Life": The Aktion *T-4 Program*

One of the most extreme examples of the consequences of stigmatization experienced by persons suffering with mental illness, among them many diagnosed with schizophrenia, is the inhumane treatment and merciless killing of patients under the so-called *Aktion* T-4 program of the Third Reich. During this period, from 1939 through 1941, schizophrenia was decreed a hereditary disease and those classified as schizophrenics were considered "unworthy of life."

As Greg Eghigian notes in his book *From Madness to Mental Health* (2010), Hitler and the Nazi Party heavily borrowed from earlier racist, Social Darwinist, and eugenic ideologies, based on the work of now infamous authors who, since the nineteenth century, discussed what they believed to be the "racial implications of natural selection."[37] In Germany, they defended the idea of "racial hygiene," following Alfred Ploetz (1860–1940) and Wilhelm Schallmayer (1857–1919), leading up to a program involving science, medicine, and public policy to promote what they considered to be "racial health."[38] In this dehumanizing context, the Nazi regime passed a 1934 law calling for the "compulsory sterilization of those deemed 'hereditarily ill,'" which, among sufferers from other illnesses, included persons diagnosed with schizophrenia.

As stated in §12 of the sterilization law, the court's decision could be carried out "against the will of the person to be sterilized," with state physicians being authorized to enlist police authorities to "carry out necessary measures," and to resort to "the application of direct force" if other nonviolent measures proved to be insufficient.[39] Significantly, the text specified the conditions under which such measures were taken, stating that "persons taking part in the legal proceedings or in carrying out the surgical operation are obligated to keep these secret," adding that "anyone violating confidentiality will be sentenced to prison for up to one year or given a fine."[40] As Eghigian notes, within the span of a year, no less than 80,000 individuals – and, during the whole period the sterilization law was in place, a total of 400,000 – were sterilized under the law, against their consent, with some 75–80 percent of this group diagnosed with "moral feeble-mindedness."[41]

During World War II, Hitler and Karl Brandt, his personal physician, further initiated a program that would carry out the medical and merciless killing of "individuals deemed to be living a 'life unworthy of life.'" This program, known under its title *Aktion* T-4, was an operation involving directors of asylums, psychiatrists, nurses, and hospital staff as well as pediatricians. As has been widely documented, it was "responsible for the killings of around one-third of the institutionalized psychiatric population – men, women, and children – by means of starvation, medication overdose, or gassing." Although it was discontinued in 1941, the killings persisted, albeit "shrouded in more secrecy than ever."[42] In addition, the so-called 14f13 program transferred numerous T-4 personnel to Eastern Europe where, as Eghigian notes, "their experience was used to run a new SS operation aimed at killing concentration-camp inmates incapable of hard labor or suffering from incurable diseases"; indeed, some 200,000 people were killed under the authorization of both these programs.[43]

In a letter to the "Reich Committee for the Scientific Registration of Severe Hereditary and Constitutional Afflictions," dated July 6, 1940, Dr. Irmfried Eberl, the director of the gassing facilities in Brandenburg and Bernburg, discussed the draft of a possible euthanasia law.[44] This law, for which an alternative (and subsequently abandoned) title was, the "Law on the Killing of Those Incapable of Living," aimed to carry out the "assistance in dying" [*Sterbehilfe*] of individuals deemed not only "unfit for living" but also unsuited for "productive activity." As indicated in §2 of the law, this included "all schizophrenics, as long as they are capable of no or only mechanical occupational activity."[45] Other categories included "feeble-minded" individuals, syphilitic patients, persons suffering from "senile dementia," epileptics "who either have frequent seizures or manifest significant changes in character," all "criminals who require psychiatric institutionalization," and, finally, "all remaining mental disturbances that are not suited to productive activity."[46] As stated in an internal T-4 document, circulated under the ominous title "Removal According to a Strict Standard: Medical Examination Report Standards of Bouhler/Brandt," only war veterans who "served on the front, were wounded, or ... received decorations," were not to be included on this list.[47]

A Dangerous Diagnosis

Even where it does not anticipate or is no longer perversely used to legitimatize eugenics, including the devastating practices and outcomes of German National Socialism, the mere diagnosis of "schizophrenia," taken as a natural kind, a distinct disease entity or category, with a deteriorating outcome, is increasingly considered by many – patients and families, mental health professionals as well as advocates representing diagnosed individuals – as detrimental to the wellbeing of these sufferers. Some even identify themselves as "schizophrenia-diagnosis survivors" and emphasize their recovery not from the illness, but from the diagnosis itself.[48]

A number of recent studies have underlined the impact of the diagnosis of schizophrenia not only on the individual's quality of life, but also on the onset, course, and outcome of the disease itself. Rüsch and his colleagues argue, for example, that stigma can precipitate initial episodes of psychosis, trigger relapses, and contributes to a more severe path for the disease in all of its facets.[49] A 2010 study also found that the existence of internalized stigma was correlated with the severity of psychiatric symptoms, and negatively associated with patients' adherence to the proposed treatment program.[50] Prevalent social and institutional stigma, it was discovered, had an impact on the onset of the disorder, and, indeed, on its negative prognosis.[51] Increased stress, delays in seeking treatment, and vulnerability to relapse, were all revealed to be directly related to the presence and role of stigma.[52]

Moreover, the "negative social interactions and discrimination" that go hand in hand with stigma, it was discovered, can dramatically increase the risk of so-called "delusional ideation."[53] As it turned out, this was the case for both effective and perceived discrimination. A 2009 study documented, moreover, that "the observed risk for schizophrenia in minority groups increases with the level of discrimination endured."[54] And for the first time, a 2003 Dutch study established a further link between perceived discrimination and delusional ideation. According to the authors, their discovery of this prospective evidence was "suggestive of a causal link."[55] As they concluded, "perceived discrimination may ... contribute to the high observed rates of psychotic disorder in exposed minority populations."[56] Another 2015 study observed a link between being at "high risk" of developing schizophrenia, reporting "higher stigma-related harm," and, finally, making the transition from being "high risk" to being diagnosed, with schizophrenia.[57]

Lastly, as already indicated, research has increasingly shown that the sheer fear of stigma can in itself act as a significant barrier to seeking treatment by (and for) patients diagnosed with schizophrenia. A 2011 study, following the premise that medication adherence is "primarily determined by beliefs," examined over 200 participants with a DSM-IV diagnosis of schizophrenia or schizoaffective disorder, and assessed treatment adherence and symptom severity. The study found that attitudes towards illness were a direct predictor of adherence to treatment.[58] Against the background of the accumulated results of empirical research undertaken over the course of several years in different geographical regions and social milieus, many advocates conclude, on reasonable grounds, that reducing both public *and* internalized stigma is thus necessary to increase treatment participation and guarantee more positive clinical/therapeutic outcomes.

Self-Stigma

Internalizing the exterior – social or institutionalized – stigma related to the diagnosis of schizophrenia inevitably leads to self-stigma, which is irrevocably correlated with a decrease in self-esteem. Research findings, moreover, point to a direct connection between the existence of self-stigma and reduced access to social and material resources, which in turn adds to increased anxiety and, hence, creates a deteriorating situation for those afflicted and diagnosed with the disease carrying the stigma.[59] What ensues is social isolation, which has long been known to heighten the risk for poor health outcomes in patients.[60] As Colori movingly writes, due to his mental condition, he lived in an almost complete isolation from age 19 through 25, "because I was unable to function well enough to interact with people and have friends." Isolation and loneliness, he explains, were one of the most difficult and painful parts of dealing with his condition "and having the knowledge that disclosing my diagnosis may recreate these feelings … had the ability to create a great deal of fear."[61]

In this context and for our purposes, it is important to note that according to some researchers, self-stigma is experienced much more strongly in patients diagnosed with schizophrenia than in those who have been diagnosed with other mental conditions.[62] Roughly one out of every three patients labeled as suffering from schizophrenia reported self-stigma, in comparison to one out of every five patients diagnosed with bipolar disorder.[63] These latter patients with a higher self-esteem score had families that also were more supportive and involved in their everyday life. Patients with a diagnosis of schizophrenia, by contrast, testified not only to believing that they were less socially accepted, but that likewise they were to be *blamed* for this very circumstance, as they themselves were not inclined to engage in social interactions.[64]

Kraepelin and Bleuler, alongside Freud and others, viewed social withdrawal and poor overall functioning as the central features of schizophrenia. More recently, researchers have argued that stigma, while unmentioned by these early twentieth-century authorities, must have been already deeply involved in the very picture they painted, playing its role in the vicious circle we have summarized above. Stronger self-stigmatizing attitudes, found mostly among patients diagnosed with schizophrenia, tend to lead to further social exclusion and, thereby, to greater suffering and experienced harm in their general level of functioning in everyday life.[65]

"Schizophrenic Skins:" Racial Stigma

One more central element to take into consideration is the racial stigma linked to the diagnosis of schizophrenia. More specifically, in the United States, schizophrenia is perceived as a dangerous, chronic condition, with racial prejudice being hardwired into the diagnosis. In fact, African Americans are three times more likely than whites to be clinically diagnosed with schizophrenia. This difficult topic has been extensively covered by Jonathan Metzl in his book *The Protest Psychosis: How Schizophrenia Became a Black Disease*, which shows how the anxieties of the civil rights era and the racialized logic of the 1960s and 1970s led to schizophrenia becoming associated with violence. In those years, the disease came to represent a "threat to civilized society," creating a "rhetorical transformation from an illness of white feminine docility to one of black male hostility."[66] As Metzl concludes, during the civil rights era, schizophrenia "literally, and then figuratively, became a black disease. And prisons emerged where hospitals once stood."[67] The rise in the numbers of people diagnosed with schizophrenia, he further observes, was a result of "changes in diagnostic criteria," *not* in patients' clinical symptoms.[68]

Working with the premise that the material reality of schizophrenia is shaped by social, political, and institutional factors – in addition to chemical or biological ones – Metzl shows how psychiatric definitions of insanity continue to "police racial hierarchies, tensions, and unspoken codes," while separating normal from abnormal behavior.[69] He argues that even in an era dominated by neuroscience, diagnosis remains a "projective act," that combines scientific understanding with a complex set of "ideological and ... political assumptions," which then become difficult to identify when covered up with the discourse and seemingly "objective rubric" of biological science.[70] For instance, in the 1960s and 1970s, as Metzl further demonstrates, the newly narrowed frame surrounding paranoid schizophrenia, helped create the category of "angry, black, male schizophrenic subjects," while women, neurotics, manic depressives, and other "nonthreatening" persons were cast into expanding categories of depression, bipolar disorder, or anxiety disorders; as a consequence, racial concerns – and, as Metzl notes, "at times overt racism" – were directly and indirectly written into the diagnostic language of the second half of the twentieth century.[71] A 2005 article in the *Washington Post*,[72] for example, described a large government study led by John Zeber that analyzed 134,523 case files and uncovered striking categorical differences. The article found that doctors diagnosed schizophrenia in African American patients (especially men) four times as often as in white patients.[73] As Metzl claims, still nowadays we find that, in the United States, persons with schizophrenia are negatively perceived as being "unduly hostile or violent," irrespective of the well-documented fact that they are "exponentially more likely" to be the victims, rather than the perpetrators, of violent acts.[74] Research suggests that even African American doctors over-diagnose schizophrenia in African American men, and that the latter receive higher dosages of antipsychotic medications than do white patients, precisely because they are more likely to be described as being "hostile or violent."[75]

Only during the civil rights era (c.1950–63) was the diagnosis that originally connoted "white American neurosis" altered due to historical currents that marked certain bodies and psyches as "crazy in particular ways."[76] From a general broad condition manifested by "emotional disharmony," that negatively impacted white people's abilities to "think and feel," rendering them "unruly children,"[77] schizophrenia became in the 1960s a disorder affecting "Negro men." But the "black forms of the illness" were marked, precisely, not by docility but by rage, volatility and aggression.[78] As Metzl observes, during this time patients who should have been treated based on their "character and intellect" were interned due to the color of their "suddenly schizophrenic skins."[79] In the 1980s and 1990s, psychiatric and medical journals would extensively document that medical doctors diagnosed paranoid schizophrenia in African American men "five to seven times more often" than in white men, and also "more frequently than in other ethnic minority groups."[80]

In the same time period, anti-psychiatrists such as David Cooper, R. D. Laing, Joseph Berke, and Leon Redler were already known for defining schizophrenia as a "predominant form of *socially stigmatized madness*."[81] Metzl, for his part, argues that the very diagnosis of schizophrenia is stigmatizing on two different levels: first, it is a diagnosis that assumes poor outcomes, but, secondly, it is also one of the systematic ways in which the medical system "forces acceptance of hegemonic descriptors of well-being" at the expense of "autobiographies of protest or survival."[82] In other words, as Metzl goes on to explain, drawing out the diagnosis's logical consequence, to enter the doctor's rhetorical system, is to "give up the fight."[83] In the end, however, Metzl's conclusion is nuanced. In his account, stigma does not directly link schizophrenia to black men. Rather, in the transformation "from clinical diagnosis to cultural trope to protest metaphor," schizophrenia developed meanings associated with race as well.[84] In sum, in the United States, unlike other psychiatric disorders, schizophrenia became an ideology-imbued diagnosis that was effectively used to stigmatize those who protested during the civil rights period and after. Udodiri Okwandu, a historian from

Harvard University, more specifically showed how forms of urban rioting during a somewhat later period (1960–75) were biomedicalized and were conceptualized as related to the (black) brain.[85]

The Case of "Sluggish Schizophrenia" in the Soviet Union

Another example demonstrates the potential political use and abuse of the diagnosis of schizophrenia through the mechanism of stigma. In the postwar Soviet Union, the diagnosis of "sluggish schizophrenia" was leveled at several hundreds of people, whose "dissident" activities – rather than medical symptoms – led to their eventual confinement in psychiatric hospitals.[86] While at the time, some argued that this diagnosis was in all likelihood invented at the behest of the KGB,[87] in a new history of the term "sluggish schizophrenia," Benjamin Zajicek associates the introduction of this terminology with a more general crisis of Russian psychiatry at the beginning of the twentieth century.[88] This crisis itself was due to the apparent inability of medical and clinical professionals, as well as hospitals and scholarly journals, to draw clear conceptual and diagnostic boundaries around the category of schizophrenia.

The term "sluggish schizophrenia"[89] referred to a *milder* form of schizophrenia. The diagnostic category was coined in the 1930s, as part of Soviet psychiatrists' efforts to narrow down the concept of schizophrenia, in hopes of joining in the utopian ideology leading up to, and giving further legitimacy to, the communist-led Revolution. As Zajicek explains, "with the Bolshevik government ideology, the belief that illness – and mental illness in particular – was caused in large part by social conditions rooted in the class-based exploitation of the old society" represented a unique challenge for psychiatrists, who wished to align themselves with the perspective of a classless society and a new status quo. Many of them, Zajicek goes on to note, took great "ideological pride in helping to lay the foundations for the future socialist civilization by taking their expertise out of asylums and hospitals and into communities and workplaces, helping people avoid habits and environments that might cause mental illness and detecting mild cases of mental disorder in time, to arrest their development."[90]

The diagnosis became infamous only much later, during the Brezhnev era, when it was treated as "the diagnosis of choice used to place political dissidents into involuntary psychiatric treatment."[91] Many scholars have pointed out this abject abuse of the term "sluggish schizophrenia,"[92] but Zajicek counters that the crisis, which the designation came to solve (and that makes it still so relevant to the current debates about the diagnosis of schizophrenia), was the realization among psychiatrists at the time that, ill-defined as it was during the first decade of the twentieth century, the concept of schizophrenia had become far too broad and needed to be narrowed down.[93]

However, with a shift from the utopian hopes of the 1920s to its statist solidifications in more conservative – and, ultimately, Stalinist – institutions and policies, the focus of the young republics' psychiatrists on so-called early or mild phases of the disease, in order to prevent further deterioration, was confronted by increasing opposition from government authorities. As Zajicek explains: "Party activists began to criticize the notion that there was a *continuum* between schizoid types, schizoid psychopathy, and schizophrenia, and to criticize psychiatrists for 'biologizing' normal variations of personality, when they should be focusing strictly on people suffering from major psychiatric diseases."[94] Psychiatrists were now expected (and directed) to solve the problem of the overcrowded asylums and the many chronic patients that occupied them, rather than studying and treating the supposed variations and subtleties of early and milder stages of mental illnesses they had focused on in their earlier revolutionary zeal.[95]

Interestingly, members of the Party were not the only ones to criticize the continuum model. As Zajicek notes, early on, the Leningrad psychiatrist V. P. Osipov claimed that the preoccupation with diagnoses of presumed *mild cases* had resulted in an "epidemic of psychiatrists 'frivolously' over-diagnosing Soviet citizens with schizophrenia."[96] This same vagueness of the term's attribution (and the diagnosis it stood for) inadvertently caused an undesirable situation, where speaking of mild symptoms and syndromes could all too "easily be abused by corrupt officials."[97] Indeed, Osipov and Zajicek offer numerous "chilling examples of Soviet citizens being diagnosed with mild schizophrenia after clashing with superiors."[98]

"Sluggish schizophrenia," a diagnostic label meant for "'light, not sharply expressed forms' of disrupted 'unity of the personality,'" as a 1944 Soviet monograph cited by Zajicek has it, was revived during the Brezhnev era *to stigmatize* opponents of the regime. It was done so by Andrei Snezhnevskii, a medical doctor who exploited this particular diagnosis to pathologize those who had shown anti-Soviet behavior. In 2014, two Russian psychiatrists, Savenko and Perekov, went as far as concluding that the "stigma related to mental illness is at the level of xenophobia. The mentally ill are perceived by the Russian public as dangerous, incurable, useless, and harmful."[99] As they noted, not only did the general public still hold on to this social stigma, the discipline of psychiatry as a whole had often been "guilty" in allowing this negative association to fester during the Soviet regime.[100]

Moving Forward: Possible Solutions

As we recall from previous chapters, Bleuler's renaming of *dementia praecox* in terms of schizophrenia was at least partially related to his resistance to the dire prognosis that was ingrained in the name itself. Even though he did not completely discard the idea of a biological component to schizophrenia, Bleuler emphasized the *psychology* of the disorder, thus suggesting a potentially reversible course of the illness. Indeed, one of the many obstacles to reducing the stigma for people suffering from schizophrenia, it was soon realized, had to come from a radical change in attitudes and practices that mental health professionals tended to hold and remain committed to. The most salient among them related to the original view of schizophrenia, according to which most of the patients diagnosed with the disease simply did not improve.

Although the more recent focus on the neurobiology of the diagnosis supposedly reduces the shame attached to behavior that is deemed deviant, it also runs the risk of turning individuals with mental illness into "almost a different species," increasing the desire for social distance from them. A study that interviewed over 7,000 subjects in Germany, Russia, and Mongolia, has amply documented the collateral damage inflicted by scientific approaches, as an incidental result of their efforts to naturalize both the deeper origins of the disease, and its manifest symptoms.[101] As Rüsch et al. put it, with the introduction of these neurobiological explanations, interpretations, and treatments of schizophrenia, "the sense of separation between 'us' and 'them' could be increased by pointing out a genetic, unchangeable etiology and the hope for recovery could be reduced."[102] This return to the early view first espoused by Kraepelin, which describes mental illness in biomedical rather than psychosocial terms, has also been found to lead to "harsher behavior towards people with mental illness."[103] Most of the research done on the detrimental impact of theories espoused by mental health professionals on the daily life of patients and the public perception of illness, clearly confirms that the discourse explaining mental illness based on "genetic" or "neurological" factors not only tends to be "overly simplistic," scientifically speaking, but in individual and social psychological terms, also tends to produce and proliferate stigma.[104]

Besides the name change, which we will examine below, the three main strategies found to be most effective in counteracting and reducing stigma are protest, education, and increasing contact with patients suffering from schizophrenia.[105] In 1996, the World Psychiatric Association started an international anti-stigma program specifically designed to counter the discrimination linked to schizophrenia. Its aim was to increase awareness and education about the nature of this particular mental illness and its available treatments, and to generate action that would reduce discrimination and prejudice.[106] In Europe and the United States, consumer groups have also "actively targeted stigma" in order to improve the lives of those suffering from mental illness.[107]

In terms of "protest," in the United States, the National Alliance on Mental Illness (NAMI) has been carrying out an anti-stigma campaign under the name "stigmabusters," which protests against media representations of mental illness and demands better legal protection for individuals, together with improved housing and employment conditions. In Germany, a Munich-based alliance for people suffering from mental illness, an initiative previously called the "Bavarian Anti-Stigma Action" or BASTA (which also means "stop"), carries out protest campaigns that use email alerts to notify members about stigmatizing advertisements or messages in the media. As Rüsch et al. note, 80 percent of the discrimination cases that BASTA contested in public were successfully stopped and resulted in official apologies from the companies or media institutions that had action taken against them.[108] In addition to these effective initiatives, education programs have involved bringing what they call "mental health consumers" to schools and police academies, educating the media, and organizing art exhibitions.

Leipzig-based initiative called "Irrsinnig Menschlich" ("Madly Human") has also carried out local and national anti-stigma initiatives, such as the "Crazy? So what!" school project, aimed at improving student awareness of mental health issues. Similarly, the international film workshop, "Against the images in our heads," sought to highlight cinematographic examples illustrating individual and public efforts at reducing stigma.[109]

An often-cited obstacle to reducing social stigma is lack of social contact with stigmatized individuals, which leads to a "lack of empathy."[110] For example, if the only encounters one has with persons suffering from schizophrenia is "a homeless individual with profound thought disorganization on the street," as Hoftman argues, then one faces "stereotyped representations of people with mental illness" which in turn, only reinforces the negative beliefs that "the entire group consists of deviant, dangerous individuals."[111] Coliri, an expert from experience, tells us that when he let people shape their perception of him based on long-term experience with them, and only later disclosed his diagnosis, he created a "positive frame of reference for schizophrenia," that overshadowed the popular and stigmatized view of the disorder.[112]

Some anti-stigma initiatives aiming to promote empathy and sympathy for patients by reducing social distance, have shown how complex this undertaking can be. In one experiment, non-schizophrenic individuals were exposed to simulations of auditory hallucinations. The experiment concluded that having experienced simulations of AVHs *oneself* indeed created "more empathy and respect towards schizophrenic patients," but, at the same time, also led to a greater desire for social distancing. As a net result, the experiment thus had a "contradictory effect" on stigma.[113] Yet another study involved playing videos that displayed schizophrenic patients talking about their recovery, which decreased stigmatizing responses in viewers. By contrast, videos in which patients described their acute symptoms, while increasing viewers' feelings of sympathy, did "not necessarily translate into reductions in stigma."[114] In sum, then, it was concluded that it should not be assumed that increases in empathy or sympathy *necessarily* involve a decrease in stigmatizing reactions or, for that matter, in social distance.[115]

Minding Our Words: Considering a Name Change

In addition to the proposed increasing of contact, education, and protest, a more controversial initiative, which stems directly from anti-stigma endeavors and points towards the decline of schizophrenia as a diagnosis, is the serious consideration of a name change. As we have seen, the diagnosis itself has been pinpointed by many observers, medical professionals, patients, their family members, and advocacy groups, as an immediate cause of stigmatization. In addition, numerous researchers and scientists have questioned both its theoretical validity and practical utility. Many among these various parties to the controversy have, therefore, claimed that the name "schizophrenia" should be dropped altogether in favor of an alternative, more appropriate – that is, more informative and less stigmatizing – diagnosis.

As Norman Sartorius from the Association for the Improvement of Mental Health Programmes, in Geneva, Switzerland, and his colleagues remind us, in medicine, "words" can "hurt."[116] With schizophrenia, doctors often hesitate to give the diagnosis to their patients, precisely because it is "linked to notions of dangerousness; incurability and unpredictability," suggesting hopelessness and even giving the impression that there is "no point in following recommendations concerning their lifestyle or the treatment of their illness."[117] Thus, when it comes to reducing stigma or improving patients' lives, "the changes of names of mental disorders, particularly, if accompanied by changes of the concepts of the disease by an appropriate education of medical staff and by the provision of evidence to the patients, their families, and their communities, can be very helpful."[118]

While some advocates of dropping the term are driven in part by recent insights in neurobiology and epigenetics, and by the idea that social adversity becomes biologically embedded (or as the saying goes, "experiences can get under one's skin"), others claim that schizophrenia is nothing but a manifestation of chronic stress, relational and social traumas, social isolation and exclusion, social defeat and economic adversity, low self-esteem, prenatal stress, migration, and other external or environmental factors. They reject the idea of a specific genetic interpretation for the pathologies in terms of natural kinds and types. Many proponents of changing the name thus simultaneously call for a shift away from a biological explanation of schizophrenia, and towards a "vulnerability to stress" model.

Leading up to the DSM-5, proposals for a viable alternative label for schizophrenia were offered both in Europe and in the United States. Despite their significant divergences, most proponents of the name change agreed on the need to find a label that would reduce social and self-stigma in patients suffering from schizophrenia. A 2013 paper written from the perspective of mental health consumers and patients, all of them forming part of the Dutch patient society Anoiksis (Gk: "opening"; an organization that initiated a campaign for the alternative label "Psychosis Susceptibility Syndrome" or PSS, and whose members suggest moving beyond labels and diagnoses, looking at what it may feel like to be in a state of "mental openness"), drew an immediate and unbreakable link between social stigma and internalized self-stigma. The paper claimed that the label schizophrenia is not only "out of date and out of touch with modern science," but also directly experienced by patients as "encapsulating the hindrance to … self-acceptance," standing in the way of "healthy self-regard."[119] Several other initiatives and steps in the same direction have been undertaken in the Far East as well as the West and merit further discussion.

From Split Mind to Integration Disorder: A Terminological Change in East Asia

Suggestive – and often successful – proposals for a different nomenclature, replacing the term "schizophrenia" with more plausible alternatives, have been made in Hong Kong, Japan, Korea, and Singapore. These proposals occurred as part of a "major social experiment" aimed at reducing stigma and promoting a different concept, both of the disease and of doctor–patient relations.[120] This original effort to destigmatize patients was rooted in a shared determination to turn *away* from the Kraepelinian tradition of defining *dementia praecox* – and then schizophrenia – on the basis of a biological and hereditary model, and *toward* a more viable and responsible concept, based on a *dimensional* model that would center instead on "vulnerability to stress." A governing idea behind this name change was that it would also improve "collaboration in treatment, facilitate rehabilitation, and enable the inclusion of patients in their community and other social networks."[121]

Japan was the first country to adopt a different terminology in August 2002, a process that began in the 1990s, with a formal request of the National Federation of Families with Mentally Ill in Japan (NFFMIJ) addressed to the Japanese Society of Psychiatry and Neurology (JSPN).[122] The previous Japanese term for schizophrenia, *Seishin-Bunretsu-Byo* (meaning "mind-split disease"), assumed it to be hereditary and untreatable. Schizophrenia was characterized by severe mental deterioration, lack of volition, and incompetence in social and personal roles. The new term, *Togo-Shitcho-Sho* (meaning "integration disorder"), was defined by alluding to a cluster of symptoms considered to be amenable to treatment, thus turning away from the Kraepelinian model and suggesting that patients, instead of being doomed due to a dire prognosis, might even expect a full and lasting recovery, if properly treated.

In Japan, the logic behind the renaming stemmed from a series of theoretical and practical considerations, among them, and most prominently, "the ambiguity of the old term, the recent advances in schizophrenia research, and the deep-rooted negative image of schizophrenia." A driving motivation behind the process was to remove the diagnosis's stigmatizing consequences for patients and families, and the "harmful impact" it could have on the recovery process itself, which made the use and mention of the term schizophrenia problematic in obtaining successful treatment outcomes.[123] As Mitsumoto Sato shows in his study "Renaming schizophrenia: A Japanese perspective," before the name change, numerous psychiatrists in Japan hesitated to inform patients of their diagnosis, due to its "possible negative consequences on treatment adherence and outcome."[124] In fact, as Ono et al. further noted, only 7 percent of JSPN Council members informed all their patients of the diagnosis and 37 percent informed only the patients' families.[125] It is important to point out these percentages and the unintended consequences they led to, since in Japan, so these scholars document, "approximately 167,000 patients with schizophrenia … spent more than one year in a psychiatric ward (on average) without knowing what their diagnosis was."[126]

But even more importantly, one of the most harmful aspects of the given – if often hidden – diagnosis, was that it tended to identify the patient as someone with a "disorganized personality," even after recovery or full remission, obliquely labeling them as "an essentially ill person" throughout their life.[127] Indeed, up to the 1970s, in numerous psychiatry textbooks, *Seishin-Bunretsu-Byo* was essentially described with Kraepelin's concept of *dementia praecox* and was likewise characterized by a poor prognosis and a "chronic process of deterioration," that would eventually lead to "decay of personality."[128] Like *dementia praecox*, the diagnosis of *Seishin-Bunretsu-Byo* strongly emphasized "severe mental deterioration, lack of volition, and incompetence in social and personal roles" in patients, and presented schizophrenia as a hereditary and untreatable pathology. In 1996, still 77.3 percent of JSPN Council members believed that the general image of schizophrenia in the community was that of an "untreatable disease."[129]

The old term *Seishin-Bunretsu-Byo* was also tied to a history of inhumane treatment of patients, which increased its stigmatizing aspects even further. During the first half of the twentieth century, due to special legislation, the mentally ill were excluded from society.[130] The law sanctioned the private confinement of individuals who were considered dangerous. They were locked up in special cells, known as *zashiki-rou* (which looked much like animal cages) and their family members were responsible for monitoring them.[131] Despite new mental health laws that appeared in the 1950s and 1960s, which greatly improved psychiatric care, "the stigma caused by this long history of exclusion and inhumane treatment remains deeply rooted."[132]

For all these reasons, in 1993, the National Federation of Families for the Mentally Ill in Japan requested that JSPN replace *Seishin-Bunretsu-Byo* with a less stigmatizing term. In 1995, the JSPN's Committee on Concept and Terminology began exploring the request and eventually announced that the old term should be replaced by a new one.[133] In 2002, the new term *Togo-Shitcho-Sho* was selected among several alternatives and then approved by the Japanese Government as the official term.[134]

Significantly, the new term was not a mere change in terminology, but implied a whole new concept of schizophrenia altogether, that is, of "its origin, pathogenesis, course, and methods of treatment."[135] Indeed, the understanding behind the name change was that it "must be accompanied by an updating and revision of the concepts of diseases."[136] Following the "vulnerability to stress" model, the new label and its intrinsic meaning of "integration disorder" put forth a very different conception which, unlike the previous Kraepelinian model, described a condition now defined by a characteristic cluster of symptoms that are amenable to treatment, so that "patients can expect full and lasting recovery if treated with modern pharmacotherapy and given psychosocial care."[137]

As indicated by a national survey, seven months after the name change, 78 percent of psychiatric practices started to use the new term.[138] Furthermore, a study undertaken by Takahashi and colleagues found that, while prior to 2000 *Seishin-Bunretsu-Byo* was used in 72.3 percent of official documents and 3.6 percent of private documents, from 2003 onwards, the new term *Togo-Shitcho-Sho* was used in 98.0 percent of official documents and 21.7 percent of private documents.[139]

Furthermore, a 2005 study by Nishimura and Ono reported that, from 2002 to 2003, the percentage of cases in which patients were informed of the diagnosis increased from 36.7 percent to 65.0 percent, and eventually to 69.7 percent in 2004.[140] Thirteen months after the name change, a survey of 136 members of the Miyagi College of Psychiatrists also showed that 86 percent of respondents found it easier to inform patients of the diagnosis and explain the concept of the disorder with the new term. Furthermore, 82 percent of respondents found the introduction of the new name "more suitable to obtain consent to treatment from patients, useful to improve treatment compliance, effective to reduce stigma, and promising for achievement of social integration."[141] In other words, not only was the new nomenclature widely adopted, but the renaming itself had positive, observable effects, as its use undeniably "increased the frequency with which patients were informed of the diagnosis," improved the lives and treatment of the same patients, fundamentally changed the habits of mental health professionals, and contributed significantly to the education of the general community in a way that diminished social stigmatizing responses.

Although Japan is often cited as a paradigmatic example of the successful renaming of schizophrenia, similar developments also occurred in other Asian countries. In South Korea, for instance, the terminology switched from *Jeongshin-Bunyeol-Byung* (meaning "split-mind disorder," from the words *Jeongshin* or "mind" and *Bunyeol* or "split") to *Johyun-Byung* (meaning "attunement disorder"). As Kim et al. argue, the previously used term was stigmatizing both for patients and caregivers, and created similar difficulties as in Japan for mental health professionals.[142] The new term, on the contrary, implied that patients with schizophrenia, simply need to "tune" their mind as one would tune a musical instrument, and in this sense, introducing the new nomenclature was "expected to result in a reduction of prejudice and discrimination against patients with schizophrenia."[143]

In Hong Kong, the older Chinese name for schizophrenia, *Jin-Shen-Fen-Lie*,[144] (which, likewise, meant "splitting of the mind"), was similarly associated with stigma. The new name *Si-Jue-Shi-Tiao*,[145] by contrast, suggested "dysfunction of thought and perception" and implied reversibility and, hence, the potential for successful treatment. Significantly, this new name has also been described as "well accepted by the public and the professionals because it is considered to be less stigmatizing."[146] Finally, in Taiwan, in October 2012, the new Chinese term for schizophrenia, *Sī-Jué-Shī-Tiáo-Zhèng* (meaning "disorder with dysfunction of thought and perception"),[147] was also chosen by psychiatrists at the 51st Annual Meeting of the Taiwanese Society of Psychiatry.[148]

In each of these cases, progress in destigmatizing schizophrenia has been noted. In Japan, a sharp difference was noted in the "image" of the disorder. A correlative difference in the assessment of (and apparent need for) social distance also manifested itself between people who were only familiar with the newly introduced term, and those who only knew the old one. With the new term, individuals reported finding it "easier to imagine the illness" (76% vs 24%), considered it was "less severe" (23% vs 87%), felt that patients "should disclose the diagnosis" (93% vs 7%), and, finally, "did not feel that the relationship with people with schizophrenia should be stopped" (51% vs 37%).[149] Significantly, families that used the new term appeared to see "much less of a distance from people with schizophrenia" than those using the old name.[150]

These changes were not limited to the psychiatric profession. New policies were implemented by the government, and the image of schizophrenia in the Japanese media and in public opinion started to shift.[151] For example, in 2016, an analysis of the media coverage of schizophrenia in Japan, undertaken by researchers at the University of Tokyo and comparing its treatment in newspapers to the originally very different coverage of bipolar disorder, found that "the portion of articles portraying people with schizophrenia as dangerous and threatening increased until the name change, then started to decrease."[152]

It is fair to conclude, therefore, that – at least in these Asian countries – the successful introduction of the new term has led to "realistic optimism of mental health professionals as well as consumers," while it has also allowed individuals who suffer from schizophrenia to "visit mental health specialists more easily and often open the session by referring to the new term of schizophrenia."[153] This circumstance has lead Sartorius et al. to suggest that the name change – including that of the concept underlying it – can, indeed, successfully change the public image of schizophrenia, "from a concept marked by fatalistic pessimism to one characterized by realistic optimism and thus promote recovery reducing public stigma and self-stigma."[154]

From Schizophrenia to "Salience Disorder": Renaming the Diagnosis in Europe and the United States

Inspired in part by the example of Japan, South Korea, Hong Kong and Taiwan, advocates in Europe and the United States, likewise, encouraged a name change. We already mentioned the proposal made by members of the Dutch patient society Anoiksis to introduce – and, from here on, to diagnostically and clinically use with preference – the alternative label "Psychosis Susceptibility Syndrome," or PSS. In the same spirit, Jim van Os, a professor of psychiatry and psychology in the Netherlands, whom we already cited, has come to believe that "schizophrenia" should be replaced by a diagnosis based on a *quantitative* understanding of health and illness, which would mean understanding the illness as a difference of degree on a continuum, rather than (in absolute terms) a category of its own, as was conveyed by the earlier, and in some circles current nomenclature, which remains "highly suggestive of a *distinct*, genetic brain disease."[155]

Indeed, as Van Os argues, the medical profession and psychiatric disciplines have already largely moved in this more holistic direction. After all, he notes, the categories used in the DSM-5 do not represent diagnoses of discrete diseases but, rather, they describe "how symptoms can cluster, to allow grouping of patients."[156] In fact, as R. D. Laing noted as early as 1967, rather than standing for a stringent, narrowly defined concept and reference, the label "schizophrenia" had more of a pragmatic use among clinical practitioners. In his words, it was "the name for a condition that most psychiatrists ascribe to patients they call schizophrenic."[157]

Suggesting that schizophrenia has now become "just" a label, and a potentially harmful one at that, proponents of change today argue that a different designation is in order. As the argument goes, "renaming is a key strategy to change attitudes," and one could cite ample proof to illustrate that this is both possible and desirable. The reduction in stigma that followed the replacement of such terms as "idiot," "retard," or "spastic," is a case in point.[158] A further example is provided by the 2018 petition addressed by Brian Koehler, past president of the American chapter of ISPS, to the WHO and the American Psychiatric Association, under the heading "Drop the term schizophrenia," in which he highlighted the stigma linked to the diagnosis, the way in which it causes difficulties, and can even trigger "relapses" in some patients.[159]

According to writers such as Van Os and Koehler, then, the term "schizophrenia" should be abandoned altogether and, moving forward, they claim, the *spectrum* of the psychoses should be made more apparent. As Van Os concludes, the best way to inform the public and provide patients with diagnoses is to "forget about 'devastating' schizophrenia as the only *category* that matters" and start "doing justice to the *broad* and *heterogeneous psychosis spectrum* syndrome that really exists."[160]

Furthermore, Van Os insists on the idea that a new label must not merely help clarify the nature of the disorder, but must be sufficiently relatable to the general public for it to successfully reduce stigma responses. As he argues, if schizophrenia were to be called "reality distortion syndrome" or "integration dysregulation syndrome," the meaning of the words would be clear, but these names may also be stigmatizing, because the general public "cannot relate to a universal psychological function of reality or integration."[161] This is why "salience syndrome" is preferable, Van Os submits, since it can be recognized as "relating to an aspect of mentation that is universal" and, in addition, "may be a vehicle to teach the general public about the experiences we call psychotic."[162] It is interesting to note that in a Canadian study about patients' preference for this new name, 8 out of 19 participants preferred Van Os' diagnosis over schizophrenia, 5 preferred the old term, 2 liked both terms equally, and 4 rejected both labels.[163] One participant confessed that he preferred "salience disorder" because it was less common: "I would like to have another name that I could use when I will be back in society, so I could tell the truth, but they won't really understand it.

I don't want to lie so I think I'll just say I have the salience syndrome, yep, that's it."[164]

Van Os' defense of the "salience syndrome" diagnosis is linked to the claim that "a 21st century concept of psychotic disorder" should be understood as "a *variation* of normal human mentation." Like the Hearing Voices Movement, and in contradistinction to the disease-entity model of schizophrenia, Van Os therefore insists on the presence of subclinical, positive, and negative experiences of psychosis in the general population and community, and concludes that because psychotic disorders are "fuzzy in that they blur into normality," they can "be expressed quantitatively."[165]

It is important to note, however, that not all calls for a renaming of schizophrenia mobilize a continuum model. In a response to Van Os' suggestion, two British psychiatrists, Mohammed Abou-Saleh and Helen L. Millar, suggested that schizophrenia should in fact be named "Kraepelin's disease."[166] Offering their support to the effort to abandon the term schizophrenia, they called on the authors of the then upcoming ICD-11 to replace it with either "Kraepelin-Bleuler disease," "Bleuler's syndrome,"[167] or with their own suggestion: "Kraepelin's disease/syndrome," in much the same way as eponyms such as Alzheimer, Parkinson, Wernicke, Korsakoff, Wilson and Down are used in the field. They also supported dropping the diagnoses of "schizoaffective disorder" and "schizophreniform disorders," and replacing them with the term "psychosis."[168]

Dropping the Term "Schizophrenia": The Case of the ISPS

As we discussed in the preface to this book, an example of an actual name change occurred in 2012, when members of the International Society for the Psychological Treatments of the Schizophrenias and other Psychoses (established in 1956, with the mission of "promoting recovery and healing through psychological and social approaches to persons experiencing psychosis and extreme states"[169]) voted overwhelmingly to remove the word schizophrenia from the society's name. The organization renamed itself the International Society for Psychological and Social Approaches to Psychosis. In the debates preceding this change, the specters of Kraepelin and Bleuler loomed large. Indeed, some argued that although the term schizophrenia had originally been coined as an alternative to the pessimistic Kraepelinian view of a degenerative mental condition, it had come to represent a distinct organic, biological disease with equally limited chances of real recovery. The case of the ISPS thus offers a telling example of how the representation of schizophrenia, both historically and conceptually, came to oscillate between both poles of the structural dichotomy we have been drawing out: one identifying and isolating a specific disease (relegated to a natural kind or discrete entity), the other supporting the idea of a continuous spectrum of psychic phenomena that spans the normal and abnormal (and, if not merely based on fuzzy categories, ideally differentiated either in quantitative or qualitative terms).

In any case, on numerous occasions, the disease model of schizophrenia has been described by proponents of the name change as directly contributing to the stigmatizing effects of the diagnosis itself. As David Kennard, a psychologist, chair of ISPS-UK, writes, for instance:

> Research studies consistently find that prejudice and fear are very much related to the biological/illness framework associated with the term "schizophrenia." Attempts to reduce prejudice by teaching that "mental illness is an illness like any other" have actually been found to increase prejudice, while explaining hallucinations or delusions as understandable reactions to life events has been found to reduce prejudice.[170]

There seems to be no simple way out of this predicament. And while we have noted the encouraging results in several Asian countries, in the West, the question of the name change still remains an ongoing debate, as does the controversy regarding the explanatory model best suited to understand the disorder thus far named "schizophrenia."

This much is clear: the name change that occurred in Japan and in other countries reveals how psychiatric diagnoses are heavily loaded with stigma, while renaming them can lead to encouraging opportunities. In fact, the unquestionable benefits of renaming include reducing self-stigma and social stigma, improving doctor–patient relationships as well as the image of the profession of psychiatry overall.[171] That said, it has also been pointed out that changing the name of the diagnosis alone is hardly enough. Rather, for such a particular change in nomenclature to be truly successful, "it must be seen and experienced as part of a change of the health system," more generally.[172] Yet there should be no doubt that this might very well be accomplished as part of this strategy.

Due to the multileveled impact of stigma in general, many observers emphasize the necessity of an equally multileveled effort when it comes to reducing the specific stigma associated with schizophrenia. Hoftman, for instance, advocates "concerted efforts at the individual (affected person and family unit), interpersonal (schools, workplaces, clinics, hospitals, mental health professionals), and institutional levels (media, advocacy groups, policy changes, new legislation)."[173] If anything, what the debate over the name change shows, beyond the obvious divergences in theoretical positions and espoused methods of its advocates, is that it goes beyond mere semantics and inevitably raises questions regarding "the core concepts underlying psychiatric nosology."[174]

Yet, again, other studies have tempered the initial enthusiasm inspired by the name change, and have, instead, underlined its equally undeniable ambiguous effects. To give just one example, a study found that while the stereotype of dangerousness was more freely ascribed to "schizophrenia" than to "integration disorder," the latter expression unexpectedly elicited "a greater desire for social distance than schizophrenia." The authors therefore concluded that the introduction of the designation "integration disorder" had its own share of "mixed effects."

Towards the Future: A Destigmatizing Story

As we have seen in this chapter, individuals with mental illness in general, and with schizophrenia in particular, suffer harsh stigmatization that significantly decreases their life opportunities and severely harms their prospects of independent functioning.[175] Already in 1963, Goffman wrote that by definition, "we believe the person with a stigma is not quite human. On this assumption … we effectively, if often un-thinkingly, reduce his life chances. We construct a stigma theory, an ideology to explain his inferiority and account for the danger he represents, sometimes rationalizing an animosity based on other differences."[176] As Ronald Bassman, a psychologist and a self-described psychiatric survivor, puts it: "when you become a mental patient, you are no longer regarded as a whole person with an individual mix of strengths and weaknesses … [The doctor's] medical orders were directed at my parents, not me, and stated with an absolute authority"; and, as he adds, "I was devastated."[177] In response to these troubling observations, it has been argued that "successful long-term anti-stigma campaigns are necessary to reduce public stigma in society."[178] However, this does not merely involve reducing social stigma. As we saw, the explanatory biological model chosen to understand schizophrenia is itself intimately tied to the potentially stigmatizing effects that the diagnosis can have on patients' lives. Indeed, while many studies assert that people who stigmatize schizophrenia should be taught that the illness is a biomedical condition "similar to diabetes or heart disease," several advocates of the name change claim that such an approach can, in fact, have the opposite effect and increase stigma rather than decrease it.[179] In any case, if a decrease in stigma is to occur, changing the name of the disease will unquestionably have to involve changing the concept of the disease that underlies it.

Because mental illness stigma acts on multiple levels, the supporters of anti-stigma campaigns conclude that multilevel efforts are needed to overcome it, which involves change in legislation, policy, and mental health professionals' attitudes and practices, as well as media representations.[180] Increasing research funding, enlisting advocates to protect patients, enhancing patient empowerment, encouraging contact with patients, and "empathy enhancement" are all possible, they argue, and, indeed, necessary improvements that ought to successfully accompany the renaming of schizophrenia.[181] Activists hope that patients' narratives might contribute to this general destigmatizing process. As Bassman goes on to note in his moving testimony:

> Among our large group of closeted ex-patients are lawyers, teachers, mechanics, doctors, carpenters, plumbers and psychologists. We are your neighbors, ministers and friends, living and working in your communities. Many thousands choose not to reveal their past … I choose to speak and write about my experiences so that others who have been diagnosed and treated for serious mental illness will be able to see new hope and possibility.[182]

Such testimonies, activists believe, might encourage more open attitudes, both in terms of self-disclosure on the part of individuals who are suffering and, no less important, on the part of those who interact with them.

The encouraging destigmatizing effects of the name changes in Asia and the ripple effect these created in Europe and the United States are further grounds, so it is suggested, to hope that *the decline of schizophrenia* as a diagnosis will prompt an eventual reduction of the stigma that it currently carries with it, and thereby enable an ongoing reshaping both of the concept and of the attitudes toward it.

Chapter 7
The Ethics of a Diagnosis

> Now I must arrive at the time of my change from scientific rationality of thinking into the delusional thinking characteristic of persons who are psychiatrically diagnosed as "schizophrenic" or "paranoid schizophrenic." … I later spent times of the order of five to eight months in hospitals … And it did happen that when I had been long enough hospitalized, I would finally renounce my delusional hypotheses and revert to thinking of myself as a human of more conventional circumstances and return to mathematical research. … However, this is not entirely a matter of joy as if someone returned from physical disability to good physical health. One aspect of this is that rationality of thought imposes a limit on a person's concept of his relation to the cosmos. For example, a non-Zoroastrian could think of Zarathustra as simply a madman who led millions of naive followers to adopt a cult of ritual fire worship. But without his "madness" Zarathustra would necessarily have been only another of the millions or billions of human individuals who have lived and then been forgotten. (John Nash, 1994, an autobiography published in the book *Les Prix Nobel/Nobel Lectures/The Nobel Prizes*, written at the time of the award)

> I've always believed in numbers and the equations and logics that lead to reason. But after a lifetime of such pursuits, I ask, "What truly is logic? Who decides reason?" My quest has taken me through the physical, the metaphysical, the delusional – and back. And I have made the most important discovery of my career, the most important discovery of my life: It is only in the mysterious equations of love that any logic or reasons can be found. (The fictional Nobel Prize speech of Prof. John Nash, in Ron Howard's 2001 film *A Beautiful Mind*)

When John Nash, the 1994 Nobel Prize laureate in Economic Sciences, was 30 years old, he suffered a shattering episode of psychosis. During the following three decades, he experienced severe delusion, hallucinations, disorganized thoughts and feelings, and a broken will. His biographer, Sylvia Nasar writes of him: "In the grip of this 'cancer of the mind,' as the universally dreaded condition is sometimes called, Nash abandoned mathematics, embraced numerology and religious prophecy, and believed himself to be a 'messianic figure of great but secret importance.'"[1] Nash was diagnosed with schizophrenia and became the inspiration for Nasar's biography and Ron Howard's 2001 film, *A Beautiful Mind.* Although Nash's life story is considered a living proof of biomedical psychiatry's triumphant success, as it portrayed the individual as being able to ultimately overcome the bizarre and torturous world of delusions and, instead, live a fulfilling meaningful life with loved ones, Nash's own account suggests otherwise. In fact, it provides ample alternative proof that the difference between the delusional world of those who are diagnosed with mental illness, on the one hand, and the rationality of the scientists, on the other, cannot be compared with the contrast between physical disability and good physical health. The above epigraph draws a parallel between the constraints that the delusional world enforces on scientific research and on one's personal liberty, on the one hand, and the limitations that rational thought imposes on one's relation to the world, on the other. It makes apparent that the difference between madness and reason is far more complicated than the simple opposition of delusion and rationality, disability and genius, or illness and health, would seem to suggest.

This book has presented the historical effort to differentiate between normal mentality and the abnormal that began with the ancients. In the Hebrew Scriptures, Greco-Roman medical treatises and philosophical works, early Christian texts, medieval medical and legal discussions, and early modern essays, we discovered how madness and mental health were viewed by sufferers and healers alike. In many passages, we found a general *duality* in the perception of the difference between normal states of mind, on the one hand, and the deviation from the socially and culturally – indeed, the philosophically, theologically, and scientifically – accepted norm, with its presumably rational standards and criteria, on the other. One perception, we suggested, views unusual mental states as categorically different, while the other sees them as located on a continuum or spectrum, differing from the norm not in kind, but in degree. Seen in such light, madness is not the *other* of reason, but one of its more distant, and less familiar, variegated shadings.

During the nineteenth century, an accelerated process of classifying psychiatric illnesses began in Europe, following previous efforts at cataloguing difference in other sciences, notably botany. *Dementia praecox* became one of the twin-nosographical pillars and leading concepts that Emil Kraepelin, the father of modern psychiatry, introduced in his effort to modernize psychiatry. By virtue of its very definition, this first pillar was associated with a dire prognosis, a steady and progressive deteriorating course, due to its biological cause. In short, *dementia praecox* was "a diagnosis of hopelessness from its creation," to quote Richard Noll.[2] Kraepelin's second pillar (that of manic-depressive insanity), by contrast, was characterized by a cyclical course and deemed to have better outcomes.

Influenced by his work with patients at the Burghölzli clinic and by Freud's ideas on the meaningfulness of psychiatric symptoms, Bleuler's introduction of the term "schizophrenia," which he coined in 1908, struck the first blow against this twin-pillar construction. The new diagnosis did not refer to a single, fixed entity. Rather, it invoked a *group* of disorders (i.e., the "schizophrenias"), just as it no longer implied an inescapable outcome. Bleuler thereby theoretically allowed for – and practically entertained – the real possibility of a variety of conditions with very different courses, including that of full recovery. This radical challenge to Kraepelin's presumed ability to distinguish between "hopeless" cases and those worth our efforts, together with the lesson learned from psychoanalysis's hypothesis of the continuity between normal mental life and the neuroses (a continuity that Bleuler and Jung would expand to include the psychoses), exposed modern psychiatry's foundations to the suspicion that it was merely built on quicksand. Later on, this realization would lead to the more vehement attacks of anti-psychiatry advocates upon the premises of psychiatry, especially its ability to distinguish the sane from the insane.

In the 1970s, neo-Kraepelinian psychiatrists, as they came to be known, invested their efforts in strengthening the foundations (or "pillars") of the psychiatric classification of disorders, multiplying the overall number of diagnosable conditions. But, as we saw, these tectonic shifts, which they brought about especially during the following two decades, led to an eventual collapse of the scientific – and in part institutional – edifice that had sheltered the psychiatric system of classification for over a century. As a result of this process, it is now often suggested that the conceptual and institutional "pillars" originally constructed by Kraepelin had come crumbling down.[3] In fact, it was argued that the very concept of schizophrenia, to the extent that it relied on them and was fundamentally defined and restricted by them, has disintegrated in tandem.[4]

These substantial movements resulted from the efforts of numerous, heterogeneous, but synergistic forces, that shared little in common aside from a growing discontent with the classification of schizophrenia as a clear and distinct, discrete category of illness, worthy of its name and useful for doctors and patients alike.

All of those involved in the broader, if disparate, movement of discontent with the psychiatric diagnosis of schizophrenia – be they psychoanalysts, psychodynamic psychiatrists, neuropsychiatrists, research psychologists, philosophers of mind, philosophers of science, as well as laypeople, journalists, advocates, patients or service-users, and their families – pressed for a revision of the psychiatric classification system, whose deeper historical and intellectual roots, as well as institutional context, we have briefly sketched in the chapters above. In their resistance to the paradigmatic, established view, they did not so much try to add to the number of "pillars" (or diagnoses), nor did they attempt to merely rearrange their position vis-à-vis each other, digging the pillars in deeper, so to speak. Rather, the aim was to take what was valid and valuable among the remaining *building blocks*, and construct a whole new conceptual edifice altogether. Ideally, it was deemed, this new model would have far greater diagnostic and clinical – that is, pragmatic – use, and thus, far more truth to it.

Motivated at times by opposing views of human nature (and of the primary causes of the extreme states of mind that they sought to explain, diagnose, heal, and prevent), these professionals and service users were all driven by a shared ambition: to radically shift the psychiatric diagnostic system from the older categorical system of classification to a dimensional, spectrum-based model. This paradigm shift required that one accept the pathological as a *variation of* – rather than an *exception to* – the normal. This difference in degree – rather than in kind – also meant that diagnoses and their criteria were devoid both of *fixity* (i.e., unchanging determinateness) and *finality* (i.e., inescapable determinism), unlike what the preceding categorical system of classification had all too often claimed for its concepts and prognoses.

As the psychiatrist Joseph Pierre demonstrates in his writings, in the duality between medical paradigms relying on distinct categories and those based on a continuum between the normal and the pathological, the latter paradigm became more prevalent (for reasons that are still largely unclear or need further explanation and elucidation).[5] Even seemingly obvious natural categories, such as those pertaining to the distinction between life and death, are now equally challenged and placed on a spectrum. As human beings, we tend to see and construe boundaries between "things," Pierre explains, but the reality is that most "things" can be conceptualized along *both* categorical *and* dimensional lines. The distinction – and apparent duality – between light "particles" and "waves," discovered by twentieth-century physics, more precisely, quantum mechanics, is a case in point.[6] The turn to the spectrum and its continuum, whose history, origins, and unfolding we have retraced here, takes up a similar place. Just as the particle-wave duality necessitated revisions in the understanding of the basic concepts and fundamental methods of theoretical physics, the revolution in psychiatric classification likewise seems to bring with it the dominance of the fixed and fateful category – indeed, of the historical name – of schizophrenia.

In our introduction, we illustrated the conceptual problem – and practical role – of "dual vision" in the history and understanding of unusual states of mind, by looking at a well-known ambigram. As can be gleaned from Joseph Jastrow's famous sketches and interpretations of the so-called duck-rabbit image, ambiguous figures illustrate that those alternative perceptions are not just the products of how different stimuli register on our visual field. Rather, they show that what we see is, first and foremost, perceived *with the mind's eye*. In other words, expectations, knowledge, and the direction of our attention all take part in what we are not only able, but also especially willing or desiring, to see.[7] Just as children, who on Easter Sunday are more likely to identify a rabbit while they more readily see ducks on an average Sunday,[8] scholars and practitioners in their respective fields also tend to see one or the other of the available views on the matter in question. In so doing, it seems, they follow the spirit of the time, the *Zeitgeist*, the conventions (customs and habits), and perhaps even the prejudices of their own age. And, as with other images that one looks at intensely and at great length, the more one observes the rabbit (with everything it conjures up and comes to epitomize paradigmatically), the more one learns about and comes to appreciate its richness, its internal complexity. Like its counterpart (i.e., the duck), the rabbit evolves and, by its nature, is neither fixed nor fated (and, lest we forget, as a picture, it is only a mere figurative drawing of the living creature itself).

During their extensive practical training, clinicians (myself included) who work with individuals suffering from what we have too crudely come to name "schizophrenia," learn that "if it looks like a duck, swims like a duck, and quacks like a duck, then, in all probability, it is a duck."

As we saw, with the shift from duck to rabbit – from categories to continuum – also came a demand to discard the diagnosis of schizophrenia altogether, or at the very least, to experiment and rename it. As this brief history has demonstrated, the term "schizophrenia" increasingly came to be seen as a concept that was never fully validated. As patients and families, doctors and philosophers, had long decried – and as extensive empirical research had also convincingly documented – the name, concept, and diagnosis *itself* came to be seen and experienced as injurious, due to the stigma it sustained and implanted, not least in patients' sense of self. In light of these circumstances, it is not surprising that when the *Schizophrenia Digest* published a call for name change suggestions, over 160 alternatives were proposed to replace the resented "S-word," that is, both its name and its concept.[9] In response to these many suggestions, Michael First, professor of clinical psychiatry at Columbia University and editor of the DSM-IV, replied: "If one of those names was phenomenal, and everyone in the field got behind it, it would probably make it in."[10] But this has not happened yet.

Given that psychiatry is still lacking a clear biological measure for most of its conditions and that symptoms of mental disorders often only depart from "normal" behavior in degrees, the Danish philosopher of science, Anke Bueter, suggests that patients' knowledge should be taken into consideration in the efforts to revise and rename psychiatric diagnoses. Bueter argues against Robert Spitzer, the architect of the DSM-III, who called these efforts to involve patients in such decisions "politically correct nonsense."[11] For Bueter, however, such an integration would correct the injustice done by undermining patients' and caregivers' "capacity as knowers." After all, she argues, it is patients who must live with the name and they are the ones who experience its stigma firsthand.[12] By using first-person accounts and narrative, Bueter argues that psychiatrists can provide "corrective means against implicit value ladenness, inaccuracies, or incompleteness."[13] For her, the marginalization of patients as knowers, for example by excluding them from taxonomic decisions, merely reinforces the prejudice that the credibility of their testimonies is deeply compromised by virtue of them being mentally ill. In short, such marginalization and exclusion further spread the discriminatory idea that it is fundamentally not worth listening to them at all. As in stigma, this can then turn into their own lack of trust in the value of their knowledge. This injustice, Bueter argues, needs to be corrected.

Other ethical discussions dealt with the question of the "usefulness" of the term schizophrenia, not only in terms of the bureaucratic and technical needs (such as its usefulness for the purpose of insurance reimbursements or for the distribution of disability benefits), but also in relation to even higher-stakes questions of life and death. Like many other patients diagnosed with schizophrenia who have been and continue to be psychiatrically treated with medications in order to alleviate their symptoms, Orlean, the patient we introduced in our preface, died when she was only 47 years old, due to complications caused by her condition but also by its treatment. By contrast, John Nash, who refused to take antipsychotic drugs after 1970, would go on to live until he was 86 years old, when he was tragically killed, together with his wife, in a taxi crash in New Jersey.

What if, instead of being treated exclusively for her condition of suffering "schizophrenia," Orlean had been healed from her smoking addiction? Helped with her weight gain? Encouraged to address her lack of physical exercise? Had been offered a listening ear for her broken heart? According to Nash, his recovery was not due to any kind of medical treatment: "I emerged from irrational thinking," he said in 1996, "ultimately without medicine other than the natural hormonal changes of aging."[14] With similar reports in mind, no doubt, Allen Frances, a psychiatrist who was central to the making of the DSM-IV and was concerned with the over-diagnosis and medicalization of ordinary life,[15] asks the obvious and, come to think of it, rhetorical question: what does it mean to call a diagnosis or label *useful* for the patient, if, in fact, "a drug for schizophrenia improves life, but in the process shortens it"? And, if this is often the case or always the risk: "who decides how the utilities should play out?"[16]

With the shift from categories to spectrum, the continued diagnosis of less severe forms of schizophrenia (such as "psychosis risk syndrome" or other so-called "high risk" conditions) raises further serious ethical questions. We must ask what, if any, lost benefits there may be to having concluded that no diagnosis of schizophrenia was warranted (as is the case for the "false negative"); but also, conversely and more significantly, what psychological and social price is paid for making a positive diagnosis of this illness all too lightly. After all, the diagnosis in question is all too often experienced by patients as "a diagnosis of death," as one American patient, suffering from its symptoms and consequences, movingly named it.[17]

Psychiatric diagnoses, Frances reminds us, "have an enormous influence in widely diverse decisions that impact directly on public health, the distribution of scarce mental health and school resources, and even the protection of constitutional rights."[18] Psychiatrists aspire to "do no harm," but given that "harm" is a contested category in and of itself, and that the process of creating and changing psychiatric diagnoses will always remain an exceedingly complex endeavor, Warren Kinghorn, a psychiatrist from Duke University School of Medicine, suggests that those who contemplate revising classification systems "should, at the very least, provoke humility and non-defensive soul-searching."[19]

If humility and soul-searching have been taken into account in the latest efforts to reconstruct the prevailing system of classifications, the path forward remains a question to be grappled with. Whether in the determination of the RDoC to biologize, geneticize, and, finally, medicalize human difference; the attempts of the HiTop consortium to move from pathological psychological categories to dimensions, signs, and symptoms; or the endeavor of patients, service users, and their advocates to see their experience and behavior as a mere variant on a larger normal scale; it seems that, in the recent shift from categories to spectrums and dimensions, the diagnosis of "schizophrenia" is gradually meeting its end.

Assuming that we are indeed witnessing the crumbling of a structure and diagnostic edifice whose foundations were first laid by Kraepelin in his construction of the two "pillars," and with it the inevitable disintegration of the very diagnosis of schizophrenia, what, exactly, would be the prudent – indeed, ethically responsible – way to respond to this outcome? And, while avoiding building yet another "house of cards," as Thomas Szasz famously accused psychiatry of attempting to do time and again,[20] would it not be equally necessary – a sign of wisdom and lessons learned – to acknowledge that so many of its elements, of its debris, and scattered building blocks, so to speak, remain of importance for us, that is, for the present and future uses we may find for them still?

Surely, these basic elements are not mere labels, or cards to frivolously gamble with. How, then, do we bring them together with what they supposedly designate? In other words, how do we put them back into play? Moreover, what place do we give to building blocks (biomarkers as well as cognitive-psychological skills and historical social, economic, and cultural elements) that are newly discovered or are the result of scientific progress?

Those in the RDoC project, for instance, who study mental disorders by exploring basic dimensions of functioning, all of which span the full spectrum of human behavior from the normal to the abnormal, continue to believe in the biology of mental illness. Indeed, they profess deep-seated trust that their building blocks, newly found in basic research, will continue to deliver data stemming from genetics, neuroimaging, and other discoveries made by the bio-sciences. These data and this trust alone, they claim, allows them to reconstruct more valid sets of diagnoses, which, in turn, may assist in finding better methods of treatment. Thinkers along these lines trust that such "bottom-up" research, encouraged by the dimensional model, would allow far better validation of disease entities than its alternatives ever could. Although the efforts to carve out schizophrenia at nature's joints have not yielded a single biological marker or gene that would be useful in making the diagnosis on more solid grounds – indeed, as Frances has claimed, those who hunted and reported these markers and genes for schizophrenia were "forced repeatedly to retract and eat humble pie"[21] – Bruce Cuthbert, Head of the RDoC Unit Office of the NIMH, and Thomas Insel, the director of the NIMH at the time it was launched, proposed to erect "seven pillars" of psychiatric diagnosis based on their shared trust in biology.[22] Although Insel and colleagues maintained that the RDoC was "neither designed nor intended to be used for practical clinical purposes," they claimed it hoped to "produce pioneering new findings and approaches to inform future versions of psychiatric nosologies."[23]

In her recent book, entitled *Mind Fixers: Psychiatry's Troubled Search for the Biology of Mental Illness*, Anne Harrington voices skepticism about the efforts to deconstruct the diagnosis of schizophrenia and the attempts at moving resolutely forward towards a dimensional model, aided by insights from genetics and animal research.[24] As her book shows with compelling evidence, biological psychiatry's struggle to get a firmer grip on the phenomenon of schizophrenia and its symptoms has led mostly to false starts and dead ends. Harrington's proposed, alternative way forward is for psychiatry to not only concentrate its efforts on studying and treating the most *severe* cases of mental illness, including schizophrenia, but also, and particularly, to overcome the reductionist biological quest, while committing to a more open and intensive dialogue with recent relevant developments in the social sciences as well as the humanities.

One such self-proclaimed alternative to the biologically oriented RDoC is the work undertaken by the psychologically minded HiTop consortium (The Hierarchical Taxonomy of Psychopathology), whose search for building blocks is not focused on the brain or the genes, but rather on the overall psychological functioning of the individual. With regard to efforts at reconstructing the theoretical understanding and clinical treatment of schizophrenia, the members of the consortium construct spectrums that range from the normal to the pathological, from engagement to detachment, from intact reality testing to a loss of the patient's crucial ability to do so.[25]

As we discussed in chapter 4, the DSM-5 placed schizophrenia on a spectrum and thus introduced what we might call the broadest possible "category" for it. Indeed, on the one hand, it would ideally allow health care professionals to intervene before a condition turned severe (to *Catch Them Before They Fall*, as the psychoanalyst Christopher Bollas, titled his recent book).[26] Yet, on the other hand, in so doing (that is, by distributing human variants across a continuum), *any* sign of oddness or mild disorder could now receive a diagnostic label and could in itself, if also inadvertently, call for an intervention far *too early*.

The dual risks to be negotiated might thus be formulated as follows: How could one, on the one hand, do one's best to prevent deterioration in the timeliest fashion (as is standard practice in other fields of medicine) while avoiding the danger of over-diagnosing, assigning false positives, on the other hand? After all, an unintended effect of the latter would be the pathologization of the normal, lapsing into forms of "cosmetic psychiatry," or neuro or cognitive "enhancement treatments."

As we proposed, the concept of schizophrenia might come to an end with a full shift to a spectrum/dimensional paradigm. Yet, perhaps, it is worthwhile to keep the diagnosis of schizophrenia, if only as a "diagnostic kind," to use Kathryn Tabb's alternative to the pursuit of "natural kinds" in psychiatry. Here is a recent and lucid proposal that deserves our consideration.[27] While acknowledging the turn "away from the conceptual architecture of traditional psychopathology," Tabb, a philosopher of science from Bard College, sees the possibility and ample opportunities for a future where "psychiatry is increasingly functioning with a diversity of diagnostic systems." Relying on – and combining – some categorical systems, on the one hand, and those premised on spectrums and dimensions, on the other, psychiatry would be increasingly interested in – and capable of – fulfilling its "manifold and diverse demands."[28]

Together with Kenneth F. Schaffner, Tabb proposes an elegant and complex model that does justice to the possible causes of the disorder discovered by the biomedical paradigm, on the one hand, while emphasizing the role of environmental factors and cultural stressors, on the other. To these, they add causes such as lack of government-funded medical services or stigma, as well as environmental stressors such as poverty, to which we might add systemic racism.[29]

As an alternative to the "two pillars" introduced by Kraepelin and the neo-Kraepelinian classification based on the symptoms and the presumed possible outcomes of the disorder (which as we have demonstrated, led to the birth of "schizophrenia" as an established and fixed diagnosis), Schaffner and Tabb offer us nothing short of a new architecture for psychiatry, a reconstructed and more refined edifice that now includes a three-dimensional structure, with four floors. The ground floor is molecular/biochemical, the second floor is cellular and anatomical, the third is behavioral and cognitive, and the fourth is the social.

There is a final pragmatic consideration to keep in mind when considering the new psychiatric classification and the possible abolition of the diagnosis of schizophrenia. Indeed, one cannot "kill" a diagnosis unless one treats people better without it, avoiding its devastating stigma. Providing better treatment to those who need it would make a bigger difference than merely changing the name of the diagnosis. It is possible that better treatment would, almost in itself, minimize the earlier need to stigmatize or consider patients and their symptoms as categorically different, that is, as strangers, odd, or others. Again, with this in mind, what approach to the different historical and available paradigms of explaining, understanding, diagnosing, and treating patients do we favor?

It is said that in the human sciences we find "lumpers" (who search for ways of combining or holistically integrating categories, suggesting humans are more alike than different) and "splitters" (who believe in the separation, identification, and, where necessary, proliferation of categories, emphasizing difference rather than sameness). The two movements of integrating small units into larger wholes, on the one hand, and of "splitting" or "disintegrating" them on the other – the two available options in our science of classification, thus far – are nothing more than a return to Jastrow's image of the duck-rabbit. As indicated in the general introduction to this book, these dual perspectives, these movements of thought and contrasting forms of analysis and interpretation – and, by extension, of diagnosis and treatment – have, perhaps, much older, indeed, ancient philosophical credentials.

Originally, they may lie in the metaphysical understanding of a unified or discrete nature (which in itself never changes, much less disintegrates), on the one hand, and the more open and resolutely dynamic conception and affirmation of existence, including organic and psychic life, on the other. Each original metaphysical paradigm casts its shadow over the other, and the subsequent scientific and psychological theories and practices that base themselves on one of them. These paradigms *either* favor the closed and static, the determinable and predetermined, *or* the open and dynamic, the indeterminable and unpredictable. That said, life and healing, call it pragmatist hope and meliorism, lie in our ability and effort to move between these two age-old paradigms to the ultimate benefit of the people who suffer.

Inspired by the Greek philosopher Empedocles, Freud, with his dual drive theory, assumed that there were two contrasting principles of nature at work in the life of the universe and of the mind. These principles (or in Greek, "causes"), Empedocles called φιλια (love) and νικοs (strife), which he deemed to be in eternal conflict. In Freud's rendition, the first strove to "unite the atoms" in ever greater units, while the second sought to "dissolve these fusions and to separate the atoms of the elements."[30] On the basis of this metaphysical, near-cosmic intuition, in the footsteps of Freud, the psychoanalytic theory and clinical practice developed by Klein and her immediate followers most significantly imagined the life of the mind to be in a continuous process of *oscillation* between these otherwise non-contingent drives of *splitting* and *integration*.

As I hope to have convincingly demonstrated in this book, both the word schizophrenia, whose very origin and etymology suggests the idea of "splitting" (of the mind, the person, and, perhaps of all our discourse about them), and the label "integration disorder" (one of the alternative terms suggested to rename it), contain within them a disarmingly neat and abbreviated definition of the very processes that psychoanalysts such as Klein and Bion made central to the understanding of the most fundamental struggle of *all* human psyches. The alternation between extreme poles – pulling, and perhaps also pushing, in opposite directions – structures our psychic lives, whether we have been given a psychiatric diagnosis or not. Moreover, in their view, sanity, creativity, and love, to use the ingredients Nash mentioned in this chapter's epigraph, are not within the realm of one drive or the other exclusively. Rather, they can be found in the fluctuations and flux between them, or in other words, in the universal and interminable efforts to integrate the splits, to repair the ruptures.

If, as Kenneth Kendler and Michael O'Donovan suggest with regard to the presumed genetic risks of schizophrenia, "there is no '*them*' and '*us*,' only subtle shades of gray"[31] – and, moreover, if Alice Maher and Louis Oppenheim,[32] in their efforts to destigmatize schizophrenia, conclude that "*They're Us*" (to cite the banner of their campaign) – then, indeed, schizophrenia is "*our* most troubling madness," as Luhrmann and Marrow put it concisely.[33]

Eugen Bleuler did not only coin the term schizophrenia, he also offered one of the greatest innovations in the understanding of extreme mental states. As his son Manfred Bleuler would claim, his father had a strong belief that symptoms were expressions of the individual's inner life. He thus "studied the schizophrenic's life essentially in the same way as we study the inner life of neurotics, of healthy men, and of *ourselves*."[34]

The appearance and possible disappearance of schizophrenia as a diagnosis may well reflect ongoing and oscillating shifts in our understanding and interpretation of much older metaphysical structures, based on the aforementioned competing conceptual models.

The contrasting and opposing explanations of the admittedly *eccentric* nature of schizophrenia, we have argued, reveal a much deeper structural antithesis. Indeed, historically – and, in all likelihood, continuously – it pits continuity against discontinuity, equilibrium against disequilibrium, and, perhaps ultimately, vitalism or spiritualism against mechanism or reductionism. That these distinctions, thus far, seem both *unavoidable* and *fallible* or, indeed, *revisable*, depending on contingent historical situations, scientific and sociocultural, conceptual and analytical grounds, makes it a fundamental critical – and clinical – imperative for us, contemporary theorists and practitioners, to use them with diligence and the greatest possible care. Indeed, it is in the space or interval of such metaphysical and epistemic uncertainty that *hope* – our very freedom and responsibility in psychic matters – is firmly lodged.

Theorizing and treating schizophrenia, as well as whatever might come to refine or replace its diagnosis and terms, requires us to be – *at a minimum* – of "two minds." As in Jastrow's drawing, we can and should see now the duck, now the rabbit, realizing that the patient is now "really different," and now "in essence the same" as us. In any case, he or she is far more complete than our inevitable partial vision suggests, and as such will elude us, in part, forever.

Notes

Preface

1 The term "disease entity" or *species morborum* refers to a *natural kind* of disease. Just as there are *species* of animal or plants, and *classes* of chemical substance, there are also *kinds* or *classes* of disease. In the same way that biology constructs *taxonomies* or that chemistry arranges the elements in a *periodic table*, medicine arranges diseases in a systematic order by *nosology*.
2 I. F. Brockington, "Schizophrenia: Yesterday's concept," *European Psychiatry* 7, 5 (1992): 203–7.
3 Richard Bentall, *Madness Explained: Psychosis and Human Nature* (London: Penguin, 2004), 107.
4 Rina Dutta, Talya Greene, Jean Addington, et al., "Biological, life course, and cross-cultural studies all point toward the value of dimensional and developmental ratings in the classification of psychosis," *Schizophrenia Bulletin* 33, (2007): 868–76.
5 Erik Simonsen, "Personality and psychosis," in J. O. Johannessen, B. V. Martindale and J. Cullberg (eds.), *Evolving Psychosis* (London: Routledge, 2006), 37.
6 B. Martindale, "Response: A historical note," in *ISPS UK Newsletter* June 12–13, 2007.

Introduction The Ends of a Diagnosis

1 Louise Wilson, *This Stranger, My Son* (New York: G.P. Putnam, 1968), 10.
2 Thomas S. Kuhn, *The Structure of Scientific Revolutions*, 4th edn, with an Introduction by Ian Hacking (Chicago, IL: University of Chicago Press, 2012), 111.
3 Orna Ophir, *Psychosis, Psychoanalysis and Psychiatry in Postwar USA: On the Borderland of Madness* (New York: Routledge, 2015).
4 Thomas Szasz, *Schizophrenia: The Sacred Symbol of Psychiatry* (New York: Basic Books, 1976).
5 Guy M. Goodwin and John R. Geddes, "What is the heartland of psychiatry?," *British Journal of Psychiatry* 191, 3 (2007): 189–91.
6 Paul Eugen Bleuler, "Die Prognose der Dementia praecox (Schizophreniegruppe)," *Allgemeine Zeitschrift für Psychiatrie und psychischgerichtliche Medizin* 65 (1908): 436–64. See also Paul Eugen Bleuler, *Dementia Praecox or the Group of Schizophrenias*, trans. J. Zinkin (New York: International Universities Press, 1950 [1911]).
7 Johann Christian Reil, "Über den Begriff der Medicin und ihre Verzweigungen, besonders in Beziehung auf die Berichtigung der Topik der Psychiaterie" ("On the Term of Medicine and its Ramifications, Particularly with Regard to the Revision of the Topic in Psychiatry"), in J. C. Hoffbauer (ed.), *Beyträge zur Beförderung einer Kurmethode auf psychischem Wege* ("*Contributions to the Advancement of a Treatment Method by Psychic Ways*") (Halle: Curt'sche Buchhandlung, 1808), 161–279.

8 Plato, *Phaedrus*, XXI, 264e–266b, trans. R. Waterfield (Oxford: Oxford University Press, 2002), 52–6.

9 Seeking an answer to the question of whether it is the lover who should be favored or the non-lover, Socrates divides madness into sinister madness – caused by human ailments – on the one hand, and that which is divine or sent by the gods, on the other. Plato, *Phaedrus*, 244a, 25.

10 Ibid., 265b, 54–5.

11 German E. Berrios, "Classifications in psychiatry: A conceptual history," *Australian and New Zealand Journal of Psychiatry* 33, 2 (1999): 145–6. See also Kenneth S. Kendler, "An historical framework for psychiatric nosology," *Psychological Medicine* 39, 12 (2009): 1935–41.

12 See Ian Hacking, "Lost in the forest," *London Review of Books*, 35, no. 15 (2008) and *The Social Construction of What* (Cambridge, MA: Harvard University Press, 1999), 83.

13 Hacking, *The Social Construction of What*, 113.

14 Daniel Mason and Honor Hsin, "'A more perfect arrangement of plants': The botanical model in psychiatric nosology, 1676 to the present day," *History of Psychiatry* 29, 2 (2018): 131–46.

15 Ian Hacking, *Mad Travelers: Reflections on the Reality of Transient Mental Illness* (Charlottesville, VA: University of Virginia Press, 1998), 55.

16 The equivalent to the *International Classification of Diseases* (ICD) issued by the World Health Organization (WHO).

17 Knud Faber, *Nosography in Modern Internal Medicine* (New York: Paul B. Hoeber, 1923), vii, cited in Charles Rosenberg, *Our Present Complaint: American Medicine Then and Now* (Baltimore, MD: Johns Hopkins University Press, 2007), 17.

18 Rosenberg, *Our Present Complaint.*

19 Amy June Sousa, "Diagnostic neutrality in psychiatric treatment in North India," in Tanya M. Luhrmann and Jocelyn Marrow (eds.), *Our Most Troubling Madness: Case Studies in Schizophrenia Across Cultures* (Oakland, CA: University of California Press, 2016), 47.

20 Anonymous, "First person account," *Schizophrenia Bulletin*, 7, 1 (1981): 196–7.

21 Rosenberg, *Our Present Complaint*, 33.

22 Andrew Krystal, Duke University, cited in Clare Wilson, "Losing the labels: Psychiatry's scientific revolution," *New Scientist* 222, 2968 (2014): 10–11.

23 Javier Escobar, "An insider's view of the new diagnostic and statistical manual of North American psychiatry (DSM-5)," *Colombia Medica* 44, 2 (2013): 129–31.

24 See Ian Hacking, "Making up people," in T. C. Heller, M. Sosna and D. E. Wellbery (eds.), *Reconstructing Individualism* (Stanford, CA: Stanford University Press, 1986), 161–71.

25 Hacking, "Making up people," 169.

26 G. Der, S. Gupta and R. M. Murray, "Is schizophrenia disappearing?," *The Lancet* 335, 8688 (1990): 513–16.

27 Raymond C. Lake, *Schizophrenia Is a Misdiagnosis: Implications for the DSM-5 and the ICD-11* (New York: Springer, 2012).

28 Jim van Os, "'Schizophrenia' does not exist," *British Medical Journal* 352 (2016): i375.

29 Simon McCarthy-Jones, "The concept of schizophrenia is coming to an end," *The Independent*, 4 September 2017.

30 Robin Murray, "Mistakes I have made in my research career," *Schizophrenia Bulletin*, 43, 2 (2017): 253–6.
31 Kuhn, *The Structure of Scientific Revolutions*.
32 Joao P. De Aquino and David A. Ross, "Using biology to reconstruct psychiatric nosology from the bottom up," *Biological Psychiatry* 82, 10 (2017): 71–4.
33 Per Bergsholm, "Is schizophrenia disappearing? The rise and fall of the diagnosis of functional psychoses: an essay," *BMC Psychiatry* 16, 387 (2016): 2–9.
34 NIMH's Research Domain Criteria (RDoC); see https://www.nimh.nih.gov/research/research-funded-by-nimh/rdoc/about-rdoc.shtml, and Bruce N. Cuthbert, "The NIMH Research Domain Criteria (RDoC): New concepts for mental disorders," *Psychiatric Times* 34, 5 (2017).
35 Richard Noll, *American Madness: The Rise and Fall of Dementia Praecox* (Cambridge, MA: Harvard University Press, 2011), 282.
36 Hierarchical Taxonomy of Psychopathology (HiTOP): See R. Kotov, R. F. Krueger, D. Watson, et al., "The Hierarchical Taxonomy of Psychopathology (HiTOP): A dimensional alternative to traditional nosologies." *Journal of Abnormal Psychology* 126, 4 (2007): 454–77.
37 Nikolas Rose, *Our Psychiatric Future* (Cambridge: Polity Press, 2019), 92.
38 Hacking, *Mad Travelers*, 87.
39 Norman Sartorius, Helen Chiu, Kua Ee Heok, et al., "Name change for schizophrenia," *Schizophrenia Bulletin* 40, 2 (2014): 255–8.
40 Tanya M. Luhrmann, *Of Two Minds: The Growing Disorder in American Psychiatry* (London: Picador, 2000).

Chapter 1 From the Bible to Bleuler

1 We use the term "patient" as it connotes *pati* or suffering.
2 Roy Porter, "The patient's view: Doing medical history from below," *Theory and Society* 14, 2 (1985): 175–98.
3 Mark Ellerby, "Schizophrenia: Stigma and the impact of literature," *Schizophrenia Bulletin* 44, 3 (2018): 466–7.
4 Emil Kraepelin, *Dementia Praecox and Paraphrenia*, trans. R. Mary Barclay; ed. George M. Robertson (New York: Krieger Publishing, 1971 [1919]), 242.
5 Susan Weiner, "The details in schizophrenia," *Schizophrenia Bulletin* 44, 4 (2018): 707–9.
6 Ibid.
7 Ibid.
8 Ibid.
9 See Tanya M. Luhrmann and Jocelyn Marrow (eds.) *Our Most Troubling Madness: Case Studies in Schizophrenia Across Cultures* (Oakland, CA: University of California Press, 2016).
10 See John Weir Perry, *The Far Side of Madness* (Englewood Cliffs, NJ: Prentice-Hall, 1974).
11 D. V. Jeste, R. Carman, J. B. Lohr, and R. J. Wyatt, "Did schizophrenia exist before the eighteenth century?," *Comprehensive Psychiatry*, 26 (1985): 493–503, 502.
12 Michel Foucault, *Madness and Civilization: A History of Insanity in the Age of Reason* (New York: Random House, 1965), 254.
13 Madalina Vârtejanu-Joubert, "Representations of madmen and madness in Jewish sources from the pre-exilic to the Roman-Byzantine period," in G. Eghigian (ed.),

The Routledge History of Madness and Mental Health (New York: Routledge, 2017), 38. See also Madalina Vârtejanu-Joubert, *Folie et société dans l'Israël antique* (Paris: L'Harmattan, 2004).

14 Deuteronomy 28:28.

15 Vârtejanu-Joubert, "Representations of madmen," 20.

16 Daniel 4:33.

17 Mark 5:2–9.

18 Mark 5:9.

19 Mark 5:15.

20 Samuel, 14:12.

21 George Rosen, *Madness in Society* (Chicago, IL: University of Chicago Press, 1968), 11.

22 Karl Jaspers, "Der Prophet Ezechiel, Eine pathographische Studie," in *Arbeiten zur Psychiatrie, Neurologie und ihre Grenzgebieten: Festschrift für Kurt Schneider* (Heidelberg: Verlag Scherer, 1947), 77–85. See also George Stein, "The voices that Ezekiel hears – Psychiatry in the Old Testament," *British Journal of Psychiatry* 196, 2 (2010): 101.

23 Samuel 14:10.

24 Samuel 10:9.

25 Daniel 4:16.

26 Isaiah 28:21.

27 Vârtejanu-Joubert, "Representations of madmen," 29.

28 Hagiga 3b, quoted in Vârtejanu-Joubert, "Representations of madmen," 34.

29 Vârtejanu-Joubert, "Representations of madmen," 34.

30 Caelius Aurelianus, *On Acute Diseases and on Chronic Diseases*, trans. I. E. Drabkin (Chicago, IL: University of Chicago Press, 1950).

31 Plato, *Phaedrus*, 265b2–6.

32 *Phaedrus*, 244b6–7.

33 Plato, *Laws*, XI, 934c7, trans. T. L. Pangle (Chicago, IL: University of Chicago Press, 1988), 337.

34 Chiara Thumiger, "Ancient Greek and Roman traditions," in *The Routledge History of Madness and Mental Health*, 42–61.

35 *Hysteria in Virgins*, quoted in Mary R. Lefkowitz and Maureen B. Fant (eds.), *Women's Life in Greece and Rome: A Source Book in Translation*, 3rd edn (Baltimore, MD: Johns Hopkins University Press, 2005), 243.

36 Ibid.

37 Ibid., 242.

38 Hippocrates, *The Sacred Disease*, Loeb Classical Library, Vol II, trans. W. H. S. Jones, P. Potter, W. D. Smith and E. T. Withington (Cambridge, MA: Harvard University Press, 1923).

39 Ibid., 175

40 Thumiger, "Ancient Greek and Roman traditions," 48.

41 Ibid.

42 *The Sacred Disease*, 177.

43 Ibid.

44 Ibid.

45 Celsus, *De Medicina*, III, 18. See Celsus, *On Medicine*, Vol. III: Books 7–8, trans. W. G. Spencer. Loeb Classical Library (Cambridge, MA: Harvard University Press, 1938), 336.
46 Thumiger, "Ancient Greek and Roman traditions," 51.
47 Ibid., 52.
48 Galen, *On the Passions and Errors of the Soul*, trans. P. Harkins (Columbus, OH: Ohio State University Press, 1963).
49 Ibid., 43.
50 Ibid., 46–7.
51 Ibid., 46. In Plato's metaphor of the tripartite soul, the charioteer drives a pair of winged horses, one of which is noble and good (the spirited part) while the other is the opposite (the appetitive part).
52 Although the origin of the six non-naturals can be traced back to Galen's "Ars medica," he does not use the term "non-naturals." It was in the Islamic world, which received Greek medicine through translation, that the number and the contents of these factors was established as theory.
53 Galen, *The Capacities of the Soul Depend on the Mixtures of the Body*, in Thumiger, "Ancient Greek and Roman traditions," 54. See Peter Singer, *Galen, Psychological Writings* (Cambridge: Cambridge University Press, 2013).
54 Margery Kempe, *The Book of Margery Kempe*, trans. John Skinner (New York: Image Books/Doubleday, 1998).
55 Claire Trenery and Peregrine Horden, "Madness in the Middle Ages," in *The Routledge History of Madness and Mental Health*, 62–80.
56 Avicenna, *Canon medicinae (latine): a Gerardo Cremonensi translatus* (Venice: Bonetus Locatellus, 1490), 257 in Trenery and Horden, "Madness in the Middle Ages," 66.
57 Ibid., 67.
58 Ibid.
59 Ibid.
60 Penelope Doob, *Nebuchadnezzar's Children: Conventions of Madness in Middle English Literature* (New Haven, CT: Yale University Press, 1974).
61 Sylvia Huot, *Madness in Medieval French Literature: Identities Found and Lost* (Oxford: Oxford University Press, 2003), 10.
62 Barbara Cassin, Emily Apter, Jacques Lezra and Michael Wood, *Dictionary of Untranslatables: A Philosophical Lexicon* (Princeton, NJ: Princeton University Press, 2014), 615.
63 Sander Gilman, *Seeing the Insane: A Visual and Cultural History of Our Attitudes Toward the Mentally Ill* (Brattleboro, VT: Echo Point Books and Media, 2014), xi.
64 Cassin, *Dictionary of Untranslatables*, 617.
65 *The Book of Margery Kempe*, trans. John Skinner (New York: Image Books/Doubleday, 1998).
66 Ibid., 276.
67 Ibid., 70.
68 Ibid., 248.
69 Trenery and Horden, "Madness in the Middle Ages," 74.

70 Ibid. See also Peregrine Horden, "Responses to possession and insanity in the earlier Byzantine world," *Social History of Medicine* 6 (1993): 177–94.
71 Michael W. Dols, *Majnūn: The Madman in Medieval Islamic Society* (Oxford: Clarendon Press, 1992), 475.
72 Hannah Allen, "A narrative of God's gracious dealings with that choice Christian," 1683, in *Voices of Madness: Four Pamphlets, 1683–1796*, ed. Allan Ingram (Stroud, Glos.: Sutton, 1997).
73 Elizabeth Mellyn, "Healers and healing in the early modern health care market," in *The Routledge History of Madness and Mental Health*, 83–100.
74 Lauren Kassell, Michael Hawkins, Robert Ralley, et al. (eds.), "CASE16959," in *The Casebooks of Simon Forman and Richard Napier, 1596–1634: A Digital Edition*, https://casebooks.lib.cam.ac.uk/cases/CASE1659.
75 Mellyn, "Healers and healing," 99.
76 Ibid., 91.
77 George Mora, "Paracelsus' psychiatry: On the occasion of the 400th anniversary of his book 'Diseases that Deprive Man of His Reason' (1567)," *American Journal of Psychiatry* 124 (1967): 803–14.
78 Mellyn, "Healers and healing," p. 91.
79 Ibid.
80 Philippe Pinel, *A Treatise on Insanity*, trans. D. D. Davis (Sheffield: W. Todd, 1806), 2.
81 Ibid.
82 German E. Berrios and Ivana S. Marková, "The epistemology and classification of 'madness' since the eighteenth century," in *The Routledge History of Madness and Mental Health*, 115–34.
83 Carl Linnaeus, *Genera Morborum* [*Classification of Diseases*] (Upsaliæ, 1759), 1.
84 Richard Pulteney, "A general view of the writings of Linnæus," 178–9. https://quod.lib.umich.edu/e/ecco/004894125.0001.000/1:3.4?rgn=div2;view=fulltext
85 William Cullen, *Synopsis Nosologiae Methodicae*, Vol. 1, 4th edn (Edinburgh: W. Creech, 1785), 182. Quoted in Berrios and Marková, "The epistemology and classification of 'madness'," 118.
86 Ibid., 118.
87 Philippe Pinel, *Medico-Philosophical Treatise on Mental Alienation or Mania*. Vol. 2, 2nd edn, trans. G. Hickish, D. Healy and L. C. Charland (Chichester: Wiley-Blackwell, 2008), 54.
88 Ibid., 62.
89 G. E. Berrios, "The nineteenth-century nosology of alienism, history and epistemology," in Kenneth S. Kendler and Josef Parnas (eds.), *Philosophical Issues in Psychiatry II: Nosology* (Oxford: Oxford University Press, 2012), 101–23.
90 Ibid., 121.
91 See Andrew Scull, *Madness in Civilization: A Cultural History of Insanity from the Bible to Freud, from the Madhouse to Modern Medicine* (Princeton, NJ: Princeton University Press, 2015).
92 William Parry-Jones, *The Trade in Lunacy: A Study of Private Madhouses in England in the Eighteenth and Nineteenth Centuries* (London: Routledge & Kegan Paul, 1972).
93 Berrios and Marková, "The epistemology and classification of 'madness'," 122.

94 Edward Shorter, *A History of Psychiatry: From the Era of the Asylum to the Age of Prozac* (New York: John Wiley & Sons, 1997).

95 Berrios and Marková, "The epistemology and classification of 'madness'," 123.

96 Andrew Abbott, *The System of Professions: An Essay on the Division of Expert Labor* (Chicago, IL: University of Chicago Press, 1988).

97 Berrios and Marková, "The epistemology and classification of 'madness,'" 121.

98 Ibid.

99 Ibid., 124.

100 See E. Mendel, *Leitfaden der Psychiatrie* (Stuttgart: Ferdinand Enke, 1902), 121, quoted in Berrios and Marková, "The epistemology and classification of 'madness'," 124.

101 P. J. Möbius, *Abriss der Lehre von den Nervenkrankheiten* (Leipzig: Ambrosius Abel, 1893), 71ff, quoted in Berrios and Marková, "The epistemology and classification of 'madness'," 124.

102 Berrios and Marková, "The epistemology and classification of 'madness'," 125.

103 Edward Shorter, "Primary care," in Roy Porter (ed.), *The Cambridge Illustrated History of Medicine* (Cambridge: Cambridge University Press, 1996), 118–53.

104 See Roy Porter, "What is disease," in *The Cambridge Illustrated History of Medicine*, 95.

Chapter 2 The Birth of "the Schizophrenias"

1 Emil Kraepelin, *Lectures on Clinical Psychiatry* (New York: William Wood & Co., 1904), 21–2.

2 Emil Kraepelin and Paul B. Hoff, *Memoirs*, eds. H. Hippius, G. Peters and D. Ploog (Berlin: Springer, 1987), 11.

3 Emil Kraepelin, *Psychiatrie: Ein Lehrbuch für Studierende und Aerzte*, 6th edn (Leipzig: Barth, 1899); Emil Kraepelin, *Psychiatry: A Textbook for Students and Physicians*, trans. H. Metoui and S. Ayed (Canton, MA: Science History Publications, 1990). See also *Psychiatrie*, 8th edn (Leipzig: Barth, 1909), and *Dementia Praecox and Paraphrenia*, trans. R. Mary Barclay; ed. G. M. Robertson (1919; repr. New York: Krieger Publishing, 1971).

4 Richard Noll, *American Madness: The Rise and Fall of Dementia Praecox* (Cambridge, MA: Harvard University Press, 2011), 48.

5 Emil Kraepelin, "Ziele und Wege der klinischen Psychiatrie [Autoreferat, Diskussion]," in *Allgemeine Zeitschrift für Psychiatrie und psychisch-gerichtliche Medicin* 53, 5 (1897): 840–8.

6 Kraepelin, *Memoirs*, 60–1.

7 Philip K. Dick, *Martian Time-Slip* (Boston: Mariner Books: 2012 [1964]), 120.

8 See G. E. Berrios, "'The clinic-diagnostic perspective in psychopathology,' by K. Kahlbaum (1878)," in *History of Psychiatry*, 18, 2 (2007), 231–3.

9 Kraepelin, *Psychiatrie: Ein kurzes Lehrbuch für Studierende und Aerzte*, 4th edn (Leipzig: Abel, 1893), in Erik Engstrom, "Emil Kraepelin's inaugural lecture in Dorpat: Contexts and legacies," *TRAMES* 20, 4 (2016): 337–50.

10 Kraepelin, *Lectures on Clinical Psychiatry*, 21–2.

11 E. Kraepelin and A. R. Diefendorf, *Clinical Psychiatry: A Textbook for Students and Physicians, Abstracted and Adapted from the 7th German Edition of Kraepelin's Lehrbuch der Psychiatrie* (New York: Macmillan Co., 1907), 219.

12 Joao P. de Aquino and David A. Ross, "Using biology to reconstruct psychiatric nosology from the bottom up," *Biological Psychiatry* 82, 10 (2017): 71–4.

13 Oscar Vogt, "Gründung eines Kraepelin-Preises und seine erste Verleihung bei der Weihe des Neubaues der Deutschen Forschungsanstalt für Psychiatrie (Kaiser Wilhelm-Institut) in München am 13. Juni 1928," *Zeitschrift für die gesamte Neurologie und Psychiatrie* 117 (1928): 195–201.

14 Kraepelin writes that we must "abandon for all time a systematic demarcation of mental disorders along the lines of Linnaeus" (in Kraepelin, *Psychiatrie: Ein kurzes Lehrbuch für Studierende und Aerzte*, 3rd and 4th edns, quoted in E. Engstrom and K. Kendler, "Emil Kraepelin: Icon and reality," *American Journal of Psychiatry* 172, 12 (2015): 1193.

15 Noll, *American Madness*, 62–3. Noll shows it was the German physician Heinrich Schüle (1840–1916), of the Illenau asylum in Baden, who first used the term *dementia praecox* in the 1886 third edition of his textbook on clinical psychiatry. There, he referred to hereditarily predisposed individuals who were "wrecked on the cliffs of puberty" and developed acute dementia, while others developed *hebephrenia*. *Dementia praecox* and *hebephrenia* were therefore terms for different conditions, one acute and one chronic. See ibid., 63.

16 Ibid., 67.

17 See Kraepelin, *Psychiatrie: Ein kurzes Lehrbuch für Studierende und Aerzte*, 2nd edn (Leipzig: Abel, 1887), quoted in Engstrom and Kendler, "Emil Kraepelin: Icon and reality," 1193.

18 Ibid.

19 Emil Kraepelin, *Clinical Psychiatry: A Textbook for Students and Physicians, Abstracted and Adapted from the 7th German Edition of Lehrbuch der Psychiatrie* (New York: Macmillan, 1923).

20 P. H. Wender, "Dementia praecox: The development of the concept," *American Journal of Psychiatry* 119 (1963): 1143–51.

21 Noll, *American Madness*, 53.

22 The editor of the 1919 English translation of *Dementia Praecox and Paraphrenia*, George M. Robertson (a lecturer on mental diseases at the University of Edinburgh and physician at the Royal Asylum in Morningside), explicitly mentioned Kraepelin's idea that *dementia praecox* was a *distinct disease*, linking it to insanity with a clear biological marker. Robertson compared Kraepelin's contribution to Antoine Lauren Bayle's 1822 bold assertion that neurosyphilis was a distinct disease entity. Comparing *dementia praecox* with GPI, Robertson argued that after a century of observations during which the latter had "yielded up most of its secrets," the most important practical problem for psychiatry remained the former.

23 The Wassermann test is an antibody test for syphilis, named after the bacteriologist August Paul von Wassermann, based on complement fixation. It was the first blood test for syphilis.

24 Hannah S. Decker, "How Kraepelinian was Kraepelin? How Kraepelinian are the neo-Kraepelinians? – From Emil Kraepelin to DSM-III," *History of Psychiatry* 18, 71 (2007): 337–60.

25 Engstrom and Kendler, "Emil Kraepelin: Icon and reality," 1190.

26 Kenneth S. Kendler, "The development of Kraepelin's concept of dementia praecox. A close reading of relevant texts," *JAMA Psychiatry* 77, 11 (2020): 1181–7.

27 See Emil Kraepelin, "The manifestations of insanity," trans. and introduction by Dominic Beer, *History of Psychiatry* 3, 12 (1992): 504–8.
28 Ibid., 507.
29 Ibid.
30 Noll, *American Madness*, 64.
31 Eugen Bleuler, "Die Prognose der Dementia praecox (Schizophreniegruppe)," quoted in Roland Kuhn, "Eugen Bleuler's concepts of psychopathology," trans. H. Cahn, *History of Psychiatry* 15, 3 (2004): 361–6.
32 Assen Jablensky, "The diagnostic concept of schizophrenia: Its history, evolution, and future prospects," *Dialogues in Clinical Neuroscience* 12, 3 (2010): 271–87.
33 Eugen Bleuler, *Dementia Praecox or the Group of Schizophrenias*, 8th edn, trans. J. Zinkin (1950; New York: International Universities Press, 1969), 7–8.
34 Kuhn, "Eugen Bleuler's concepts of psychopathology," 361.
35 Bleuler, "Die Prognose der Dementia Praecox (Schizophreniegruppe)," in Kuhn, 361–6.
36 Ibid. See also *Lehrbuch der Psychiatrie* (Berlin: Springer, 2016) and *Dementia Praecox or the Group of Schizophrenias*, trans. J. Zinkin (1911; New York: International Universities Press, 1950).
37 See also Gabriele Stotz-Ingenlath, "Epistemological aspects of Eugen Bleuler's conception of schizophrenia in 1911," *Medicine, Healthcare and Philosophy* 3 (2000): 153–9.
38 Bleuler, *Dementia Praecox or the Group of Schizophrenias*, 9.
39 Ibid., 95.
40 Ibid., 14.
41 Ibid., 17.
42 Ibid., 21, italics in original.
43 Ibid., 22, italics in original.
44 Ibid., italics in original.
45 Ibid., 22–3.
46 Ibid., italics added.
47 Ibid., 40.
48 Ibid.
49 Ibid., 47.
50 Ibid., 50.
51 Ibid.
52 Ibid.
53 Ibid., 56.
54 Ibid.
55 Ibid., 67.
56 Manfred Bleuler, "Eugen Bleuler and schizophrenia," *British Journal of Psychiatry* 144 (1984): 327–8.
57 Bleuler, *Dementia Praecox or the Group of Schizophrenias*, 471–2.
58 Ibid.
59 Ibid., 470–1.
60 Ibid., 486; 482.
61 Ibid., 475.
62 Ibid.
63 Ibid., 472.

64 Ibid., 476.
65 Ibid., 476–7.
66 Ibid., 462, italics added.
67 See T. G. Dalzell, "Eugen Bleuler 150: Bleuler's reception of Freud," *History of Psychiatry* 18, 72 Pt 4 (2007): 471–82.
68 After spending some time at the Salpêtrière hospital in Paris, where he had studied with its director of psychological laboratories, Pierre Janet (1859–1947), Jung returned to Zurich and moved into a flat in the Burghölzli clinic next to Bleuler's, with whom he worked closely.
69 C. G. Jung, *Zur Psychologie und Pathologie sogenannter okkulter Phänomene* (Dissertation, University of Zurich, 1902). See also A. Möller, C. Scharfetter and D. Hell, "Development and termination of the working relationship of C. G. Jung and Eugen Bleuler, 1900–1909," *History of Psychiatry* 13, 4 (2002): 445–53.
70 Jung, Foreword to *Über die Psychologie der Dementia praecox: Ein Versuch* (Halle: Verlagsbuchhandlung C. Marhold, 1907). English translation, *The Psychology of Dementia Praecox*, in *The Collected Works of C. G. Jung*, vol. 8, trans. R. F. C. Hull (Princeton, NJ: Princeton University Press, 1974), 3.
71 Stephan Heckers, "Bleuler and the neurobiology of schizophrenia," *Schizophrenia Bulletin* 37, 6 (2011): 1131–5.
72 Eugen Bleuler, Preface to *Dementia Praecox or the Group of Schizophrenias*, vii.
73 Ibid., 1.
74 Dalzell, "Eugen Bleuler 150: Bleuler's reception of Freud."
75 Sigmund Freud, "Psychoanalytische Bemerkungen über einen autobiographisch beschriebenen Fall von Paranoia (Dementia Paranoides)," *Jahrbuch für psychoanalytische und psychopathologische Forschungen* 3, 1 (1911): 9–68.
76 See D. P. Schreber, *Memoirs of My Nervous Illness* (New York: New York Review Books, 2000).
77 Eugen Bleuler, "Psychoanalytische Bemerkungen über einen autobiographisch beschriebenen Fall von Paranoia (Dementia paranoides)," *Jahrbuch für psychoanalytische und psychopathologische Forschungen*. Bd. III. *Zentralblatt für Psychoanalyse* 2 (1912): 343–8. See also T. G. Dalzell, *Freud's Schreber Between Psychiatry and Psychoanalysis* (London: Karnac Books, 2011).
78 Angela Woods, "'I suffer in an unknown manner that is hieroglyphical': Jung and Babette *en route* to Freud and Schreber," *History of the Present* 1, 2 (2011): 244–58.

Chapter 3 Psychoanalysis and Schizophrenia

1 Carl G. Jung, *Collected Work of C. G. Jung, Volume 3: Psychogenesis of Mental Disease*, trans. R. F. C. Hull (Princeton, NJ: Princeton University Press, 1982 [1920]), 158.
2 Jung, Letter to Freud, dated January 8, 1907, in *The Freud/Jung Letters: The Correspondence between S. Freud and C. G. Jung*, edited by William McGuire (London: Hogarth Press and Routledge & Kegan Paul, 1974), 21.
3 See Jung, *Psychoanalysis and Association Experiments*, trans. D. Stein and D. Riviere (Princeton, NJ: Princeton University Press, 1973 [1906]).
4 Jung, *The Collected Works of C. G. Jung, vol. 3*, 162.
5 Jung, "The association method," *American Journal of Psychology* 31 (1910): 219–69.

6 Bleuler, "Significance of association experiments," trans. M. D. Eder, in C. G. Jung (ed.), *Studies in Word-Association* (London: Routledge and Kegan Paul, 1969 [1906]), 6.
7 Freud, Letter to Jung, dated December 6, 1906, in *The Freud/Jung Letters*, 13.
8 Hilda C. Abraham and Ernst L. Freud (eds.), *A Psychoanalytic Dialogue: The Letters of Sigmund Freud and Karl Abraham, 1907–1926* (New York: Basic Books, 1965), 11.
9 Freud, Letter to Jung, dated June 21, 1908, in *The Freud/Jung Letters*, 158.
10 George Makari, *Revolution in Mind: The Creation of Psychoanalysis* (New York: HarperCollins, 2008), 194.
11 Freud, Letter to Jung, dated April 7, 1911, in *The Freud/Jung Letters*, 414.
12 Bleuler, "The prognosis of dementia praecox: the group of schizophrenias," (1908) in J. Cutting and M. Shepherd (eds.), *The Clinical Roots of the Schizophrenia Concept: Translations of Seminal European Contributions on Schizophrenia* (Cambridge: Cambridge University Press, 1987), 59.
13 E. Bleuler, *Affectivity, Suggestibility, Paranoia*, trans. C. Ricksher (Utica, NY: State Hospitals Press, 1912; German publication 1906).
14 Jung, *The Psychology of Dementia Praecox* (1907), in *The Collected Works of C. G. Jung*, vol. 8, trans. R. F. C. Hull (Princeton, NJ: Princeton University Press, 1974).
15 Jung, Letter to Freud dated April 11, 1907, in *The Freud/Jung Letters*, 30.
16 Jung, Letter to Freud dated June 4, 1907, in *The Freud/Jung Letters*, 58.
17 Jung, Letter to Freud dated June 26, 1908, in *The Freud/Jung Letters*, 160–1.
18 Ibid., 161.
19 Freud, Letter to Oskar Pfister, dated September 14, 1926, in *Psychoanalysis and Faith: The Letters of Sigmund Freud and Oskar Pfister*, ed. H. Meng and E. L. Freud, trans. E. Mosbacher (New York: Basic Books, 1963), 105–6.
20 Ibid., 106.
21 David J. Lynn, "Freud's analysis of A.B., a psychotic man, 1925–1930," *Journal of the American Academy of Psychoanalysis and Dynamic Psychiatry* 21, 1 (1993): 63–78.
22 Sigmund Freud, *Psychoanalysis and Faith: The Letters of Sigmund Freud and Oskar Pfister*, ed. H. Meng and E. Freud (New York: Basic Books, 1963), 96.
23 See Lynn, "Freud's analysis of A.B., a psychotic man," 69.
24 Freud, Letter to Oskar Pfister, 1926, in *Psychoanalysis and Faith*, 106.
25 Freud, Letter to Jung, dated February 17, 1908, in *The Freud/Jung Letters*, 121.
26 Abraham and Freud (eds.), *A Psychoanalytic Dialogue*, 11.
27 Sigmund Freud, "Psycho-analytic notes on an autobiographical account of a case of paranoia (dementia paranoides)," in *The Standard Edition of the Complete Psychological Works of Sigmund Freud, Volume XII (1911–1913): The Case of Schreber, Papers on Technique and Other Works*, 1–82.
28 Daniel Paul Schreber, *Denkwürdigkeiten eines Nervenkranken* (1903), English trans., *Memoirs of My Nervous Illness* (New York: New York Review Books, 2000).
29 Freud, "Psycho-analytic notes," 9.
30 In fact, Schreber had died in 1911, just a few months before Freud's essay saw the light of day.
31 Schreber, *Memoirs*, quoted in Freud, "Psycho-analytic notes," 12.
32 Ibid., 36.
33 Ibid., 13.

34 Ibid., 14.
35 Ibid., 13–14.
36 Ibid., 15.
37 Ibid.
38 Ibid.
39 Ibid., 16.
40 Ibid., 18, emphasis added.
41 Ibid., 21, emphasis added.
42 Ibid., emphasis added.
43 Ibid., 35.
44 Ibid., emphasis added.
45 Ibid., 43.
46 Ibid.
47 Ibid.
48 Ibid., 46, emphasis added.
49 Ibid., 49.
50 Freud gives an example borrowed from Jung, who discusses a schizophrenic patient who, instead of cathecting his doctor (that is, investing his libido in the figure of the healer), was convinced that "all Dr. J.'s" are fundamentally the same. See ibid., 50.
51 Ibid., 52.
52 Ibid., 53.
53 Ibid.
54 Where the latter is portrayed as a whore who speaks to him in human language, and in which the "sun turns pale before him." See ibid., 54.
55 And, lest we forget, the sun or sun god plays a central role in Freud's own later self-described "historical novel," namely *Der Mann Moses und die monotheistische Religion* (*Moses and Monotheism*), which all but anchors biblical religion in a solar myth of sorts.
56 Freud, "Psycho-analytic notes," 55.
57 Ibid.
58 Ibid., 57.
59 Ibid.
60 Ibid., 59, emphasis added.
61 Ibid., 66, emphasis added.
62 Ibid., 68.
63 Jung, *The Psychology of Dementia Praecox*, 36.
64 Ibid., 98.
65 In McGuire, *The Freud/Jung Letters*, 20.
66 Jung, Letter to Freud, dated April 17, 1907, in *The Freud/Jung Letters*, 36.
67 Freud, Letter to Jung, dated January 27, 1908, in *The Freud/Jung Letters*, 115–16.
68 Jung, Letter to Freud, dated April 18, 1908, in *The Freud/Jung Letters*, 138–9.
69 Quoted in Ernest Jones, *The Life and Work of Sigmund Freud*, vol. III, *The Man* (New York: Basic Books, 1955), 488, emphasis added.
70 Karl Abraham, "On the significance of sexual trauma in childhood for the symptomatology of dementia praecox" (1907), in *Clinical Papers and Essays on Psycho-Analysis* (London: Maresfield Reprints, 1979), 19.

71 In Hilda Abraham, "Karl Abraham: An unfinished biography," *The International Review of Psycho-Analysis* 1 (1974): 35.
72 Karl Abraham, "The experiencing of sexual traumas as a form of sexual activity," in *Selected Papers of Karl Abraham*, trans. Douglas Bryan and Alix Strachey (London: Maresfield Library, 1972), 62.
73 Abraham, "Karl Abraham: An unfinished biography," 38.
74 Karl Abraham, "The psycho-sexual differences between hysteria and dementia praecox" (1908), in *Selected Papers of Karl Abraham*, trans. Douglas Bryan and Alix Strachey (London: Maresfield Library, 1972), 79.
75 Ibid., 73–4.
76 Karl Abraham and Sigmund Freud, *A Psycho-Analytic Dialogue: The Letters of Sigmund Freud and Karl Abraham, 1907–1926* (New York: Basic Books, 1965), 9–10.
77 Ibid., 44–5.
78 Freud, "Psycho-analytic notes," 68.
79 Ibid., 70.
80 Ibid.
81 Ibid., 70–1.
82 Ibid., 71.
83 Ibid., 72.
84 Ibid., 75.
85 Ibid.
86 Ibid., 82.
87 Sigmund Freud, "The claims of psycho-analysis to scientific interest" (1913), in *The Standard Edition of the Complete Psychological Works of Sigmund Freud, Vol. XIII (1913–1914): Totem and Taboo and Other Works*, 163–90.
88 Ibid., 174, emphasis added.
89 Ibid.
90 Ibid., 175.
91 Sigmund Freud, "A metapsychological supplement to the theory of dreams," and "A case of paranoia running counter to the psycho-analytic theory of the disease" (1915), in *The Standard Edition of the Complete Psychological Works of Sigmund Freud, Vol. XIV (1914–1916): On the History of the Psycho-Analytic Movement, Papers on Metapsychology and Other Works*, 261–72.
92 Freud, "The unconscious," (1915), in *The Standard Edition of the Complete Psychological Works of Sigmund Freud, Volume XIV*, 196.
93 Ibid., 199–200.
94 Viktor Tausk (1879–1919) was a psychiatrist and psychoanalyst, born in Slovakia. At the encouragement of Freud, in 1908, he moved to Vienna and began psychoanalytic training. He became interested in the psychoses when Jung published *The Psychology of Dementia Praecox* in 1907 and the rupture with Freud began. Tausk ended up committing suicide in Vienna. He is best known for his 1919 article, "On the origin of the 'influencing machine' in schizophrenia," in *Psychoanalytic Quarterly* 2, 519–56.
95 Freud, "The unconscious," 198, italics in the original.
96 Ibid.
97 Ibid., 199.
98 Ibid.

99 Ibid., 200.
100 Ibid., 203, emphasis added.
101 Ibid.
102 Ibid., 204.
103 Freud, "The loss of reality in neurosis and psychosis" (1924), in *The Standard Edition of the Complete Psychological Works of Sigmund Freud, Volume XIX (1923–1925): The Ego and the Id and Other Works*, 183.
104 See Strachey, editor's note to "Fetishism," *SE* 19:150, who mentions Freud's unfinished, posthumously published paper, "Splitting of the ego in the process of defence" (1940).
105 Sigmund Freud, "Constructions in analysis" (1937), in *The Standard Edition of the Complete Psychological Works of Sigmund Freud, Volume XXIII (1937–1939): Moses and Monotheism, An Outline of Psycho-Analysis and Other Works*, 267.
106 Ibid., 267–8.
107 Sigmund Freud, "An outline of psycho-analysis," in *The Standard Edition of the Complete Psychological Works of Sigmund Freud, Volume XXIII (1937–1939): Moses and Monotheism, An Outline of Psycho-Analysis and Other Works*, 202.
108 Nathaniel London, "An essay on psychoanalytic theory: Two theories of schizophrenia. Part I: Review and critical assessment of the development of the two theories," *International Journal of Psychoanalysis* 54 (1973): 169–78 and "An essay on psychoanalytic theory: Two theories of schizophrenia. Part II: Discussion and restatement of the specific theory of schizophrenia," *International Journal of Psychoanalysis* 54 (1973): 179–93.
109 London, "An essay on psychoanalytic theory: Two theories of schizophrenia. Part I," 171.
110 Ibid.
111 Ibid., 172.
112 Abraham and Freud (eds.), *A Psychoanalytic Dialogue*, 11.
113 Orna Ophir, *Psychosis, Psychoanalysis and Psychiatry in Postwar USA: On the Borderland of Madness* (New York: Routledge, 2015), 54.
114 J. S. Grotstein, "The psychoanalytic concept of schizophrenia: I. The dilemma," *International Journal of Psychoanalysis* 58 (1977): 403–25; and "The psychoanalytic concept of schizophrenia: II. Reconciliation," *International Journal of Psychoanalysis* 58 (1977): 427–52.
115 Grotstein, "The psychoanalytic concept of schizophrenia: I. The dilemma," 405, emphasis added.
116 N. C. Andreasen, "The American concept of schizophrenia," *Schizophrenia Bulletin* 15, 4 (1989): 520.
117 L. Rzesnitzek, "'Early psychosis' as a mirror of biologist controversies in post-war German, Anglo-Saxon, and Soviet psychiatry," *Frontiers in Psychology* 4 (2013): 3.
118 J. Zubin and B. Spring, "Vulnerability: A new view of schizophrenia," *Journal of Abnormal Psychology* 86, 2 (1977): 103–26. See also J. Zubin, S. Steinhauer and R. Condray, "Vulnerability to relapse in schizophrenia," *British Journal of Psychiatry. Supplement* 161, 18 (1992): 13–18.
119 Harry Stuck Sullivan, *Conceptions of Modern Psychiatry* (New York: Norton, 1947), 16.
120 Harry Stuck Sullivan, *Schizophrenia as a Human Process* (New York: Norton, 1962), 224.

121 Herbert Rosenfeld, "Transference phenomena and transference-analysis in an acute catatonic schizophrenic patient," *International Journal of Psychoanalysis*, 33 (1952): 457–64.
122 Sigmund Freud, "Civilization and its discontents," in *The Standard Edition of the Complete Psychological Works of Sigmund Freud, Volume XXI (1927–1931): The Future of an Illusion, Civilization and its Discontents, and Other Works*, 118.
123 Melanie Klein, "Notes on some schizoid mechanisms," *International Journal of Psychoanalysis* 27 (1946): 99–110.
124 Ibid., 109.
125 Ibid.
126 Ibid.
127 Ibid.
128 Ibid.
129 Elliott Jacques, "Schizophrenia: An interpersonal and Kleinian viewpoint," in William F. Flack, Jr., Daniel R. Miller and Morton Wiener (eds.), *What Is Schizophrenia?* (New York: Springer, 2001), 91–6.
130 Françoise Davoine, "The lessons taught by hospitalized patients on the psychoanalysis of psychosis and trauma," a lecture delivered at the Freud Museum in London, in a conference dedicated to psychoanalysis and the psychoses, September 2018.
131 Barbara Cassin, Emily Apter, Jacques Lezra and Michael Wood, *Dictionary of Untranslatables: A Philosophical Lexicon* (Princeton, NJ: Princeton University Press, 2014), 211.
132 Bleuler, "The prognosis of dementia praecox," 59.
133 Bleuler, *Dementia Praecox or the Group of Schizophrenias*, trans. J. Zinkin, 1950, 8th edn (New York: International Universities Press, 1969), 8.
134 See the title of Klein's brilliant 1930 account of her work with a very disturbed young boy, named Dick: "The importance of symbol-formation in the development of the ego," *International Journal of Psychoanalysis* 11 (1930): 24–39.
135 Melanie Klein, "The Psycho-Analytic Play Technique (1955)," in *Envy and Gratitude and Other Works 1946–1963* (London: Hogarth Press, 1975), p. 140.
136 Ophir, *Psychosis, Psychoanalysis and Psychiatry in Postwar USA.*
137 Freud, "Constructions in analysis," in *The Standard Edition of the Complete Psychological Works of Sigmund Freud, Volume XXIII (1937–1939): Moses and Monotheism, An Outline of Psycho-Analysis and Other Works*, 269.
138 Katharina Trede, "150 years of Freud-Kraepelin dualism," *The Psychiatric Quarterly* 78, 3 (2007): 237–40.

Chapter 4 A Moving Target

1 Elyn R. Saks, *The Center Cannot Hold* (New York: Hyperion, 2007), 40, 328, emphasis added.
2 Guy A. Boysen and Ashley Ebersole, "Expansion of the concept of mental disorder in the DSM-5," *Journal of Mind and Behavior* 35, 4 (2014): 225–44.
3 Elyn R. Saks, *The Center Cannot Hold* (New York: Hyperion, 2007), 328–9.
4 Ian Hacking, *The Social Construction of What?* (Cambridge, MA: Harvard University Press, 2000), 113.
5 Ian Hacking, *Mad Travelers: Reflections on the Reality of Transient Mental Illness* (Charlottesville, VA: University of Virginia Press, 1998), 1.

6 Richard Noll, *American Madness: The Rise and Fall of Dementia Praecox* (Cambridge, MA: Harvard University Press, 2011), 10.
7 Ibid.
8 Adolf Meyer, "Constructive formulation of schizophrenia," *The American Journal of Psychiatry* 78, 3 (1922): 355–64.
9 Adolf Meyer, *Psychobiology, A Science of Man* (Springfield, IL: Charles C. Thomas, 1957), 180–1.
10 Susan D. Lamb, *Pathologist of the Mind, Adolf Meyer and the Origins of American Psychiatry* (Baltimore, MD: Johns Hopkins University Press, 2014), 101.
11 Ibid.
12 Ruth Leys further suggests that for Meyer even "types" were "types of one," as is suggested by the "life chart," the new technological tool he developed for the representation of the patient. See Ruth Leys, "Types of one: Adolf Meyer's life chart and the representation of individuality," *Representations* 34 (1991): 1–28. A "life chart" of a case of schizophrenia appears on page 15 of the article. See also Ruth Leys, "Meyer, Jung, and the limits of association," *Bulletin of the History of Medicine* 59, 3 (1985): 345–60.
13 N. C. Andreasen, "The American concept of schizophrenia," *Schizophrenia Bulletin* 15, 4 (1989): 520.
14 Eugen Bleuler, *Dementia Praecox or the Group of Schizophrenias* (New York: International Universities Press, 1950).
15 Eugen Bleuler, *Textbook of Psychiatry* (New York: The Macmillan Company, 1924), 436.
16 William Guy and Michael H. Finn, "A review of autofellatio," *Psychoanalytic Review* 41, 4 (1954): 354–5, emphasis added.
17 APA, *DSM-I*, 24. One of the main goals of the creators of the DSM-I was to differentiate between "organic psychoses" (mental disorders involving an organic brain disturbance) and "functional psychoses" (which are not due to a primary disturbance in the brain function), a distinction that predated Kraepelin. Whether the reaction is psychotic, neurotic, or behavioral was secondary to this basic division. See M. D. Beer, "Psychosis: A history of the concept," *Comprehensive Psychiatry* 37, 4 (1996): 273–91.
18 Allan V. Horwitz, "*DSM-I* and *DSM-II*," in R. L. Cautin and S. O. Lilienfeld (eds.), *The Encyclopedia of Clinical Psychology* (Chichester: Wiley Blackwell, 2015); G. N. Grob, "Origins of DSM-I: A study in appearance and reality," *American Journal of Psychiatry* 148, 4 (1991): 421–31 and E. Shorter, "The history of nosology and the rise of the Diagnostic and Statistical Manual of Mental Disorders," *Dialogues in Clinical Neuroscience* 17, 1 (2015): 59–67.
19 Indeed, some argue that psychoanalysts formed a minority on the editorial committee responsible for DSM-I, which was of little use to psychoanalysts overall, and that the final publication was ultimately more infused with Kraepelinian concepts than with psychoanalytic ones. See R. Cooper and R. K. Blashfield, "Re-evaluating DSM-I," *Psychological Medicine* 46, 3 (2016): 449–56.
20 American Psychiatric Association, *Diagnostic and Statistical Manual of Mental Disorders* (Washington, DC: American Psychiatric Association, 1952), 26.
21 Ibid.
22 Ibid.
23 Ibid.
24 Ibid.

25 Ibid., 40.
26 APA, *DSM-II. Diagnostic and Statistical Manual of Mental Disorders*, 2nd edn (Washington, DC: American Psychiatric Association, 1968), vii.
27 Robert K. Herbert and Karen Z. Waltensperger, "Schizophrasia: Case study of a paranoid schizophrenic's language," *Applied Psycholinguistics* 1 (1980): 81–93.
28 APA, *DSM-II*, 9.
29 Ibid., viii.
30 Ibid.
31 Ibid., ix.
32 Ibid., emphasis added.
33 The psychoses are further differentiated into: (1) psychoses associated with organic brain syndromes (such as senile and pre-senile dementia, alcoholic psychoses, psychoses associated with intracranial infection, etc.); (2) psychoses not attributed to physical conditions; (3) affective psychoses; (4) paranoid states; and finally (5) other psychoses (reactive in their nature).
34 APA, *DSM-II*, 23.
35 This is the second group of psychoses: "psychoses not attributed to physical conditions."
36 APA, *DSM-II*, 33.
37 Ibid.
38 Interestingly, "schizophrenia latent type" (a diagnosis reserved for those with clear symptoms of schizophrenia but no previous history of psychosis) contains what was previously referred to as "incipient," "pre-psychotic," "pseudoneurotic," "pseudopsychopathic," or "borderline" schizophrenia. Terms such as "prodrome" and "prodromal" (which were previously used to define the early stages of the disorder) disappeared from the classification in the DSM-II, without explanation.
39 Norman Sartorius, Robert Shapiro and Assen Jablensky, "The international pilot study of schizophrenia," *Schizophrenia Bulletin* 1, 11 (1974): 21–34. The study took place in Colombia, Czechoslovakia, Denmark, India, Nigeria, China, the Union of Soviet Socialist Republics, the United Kingdom, and the United States, examining 1,202 patients, 811 having received the diagnosis of schizophrenia.
40 Assen Jablensky and Norman Sartorius, "Is schizophrenia universal?," *Acta Psychiatria Scandinavia* Suppl. 344 (1988): 65–70.
41 Alex Cohen, Vikram Patel, R. Thara and Oye Gureje, "Questioning an axiom: Better prognosis for schizophrenia in the developing world?," *Schizophrenia Bulletin* 34, 2 (2008): 229–44.
42 Assen Jablensky and Norman Sartorius, "What did the WHO studies really find?," *Schizophrenia Bulletin* 34, 2 (2008): 253–5.
43 Robert E. Kendell, J. Cooper, A. Gourlay, J. Copeland, L. Sharpe and B. Gurland, "Diagnostic criteria of American and British psychiatrists," *Archives of General Psychiatry* 25 (1971): 128.
44 Ibid.
45 Ibid., 129.
46 Ibid.
47 Ibid.
48 Orna Ophir, *Psychosis, Psychoanalysis and Psychiatry in Postwar USA: On the Borderland of Madness* (New York: Routledge, 2015), ch. 4.

49 Kenneth S. Kendler and Kenneth F. Schaffner, "The dopamine hypothesis of schizophrenia: An historical and philosophical analysis," *Philosophy, Psychiatry, & Psychology* 18, 1 (2011): 41–63; K. Kendler, "The dopamine hypothesis of schizophrenia: An updated perspective," in Kenneth S. Kendler and Josef Parnas (eds.), *Philosophical Issues in Psychiatry III: The Nature and Sources of Historical Change* (Oxford: Oxford University Press, 2015).

50 Hannah S. Decker, "How Kraepelinian was Kraepelin? How Kraepelinian are the neo-Kraepelinians? From Emil Kraepelin to DSM-III," *History of Psychiatry* 18, 3 (2007): 337–60.

51 K. Kendler, R. Muñoz and G. Murphy, "The development of the Feighner Criteria: A historical perspective," *American Journal of Psychiatry* 167 (2010): 134–42.

52 J. P. Feighner, R. Muñoz, G. Winokur, R. A. Jr, Woodruff, S. B. Guze, and E. Robins, "Diagnostic criteria for use in psychiatric research," *Archives of General Psychiatry* 26, 1 (1972): 57–63.

53 David L. Rosenhan, "On being sane in insane places," *Science* 179, 4070 (1973), 250–8.

54 Ibid., 251.

55 Ibid., 252.

56 Ibid., 250.

57 Susannah Cahalan, *The Great Pretender: The Undercover Mission That Changed Our Understanding of Madness* (New York: Little, Brown, 2019).

58 R. D. Laing and Aaron Esterson, *Sanity, Madness and the Family* (New York: Basic Books, 1963); Michel Foucault, *Madness and Civilization: A History of Insanity in the Age of Reason* (New York: Random House, 1965); Erving Goffman, *Asylums: Essays on the Social Situations of Mental Patients and Other Inmates* (New York: Doubleday, 1961); Erving Goffman, *Stigma: Notes on the Management of Spoiled Identity* (Harmondsworth: Penguin Books, 1963); Thomas Szasz, *The Myth of Mental Illness* (New York: Harper & Row, 1961).

59 APA, *Diagnostic and Statistical Manual of Mental Disorders*, 3rd edn (Washington, DC: American Psychiatric Association, 1980), 185.

60 Thomas H. McGlashan and Christopher J. Keats, *Schizophrenia: Treatment Process and Outcome* (Washington, DC: American Psychiatric Press, 1989), 13, 94.

61 APA, *DSM-III*, 6, emphasis added.

62 Ibid.

63 Goffman, *Stigma.*

64 APA, *DSM-III*, 6.

65 Ibid.

66 Ibid., 6.

67 Ibid., 8.

68 Ibid., 181.

69 Schneider's "first-rank symptoms" were an addition to the diagnosis of schizophrenia that became popular in Europe in the mid-twentieth century and in the 1980s in the United States. According to Schneider, any one of the following eight symptoms is pathognomonic of schizophrenia: auditorization of thought (hearing one's own thoughts); auditory hallucinations that form a "running commentary" on the patient's thoughts and activities; thought withdrawal; thought insertion; thought broadcasting; somatic hallucinations that the patient attributes to the will, influence, or motive of

outside agencies; delusional perceptions; all events in the sphere of feeling, drive, and volition that are experienced as made or influenced by others. See Wayne S. Fenton, Thomas H. McGlashan and Robert K. Heinssen, "A comparison of DSM-III and DSM-III-R schizophrenia," *American Journal of Psychiatry* 145, 11 (1988): 1446–9.

70 APA, *DSM-III*, 181.

71 Ibid., emphasis added.

72 Ibid.

73 Kevin Alan Lee, *The Split Mind: Schizophrenia from an Insider's Point of View* (Nottingham: Nottingham University Press, 2011), 8.

74 McGlashan and Keats, *Schizophrenia: Treatment Process and Outcome.*

75 Lee, *The Split Mind*, 129.

76 Ibid., 132.

77 APA, *DSM-III*, 182.

78 Herbert and Waltensperger, "Schizophrasia."

79 APA, *DSM-III*, 188.

80 Norma MacDonald, "The other side: Living with schizophrenia," *The Canadian Medical Association Journal* 82 (1960), 218–21, p. 218.

81 As seen in the phenomena of affective "blunting" and "flattening."

82 Lee, *The Split Mind*, 136–7.

83 Antipsychotics also allowed for deinstitutionalization, as patients were sedated enough to be released from custodial care to community mental health centers. "Deinstitutionalization" became a rationale for simply closing down the hospitals. In turn, American psychiatrists got particularly hooked on prescribing medication, dispensing with their custodial duties and much of their pastoral role. Now it is very difficult to get inpatient psychiatric care in the United States. One must present as gravely disabled, the golden ticket being dangerous suicidal ideation. See Gerald Grob, "The forging of mental health policy in America: World War II to new frontier," *Journal of the History of Medicine and Allied Sciences* 42 (1987), 410–46.

84 APA, *DSM-III*, 184. Bleuler's fourth and last "A," namely "autism," was used in DSM-III to describe this condition in its most severe appearance.

85 Lee, *The Split Mind*, 140.

86 Cutting nature further at its joints, the manual divided the phases of the disorder into three distinct segments: "prodromal phase" from the DSM-I, adding a list of the functions that were deemed in decline. Second, it stipulated an active phase of "florid psychotic symptoms," and finally, it assumed a "residual phase" after the psychosis has subsided. The DSM-III also added a digit to the diagnostic code of schizophrenia, in order to indicate more precisely the kind of course (chronic, sub-chronic, etc.) the illness might end up taking. APA, *DSM-III*, 192.

87 Ibid., 186.

88 Andreasen, "The American concept of schizophrenia."

89 Hannah Decker, *The Making of DSM-III®: A Diagnostic Manual's Conquest of American Psychiatry* (New York: Oxford University Press, 2013), 179, emphasis added.

90 J. P. Feighner et al., "Diagnostic criteria for use in psychiatric research."

91 R. L. Spitzer, J. Endicott and E. Robins, "Research diagnostic criteria: Rationale and reliability," *Archives of General Psychiatry* 35, 6 (1978): 773–82. Paradoxically, however, the increased precision and differentiation of diagnostic criteria would also allow clinicians to express diagnostic uncertainty wherever needed.

92 S. Kawa and J. Giordano, "A brief historicity of the Diagnostic and Statistical Manual of Mental Disorders: Issues and implications for the future of psychiatric canon and practice," *Philosophy, Ethics, and Humanities in Medicine* 7, 1 (2012): 1–9.
93 Noll, *American Madness*, 278–9.
94 W. N. Goldstein, "DSM-III and the diagnosis of schizophrenia," *American Journal of Psychotherapy* 37, 2 (1983): 168–81.
95 Ibid.
96 Ibid.
97 APA, *Diagnostic and Statistical Manual of Mental Disorders, III-R Edition* (Washington, DC: American Psychiatric Association, 1987), 187.
98 Ibid., xx.
99 Ibid.
100 Fenton et al., "A comparison of DSM-III and DSM-III-R schizophrenia," 1446.
101 Ibid., 1447.
102 Ibid., 1448.
103 The expression "death by a thousand qualifications" refers to a logical fallacy, where a term is used to define something, but there are so many qualifications to the definition that the original term becomes meaningless. See Antony Flew, "Theology and falsification" (1950), in Antony Flew and Alasdair C. MacIntyre (eds), *New Essays in Philosophical Theology* (London: SCM Press, 1968).
104 Fenton et al., "A comparison of DSM-III and DSM-III-R schizophrenia," 1448.
105 R. L. Spitzer, M. Gibbon, A. E. Skodol, J. B. W. Williams and M. B. First (eds.), *DSM-IV Casebook: A Learning Companion to the Diagnostic and Statistical Manual of Mental Disorders*, 4th edn (Washington, DC: American Psychiatric Association, 1994), 32–3.
106 Ibid., 34.
107 APA, *Diagnostic and Statistical Manual of Mental Disorders*, 4th edn (Washington, DC: American Psychiatric Association, 1994), 274–5, emphasis added. The "positive symptoms," for their part, are further divided into two distinct dimensions, the "psychotic *dimension*" (which includes delusions and hallucinations), and the "disorganization *dimension*" (which includes disorganized speech and behavior), with the implicit hope of identifying their underlying *neural* mechanisms.
108 These functions include: cognitive and emotional, perception, inferential thinking, language and communication, behavioral monitoring, affect, fluency and productivity of thought and speech, hedonic capacity, volition and drive.
109 Similarly, "distortions or *exaggerations* of inferential thinking" are followed by "delusions" (in parentheses), "language and communication" is followed by "disorganized speech," and "behavioral monitoring" by "grossly disorganized or catatonic behavior." Ibid., 275.
110 Ibid., emphasis added.
111 Ibid., 277, emphasis added.
112 Ibid.
113 Ibid.
114 Ibid., emphasis added.
115 Ibid., 276.

116 That said, the spectrum allows for different stages, such that disorganized thinking or speech may reveal themselves as less severe during the prodromal phase, that is, *before* major symptoms are manifested, and also *after* the acute phase, in other words, during the residual periods of schizophrenia.

117 Ibid.

118 The assessment of functioning, in this edition, is found in a renewed "Axis V," that suggests using a tool called the Global Assessment of Functioning (GAF) scale with respect only to psychological, social, and occupational functionality (ibid., 30–1). The GAF scale runs from 1 to 100 and it is suggested that it be used when tracking progress in rehabilitation, independent of the severity of the symptoms. Other numerical scales, such as the Occupational Functioning Assessment Scale (SOFAS) or the Global Assessment of Relational Functioning (GARF) scale, are also advised in the DSM-IV's Appendix. These add to the manual's avowed shift toward a more quantitative assessment of mental illness in general, and schizophrenia in particular.

119 Ibid., 280.

120 Ibid.

121 Ibid.

122 Ibid., 282.

123 Ibid., 283.

124 Jim van Os and Hélène Verdoux, "Diagnosis and classification of schizophrenia: Categories versus dimensions, distributions versus disease," in R. Murray, P. Jones, E. Susser, J. van Os and M. Cannon (eds.), *The Epidemiology of Schizophrenia* (Cambridge: Cambridge University Press, 2003), 364–408.

125 Hacking, *The Social Construction of What?*

126 Nick O. Haslam, "Kinds of kinds: A conceptual taxonomy of psychiatric categories," *Philosophy, Psychiatry & Psychology* 9 (2002): 203–17; "Natural kinds, human kinds, and essentialism," *Social Research* 65 (1998): 291–314; "Psychiatric categories as natural kinds: Essentialist thinking about mental disorders," *Social Research* 67 (2000): 1031–58.

127 Rachel V. Cooper, "What is wrong with the DSM?," *History of Psychiatry* 15, 1 (2004): 5–25; *Classifying Madness: A Philosophical Examination of the Diagnostic and Statistical Manual of Mental Disorders* (Dordrecht: Springer, 2005); "Psychiatry as a value-laden science," in *Psychiatry and Philosophy of Science* (London: Acumen, 2007); "Are there natural kinds in psychology?" in R. Groff (ed.), *Revitalising Causality: Realism about Causality in Philosophy and Social Science* (London: Routledge, 2007); "Is psychiatry classification a good thing?," in Kenneth S. Kendler and Josef Parnas (eds.), *Philosophical Issues in Psychiatry II: Nosology* (Oxford: Oxford University Press, 2012), 61–70.

128 John Z. Sadler, *Values and Psychiatric Diagnosis* (Oxford: Oxford University Press, 2004).

129 Kenneth S. Kendler, "The dappled nature of causes of psychiatric illness: Replacing the organic-functional/hardware-software dichotomy with empirically based pluralism," *Molecular Psychiatry* 17 (2012): 377–88; K. S. Kendler, P. Zachar and C. Craver, "What kinds of things are psychiatric disorders?" *Psychological Medicine* 41, 6 (2011): 1143–50; Kenneth S. Kendler and Josef Parnas (eds.), *Philosophical Issues in Psychiatry: Explanation, Phenomenology and Nosology* (Baltimore, MD: The Johns Hopkins University Press, 2008).

130 P. Zachar, "Psychiatric disorders are not natural kinds," *Philosophy, Psychiatry & Psychology* 7 (2000): 167–94.

131 See also M. First, "Reorganizing the diagnostic groupings in DSM-V and ICD-11: A cost/benefit analysis," *Psychological Medicine* 39 (2009): 2091–7; Nick Haslam, "Kinds of kinds: A conceptual taxonomy of psychiatric categories," *Philosophy, Psychiatry & Psychology* 9, 3 (200): 203–17; S. E. Hyman, "The diagnosis of mental disorders: The problem of reification," *Annual Review of Clinical Psychology* 6 (2010): 155–79; A. Jablensky, "A meta-commentary on the proposal for a meta-structure for DSM-V and ICD-11," *Psychological Medicine* 39 (2009): 2099–103; P. E. Meehl, "Bootstraps taxometrics: Solving the classification problem in psychopathology," *American Psychologist* 50, 4 (1995): 266–75; J. M. Pierre, "The borders of mental disorder in psychiatry and the DSM: Past, present, and future," *Journal of Psychiatric Practice* 16 (2010): 375–86; Sadler, *Values and Psychiatric Diagnosis*.

132 These values were of an aesthetic, epistemological, ethical, ontological, and pragmatic nature.

133 P. E. Meehl, "Bootstraps"; J. Ruscio, N. Haslam, A. M. Ruscio, *Introduction to the Taxometric Method: A Practical Guide* (Mahwah, NJ: Lawrence Erlbaum Associates, 2006); L. K. Muthén and B. O. Muthén, *Mplus Version 5.0*, computer program (Los Angeles, CA: 2007).

134 T. Insel, B. Cuthbert, M. Garvey, et al., "Research domain criteria (RDoC): Toward a new classification framework for research on mental disorders," *American Journal of Psychiatry* 167, 7 (2010): 748–51.

135 Ian Hacking, "Lost in the forest – Who needs the DSM?," *London Review of Books* 35, 15 (2013).

136 Elizabeth H. Flanagan, Lesley Anne Solomon, Amy Johnson, Priscilla Ridgway, John S. Strauss, and Larry Davidson, "Considering *DSM-5*: The personal experience of schizophrenia in relation to the *DSM-IV-TR* criteria," *Psychiatry: Interpersonal and Biological Processes* 75, 4 (2012): 375–86.

137 W. Ahn, E. H. Flanagan, J. K. Marsh, C. A. Sanislow, "Beliefs about essences and the reality of mental disorders," *Psychological Science* 17 (2006): 759–66; Nancy S. Kim and Woo-kyoung Ahn, "Clinical psychologists' theory-based representations of mental disorders predict their diagnostic reasoning and memory," *Journal of Experimental Psychology. General* 131 (2002): 451–76.

138 Flanagan et al., "Considering *DSM-5*," 375.

139 Ken Steele and Claire Berman, *The Day the Voices Stopped: A Memoir of Madness and Hope* (New York: Basic Books, 2001), 140.

140 Jim van Os and Carol Tamminga, "Deconstructing psychosis," *Schizophrenia Bulletin* 33, 4 (2007): 861–2.

141 Darrel A. Regier, "Time for a fresh start? Rethinking psychosis in *DSM-V*," *Schizophrenia Bulletin* 33, 4 (2007): 843–5.

142 Carol A. Tamminga, Paul J. Sirovatka, Darrel A. Regier and Jim van Os, *Deconstructing Psychosis: Refining the Research Agenda for DSM-V* (Arlington: American Psychiatric Association, 2010), xxii.

143 John W. Barnhill, *DSM-5 Clinical Cases* (Arlington, VA: American Psychiatric Publishing, 2014).

144 Ibid.

145 Ibid.

146 Already in 2002, the APA had published *A Research Agenda for DSM-V*, explicitly announcing that researchers in psychiatry needed a different style of classification. But it was left unclear what sort of classification might be better suited to the phenomena and symptoms in question. In fact, the publication concluded that some "as yet unknown paradigm shift may need to occur." See D. Kupfer, M. First and D. Regier, *A Research Agenda for DSM-V* (Washington, DC: American Psychiatric Association, 2002), xix.

147 APA, *Diagnostic and Statistical Manuel of Mental Disorders*, 5th edn (Arlington, VA: American Psychiatric Association, 2013), emphasis added.

148 Ibid.

149 Ibid., 12.

150 Ibid., 20.

151 In her analysis of the new manual, for instance, philosopher of science Rachel Cooper points out some of these radical revisions. See Rachel Cooper, "What is wrong with the DSM?"

152 D. J. Kupfer, E. A. Kuhl and D. A. Regier, "DSM-5 – The future arrived," *JAMA* 309, 16 (2013): 1691–2.

153 APA, *DSM-5*, 20, emphasis added.

154 Ibid. Distress or impairment are, in other words, included in the DSM-5 diagnostic criteria because no other bio-indications can be found to clearly draw the line between the normal and the pathological. A voice-hearer who is not harmed by his voices can, accordingly, be considered impaired but not necessarily disabled.

155 Ibid., 25; xlii.

156 Ibid., xlii.

157 Ibid., 85.

158 Ibid. 87.

159 Ibid., 810.

160 Rajiv Tandon, Wolfgang Gaebel and Deanna M. Barch, et al., "Definition and description of schizophrenia in the DSM-5," *Schizophrenia Research* 150, 1 (2013): 3.

161 Three-dimensional clusters of symptoms that were already proposed in the DSM-IV – the psychotic (hallucinations/delusions), disorganized, and negative (deficit) dimensions – are also presented in the DSM-5 as the core symptoms of schizophrenia. To underscore their significance and therapeutic applicability, a numerical scale of their severity is added in its pages. Instead of the "mild, moderate and severe" symptoms identified in the DSM-IV, the DSM-5 uses a 5-point scale of severity, ranging from 0 (not present) to 4 (present and severe). APA, *DSM-IV*, 40.

162 Ibid.

163 Ming T. Tsuang, Jim van Os, Rajiv Tandon, et al., "Attenuated psychosis syndrome in DSM-5," *Schizophrenia Research* 150, 1 (2013): 31–5. Similar developments happened with the Ultra-High-Risk (UHR) criterion. See P. Fusar-Poli, W. T. Carpenter, S. W. Woods and T. H. McGlashan, "Attenuated psychosis syndrome: ready for DSM-5.1?," *Annual Review of Clinical Psychology* 10 (2014): 155–92, emphasis added.

164 Allen J. Frances, "Psychosis risk syndrome: Just as risky with a new name," *Psychology Today*, July 30, 2010, https://www.psychologytoday.com/us/blog/dsm5-in-distress/201007/psychosis-risk-syndrome-just-risky-new-name; Tony P. George, "Psychiatry 2013 and

DSM-5," *Psychiatric Times* 30, 12. https://www.psychiatrictimes.com/view/psychiatry-2013-and-dsm-5.

165 Juan Francisco Rodríguez-Testal, Cristina Senín-Calderón and Salvador Perona-Garcelán, "From DSM-IV-TR to DSM-5: Analysis of some changes," *International Journal of Clinical and Health Psychology* 14 (2014): 221–31. Indeed, the DSM-5 insistently refers to Neurodevelopmental disorders, Neurocognitive disorders, Functional neurological symptom disorder, and so on.

166 Barnaby Nelson, "Attenuated psychosis syndrome: Don't jump the gun," *Psychopathology* 47, 5 (2014): 292–6.

167 Arthur Maciel Nunes Gonçalves, Clarissa de Rosalmeida Dantas, Claudio E. M. Banzato and Ana Maria Galdini Raimundo Oda, "A historical account of schizophrenia proneness categories from DSM-I to DSM-5 (1952–2013)," *Revista Latinoamericana de Psicopatologia Fundamental* 21, 4 (2018): 798–828.

168 Patrick D. McGorry, "News brief: Attenuated psychosis syndrome left out of DSM-5 main text," in: A. M. N. Goncalves et al. "Values and DSM-5: looking at the debate on attenuated psychosis syndrome," *BMC Medical Ethics* 17, 7 (2016). Gale Academic OneFile, link.gale.com/apps/doc/A440765599/AONE?u=nysl_oweb&sid=googleScholar&xid=40fcd684.

169 Patrick D. McGorry, "'A stitch in time' … the scope for preventive strategies in early psychosis," *European Archives of Psychiatry and Clinical Neuroscience* 248 (1998): 28–9.

170 Ibid., 29.

171 David J. Kupfer and Darrel A. Regier, "Neuroscience, clinical evidence, and the future of psychiatric classification in DSM-5," *American Journal of Psychiatry* 168, 7 (2011): 672–4.

172 K. McNally, "Definitions of schizophrenia, 1908–1987: The failed essentialism," *Theory & Psychology* 22, 1 (2012): 91–113.

173 N. Kapur, J. Cooper, R. C. O'Connor and K. Hawton, "Non-suicidal self-injury v. attempted suicide: New diagnosis or false dichotomy?," *British Journal of Psychiatry* 202, 5 (2013): 326–8, in Rodríguez-Testal, Senín-Calderón and Perona-Garcelán, "From DSM-IV-TR to DSM-5: Analysis of some changes," *International Journal of Clinical and Health Psychology* 14, 3 (2014): 221–31.

174 K. Kendler, D. Kupfer, W. Narrow, K. Phillips and J. Fawcett, *Guidelines for Making Changes to DSM-V* (Washington, DC: APA, 2009).

Chapter 5 Hearing Voices

1 Valerie Fox, "First person account: A glimpse of schizophrenia," *Schizophrenia Bulletin* 28, 2 (2002): 363–5.

2 In this sense, people who hear nonverbal voices or sounds, such as laughter, cries, or wails, do not, strictly speaking, count as voice-hearers.

3 Kevin Alan Lee, *The Split Mind: Schizophrenia from an Insider's Point of View* (Nottingham: Nottingham University Press, 2011), 127–8.

4 Simon McCarthy-Jones, *Hearing Voices: The Histories, Causes and Meanings of Auditory Verbal Hallucinations* (Cambridge: Cambridge University Press, 2012), 5. McCarthy-Jones as well as Christopher Cook took part in a large interdisciplinary study of voice-hearing based in Durham University. See https://hearingthevoice/about-the-project.

5 Ibid., 10.
6 Ibid., 2.
7 See, for instance, I. Leudar and W. Sharrock, "Changing the past?," *History of the Human Sciences* 16 (2003): 105–21.
8 Mikkel Borch-Jacobsen, "Making psychiatric history: Madness as folie à plusieurs," *History of the Human Sciences* 14 (2001): 20.
9 See McCarthy-Jones, *Hearing Voices*, 10.
10 Christopher Cook, *Hearing Voices, Demonic and Divine: Scientific and Theological Perspectives* (Oxon, UK: Routledge, 2019), 8.
11 Genesis, 3:9–19.
12 Richard Friedman, *The Disappearance of God: A Divine Mystery* (Boston, MA: Little Brown and Company, 1995).
13 Exodus 20:19.
14 Cook, *Hearing Voices, Demonic and Divine*, 67.
15 Ibid., 75.
16 E. R. Dodds, *The Greeks and the Irrational* (Berkeley, CA: University of California Press, 1951), 116. As McCarthy-Jones specifies, voices issuing commands are the most common type heard in psychiatric populations today, which according to him reveals a continuity in voice-hearing that stretches back across the millennia. See McCarthy-Jones, *Hearing Voices*, 17.
17 Plato, quoted in A. A. Long, "How does Socrates' divine sign communicate with him?," in S. Ahbel-Rappe and R. Kamtekar (eds.), *A Companion to Socrates* (London: Blackwell, 2009), 64.
18 Ibid., 70.
19 M. L. McPherran, *The Religion of Socrates* (University Park, PA: Penn State University Press, 1993), 133.
20 Long, "How does Socrates' divine sign communicate with him?," 63.
21 Aristotle, *On Dreams*, trans. J. I. Beare, in *The Complete Works of Aristotle: The Revised Oxford Translation* (Princeton, NJ: Princeton University Press, 1984 [1908]), 732, in McCarthy-Jones, *Hearing Voices*, 17–18.
22 Aristotle, *On Dreams*, 732.
23 McCarthy-Jones, *Hearing Voices*, 21.
24 M. A. O'Brien, *Madness in Ancient Literature* (Whitefish, MT: Kessinger Publishing, 2003 [1924]).
25 Ibid.
26 Cook, *Hearing Voices, Demonic and Divine*, 81.
27 Ibid., 82.
28 Ibid., 84; 86.
29 Ibid., 95.
30 Ibid., 102.
31 McCarthy-Jones, *Hearing Voices*, 24.
32 Ibid., 24–5.
33 *Nephesh* in Hebrew, *psuche* in Greek: "living, thinking being."
34 *Ne shamah* in Hebrew: "wind"; *pneuma* in Greek: "breeze."
35 Eph. 3:16, in McCarthy-Jones, *Hearing Voices*, 25.
36 E. Underhill, *Mysticism: A Study in the Nature and Development of Man's Spiritual Consciousness* (London: Methuen, 1911), 328.

37 Underhill, in McCarthy-Jones, *Hearing Voices*, 25.
38 Augustine, *The Literal Meaning of Genesis*, Vol II, trans. J. H. Taylor (Ramsey, NJ: Paulist Press, 1982), 186.
39 J. Finnis, *Aquinas* (Oxford: Oxford University Press, 1998), in McCarthy-Jones, *Hearing Voices*, 25.
40 Underhill, in McCarthy-Jones, *Hearing Voices*, 25.
41 Ibid., 25.
42 A. Obermeier and R. Kennison, "The privileging of *visio* over *vox* in the mystical experiences of Hildegard of Bingen and Joan of Arc," *Mystics Quarterly* 23 (1997): 137–63.
43 Underhill, *Mysticism*, 277.
44 Riehle, 1977, in Obermeier and Kennison, "The privileging of *visio* over *vox*," 143.
45 Hildegard of Bingen, *Scivias*, trans. Mother Columba Hart and Jane Bishop (Mahwah, NJ: Paulist Press, 1990), 59.
46 Hildegard of Bingen, cited in A. H. King-Lenzmeier, *Hildegard of Bingen: An Integrated Vision* (Minnesota, MN: Liturgical Press, 2001), 27.
47 Moshe Sluhovsky, *Believe Not Every Spirit: Possession, Mysticism, and Discernment in Early Modern Catholicism* (Chicago, IL: University of Chicago Press, 2007).
48 Sluhovsky, *Believe Not Every Spirit*, in McCarthy-Jones, *Hearing Voices*, 26.
49 McCarthy-Jones, *Hearing Voices*, 27.
50 Aquinas, *Summa Theologiae*, Ia q. 111 a. 3.
51 Ibid., Ia q. 111 a. 4.
52 Ibid., IIa IIae q. 172 a. 5.
53 Ibid., IIa IIae q. 171 a. 1.
54 McCarthy-Jones, *Hearing Voices*, 29. Nevertheless, a person able to correctly interpret their own hallucinations is a "more excellent prophet" than one who simply interprets another's hallucination, as he "both lifts the veil of darkness (i.e., has a perceptual experience) and removes the veil of ignorance (i.e., correctly interprets it)."
55 Ibid., 28.
56 Ibid., 36.
57 Ibid., 30.
58 Renate Blumenfeld-Kosinski, *Poets, Saints, and Visionaries of the Great Schism* (University Park, PA: Pennsylvania State University Press, 2006).
59 Ibid.
60 Rudolf Schüssler, "Jean Gerson, moral certainty and the Renaissance of ancient scepticism," *Renaissance Studies* 23 (2009): 445–62.
61 McCarthy-Jones, *Hearing Voices*, 31.
62 Julian of Norwich, *Revelations of Divine Love*, trans. Barry Windeatt (Oxford: Oxford University Press, 2015 [1675]), 22.
63 Ibid., 32.
64 Margery Kempe, *The Book of Margery Kempe*, trans. Anthony Bale (Oxford: Oxford University Press, 2015), 119.
65 *Jeanne d'Arc, Maid of Orleans, Deliverer of France*, ed. T. Douglas Murray (New York: McClure, Phillips & Co., 1902), 10.
66 Ibid., 33.

67 Jean Gerson, *Jean Gerson: Early Works*, trans. B. P. McGuire (New York: Paulist Press, 1998), 339.
68 A. C. Jacobson, "The case of Joan of Arc: Was the Maid insane?," *Medieval Times* 45 (1917): 163–5.
69 D. K. Henderson, *Psychopathic States* (New York: Norton, 1939).
70 C. Allen, "The schizophrenia of Joan of Arc," *History of Medicine* 6 (1975): 4–9.
71 F. O. Henker, "Joan of Arc and DSM III," *Southern Medical Journal* 77 (1984): 1488–90.
72 Leo Sherley-Price, "Introduction," in Walter Hilton, *The Ladder of Perfection* (London: Penguin, 1988), 10.
73 In Cook, *Hearing Voices, Demonic and Divine*, 124.
74 In McCarthy-Jones, *Hearing Voices*, 39.
75 K. Ward, "The Reformation," talk given at Gresham College. Available at: www.gresham.ac.uk/lectures-and-events/the-reformation.
76 Other reformers included John Calvin and Ulrich Zwingli, for instance.
77 In McCarthy-Jones, *Hearing Voices*, 40.
78 Luther, cited in H. C. E. Midelfort, *A History of Madness in Sixteenth-Century Germany* (Stanford, CA: Stanford University Press, 1999), 91.
79 Ibid.
80 Ibid.
81 Keith Thomas, *Religion and the Decline of Magic: Studies in Popular Beliefs in Sixteenth- and Seventeenth-Century England* (London: Weidenfeld & Nicolson, 1971).
82 Michael MacDonald, *Mystical Bedlam: Madness, Anxiety, and Healing in Seventeenth-Century England* (Cambridge: Cambridge University Press, 1983), 170.
83 William Battie, *Treatise on Madness* (London: Brunner/Mazel, 1758), 6, in McCarthy-Jones, *Hearing Voices*, 55.
84 McCarthy-Jones, *Hearing Voices*, 57.
85 Teresa of Ávila, *The Book of My Life*, trans. Mirabai Starr (Boston, MA: New Seeds Books: 2007), 132.
86 Saint John of the Cross, *The Ascent to Mount Carmel* (Brewster, MA: Paraclete Press, 2010), 103, in McCarthy-Jones, *Hearing Voices*, 46.
87 McCarthy-Jones, *Hearing Voices*, 57.
88 Ibid.
89 Ibid., 95.
90 I. Leudar and P. Thomas, *Voices of Reason, Voices of Insanity: Studies of Verbal Hallucinations* (London: Routledge, 2000).
91 Underhill, *Mysticism*, 322.
92 Åsa Jansson, "Voice-hearing in 19th-century psychiatry," *The Lancet* 392 (2018): 1618–19.
93 John Conolly, "Clinical lectures on the principal forms of insanity delivered in the Middlesex Lunatic Asylum at Hanwell," quoted in Jansson, "Voice hearing in 19th-century psychiatry," 1618.
94 Ibid., 1619.
95 Ibid.
96 Emil Kraepelin, *Dementia Praecox and Paraphrenia*, trans. R. Mary Barclay; ed. George M. Robertson (New York: R. E. Krieger Publishing, 1971 [1919]) in Jansson, "Voice hearing in 19th century psychiatry," 1619.

97 Kraepelin, *Dementia Praecox*, 9.

98 Eugen Bleuler, *Dementia Praecox or the Group of Schizophrenias*, 8th edn, trans. J. Zinkin (1950; New York: International Universities Press, 1969).

99 Ibid., 389.

100 Ibid., 392; 388.

101 Ibid., 460.

102 Jung, *The Psychogenesis of Mental Disease*, trans. R. F. C. Hull (London: Routledge & Kegan Paul, 1960), 178.

103 Which he describes as "superficial and unwarranted." Ibid., 206.

104 Ibid.

105 McCarthy-Jones, *Hearing Voices*, 83.

106 Benjamin Gray, "Hidden demons: A personal account of hearing voices and the alternative of the Hearing Voices Movement," *Schizophrenia Bulletin* 34, 6 (2008): 1006–7.

107 Kurt Schneider, *Psychischer Befund und psychiatrische Diagnose* (Leipzig: Thieme, 1939).

108 Ibid., and Kurt Schneider, *Clinical Psychopathology*, trans. M. W. Hamilton, 5th edn (New York: Grune & Stratton), in Heinz Katschnig, "Psychiatry's contribution to the public stereotype of schizophrenia: Historical considerations," *Journal of Evaluation in Clinical Practice* 24, 5 (2018): 1093–100.

109 Schneider, in Katschnig, "Psychiatry's contribution to the public stereotype of schizophrenia," 1094.

110 Ibid., 1097.

111 Ibid.

112 Ibid.

113 These were the pure – or, say, existential – and the symptomatic – or, say, somatic phenomena. While both fields relied on different axioms or postulates, neither had corroborated its respective hypothesis sufficiently to silence the other, much less to cover the complete terrain of mental distress and/or illness. See Werner Janzarik, "Jaspers, Kurt Schneider and the Heidelberg school of psychiatry," trans. R. Viviani and G. E. Berrios, *History of Psychiatry* IX (1998): 241–52; 246.

114 Schneider, in Katschnig, "Psychiatry's contribution to the public stereotype of schizophrenia," 1094

115 Ibid., 1097.

116 Ibid.

117 Ibid.

118 Ibid.

119 Orna Ophir, *Psychosis, Psychoanalysis and Psychiatry in Postwar USA: On the Borderland of Madness* (New York: Routledge, 2015), 71.

120 S. Kety, "The syndrome of schizophrenia: Unresolved questions of opportunities of research," *British Journal of Psychiatry* 136, 5 (1980): 421–36.

121 *DSM-III*, 182–3.

122 Ibid., 207; 211.

123 Ibid., 188.

124 Ibid., 306.

125 McCarthy-Jones, *Hearing Voices*, 87.

126 Ophir, *Psychosis, Psychoanalysis and Psychiatry in Postwar USA*, 133–70.

127 McCarthy-Jones, *Hearing Voices*, 88.

128 On the one hand, the biomedical or biopsychiatric pole attributed the causes of voice-hearing to a form of organic illness that could be identified – that is, carved at nature's joints – while, on the other hand, there was a growing awareness of the need to adopt or supplement the official model with an alternative interpretation and appreciation of these phenomena, in light of cultural, along with psychological and social, factors, distinct from biological determinants (whether natural kinds or cut-outs, call them markers, of sorts).

129 Massoud Stephane, Paul Thuras, Henry Nasrallah and Apostolos P. Georgopoulos, "The internal structure of the phenomenology of auditory verbal hallucinations," *Schizophrenia Research* 61, 2–3 (2003): 186.

130 S. Wahass and G. Kent, "A cross-cultural study of the attitudes of mental health professionals towards auditory hallucinations," *International Journal of Social Psychiatry* 43, 3 (1997): 190–1.

131 Ibid., 190.

132 T. M. Luhrmann, R. Padmavati, H. Tharoor and A. Osei, "Differences in voice-hearing experiences of people with psychosis in the USA, India and Ghana: Interview-based study," *The British Journal of Psychiatry* 206, 1 (2015): 41–4.

133 Ibid., 41.

134 Ibid., 42.

135 Ibid.

136 Ibid.

137 Ibid.

138 Ibid.

139 Ibid., 42–3.

140 For a striking early illustration of the cultural framework underlying spirit possession and possession rituals in Accra, Ghana, see Jean Rouch's famous documentary, "Les Maîtres Fous," 1955.

141 Luhrmann et al., "Differences in voice-hearing experiences," 43.

142 Ibid., 42.

143 Ibid.

144 Ibid., 44

145 Ibid.

146 Ibid., 43.

147 Ibid., 44. See also J. A. Jenner, G. van de Willige and D. Wiersma, "Effectiveness of cognitive therapy with coping training for persistent auditory hallucinations: A retrospective study of attenders of a psychiatric out-patient department," *Acta Psychiatrica Scandinavica* 98 (1998): 384–9; and Julian Leff, Geoffrey Williams, Mark Huckvale, Maurice Arbuthnot and Alex P. Leff, "Avatar therapy for persecutory auditory hallucinations: What is it and how does it work?," *Psychosis* 6, 2 (2014): 166–76.

148 Luhrmann et al., "Differences in voice-hearing experiences," 44. See also Craig Morgan, Kwame McKenzie and Paul Fearon (eds.), *Society and Psychosis* (Cambridge: Cambridge University Press, 2008).

149 Luhrmann et al., "Differences in voice-hearing experiences," 44.

150 Ibid. See Marius Romme and Sandra Escher, *Accepting Voices* (London: Mind, 1993).

151 Jason Jepson, "Surviving the voices," *Schizophrenia Bulletin* 44, 4 (2018): 706.

152 McCarthy-Jones, *Hearing Voices*, 316.

153 As Frank notes, "postmodern times are when the capacity for telling one's own story is reclaimed." Arthur Frank, *The Wounded Storyteller* (Chicago, IL: University of Chicago Press, 1995), 7.

154 Ibid., xiii.

155 J. Dillon and R. May, "Reclaiming experience," *Clinical Psychology* 17 (2002): 25–77.

156 As McCarthy-Jones notes, "One participant, Anna, stated that she had to go through voice-hearing in order to get through the traumatic experiences of her childhood: 'the psyche knows best what it needs, and if it needs voices then you get voices. I needed voices' … Another participant, Yolanda, felt her voices, which came on after a split from her boyfriend, started because she needed to 'observe that [her] body was so tired.' Such meanings facilitate coping with AVHs, and make sense of the experience in the context of the voice-hearer's own life." McCarthy-Jones, *Hearing Voices*, 369; 320.

157 See McCarthy-Jones, *Hearing Voices*, 92, note 24.

158 Hague, in Romme and Escher, *Accepting Voices*, 198.

159 These 150 individuals even described their voices as a beneficial experience. See also A. Honig, M. Romme, B. J. Ensink, et al., "Auditory hallucinations: A comparison between patients and nonpatients," *Journal of Nervous and Mental Disease* 186, 10 (1998): 646–51; M. Romme, A. Honig, E. O. Noorthoorn and A. D. Escher, "Coping with hearing voices: An emancipatory approach," *British Journal of Clinical Psychology* 161, 1 (1992): 99–103; S. Escher, M. Morris, A. Buiks, et al., "Determinants of outcome in the pathways through care for children hearing voices," *International Journal of Social Welfare* 13, 3 (2004): 208–22.

160 M. Romme and A. D. Escher, "Hearing voices," *Schizophrenia Bulletin* 15 (1989): 209–16.

161 The Hearing Voices network was created in England in 1988, with networks now existing in over 35 countries. In 2014 in England, there were "over 180 groups hosted in a range of settings including child and adolescent mental health services, prisons, inpatient units, and the voluntary sector," and "the sixth World Hearing Voices Congress (Melbourne, Australia, 2013), which was attended by nearly 800 delegates," in: Dirk Corstens, Eleanor Longden, Simon McCarthy-Jones, Rachel Waddingham and Neil Thomas, "Emerging perspectives from the Hearing Voices Movement: implications for research and practice," *Schizophrenia Bulletin* 40, Suppl. 4 (2014), S285.

162 Ibid., S288.

163 Romme and Escher, *Accepting Voices*.

164 An annual "Voices Hearing day" is held on September 14 celebrating voice-hearing as a sign of diversity and promoting awareness and acceptance of voice-hearing in the general community.

165 See, for example, H. Sidgewick, A. Johnson, F. Myers, et al. "Report on the census of hallucinations," *Proceedings of the Society for Psychical Research* 26 (1894): 259–394; Allen Y. Tien, "Distributions of hallucinations in the population," *Social Psychiatry and Psychiatric Epidemiology* 26, 6 (1991): 287–92; and Catherine Lawrence, Jason Jones and Myra Cooper, "Hearing voices in a non-psychiatric population," *Behavioral and Cognitive Psychotherapy* 39, 3 (2009): 363–73.

166 See the Melbourne Hearing Voices Declaration 2013 and the 2014 Thessaloniki Declaration.

167 See Eleanor Sorrell, Mark Hayward and Sara Meddings, "Interpersonal processes and hearing voices: A study of the association between relating to voices and distress in clinical and non-clinical hearers," *Behavioural and Cognitive Psychotherapy* 38, 2 (2010): 127–40.

168 See Slade and Bentall, who conclude that the failure to attend to hallucinatory experiences and/or have the opportunity for dialogue about them is likely to have the effect of helping to maintain them. P. Slade and R. Bentall, "Psychological treatments for negative symptoms," *British Journal of Psychiatry* 7, Supplement (1989): 133–5.

169 Many report their voices began after experiencing trauma, sexual or physical abuse, or intense emotional experiences, such as an accident, mourning, a divorce, or pregnancy. See Eleanor Longden, Anna Madill and Mitch G. Waterman, "Dissociation, trauma, and the role of lived experience: Toward a new conceptualization of voice hearing," *Psychological Bulletin* 138, 1 (2012): 28–76; Andrew Moskowitz and Dirk Corstens, "Auditory hallucinations: Psychotic symptom or dissociative experience?," *Journal of Psychological Trauma* 6, 2 (2007): 35–63.

170 Marius Romme, Sandra Escher, Jacqui Dillon, Dirk Corstens and Mervyn Morris, *Living with Voices: 50 Stories of Recovery* (Ross-on-Wye: PCCS Books, 2009).

171 Marius Romme and Sandra Escher, *Making Sense of Voices* (London: Mind, 2000), 60.

172 Ibid.

173 Corstens et al., "Emerging perspectives from the Hearing Voices Movement," S288 and McCarthy-Jones, *Hearing Voices*, 95.

174 Corstens et al., "Emerging perspectives from the Hearing Voices Movement," S292. See Deborah Milligan, Simon McCarthy-Jones, Allan Winthrope and Robert Dudley, "Time changes everything? A qualitative investigation of the experience of auditory verbal hallucinations over time," *Psychosis* 5 (2013): 107–18.

175 Ibid.

176 Corstens et al., "Emerging perspectives from the Hearing Voices Movement," S286–7. See Dirk Corstens, Sandra Escher and Marius Romme. "Accepting and working with voices: The Maastricht approach," in Andrew Moskowitz, Ingo Schäfer and Martin J. Dorahy (eds.), *Psychosis, Trauma and Dissociation: Emerging Perspectives on Severe Psychopathology* (Oxford: Wiley-Blackwell; 2008), 319–31; Dirk Corstens and Eleanor Longden, "The origins of voices: links between life history and voice hearing in a survey of 100 cases," *Psychosis: Psychological, Social and Integrative Approaches* 5, 3 (2013): 270–85; and Eleanor Longden, Dirk Corstens, Sandra Escher and Marius Romme, "Voice hearing in biographical context: A model for formulating the relationship between voices and life history," *Psychosis: Psychological, Social and Integrative Approaches* 4, 3 (2012): 224–34. For the "Maastricht Hearing Voices Interview," see Romme and Escher, *Making Sense of Voices*.

177 See Romme et al., *Living with Voices*.

178 Corstens et al., "Emerging perspectives from the Hearing Voices Movement," S288.

179 Romme et al., *Living with Voices*, 7.

180 See Eleanor Longden, Dirk Corstens and Jacqui Dillon, "Recovery, discovery and revolution: The work of Intervoice and the Hearing Voices Movement," in Steven Coles, Sarah Keenan and Bob Diamond (eds.), *Madness Contested: Power and Practice* (Ross-on-Wye: PCCS, 2013), 161–80.

181 See Michel Foucault, *Madness and Civilization: A History of Insanity in the Age of Reason*, trans. R. Howard (London: Tavistock, 1965); abridged; *History of Madness*, ed. Jean Khalfa, trans. Jonathan Murphy and Jean Khalfa (London: Routledge, 2006).

182 Corstens et al., "Emerging perspectives from the Hearing Voices Movement," S287. See also Vanessa Beavan, John Read and Claire Cartwright, "The prevalence of voice-hearers in the general population: A literature review," *Journal of Mental Health* 20, 3 (2011): 281–92; and Lucy Johnstone, "Voice hearers are people with problems, not patients with illnesses," in Marius Romme and Sandra Escher (eds.), *Psychosis as a Personal Crisis: An Experience-Based Approach* (London: Routledge, 2011), 27–36.

183 McCarthy-Jones, *Hearing Voices*, 95.

184 Angela Woods, "The voice-hearer," *Journal of Mental Health* 22 (2013): 268.

185 Corstens et al., "Emerging perspectives from the Hearing Voices Movement," S287.

186 McCarthy-Jones, *Hearing Voices*, 309.

Chapter 6 Stigma and the Problem of Naming

1 WHO (2015) "WHO best practices for the naming of new human infectious diseases," available at: http://apps.who.int/iris/bitstream/10665/163636/1/WHO_HSE_FOS_15.1_eng.pdf?ua=1.

2 Johanne Eliacin, "Racism and immigration: An African-Caribbean woman in London," in Tanya M. Luhrmann and Jocelyn Marrow (eds.), *Our Most Troubling Madness: Case Studies in Schizophrenia Across Cultures* (Oakland, CA: University of California Press, 2016), 91.

3 Mitsumoto Sato, "Renaming schizophrenia: A Japanese perspective," *World Psychiatry* 5 (2006): 53–5.

4 See Jeffrey A. Lieberman and Michael B. First, "Renaming schizophrenia," *British Medical Journal* 334 (2007): 108; David G. Kingdon, Yoshihiro Kinoshita, Farooq Naeem, et al., "Schizophrenia can and should be renamed," *British Medical Journal* 334 (2007): 221–2; Constantin Tranulis, Tania Lecomte, Bassam El-Khoury, Anaïs Lavarenne and Daniel Brodeur-Côté, "Changing the name of schizophrenia: Patient perspectives and implications for DSM-V," *PLoS One* 8, 2 (2013): e55998; Nell Ellison, Oliver Mason and Katrina Scior, "Renaming schizophrenia to reduce stigma: Comparison with the case of bipolar disorder," *British Journal of Psychiatry* 206, 4 (2015): 341–2.

5 M. V. Karidi, D. Vassilopoulou, E. Savvidou, et al., "Bipolar disorder and self-stigma: A comparison with schizophrenia," *Journal of Affective Disorders* 184 (2015): 209–215, 209. See also Winnie W. S. Mak and Crystal F. M. Wu, "Cognitive insight and causal attribution in the development of self-stigma among individuals with schizophrenia," *Psychiatric Services* 57, 12 (2006): 1800–2; and Philip T. Yanos, David Roe, Keith Markus and Paul H. Lysaker, "Pathways between internalized stigma and outcomes related to recovery in schizophrenia spectrum disorders," *Psychiatric Services* 59, 12 (2008): 1437–42.

6 See Nicolas Rüsch, Matthias C. Angermeyer and Patrick W. Corrigan, "Mental illness stigma: Concepts, consequences, and initiatives to reduce stigma," *European Psychiatry* 20 (2005): 529–39.

7 Matthias C. Angermeyer and Herbert Matschinger, "The stereotype of schizophrenia and its impact on discrimination against people with schizophrenia: Results

from a representative survey in Germany," *Schizophrenia Bulletin* 30, 4 (2004): 1049–61.

8 Nadia Kadri, Fatiha Manoudi, Soumia Berrada and Driss Moussaoui, "Stigma impact on Moroccan families of patients with schizophrenia," *Canadian Journal of Psychiatry* 49, 9 (2004): 625.

9 Gil Dov Hoftman, "The burden of mental illness beyond clinical symptoms: Impact of stigma on the onset and course of schizophrenia spectrum disorders," *American Journal of Psychiatry: Residents' Journal* 11, 4 (2016): 7.

10 Rosenfield, 1997, in Karidi et al., "Bipolar disorder and self-stigma," 209.

11 Rüsch et al., "Mental illness stigma," 530.

12 Steve Colori, "Disclosing my diagnosis," *Schizophrenia Bulletin* 45, 2 (2019): 269–70.

13 Ibid.

14 Hoftman, "The burden of mental illness," 6.

15 Anonymous, "Why having a mental illness is not like having diabetes," *Schizophrenia Bulletin* 33, 4 (2007): 846–7.

16 Hoftman, "The burden of mental illness." See Patrick W. Corrigan, Fred E. Markowitz and Amy C. Watson, "Structural levels of mental illness stigma and discrimination," *Schizophrenia Bulletin* 30 (2004): 481–91.

17 Rüsch et al., "Mental illness stigma," 530.

18 Hoftman, "The burden of mental illness," 6.

19 Ronald Bassman, "Overcoming the impossible: My journey through schizophrenia," *Psychology Today*, February 2001.

20 Ibid. See Shekhar Saxena, Graham Thornicroft, Martin Knapp and Harvey Whiteford, "Resources for mental health: scarcity, inequity, and inefficiency," *Lancet* 370 (2007): 878–89.

21 Ibid. See Bruce G. Link, Lawrence H. Yang, Jo C. Phelan and Pamela Y. Collins, "Measuring mental illness stigma," *Schizophrenia Bulletin* 30, 3 (2004): 511–41.

22 Rüsch et al., "Mental illness stigma," 530.

23 Jonathan Metzl, *The Protest Psychosis: How Schizophrenia Became a Black Disease* (Boston, MA: Beacon Press, 2009), 198.

24 Ibid., 189.

25 Ibid.

26 Ibid.

27 Mark Ellerby, "Schizophrenia: Stigma and the impact of literature," *Schizophrenia Bulletin* 44, 3 (2018): 466.

28 Kevin Alan Lee, *The Split Mind: Schizophrenia from an Insider's Point of View* (Nottingham: Nottingham University Press, 2011), 1.

29 Rüsch et al., "Mental illness stigma."

30 Matthias C. Angermeyer and Herbert Matschinger, "Causal beliefs and attitudes to people with schizophrenia: Trend analysis based on data from two population surveys in Germany," *British Journal of Psychiatry* 186 (2005): 331–4.

31 Karidi et al., "Bipolar disorder and self-stigma," 209.

32 Erving Goffman, *Stigma: Notes on the Management of Spoiled Identity* (Harmondsworth: Penguin Books, 1963), 17.

33 Kurt Snyder, Raquel E. Gur and Linda Wasmer Andrews, *Me, Myself, and Them: A Firsthand Account of One Young Person's Experience with Schizophrenia* (New York: Oxford University Press, 2008), 106.
34 Jim van Os, "Salience syndrome replaces schizophrenia in DSM-V and ICD-11. Psychiatry's evidence-based entry into the 21st century?," *Acta Psychiatrica Scandinavica* 120 (2009): 369.
35 Ibid., 368, emphasis added.
36 Ibid.
37 Greg Eghigian, *From Madness to Mental Health: Psychiatric Disorder and Its Treatment in Western Civilization* (New Brunswick, NJ: Rutgers University Press, 2010).
38 Ibid., 294.
39 Ibid., 302.
40 Ibid., 303.
41 Ibid., 299.
42 Ibid., 304.
43 Ibid., 304.
44 Ibid., 305.
45 Ibid.
46 Ibid., 305–6.
47 Ibid., 307.
48 See Will Hall, *Outside Mental Health: Voices and Visions of Madness* (Madness Radio, 2016).
49 Rüsch et al., "Mental illness stigma."
50 James D. Livingston and Jennifer E. Boyle, "Correlates and consequences of internalized stigma for people living with a mental illness: A systematic review and meta-analysis," *Social Science & Medicine* 71, 12 (2010): 2150.
51 Hoftman, "The burden of mental illness," 5–6.
52 Catherine van Zelst, "Which environments for G × E? A user perspective on the roles of trauma and structural discrimination in the onset and course of schizophrenia," *Schizophrenia Bulletin* 34 (2008): 1106–10.
53 Hoftman, "The burden of mental illness," 6.
54 Catherine van Zelst, "Stigmatization as an environmental risk in schizophrenia: A user perspective," *Schizophrenia Bulletin* 35 (2009): 293–6.
55 Ilse Janssen, Manon Hanssen, Maarten Bak, et al, "Discrimination and delusional ideation," *British Journal of Psychiatry* 182 (2003): 74.
56 Ibid., 71.
57 Hoftman, "The burden of mental illness," 6. See Nicolas Rüsch, Karsten Heekeren, Anastasia Theodoridou, et al., "Stigma as a stressor and transition to schizophrenia after one year among young people at risk of psychosis," *Schizophrenia Research* 166 (2015): 43–8.
58 Vered Baloush-Kleinman, Stephen Z. Levine, David Roe, et al., "Adherence to antipsychotic drug treatment in early-episode schizophrenia: A six-month naturalistic follow-up study," *Schizophrenia Research* 130 (2011): 180.
59 Karidi et al., "Bipolar disorder and self-stigma," 210.
60 Hoftman, "The burden of mental illness," 6. See, for instance, Karidi et al.
61 Colori, "Disclosing my diagnosis," 270.

62 Beate Schulze and Matthias C. Angermeyer, "Subjective experiences of stigma: Schizophrenic patients, their relatives and mental health professionals," *Social Science &Medicine* 56 (2003): 299–312.

63 Gökhan Sarısoy, Ömer Faruk Kaçar, Ozan Pazvantoğlu, et al., "Internalized stigma and intimate relations in bipolar and schizophrenic patients: A comparative study," *Comprehensive Psychiatry* 54, 6 (2013): 665–72.

64 Karidi et al., "Bipolar disorder and self-stigma," 213–14.

65 Ibid., 209.

66 Metzl, *The Protest Psychosis*, xv.

67 Ibid., xxi.

68 Ibid., xvi.

69 Ibid., ix.

70 Ibid., xvii.

71 Ibid., xix.

72 Shankar Vedantam, "Racial disparities found in pinpointing mental illness," *Washington Post*, June 28, 2005, in Metzl, *The Protest Psychosis*, xix.

73 Metzl, *The Protest Psychosis*, x.

74 Ibid., xix.

75 Ibid.

76 Ibid.

77 Ibid.

78 Ibid., xviii.

79 Ibid.

80 Ibid., x–xi

81 Ibid., 134.

82 Ibid.

83 Ibid., 197.

84 Ibid.

85 Udodiri Okwandu, "Violence and the (Black) brain: Law and order politics and the biomedicalization of urban rioting and violence, 1960–1975," lecture at the DeWitt Wallace Institute for the History of Psychiatry, WCMC, New York, December 4, 2019.

86 Greg Wilkinson, "Political dissent and 'sluggish' schizophrenia in the Soviet Union," *British Medical Journal* 193, 10 (1986): 641–2.

87 Theresa C. Smith and Thomas A. Oleszczuk, *No Asylum: State Psychiatric Repression in the Former USSR* (New York: New York University Press, 1996).

88 Benjamin Zajicek, "Soviet psychiatry and the origins of the sluggish schizophrenia concept, 1912–1936," *USA History of the Human Sciences* 31, 2 (2018): 88–105.

89 вялотеку́щая шизофрени́я, *vyalotekushchaya shizofreniya*.

90 Ibid., 89.

91 Ibid.

92 See Sidney Bloch and Peter Reddaway, *Psychiatric Terror: How Soviet Psychiatry is Used to Suppress Dissent* (New York: Basic Books, 1977); David Joravsky, *Russian Psychology: A Critical History* (Oxford: Basil Blackwell, 1989); H. Lavretsky, "The Russian concept of schizophrenia: A review of the literature," *Schizophrenia Bulletin* 24 (1998): 537–57; Smith and Oleszczuk, *No Asylum*.

93 Zajicek, "Soviet psychiatry," 95.
94 Ibid., 97.
95 Ibid.
96 V. P. Osipov, "Granitsy skhizofrenii, ee miagkie formy i ikh legkomyslennoe raspoznavanie" [The borders of schizophrenia, its mild forms and their careless recognition], *Sovetskaia nevropatologiia, psikhiatriia i psikhogigiena* 4, 7 (1935): 1–30, on pp. 27–8, in Zajicek, "Soviet psychiatry," 98.
97 Zajicek, "Soviet psychiatry," 98.
98 Ibid.
99 Yu. S. Savenko and A. Ya. Perekhov, "The state of psychiatry in Russia," *Psychiatric Times* 31, 2 (2014): 51–5.
100 Ibid.
101 Sandra Dietrich, Michael Beck, Bujana Bujantugs, Denis Kenzine, Herbert Matschinger and Matthias C. Angermeyer, "The relationship between public causal beliefs and social distance to mentally ill people," *Australian and New Zealand Journal of Psychiatry* 38 (2004): 348–54.
102 Rüsch et al., "Mental illness stigma," 534.
103 Sheila Mehta and Amerigo Farina, "Is being 'sick' really better? Effect of the disease view of mental disorder on stigma," *Journal of Social and Clinical Psychology* 16 (1997): 405–19.
104 Rüsch et al., "Mental illness stigma," 535. See Jo C. Phelan, "Genetic bases of mental illness – A cure for stigma?," *Trends in Neurosciences* 25, (2002): 430–1.
105 Rüsch et al., "Mental illness stigma," 533.
106 Ibid. See www.openthedoors.com
107 Rüsch et al., "Mental illness stigma," 533.
108 Ibid., 534.
109 www.irrsinnig-menschlich.de
110 Hoftman, "The burden of mental illness," 6.
111 Ibid. See Stephen P. Hinshaw and Andrea Stier, "Stigma as related to mental disorders," *Annual Review of Clinical Psychology* 4 (2008): 367–93.
112 Coliri, "Disclosing my diagnosis," 270.
113 Shuntaro Ando, Sarah Clement, Elizabeth A. Barley and Graham Thornicroft, "The simulation of hallucinations to reduce the stigma of schizophrenia: a systematic review," *Schizophrenia Research* 133, 1–3 (2011): 8–16.
114 Ross M. G. Norman, Yixian Li, Richard Sorrentino, Elizabeth Hampson and Yang Ye, "The differential effects of a focus on symptoms versus recovery in reducing stigma of schizophrenia," *Social Psychiatry and Psychiatric Epidemiology* 52, 11 (2017): 1385–94.
115 Ibid., 1391.
116 Norman Sartorius, Helen Chiu, Kua Ee Heok et al., "Name change for schizophrenia," *Schizophrenia Bulletin* 40, 2 (2014): 255–8.
117 Ibid., 255.
118 Ibid.
119 Bill George and Aadt Klijn, "A modern name for schizophrenia (PSS) would diminish self-stigma," *Psychological Medicine* 43 (2013): 1556.
120 Sartorius et al., "Name change for schizophrenia," 257.
121 Ibid., 255.

122 Ibid.
123 Sato, "Renaming schizophrenia," 53.
124 Ibid.
125 Ono et al., cited in Sato, "Renaming schizophrenia," ibid.
126 Sato, "Renaming schizophrenia," 53.
127 Ibid.
128 Ibid.
129 Ibid., 54.
130 For instance, one finds the exclusion policy of the *Seishin-Byo-Sha-Kango-Ho* (meaning "Act to keep people with psychosis under observation") in place from 1900 to 1950, and under the later Eugenic Protection Act (1940–1996).
131 Tomoko Kanata, "Japanese mental health care in historical context: Why did Japan become a country with so many psychiatric care beds?," *Social Work/Maastkaplike Werk* 52, 4 (2016): 471–89.
132 Sato, "Renaming schizophrenia," 54.
133 Ibid., 53.
134 Sartorius et al., "Name change for schizophrenia," 255.
135 Sato, "Renaming schizophrenia," 54.
136 Sartorius et al., "Name change for schizophrenia," 255.
137 Ibid., 255. See also M. Sato (ed.), "Togo-Shitcho-Sho. What is changed from split-mind-disease" [in Japanese]. Special Committee Report (Tokyo: Japanese Society of Neurology and Psychiatry, 2002).
138 Sartorius et al., "Name change for schizophrenia," 255.
139 Tohru Takahashi, Miho Tsunoda, Mitsuhiro Miyashita, et al., "Comparison of diagnostic names of mental illnesses in medical documents before and after the adoption of a new Japanese translation of 'schizophrenia'," *Psychiatry and Clinical Neurosciences* 65 (2011): 89–94.
140 Y. Nishimura and H. Ono, "A study on renaming schizophrenia and informing diagnosis," in Y. Ono (ed.), *Studies on the Effects of Renaming Psychiatric Disorders* (Tokyo: Ministry of Health, Labor and Welfare, 2005), 6–13. Japanese text quoted in Sato, "Renaming schizophrenia," 53–5.
141 Sato, "Renaming schizophrenia," 54.
142 Sung-Wan Kim, Ji-Eun Jang, Jae-Min Kim et al., "Comparison of stigma according to the term used for schizophrenia: Split-mind disorder vs. attunement disorder," *Journal of the Korean Neuropsychiatric Association* 51 (2012): 210–17.
143 Sartorius et al., "Name change for schizophrenia," 256.
144 精神分.
145 思覺失調.
146 Ibid., 256. See Cindy P.-Y. Chiu, May M.-L. Lam, Sherry K.-W. Chan, et al. "Naming psychosis: The Hong Kong experience," *Early Intervention in Psychiatry* 4 (2010): 270–4.
147 思覺失調症.
148 Sartorius et al., "Name change for schizophrenia," 257.
149 Ibid., 256.
150 Ibid.

151 Brian Koehler, "Petition to the WHO & APA to drop the term 'schizophrenia'," available at: https://www.ispsconference.nl/2018/10/25/petition-to-the-who-apa-to-drop-the-term-Schizophrenia-brian-koehler-phd-ms/.
152 Ibid. See Ai Aoki, Yuta Aoki, Robert Goulden, Kiyoto Kasai, Graham Thornicroft and Claire Henderson, "Change in newspaper coverage of schizophrenia in Japan over 20-year period," *Schizophrenia Research* 175, 1–3 (2016): 193–7.
153 Sartorius et al., "Name change for schizophrenia," 256.
154 Ibid.
155 Jim van Os, "'Schizophrenia' does not exist," *British Medical Journal* 352 (2016): i375.
156 Ibid.
157 R. D. Laing, "The study of family and social contexts in relation to the origin of schizophrenia," in J. Romano (ed.), *The Origins of Schizophrenia* (Amsterdam: Excerpta Medica Foundation, 1967), 139.
158 David, Kennard, "Is it time for ISPS to remove the term 'schizophrenia' from its name?," *Psychosis* 1, 1 (2009): 96.
159 Koehler, "Petition to the WHO & APA."
160 Van Os, "'Schizophrenia' does not exist."
161 Van Os, "Salience syndrome," 369.
162 Ibid.
163 Constantin Tranulis, "The language we use," *Visions* 14, 1 (2018): 38.
164 Ibid.
165 Van Os, "Salience syndrome," 365, 363.
166 Mohammed Abou-Saleh and Helen L. Millar, "Rapid response: Schizophrenia does exist: It is Kraepelin's disease," *British Medical Journal* 352 (2016): i375.
167 Antonio Lasalvia, Elena Penta, Norman Sartorius and Scott Henderson, "Should the label 'schizophrenia' be abandoned?," *Schizophrenia Research* 162 (2015): 276–84.
168 Although they support the change, they nevertheless also express skepticism about the abolition of the term schizophrenia, claiming that "whilst the controversy over renaming continues, it may outlive its obituarists." See Abou-Saleh and Millar, "Schizophrenia does exist."
169 See ISPS-US 2021 newsletter website.
170 Kennard, "Is it time for ISPS to remove the term 'schizophrenia' from its name?," 96.
171 Sartorius et al., "Name change for schizophrenia," 257.
172 Ibid.
173 Hoftman, "The burden of mental illness," 7.
174 Van Os, "Salience syndrome," 363.
175 Hoftman, "The burden of mental illness," 6.
176 Goffman, *Stigma*, 15.
177 Bassman, "Overcoming the impossible."
178 Rüsch et al., "Mental illness stigma," 536.
179 Ibid., 198.
180 Hinshaw and Stier, "Stigma as related to mental disorders."
181 Ibid.; Hoftman, "The burden of mental illness," 6.
182 Bassman, "Overcoming the impossible."

Chapter 7 The Ethics of a Diagnosis

1 Sylvia Nasar, *A Beautiful Mind: The Life of Mathematical Genius and Nobel Laureate John Nash* (New York: Simon & Schuster, 1998), 16.

2 Richard Noll, *American Madness: The Rise and Fall of Dementia Praecox* (Cambridge, MA: Harvard University Press, 2011), 3.

3 Joao P. de Aquino and David A. Ross, "Kraepelin's crumbling twin pillars: Using biology to reconstruct psychiatric nosology from the bottom up," *Biological Psychiatry* 82, 10 (2017): e71–4.

4 Robin M. Murray and Alice Foerster, "Schizophrenia: Is the concept disintegrating?," *Journal of Psychopharmacology* 1, 3 (1987): 133–9.

5 Joseph M. Pierre, "Deconstructing schizophrenia for DSM-5: Challenges for clinical and research agendas," *Clinical Schizophrenia and Related Psychoses* 2 (2008): 166–74.

6 Ibid., 168.

7 Gerald M. Long and Thomas C. Toppino, "Enduring interest in perceptual ambiguity: Alternating views of reversible figures," *Psychological Bulletin* 130, 5 (2004): 748–68.

8 Peter Brugger and Susanne Brugger, "The Easter bunny in October: Is it disguised as a duck?," *Perceptual and Motor Skills* 76, 2 (1993): 577–8.

9 S. Z. Berg, "Changing the S word: Is there a better name?," *Schizophrenia Digest* (2006): 30–4, in Robert H. Chaplin, "Renaming schizophrenia," *BMJ* 334 (2007): 108.

10 Patricia-Jane Teskey, "What's in a name? A case for changing the 'S' word," *Schizophrenia Digest*, 4 (2006): 36–7.

11 Anke Bueter, "Epistemic injustice and psychiatric classification," *Philosophy of Science* 86 (2019): 1064–74.

12 Bueter suggests integrating these marginalized knowers in psychiatric classification efforts, as discarding their perspective, would result in an epistemic wrong, a special case of testimonial injustice.

13 Ibid.

14 In Nasar, *A Beautiful Mind*, 352.

15 Allen Frances, *Saving Normal: An Insider's Revolt Against Out-of-Control Psychiatric Diagnosis, DSM-5, Big Pharma, and the Medicalization of Ordinary Life* (New York: William Morrow, 2013).

16 Allen Frances, in James Phillips et al., "The six most essential questions in psychiatric diagnosis: A pluralogue part 2: Issues of conversation and pragmatism in psychiatric diagnosis," *Philosophy, Ethics, and Humanities in Medicine* 7, 8 (2012): 12.

17 Tanya M. Luhrmann and Jocelyn Marrow (eds.), *Our Most Troubling Madness: Case Studies in Schizophrenia Across Cultures* (Oakland, CA: University of California Press, 2016), 104.

18 Frances, in Phillips et al., 12.

19 Warren Kinghorn, "Commentary: The DSM and 'do no harm': Is a radical pragmatism sufficient?" in Phillips et al., "The six most essential questions in psychiatric diagnosis: A pluralogue part 2: Issues of conversation and pragmatism in psychiatric diagnosis," *Philosophy, Ethics, and Humanities in Medicine* 7, 8 (2012): 8.

20 Thomas Szasz, "Law and psychiatry: The problems that will not go away," *The Journal of Mind and Behavior* 11, 3–4 (1990): 557–64.

21 Allen Frances, in Phillips et al., "The six most essential questions in psychiatric diagnosis: A pluralogue part 1: Issues of conversation and pragmatism in psychiatric diagnosis," *Philosophy, Ethics, and Humanities in Medicine* 7, 8 (2012): 16.

22 Bruce N. Cuthbert and Thomas R. Insel, "Toward the future of psychiatric diagnosis: The seven pillars of RDoC," *BMC Med* 11 (2013) 126. Their seven pillars (the number seven *ipso facto* implying the limitation and, hence, weakness of the historical "twin" pillar model) consist of strong foundations in the basic sciences, notably genetics and neuroscience; the postulation of a normal range of mental functioning of the different dimensions, and tipping points that mark the "transition to more severe pathology," at which interventions are indicated. They offer a much wider range of inclusion in sampling, comprising, for example, all the patients in one clinic, as well as "normal" subjects, while posing very particular questions (such as investigating a specific form of memory). Most importantly, the RDoC will not be studying every diagnosis ready at hand in the DSM or ICD systems of classification, only those selected elements "for which there is considerable data." Finally, the RDoC's last pillar was that it is no longer committed to "fixed definitions of disorders." Just as it could "validate constructs that are not currently part of the RDoC matrix," it could also, with equal ease, modify in various ways the existing constructs.

23 Ibid., 7.

24 Anne Harrington, *Mind Fixers: Psychiatry's Troubled Search for the Biology of Mental Illness* (New York: Norton & Co., 2019).

25 Roman Kotov, "Schizophrenia in hierarchical taxonomy of psychopathology (HiToP): New avenues for research and treatment," *Schizophrenia Bulletin* 45, 2 (2019): S102. In this model Kotov suggested two distinct spectra – the "psychoticism spectrum" and "detachment spectrum" – with several lower-order dimensions in each of them. "Psychoticism spectrum" includes positive symptoms and spans from strong reality testing on the normal end of the spectrum, to frank psychosis on the other (further subdivided into hallucination delusions, disorganization, and dissociation). The "detachment spectrum" includes the negative symptoms, ranging from high extroversion on the healthy end, all the way to full-blown deficit syndrome on the pathological end. Detachment can then be further subdivided into apathy, social withdrawal and disinterest, the very same elements that Kraepelin found to constitute the basic "pillar" of *dementia praecox*.

26 Christopher Bollas with Sacha Bollas, *Catch Them Before They Fall: The Psychoanalysis of Breakdown* (New York: Routledge, 2013).

27 Kathryn Tabb, "Philosophy of psychiatry after diagnostic kinds," *Synthese* 196 (2019): 2177–95.

28 Scott O. Lilienfeld, "DSM-5: Centripetal scientific and centrifugal antiscientific forces," *Clinical Psychology: Science and Practice* 21, 3 (2014): 269–79.

29 Kenneth F. Schaffner and Kathryn Tabb, "Varieties of social constructionism and the problem of progress in psychiatry," in Kenneth Kendler and Josef Parnas (eds), *Philosophical Issues in Psychiatry III: The Nature and Sources of Historical Change* (Oxford: Oxford University Press, 2014), 85–106.

30 Sigmund Freud, "Analysis terminable and interminable," *International Journal of Psychoanalysis* 18 (1937): 373–405.

31 Kenneth Kendler and Michael O'Donovan, "A breakthrough in schizophrenia genetics," *JAMA Psychiatry* 71, 12 (2014): 1319–20.

32 Abstracts for the 16th ISPS Congress in Copenhagen, *Psychosis* (2009): 3–131.
33 See Luhrmann and Marrow, *Our Most Troubling Madness*.
34 M. Bleuler and R. Bleuler, "Dementia praecox oder die Gruppe der Schizophrenien: Eugen Bleuler," *The British Journal of Psychiatry* 149 (1986): 661–4.

Index